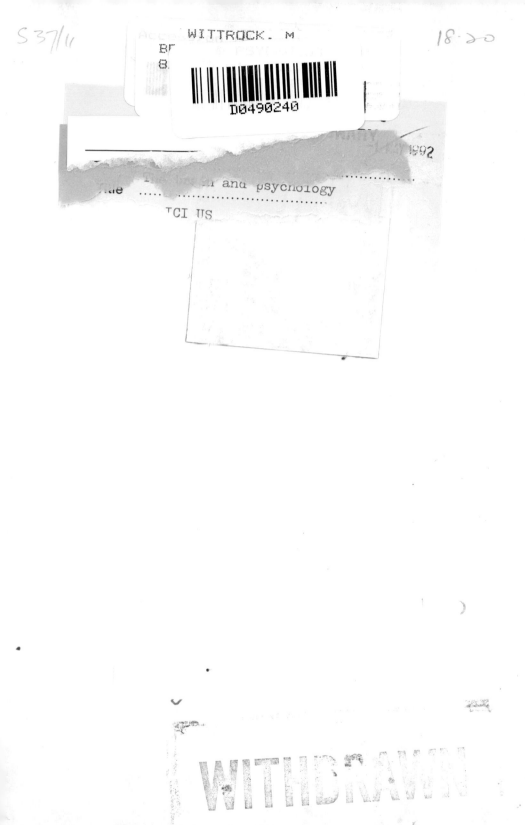

THE BRAIN AND PSYCHOLOGY

EDUCATIONAL PSYCHOLOGY

Allen J. Edwards, Series Editor
Department of Psychology
Southwest Missouri State University
Springfield, Missouri

In preparation:

James H. McMillan (ed.). The Social Psychology of School Learning

Published

M. C. Wittrock (ed.). The Brain and Psychology

Marvin J. Fine (ed.). Handbook on Parent Education

Dale G. Range, James R. Layton, and Darrell L. Roubinek (eds.). Aspects of Early Childhood Education: Theory to Research to Practice

Jean Stockard, Patricia A. Schmuck, Ken Kempner, Peg Williams, Sakre K. Edson, and Mary Ann Smith. Sex Equity in Education

James R. Layton. The Psychology of Learning to Read

Thomas E. Jordan. Development in the Preschool Years: Birth to Age Five

Gary D. Phye and Daniel J. Reschly (eds.). School Psychology: Perspectives and Issues

Norman Steinaker and M. Robert Bell. The Experiential Taxonomy: A New Approach to Teaching and Learning

J. P. Das, John R. Kirby, and Ronald F. Jarman. Simultaneous and Successive Cognitive Processes

Herbert J. Klausmeier and Patricia S. Allen. Cognitive Development of Children and Youth: A Longitudinal Study

Victor M. Agruso, Jr. Learning in the Later Years: Principles of Educational Gerontology

Thomas R. Kratochwill (ed.). Single Subject Research: Strategies for Evaluating Change

The list of titles in this series continues on the last page of this volume.

THE BRAIN AND PSYCHOLOGY

Edited by

M. C. WITTROCK

University of California, Los Angeles
Los Angeles, California

1980

ACADEMIC PRESS

A Subsidiary of Harcourt Brace Jovanovich, Publishers

New York   London   Toronto   Sydney   San Francisco

ACADEMIC PRESS, INC.
111 Fifth Avenue, New York, New York 10003

United Kingdom Edition published by
ACADEMIC PRESS, INC. (LONDON) LTD.
24/28 Oval Road, London NW1 7DX

Library of Congress Cataloging in Publication Data
Main entry under title:

The Brain and psychology.

(Educational psychology series)
Includes bibliographies and index.
1. Brain.   2. Neuropsychology.   3. Brain––
Localization of functions.   4. Cognition.
I. Wittrock, Merlin C.   II. Series: Educational
psychology series (New York)
QP376.B6963   153   79–8540
ISBN 0–12–761050–2

Contents

PART II

INFORMATION PROCESSING IN THE BRAIN

Chapter III

The Neuropsychology of Attention: Emotional and Motivational Controls

DIANE McGUINNESS AND KARL PRIBRAM

Chapter IV

Visual Perception and Memory

DAVID J. MADDEN AND ROBERT D. NEBES

Chapter V

Language and Verbal Processes

DANIEL BUB AND HARRY A. WHITAKER

Chapter VI

Cerebral Asymmetry and the Psychology of Man 245

JERRE LEVY

PART III

PSYCHOLOGY AND THE RECENT RESEARCH ON THE BRAIN

Chapter VII

Cognition and the Brain 325

MARCEL KINSBOURNE

Chapter VIII

The Developing Brain and Child Development 345

W. E. JEFFREY

Chapter IX

Learning and the Brain 371

M. C. WITTROCK

List of Contributors

Numbers in parentheses indicate the pages on which the authors' contributions begin.

THEODORE W. BERGER* (3), Department of Psychobiology, University of California, Irvine, California 92664

STEPHEN D. BERRY† (3), Department of Psychobiology, University of California, Irvine, California 92664

DANIEL BUB (211), Department of Psychology, University of Rochester, Rochester, New York 14627

W. E. JEFFREY (345), Department of Psychology, University of California, Los Angeles, California 90024

MARCEL KINSBOURNE (325), The Hospital for Sick Children, Toronto, Ontario, M5G 1X8, Canada

JERRE LEVY (245), Department of Behavioral Sciences, University of Chicago, Chicago, Illinois 60637

DIANE McGUINNESS (95), Department of Psychology, University of California, Santa-Cruz, California

DAVID J. MADDEN (141), Duke University Medical Center, Durham, North Carolina 27706

*PRESENT ADDRESS: Psychobiology Program, Department of Psychology and Department of Psychiatry, Western Psychiatry Institute and Clinic, University of Pittsburgh, Pittsburgh, Pennsylvania 15260

†PRESENT ADDRESS: Department of Psychology, Miami University, Oxford, Ohio 45056

ROBERT D. NEBES (141), Duke University Medical Center, Durham, North
    Carolina 27710

KARL PRIBRAM (95), Department of Psychology, Stanford University,
    Stanford, California 94305

RICHARD F. THOMPSON (3), Department of Psychobiology, University of
    California, Irvine, California 92664

COLWYN TREVARTHEN (33), Department of Psychology, University of
    Edinburgh, Edinburgh, E48 9TA, Scotland

HARRY A. WHITAKER (211), Department of Psychology, University of
    Rochester, Rochester, New York 14627

M. C. WITTROCK (371), Graduate School of Education, University of
    California, Los Angeles, California 90024

Preface

The study of the brain and research on human psychological behavior existed in two different worlds until relatively recently. The problems of understanding human behavior seemed to be too complex to be informed by the study of the central nervous system. For years many psychologists thought it best to study relations between environmental stimuli and human behavior, omitting from their research and theories the little-understood and difficult-to-study cognitive psychological processes and the complex neural structures and systems of the brain. If one could show that environmental stimuli control human behavior, then for reasons of parsimony there was little need to study complex cognitive processes, such as attention, learning, and memory and their neural substrates.

But recent research in cognition and in individual differences has indicated that behavior is influenced by environmental stimuli and by the learner's previous experiences, memories, attributions, motives, organized knowledge, intentions, and physiological processes. Research in memory, attention, encoding, imagery, verbal processes, cognitive styles, and information-processing strategies began to flourish and to contribute to the emerging field of cognitive science.

At a different level of study, neuropsychologists and other neuroscientists developed new research methods and techniques that led to important, sometimes dramatic, findings about the cognitive functions, neural structures, and physiological processes of the brain. Attentional mechanisms and arousal systems were identified. Cortical information-processing systems, which function in perception, learning, and memory, were discovered. The neural substrates of some of the psychological processes underlying human behavior, such as the synaptic transmission of neural impulses, became better understood.

The levels of study were different in neuroscience and in cognitive psychology, but the phenomena under study, such as attention, perception, memory, learning disabilities, and individual differences, were often closely related to each other. Precisely because different levels of related phenomena are under study in these two fields, the recent findings of the research on the human brain have become of interest to many psychologists, educational psychologists, and educational researchers who study cognition, human learning, memory, development, individual differences, attention, motivation, perception, cognitive style, and learning disorders. People in these areas can no longer afford to ignore some of the findings of the recent research on the brain.

This volume reports an important part of the recent findings of the research on the brain. The book begins with a section on the organization of the brain, including its structural and its functional organizations. The first chapter, by Richard Thompson, Theodore Berger, and Stephen Berry, introduces the anatomy, physiology, and chemistry of the brain. The authors describe and illustrate the interesting structures and fundamental processes and systems of the brain. The fascinating sequence of chemical and electrical changes in the synaptic transmission of neural impulses is presented, along with the basic anatomical structures of the different regions of the brain. This chapter provides a useful base for the chapters which follow.

Colwyn Trevarthen describes the functional organization of the brain in the second chapter of the book. He elaborates the psychological and behavioral functions of structures in the spinal cord, brainstem, cerebellum, and forebrain, especially the cerebral cortex.

The information-processing systems of the brain are described in the second section of the book, which consists of four chapters. In Chapter III, Diane McGuinness and Karl Pribram write about attention and its motivational and emotional controls. They present a sophisticated model of attention, analyzing it into three major components: arousal, activation, and effort. Their model leads to a new understanding of the brain's complicated functioning in attention, and to new ways to measure concept learning or categorization and reasoning and problem solving. Their chapter summarizes a lengthy and fruitful research program in the neuropsychology of attention.

Richard Madden and Robert Nebes report next on visual perception and memory. In the context of the recent history of research on cortical hemispheric processes, they discuss, at length, recent findings about perception that have grown from information-processing approaches to the study of vision. They introduce fundamental ideas about encoding as well. The chapter brings together related research from the two worlds of cognitive psychology and neuroscience. As a result, one can get a better understanding of each of these two worlds and of the directions in which they are proceeding.

Daniel Bub and Harry Whitaker delve into language and the brain in Chapter V. They discuss a model of language structures of the brain that has been refined over the years since Karl Wernicke introduced it in 1874. They summarize data from a variety of research approaches used in linguistics, psychology, and neurology that contribute to an understanding of some of the relations between language and the structures of the brain.

Part II concludes with a comprehensive chapter by Jerre Levy on cerebral asymmetry in cognitive processes and individual differences in brain function (Chapter VI). She organizes an enormous number of research findings about the different functions of the cortical hemispheres of the brain, a widely popular, often oversimplified, but highly complicated topic to discuss. She presents the research-based state of the art of hemispherisity, with emphasis on the research in individual differences in hemispheric brain functions, especially among right-handed and left-handed men and women.

The third and final section of the book consists of three chapters on relationships between recent research on the brain and cognitive processes of interest to psychologists. Marcel Kinsbourne, a neuroscientist, writes about cognition and the brain, about relations between the organization of the brain and the problems of psychologists, educational psychologists, and educators interested in the acquisition of behavior. From relatively stimulus-bound trial-and-error behavior, learners develop abilities to represent experience mentally, to abstract it, and to adapt fluently to new and different environments by use of their mental representations and the output mechanisms of their brains.

In Chapter VIII, Wendell Jeffrey, a developmental psychologist, discusses development and the brain. He relates recent research on the brain to some of the problems and processes of child development. He shows that attempts to influence the environments of children should be built upon knowledge about the development of the brain's cognitive mediating structures, their neural substrates, and their differences among individuals.

In the final chapter of the book, I discuss, from an educational psychological perspective, learning and the recent research on the brain. The theme of the chapter is that research in neuroscience and research in cognitive psychology lead to a new emphasis upon the generative processes of the brain and their important role in influencing learning. The theme recurs in research on encoding and memory. Implications of this theme are discussed, including a paradigm for research on teaching and instruction that includes the cognitive processes of the brain, the transformations they perform, and their effects upon learning.

In brief, Part I (Chapters I and II) introduces the basic structural and functional organization of the brain. Part II (Chapters III–VI) discusses research on the basic information-processing systems of the brain: attention, perception, encoding, and memory, including imagery and verbal processes, as well as some of the research on individual differences in information processing strategies. Finally, Part III (Chapters VII–IX) relates the research on the brain to several problems in psychology as these relationships are perceived by a brain researcher, a developmental psychologist, and an educational psychologist.

Acknowledgments

I want to thank the people who participated in the preparation of the book, including the authors of the chapters; the typists Joan Morley and Barbara Trelease; the graduate students who read and commented on my chapter, Helen Schultze, Theresa Roberts, Janet Sutton, and Elizabeth Weinberger; and Professor Allen J. Edwards, the editor of this monograph series, who was active throughout the development of the volume. A special thank you goes to my wife Nancy, to whom the book is dedicated.

PART I

THE ORGANIZATION OF THE BRAIN

In this first of three parts of the volume, the chapters on the structural organization and the functional organization of the brain introduce two different levels of study of the major systems of the brain and its complex cognitive functions. Chapter One introduces the anatomy, chemistry, and physiology of the brain, and Chapter Two introduces the functional organization of the brain. These two chapters provide holistic perspectives of the organization of the brain and introduce the often complementary findings that emerge from these two different levels of study of the brain.

Chapter I

An Introduction to the Anatomy, Physiology, and Chemistry of the Brain

RICHARD F. THOMPSON
THEODORE W. BERGER
STEPHEN D. BERRY

In all higher organisms, behavior is a reflection of the activity of the brain. In a sense, each of us is simply a brain together with a few minor input and output appendages. The brain is essentially a set of interconnecting elements—the neurons, or nerve cells. Each neuron receives information from other neurons or from sensory receptors and transmits information to still other neurons or to muscles to produce behavior. All stimuli impinging upon us, all sensations, thoughts, actions, and feelings, must be coded into the languages of the neuron. Every neuron transmits information in two quite different modes: A message is either continuous or all-or-none. A particular neuron is activated in a continuous fashion by other neurons: This is the graded-decision process, the process of *synaptic transmission*. Once the nerve cell is activated to transmit this information along its fiber to another neuron, it converts the graded-decision language into an all-or-none spike or *action potential*, the digital language of the nerve fiber. The two basic processes of neuronal activity thus depend on the action potential and synaptic transmission.

The human brain consists of some 10^{12} neurons—not too great a number. However, the number of possible interconnections among these neurons in a single human brain is greater than the total number of

3

THE BRAIN AND PSYCHOLOGY

atoms making up the entire universe! It is in their patterns of interconnections that the higher and more integrative processes—sensation,
perception, memory, emotion and motivation, thought and awareness
—develop. The two simple processes of synaptic transmission and the
action potential "spoken" by each neuron are somehow converted into
the languages of psychology.

A parallel of sorts can be drawn between the very elementary
functions of a neuron and the much more complex integrative functions
of the brain. A neuron receives information from many sources (sensation); the neuron integrates this information (processing); neurons may
be altered or "store" the information (memory); and neurons transmit
this information to other neurons, muscles, or internal organs (action or
behavior). These aspects of the activity of nerve cells will be emphasized
in the first portion of this chapter. Remember, however, that it is only in
the interconnections and interaction among the myriad of neurons and
systems of neurons in the brain that psychological processes emerge.
The major brain systems will be described in the latter portion of this
chapter.

I. The Neuron

A. Anatomy of the Neuron

As is true for all biological material, brain tissue is composed of basic
cellular elements. There are essentially two major classes of brain cells.
Only one class is believed to perform the functions previously discussed
that are the basis for psychological phenomena: the neuron. For this
reason, the present chapter will deal almost exclusively with the structure and function of neurons. The other major class, neuroglia cells,
perform primarily nutritive and supportive functions for neurons. Figure 1.1 shows schematized examples of different types of neurons
(A,B,C) and a glia cell (D).

Despite the fact that neurons may vary widely in their anatomical
characteristics, all neurons have several common features. The most
obvious structural component is the cell body, or soma (Figure 1.1A).
The soma consists of a membrane which surrounds an accumulation of
cytoplasm, together with the cell nucleus (Figure 1.2). The cell cytoplasm is composed of what is essentially a salt solution containing a
number of important organelles. The cell nucleus contains, within its
nucleolus, genetic material (DNA, RNA) that controls the fundamental

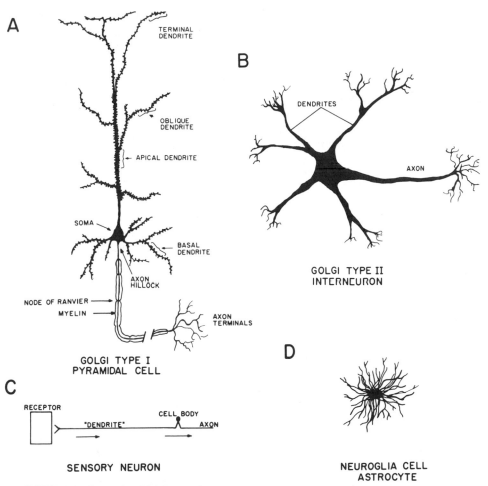

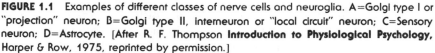

FIGURE 1.1 Examples of different classes of nerve cells and neuroglia. A=Golgi type I or "projection" neuron; B=Golgi type II, interneuron or "local circuit" neuron; C=Sensory neuron; D=Astrocyte. [After R. F. Thompson **Introduction to Physiological Psychology,** Harper & Row, 1975, reprinted by permission.]

steps in protein synthesis. Organelles within the cell are responsible for major nutritive and metabolic functions that sustain the neuron. The more important of these organelles (Figure 1.2) are (*a*) the Nissl substance, composed of rough endoplasmic reticulum surrounded by ribosomes and believed to be involved in protein synthesis; (*b*) the Golgi apparatus, believed to be involved in the synthesis of neurotransmitters (page 19); (*c*) mitochondria, sites where the major steps (oxidative

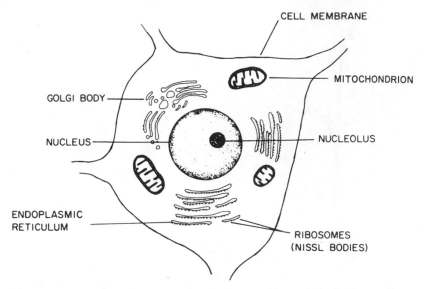

FIGURE 1.2. Major intracellular organelles of a neuron. Neurotubules and neurofilaments are not shown. [From R. F. Thompson **Introduction to Physiological Psychology**, Harper & Row, 1975, reprinted by permission.]

phosphorylation) in energy metabolism take place; and (*d*) neurotubules and neurofilaments (not shown in Figure 1.2), believed to function in cell support and axoplasmic transport.

The last of these phenomena is particularly important with respect to the other major structural components of the neuron: the dendrites, axon, and axon terminals (Figure 1.1A). Only the cell soma contains the organelles necessary for protein synthesis. As a result, these materials must be transported to the other main processes of the neuron for metabolic and functional maintenance. An active transport process operates within the neuron to move proteins produced in the cell body to the dendrites, axon, and axon terminals. In fact, if a nerve axon is tied off or pinched in the middle, the part of the nerve near the cell body will become distended as materials "back up" en route to the peripheral parts of the cell.

The dendrites constitute the second major component of neurons. Dendrites, in general, are short in the sense that they end within the region of the cell body, but they also have a very large surface area because they divide or branch extensively. For this reason, the dendritic region is often termed the dendritic "tree" (Figure 1.1A and B). The dendrites are the major receptive surface of the neuron. All incoming information from other nerve cells arrives on the dendritic and cell soma regions. Because dendrites have so much more surface area than the cell body, however, the majority of incoming information is received at the dendrite. This information is subsequently transmitted to the neuron soma. Dendritic processes vary greatly in diameter throughout their length and are sometimes covered with "spines" that are specialized evaginations of the cell membrane. It is primarily at the dendritic spine that contact is made with the output of other nerve cells.

The third major structural component of the neuron—the axon—arises from a part of the cell body termed the axon hillock. The hillock region constitutes the initial segment of the axon. In general, axons are narrower than dendrites, branch less frequently, and are much more uniform in diameter throughout their length. The axon serves as the major conduction pathway for information leaving the cell body. For this reason, axons are usually significantly longer than dendrites, sometimes reaching lengths (in humans) as great as 3 meters.

Many axons are coated with a fatty material called myelin. Myelin is actually part of a neighboring glia cell that becomes wrapped around an axon during the course of neuron cell development. A single glia cell process may cover as much as a 1-mm section of neuronal axon. Where the process from one glia cell ends, a process from another glia cell begins, so that an axon will be sheathed with myelin along its entire length except for the hillock and terminal regions. Points along the axon where two glia processes juxtapose are termed "nodes of Ranvier." Myelin has a profound influence on neuron cell function, in that myelinated axons conduct information away from the cell soma at a much faster rate than unmyelinated axons. In this sense, glia cells—through their myelin sheathing—operate to increase the speed of information transmission through the brain.

The final major component of the nerve cell is the axon terminal. When the axon reaches its target site (another nerve cell, striated muscle, or internal organ), it branches into specialized terminal endings. Each terminal ending contacts the dendritic spine or soma of another nerve cell. Nerve terminals do not actually contact the next nerve cell membrane, but transmit output information across a region where the membranes of the two cells are particularly close—the synaptic cleft or synapse. The synapse, then, is the site where information from one cell (presynaptic cell) is finally transmitted to another neuron (postsynaptic cell). If the synapse happens to be onto muscle instead of another cell, the specialized region of contact is termed a neuromuscular junction rather than a synapse. As will be discussed, the synapse (the presynaptic terminal and the postsynaptic receptor area) is believed to be the most likely site for neuronal mechanisms of learning and memory.

There are a great many structural features that typify neuron—neuronal synapses and neuromuscular junctions (Figure 1.8). Among the most general are swelling of the axon terminal at its tip, a narrowing of the extracellular space between the pre- and postsynaptic cells to about 200–500 Å (an Å or Angstrom unit equals one hundred-millionth of a centimeter), and the appearance of a large number of vesicles (300–500 Å in diameter) clumped about the presynaptic site. All synapses show these characteristics, although the details of synaptic features vary depending on whether the synapse is neuron–neuronal or neuromuscular. As we shall see later, it is the vesicles that play the key role in transmission of information between the two sites at the synapse.

On purely anatomical grounds, one may define three major classes of neurons. The first class is often termed a "projection" or *Golgi type I* neuron, and is typified by the pyramidal cell shown in Figure 1.1A. The most striking characteristic of this cell is its extremely long axon which forms connections between one major brain region and another. Pyramidal cells are unique from other projection cell types, however, in that they sometimes have two dendrites, one apical and one basal (Figure 1.1A).

A second class of neuron is often termed a "local circuit," "interneuron," or *Golgi type II* neuron (Figure 1.1B). Such cells typically have short axons that terminate within the region of the cell body and link neurons within a given brain structure to each other (rather than providing connections between regions of the brain as do projection neurons). A third class of neuron is called a *sensory* neuron (Figure 1.1C), the main function of which is to conduct sensory information concerning the periphery of the body to the central parts of the nervous system—the spinal cord and the brain. Sensory neurons are classified separately from projection and local circuit neurons because the dendrites of sensory cells are replaced by long fibers that extend to skin, muscles, or joints. There, each fiber contacts specialized sensory receptors that are responsible for transforming sensory events (e.g., touch, heat, cold, or pain) into nerve cell responses. This information is conducted to each cell soma and eventually into the spinal cord via sensory cell axons.

The soma, dendrite, axon, and axon terminals, then, are the principal anatomical aspects of the neuron. Each structural part of a neuron has a particular function in the processing of information from the external world. Most incoming information is received by the dendrites and transmitted to the cell body. The cell body serves as the major integrator of this input information, which comes from many other nerve cells (typically, thousands). The cell soma—in particular, the axon hillock region—plays a decisive role in the processing of neural information in the sense that it determines whether or not the integrated message continues to other cells through the axon. If the message is projected along the axon, it eventually reaches the axon terminals and is transmitted to other neurons or muscle tissue across the synapse.

Admittedly, this scheme is somewhat simplistic. A discussion of the physiology and chemistry of nervous system tissue, however, will show that most of the major functional aspects of the neuron fit well within such a framework.

B. Physiology of the Neuron

A proper discussion of the physiology of the neuron should be founded on one basic premise: Events and information from the external world are not represented within the brain as they exist in the external world. Rather, they are transformed or translated into a coding scheme used by neurons. The present discussion of the physiology of the neuron is really a discussion of this coding process, and of the types of signals neurons use to represent external events within the brain.

As stated previously, the neuron consists of a membrane that surrounds a small volume of cytoplasm made up of a watery salt solution and organelles. Whereas the organelles are responsible for certain metabolic operations that maintain the cell, it is the cell membrane and the salt solution that are the keys to the physiology of the neuron.

One important characteristic of the salt solution is that the inside is different from the outside of the cell membrane (Figure 1.3). The intracellular fluid has a high concentration of potassium (K^+) ions, a low concentration of chloride (Cl^-) ions, and various organic anions (i.e., protein molecules that have a negative charge and are too large to pass through the nerve membrane). The extracellular fluid has a low concentration of K^+ ions, a high concentration of Na^+ ions, and a high concentration of Cl^- ions. As a result of the relative concentrations of all ions and anions, the intracellular fluid is negative with respect to the outside of the cell membrane. In other words, there are relatively more positive ions (or fewer negative ions) outside the cell than inside the cell—enough to result in a potential difference of -70 millivolts (mV). This difference is termed the resting potential, that is, the potential difference between the intracellular and extracellular fluids when the neuron is at rest (not transmitting any information). (Any comparison of the potential difference between the intracellular and extracellular cytoplasm is termed the "potential difference across the membrane," or the *membrane potential*.) The cell membrane plays a critical role in the maintenance of this resting potential because it acts to partially separate the intracellular and extra-

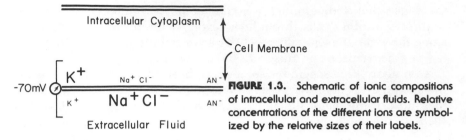

FIGURE 1.3. Schematic of ionic compositions of intracellular and extracellular fluids. Relative concentrations of the different ions are symbolized by the relative sizes of their labels.

cellular fluids, thus allowing the potential difference to persist. The cell membrane is said to be semipermeable; that is, it will allow only certain ions to pass back and forth between the intracellular and extracellular fluids. The existence of a potential difference between the inside and the outside of a cell membrane is not unique to nerve cells. Any semipermeable membrane that separates different ionic solutions will have a potential difference across that membrane.

The critical step during a neuron's reception of information is a change in the permeability of the cell membrane. For example, if a cell's dendrite is weakly stimulated by the terminals of an input neuron, what results is a small and time-limited increase in permeability to Na^+, allowing some Na^+ to enter the cell. The increase in positive ions inside the cell causes a slight shift in the membrane potential in the positive direction (Figure 1.4); that is, the intracellular fluid becomes a little less negative compared to the extracellular space. The membrane potential returns to resting level because the increase in permeability to the Na^+ is followed by a flow of K^+ out of the cell. The decrease in the number of intracellular positive ions caused by the exit of K^+ restores the intracellular negativity to resting levels. This event is termed an *excitatory postsynaptic potential*, or an *EPSP*, and typically lasts 5–20 msec.

When a neuron receives information over one of its inputs, the result may be a decrease in the membrane potential (depolarization), or an increase in the membrane potential (hyperpolarization). Whereas the former event is termed an EPSP, the latter is termed an *inhibitory postsynaptic potential* or *IPSP*. During an IPSP, the cell membrane is believed to become permeable to Cl^- ions, which enter the cell, causing an increase in the negativity of the intracellular cytoplasm.

EPSPs and IPSPs represent the first major class of brain signals and have several characteristics:

1. They are graded, meaning that their amplitude is proportional to the input; thus, there are essentially an infinite number of possible EPSP and IPSP amplitudes.

2. EPSPs and IPSPs are local potentials in the sense that they travel only a short distance from the site on the membrane where they are generated. In other words, if an EPSP is generated at one site on a cell membrane and recorded there by an electrode, the same EPSP recorded at other sites on the cell membrane appears attenuated in amplitude. The greater the distance, the larger the attenuation.

3. EPSPs and IPSPs occur only in the dendritic and cell soma regions (Figure 1.5).

Because the EPSP is graded, if the incoming stimulus is decreased in strength, an EPSP will decrease in amplitude. If the stimulus is increased in amplitude, the EPSP will increase in amplitude—but only to a point. Beyond a given stimulus strength, the EPSP changes to a qualitatively different type of brain signal: the action potential (Figure 1.4). The membrane potential at which an EPSP becomes an action potential is termed "threshold." Because a neuron must be depolarized to threshold, only EPSPs can lead to action potentials.

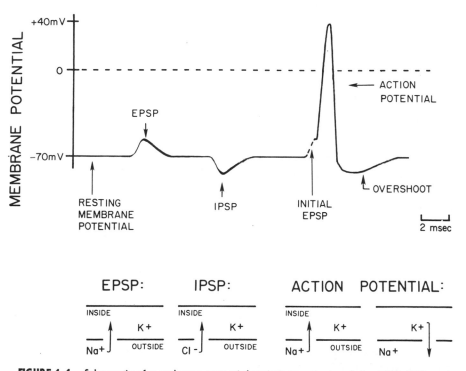

FIGURE 1.4. Schematic of membrane potential variations occurring during EPSP, IPSP, and action potential. Lower figures indicate ion currents responsible for each potential.

During the occurrence of an action potential, Na^+ enters the inside of the cell. Enough positively charged sodium ions enter to make the inside of the cell more positive than the extracellular cytoplasm—in other words, there is a reversal of the membrane potential (Figure 1.4). The intracellular fluid changes from -70 mV relative to the extracellular space in the resting state to $+40$ mV at the peak of the action potential state (Figure 1.4).

When the cell membrane potential reaches the peak of the action potential, Na^+ ions stop entering the cell and K^+ ions start leaving. K^+ leaving the cell, of course, means a decrease in the positivity of the intracellular cytoplasm. Enough K^+ leaves the cell to bring the membrane potential from $+40$ mV back to the resting potential. In fact, a slight "overshoot" occurs such that the membrane returns to -75 mV at first and then rises to -70 mV. Thus, the flow of Na^+ into the cell accounts for the increasing part of the action potential while the flow of K^+ out of the cell accounts for the decreasing part of the action potential.

This entire sequence of events, represented by the duration of the action potential, typically takes 1–2 msec. After this successive flow of Na^+ and K^+ ions, the cell membrane enters what is termed the *absolute refractory* period during which no new stimulus can initiate an action potential. The duration of the refractory period is typically 1 msec. The absolute refractory period is followed by a *relative refractory* period (lasting several milliseconds) during which a new action potential can be generated, but a much stronger stimulus than normal is necessary to do so. It is important to note that other nerve cell mechanisms, not discussed here, perform the function of redistributing K^+ and Na^+ ions during the refractory periods, so there is no permanent loss of K^+ or gain of Na^+ to the intracellular fluid after the action potential.

Action potentials represent the second major class of brain signals and have characteristics quite different from EPSPs and IPSPs. Action potentials are not graded because their amplitude is not proportional to the input. Once the input stimulus is of a given strength (enough for the membrane potential to reach threshold), the identical series of Na^+ and K^+ ion currents takes place regardless of other characteristics of the input stimulus. Thus action potentials are often described as all-or-none phenomena, in that they represent what is essentially a binary event.

Second, action potentials do not degrade with distance along the membrane. The occurrence of an action potential on one part of the membrane causes the neighboring segment of membrane to depolarize and also to reach threshold, resulting in another action potential in that neighboring part of the membrane. Because of this characteristic, action potentials are said to be "regenerative" rather than "local." The regenerative feature makes action potentials ideal for the transmission of information over long distances. This is precisely the role that action potentials play in the processing of information in the brain, and for this reason, usually occur only in neuron axons, axon terminals, and somas (Figure 1.5).

Postsynaptic potentials (EPSPs and IPSPs) and action potentials constitute the two major types of signals used by neurons. All incoming information to the dendrites and soma of a neuron results in either an EPSP or an IPSP. Both are graded signals and do not propagate further than the cell soma. As stated previously, the cell soma acts to integrate all incoming information. The nature of this integrative process is simple summation. Any EPSP acts to depolarize the cell membrane closer to the threshold point. Any IPSP causes greater hyperpolarization, driving the cell membrane further from threshold. Thus, two coincident EPSPs can result in an action potential and ensure transmission along the axon, whereas either EPSP occurring alone may not be sufficient to do so. Alternatively, IPSPs can block transmission (down the axon) by preventing the membrane potential from reaching threshold.

An important question at this point is what the nature of the transmitted message might be. For any signal to provide information it must vary, that is, not be redundant. Yet for any message to be transmitted in the nervous system, it must take the form of an action potential. All action potentials have essentially constant amplitudes and durations. How, then, can an invariant signal be used to represent variant events? The answer lies in the fact that an action potential is an all-or-none

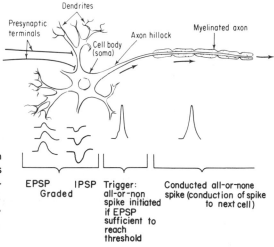

FIGURE 1.5. Summary diagram of the types of potential changes and their relative sites of occurrence in neurons. [From R. F. Thompson **Foundations of Physiological Psychology,** Harper & Row, 1967, reprinted by permission.]

phenomenon—in other words, a binary event. Information is represented by the sequence of successive action potentials; not by the occurrence of any individual action potential.

For example, different events can be represented by different numbers of action potentials per unit time, that is, the frequency of cell firing (Figure 1.6A). Alternatively, the temporal pattern or duration of a series of action potentials (Figure 1.6B and C) may be used to code events from the external world. These are only a few of many possible binary-based codes. At first, this may seem a rather limited scheme for representing all the information that a human brain is capable of storing. One analogy that may indicate its scope, however, is the modern digital computer which operates on the same binary principle.

An additional question relates to the specificity of such a coding scheme. There are a great many external objects that may be considered

A   FREQUENCY CODE

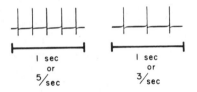

B   TEMPORAL PATTERN CODE

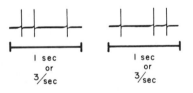

C   DURATION CODE

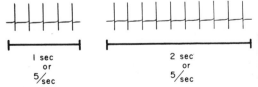

FIGURE 1.6. Examples of types of codes utilized by neurons to represent different events. See text for explanation.

unique. Human faces are perhaps the best example. We rarely confuse other individuals with our parents, spouses, children, etc. The basic question is how neurons can be "fine-tuned" to represent unique objects.

As a hypothetical example, imagine that 10 essential characteristics are necessary to specify a given object uniquely. We then require that a neuron have 10 inputs representing each of those critical features, and that all 10 resulting EPSPs be needed for the neuron to depolarize enough to reach threshold. The occurrence of an action potential in that neuron represents the identification of the unique object. Any fewer than all 10 simultaneously present characteristics, and the action potential fails to occur (the recognition is not made). A number of such "unique object" or "feature detector" neurons have been discovered in basic research on animals, some showing a great deal of specificity in the characteristics which must be present for the cell to be activated. For example, in the visual area of the cerebral cortex, some neurons will respond only to lines, others only to angles, and still others only to "tongues" (one end of a rectangular shape). An important word of caution: Although many such "feature coding" neurons exist, it does not necessarily follow that visual perception, for example, consists simply of successively more abstract feature codes in more and more specialized neurons. It seems very unlikely that specific neurons exist for specific perceptions. There is probably no "Mona Lisa" neuron—a neuron that responds only to Leonardo's painting. How the various "feature detector" neurons in the visual system interact to yield visual perception remains unknown. In any event, neurons can function flexibly enough to represent many different events through the use of binary-based coding schemes, and can also be fine-tuned sufficiently to represent very specific objects through stringent input requirements.

While synaptic potentials and action potentials are the two types of signals recorded from individual neurons, such recordings (which involve introducing electrodes directly into the brain) are not often possible or practical. The electrical changes occurring in large numbers of neurons (typically, millions) can be recorded from the surface of the skull or scalp. Such a recording is termed an *electroencephalogram,* or *EEG.* The EEG is thought to represent the summed electrical change produced by all PSPs and action potentials within a large brain area, and can be used for many diagnostic and experimental purposes. Perhaps the most well-known brain signal recorded by EEG techniques is the *alpha* response, a sinusoidal-like wave having a frequency of 8–12 Hz that indicates a state of restfulness in awake mammals. Different frequencies of EEG brain responses have also been found to correlate with

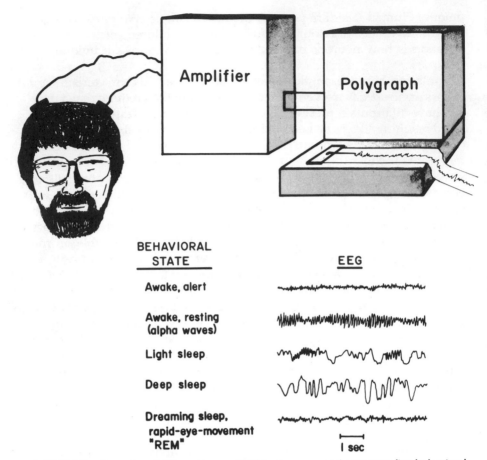

FIGURE 1.7. Examples of different types of EEG brain waves and corresponding behavioral or mental states.

different phases of sleep (Figure 1.7). It is believed that the EEG recorded at the scalp represents the summed synaptic activity (PSP) generated by many thousands of neurons in the cerebral cortex acting in concert.

C. Chemistry of the Neuron

All major input to neurons is received at the dendrite and soma, taking the form of EPSPs and/or IPSPs. If the inputs are sufficient for the cell membrane to reach threshold, an action potential is generated at the axon hillock and propogated to the axon terminals as output to the next

neuron. Both of these major steps—input and output—take place between neurons at the synapse. Neurons remain anatomically independent, however. Two cell membranes may reach close apposition at the
synapse, but the membranes are still unattached. Electrical events—like
the ionic currents that are the basis for PSPs and action potentials—
cannot traverse the synaptic gap (just as current cannot flow through a
circuit with a broken wire). How, then, is information transmitted from
one neuron to another (or to muscle) through the extracellular space of
the synapse?

The transmission is accomplished through the transformation of an
electrical event—the action potential—into a chemical event. Recall that
spherical vesicles are present on the presynaptic side of the synapse
(Figure 1.8). The vesicles are thought to contain chemical substances
termed *neurotransmitters*. When an action potential invades the axon
terminals, the vesicles merge with the cell membrane and empty their

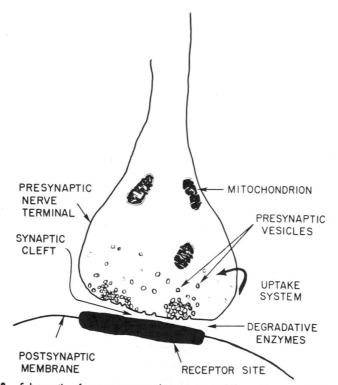

FIGURE 1.8. Schematic of neuronneuronal synapse and the major pre- and postsynaptic
elements. [After R. F. Thompson **Introduction to Physiological Psychology,** Harper & Row,
1975, reprinted by permission.]

neurotransmitter contents into the synaptic cleft. The transmitter diffuses across the small synaptic space to make contact with specialized areas of the postsynaptic membrane termed *receptor sites*. Through contact with receptors, changes are induced in the permeability of the postsynaptic cell membrane, bringing about the ionic currents necessary for PSPs and action potentials. At the postsynapic site, then, the chemical events necessary for pre- to postsynaptic transmission are retransformed into electrical (ionic) events.

The effect of a neurotransmitter on the postsynaptic receptor site is not normally long-lasting. Recall that EPSPs and IPSPs have durations ranging from approximately 5 to 20 msec. Transmitter effects are restricted by degradative enzymes present in the extracellular space that act to catabolize transmitters into their nonactive, component forms. Shortly after their release from the presynaptic terminal, then, neurotransmitters are broken down and deactivated. The relatively short time-course of EPSPs and IPSPs reflects the limited effect of transmitter on the postsynaptic membrane.

As a result of this constant release and degradation, presynaptic supplies of neurotransmitter are being depleted and must be resupplied. This is accomplished through resynthesis of the neurotransmitter from building block precursors also present in the extracellular fluid. Access to extracellular precursor supplies is accomplished through what are termed *uptake systems* that actively transport precursors through the cell membrane to the intracellular Golgi apparatus, the organelles believed to be responsible for neurotransmitter synthesis. After synthesis, the transmitter is assumed to be packaged into vesicle form for release.

The essential features of synaptic transmission—synthesis, vesicle encapsulation, release, receptor site contact, degradation, uptake, etc.—are true of all brain synapses. The specifics may vary, however, depending on the particular neuron. Different neurons are chemically different neurotransmitters. There are several major groups of transmitter types: (*a*) acetylcholine (ACH), the most well understood of all neurotransmitters, is known to function at the neuromuscular junction; it is also believed to be a brain neurotransmitter; (*b*) catecholamines, a group of neurotransmitters that includes norepinephrine, epinephrine and dopamine; (*c*) serotonin, or 5-hydroxytrytamine; and (*d*) the amino acid transmitters, specifically, gamma-aminobutyric acid (GABA), glycine and glutamic acid. Certain neurotransmitters are known to be excitatory (produce EPSPs in the postsynaptic cell), such as acetylcholine, whereas others are known to be inhibitory (produce IPSPs), such as GABA.

Recall that every transmitter is synthesized from certain precursors, released from the presynaptic terminal, broken down by degradative enzymes, and so on. Each different neurotransmitter has its corresponding set of specific precursors, receptor sites, degradative enzymes, etc. This specificity allows for the experimental and clinical manipulation of one transmitter independently of all others, through drugs.

For example, Parkinson's disease is believed to be caused by a lack of one of the catecholamines (dopamine) in a certain region of the brain. A common treatment today is to administer patients with large quantities of the precursor, L-dopa, from which dopamine is subsequently synthesized. Another of the catecholamines (norepinephrine) is hypothesized to play a critical role in psychological disorders. Low levels of catecholamines are thought to be related to depression, whereas mania is believed to be a result of high levels of norepinephrine. For this reason, depression is often treated with drugs which inhibit the degradative enzymes for catecholamines, thus increasing the level of brain norepinephrine.

Even from this brief discussion of the chemistry of the neuron, it should be clear that many variables are involved in synaptic transmission. It is this multitude of variables and their involvement in the critical step of transmission from one neuron to another that makes the synapse the most likely location for neural mechanisms that are the basis for learning. Learning may be defined as a change in nerve cell response (ultimately leading to a change in behavior) as a function of past experience. It is easy to imagine alteration of a number of synaptic variables that would change the functioning of a given neuron. For example, the release of fewer vesicles from the presynaptic terminal could lead to a smaller EPSP, making a postsynaptic action potential less likely. Increased concentration of degradative enzymes in the vicinity of the synapse would have the similar effect of decreasing the likelihood of a postsynaptic action potential. Changes in the efficiency of uptake systems could readily affect the amount of precursor available for transmitter synthesis. Increasing the sensitivity of postsynaptic receptors to a neurotransmitter could also result in altered transmission by more readily producing an action potential from a given input.

These are the types of changes that might serve as the basis for learning. In fact, for a very simple form of learning—habituation (a decrease in response as a result of repeated activation)—it has been shown that the mechanism involved is a decrease in the probability of vesicle release at the presynaptic terminal. Precisely how and where such changes are "stored" as "memory" within the neuron is still unknown.

In summary, this section on the neuron has attempted to describe its major anatomical, physiological, and chemical aspects within the framework of its role as the essential element of the brain. As stated at the beginning of this section, the neuron's major functions are receiving incoming information, integrating this input, storing the message, and, finally, transmitting the message to another part of the brain for more processing, to striated muscles for overt behavior, or to internal organs for regulation of body functions. The neuron has specialized areas for receiving incoming information (dendrites and soma), and the input takes a specialized form (i.e., EPSPs or IPSPs). Integration of input is accomplished through summation of these PSPs, which in turn determines whether the neuron transmits a message along its axon through the use of action potentials. The specific sequence of action potentials can serve as a code to represent the message. The eventual occurrence of action potentials in the nerve terminals causes the release of chemical transmitter substances into the synapse, providing input to the next neuron or to muscle. These final transmission steps are the most likely to be influenced by experience, or learning, on the part of the organism. The next section of this chapter will concentrate on how individual neurons are grouped into larger structures to make up different major parts of the brain.

II. The Central Nervous System:
The Brain and Spinal Cord

Within the central nervous system (CNS), the cell bodies of neurons tend to be organized into groups, called nuclei; their axons form interconnecting pathways, called tracts. Although neurons within a given nucleus are typically involved in similar or related functions, it is important to keep in mind that few nuclei act autonomously in the production of behavior. Instead, complex behavioral processes are organized, initiated, or modulated by neural "systems" composed of several nuclei and tracts.

Before considering the anatomy and function of specific nuclei and systems, we will look at the overall organization of the human nervous system. Figure 1.9 shows the surface topography of the CNS, with schematized representations of the peripheral and autonomic nervous systems. The peripheral nervous system is composed of the major nerves, receptors, and neuromuscular junctions outside the bony protection of the cranium and spinal vertebrae. Note that the peripheral nerves are mixed, having both motor and sensory fibers related to a particular body region, which become separated in the vicinity of the spinal cord (sensory fibers enter through the dorsal root of the spinal cord; motor fibers exit via the ventral root). The autonomic nervous system is involved in the regulation of many involuntary or vegetative bodily functions such as heart rate, salivation, and stomach contractions. It has two major divisions: the sympathetic—which arouses respiratory, cardiac, and muscular systems for vigorous activity—and the parasympathetic—which acts in the opposite direction. The autonomic *ganglia* (a term referring to collections of neural cell bodies outside the CNS proper) of the sympathetic system can be seen adjacent to each segment of the spinal column in Figure 1.9.

The labels in Figure 1.9 indicate the major subdivisions of the CNS: the spinal cord, brainstem, cerebellum, and cerebral hemispheres. One important principle of organization is that each brain structure is bilaterally symmetrical, that is, the right and left sides of the brain are mirror images. Most structures are connected to their "twins" by tracts called commissures that cross the midline of the brain. Figure 1.9 shows a midline view of the CNS. Note the relative locations of the spinal cord, brainstem, cerebellum, midbrain, and cerebral cortex. In this view, the corpus callosum, which is the largest of the commissures connecting the cerebral hemispheres, is particularly evident. The inset in this figure labels the planes of orientation and terms used to describe relative locations of brain structures (e.g., the midline view is shown as if the brain were cut in the sagittal plane; anterior or rostral denote the front).

A. The Spinal Cord

We will begin our discussion of specific brain systems with the spinal cord, which consists of the axons of major sensory and motor pathways (white matter) and a central region of gray matter (nuclei). The gray matter is composed of the cell bodies of motor neurons and of interneurons which compose the circuitry for lower level behavioral integration such as reflexes. Traditionally, the spinal cord has been thought to serve only "lower" or simpler functions, while complex or "higher" functions have been attributed to the cerebrum, especially the cerebral cortex. When the spinal cord is operating without any "higher" influences (e.g., in the case of injury or animal experimentation) the complexity of behavior is often surprising. Not only are higher order reflex sequences organized at the spinal level, but the cord itself appears capable of simple forms of associative learning in the absence of input from the brain. These facts introduce the concept of hierarchical organization of brain systems, in which the functions of "lower" or simpler regions of the CNS are under the modulatory control of more complicated systems. One extreme example of this control would be a case in which the withdrawal reflex from a painful stimulus could be overridden by another brain system in order to rescue a child in danger. Even the less

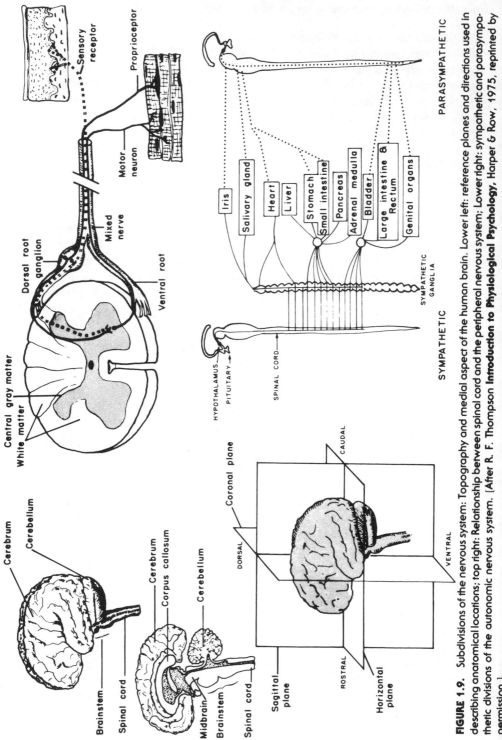

FIGURE 1.9. Subdivisions of the nervous system: Topography and medial aspect of the human brain. Lower left: reference planes and directions used in describing anatomical locations; top right: Relationship between spinal cord and the peripheral nervous system; Lower right: sympathetic and parasympathetic divisions of the autonomic nervous system. [After R. F. Thompson *Introduction to Physiological Psychology*, Harper & Row, 1975, reprinted by permission.]

Labels in figure:

Sensory receptor
Proprioceptor
Motor neuron
Mixed nerve
Dorsal root ganglion
Ventral root
Central gray matter
White matter

Cerebrum
Cerebellum
Brainstem
Spinal cord
Cerebrum
Corpus callosum
Cerebellum
Midbrain
Brainstem
Spinal cord

PARASYMPATHETIC
Iris
Salivary gland
Heart
Liver
Stomach
Small intestine
Pancreas
Adrenal medulla
Bladder
Large intestine & Rectum
Genital organs
SYMPATHETIC GANGLIA
HYPOTHALAMUS
PITUITARY
SPINAL CORD
SYMPATHETIC

Coronal plane
Sagittal plane
Horizontal plane
DORSAL
ROSTRAL
CAUDAL
VENTRAL

dramatic, everyday activities of the human brain, however, demonstrate subtle forms of hierarchical relationships among different brains systems, resulting in the flexibility and precision of behavior shown only by organisms with well-developed brains. In this context, then, the spinal cord is recognized as a complex processing region as well as a conduit for information to and from the brain itself.

B. Brainstem and Motor Systems

Inside the base of the skull, the central areas of the spinal cord expand into a very complicated region of tracts and nuclei called the brainstem, thought to be responsible for many involuntary and metabolic functions (e.g., respiration). Certain of these nuclei appear to subserve important, highly complex reflexes such as the orienting reflex. This is a stereotypic response to novel stimulation which involves head turning, eye movements, arousal, postural changes, and autonomic effects including heart rate and respiration changes. The autonomy of these brainstem regions involved in the orienting reflex, as well as the complexity of their organization, is underscored by the fact that all of these functions are aroused by some stimulus, organized, coordinated, and executed—all in a fraction of a second and often before the higher "conscious" brain is aware that the stimulus occurred.

The brainstem is also known to be involved in the control of arousal reactions in other brain areas. One brainstem region, the reticular formation (Figure 1.10), is part of a system that is responsible for activating many areas of the brain in response to sensory stimulation or upon waking from sleep. In fact, the EEG rhythms associated with various states of sleep and arousal (Figure 1.7) are thought to be controlled by the reticular activating system, which includes the reticular formation and the midline thalamus (to be discussed). Two other regions within the brainstem are necessary for the initiation of different sleep states. The locus coeruleus is involved in a norepinephrine (neurotransmitter) system initiating the rapid eye movement (REM, often associated with dreaming) phase of sleep. The raphé nuclei appear to play a role in other sleep stages (slow wave sleep), utilizing serotonin as their transmitter.

Lying dorsal to the brainstem is the cerebellum, a highly convoluted structure involved in organizing and monitoring complex patterns of skilled motor activity. Without this structure, movements become jerky and uncoordinated. Also thought to be part of a system organizing complex motor activity are the basal ganglia (caudate nucleus, globus pallidus, putamen) which lie deep within the cerebral hemispheres (Fig-

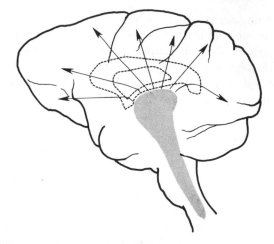

FIGURE 1.10. Schematized view of the location of the reticular activating system in the brainstem, midbrain, and cerebrum. Note the widespread influence on cortical areas. [After R. F. Thompson **Introduction to Physiological Psychology,** Harper & Row, 1975, reprinted by permission.]

ure 1.11). Damage or disruption of these areas results in tremor, abnormal rhythmic movements, and disturbance in muscle tone. One theory holds that these regions set the target, or end point, for many forms of motor movements. One disease of these structures, Parkinsonism, appears to involve the dopaminergic projection from the brainstem to the caudate nucleus. As mentioned previously, replacement of the brain dopamine can dramatically ease the symptoms of this disease.

C. The Hypothalamus and the Limbic System

Just anterior to the brainstem is a region called the hypothalamus, containing many nuclei and pathways related to metabolic, hormonal, and motivational aspects of behavior. Stimulation of this brain area can result in intense pleasure reactions or violent rage, depending on the specific nuclei affected. Animals with all brain tissue above the hypoth-

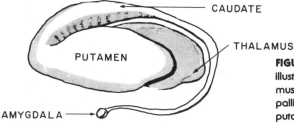

CAUDATE

THALAMUS

PUTAMEN

AMYGDALA

FIGURE 1.11. The basal ganglia, illustrated with respect to the thalamus and amygdala. The globus pallidus is located between the putamen and thalamus.

alamus removed can still exhibit complicated, highly organized patterns of emotional or motivated behavior, including autonomic effects. In many of these cases, however, the behavior is directed at an inappropriate object. An extremely important function of the hypothalamus is its control of the pituitary gland and endocrine system. Feedback loops between this region and glands throughout the body control reproductive cycles, sexual receptivity, and autonomic responses to stressful stimuli. Homeostasis (a consistent internal environment) is maintained by hypothalamic systems regulating feeding, drinking, and internal temperature. Arguments for the existence of true brain "centers" were long supported by the critical role of the hypothalamus in homeostasis.

The hypothalamus is intimately related to a group of cerebral structures known as the limbic system. The system derived its name from the fact that it forms a border or rim (Latin: *limbus*) encircling the top of the brainstem, lying between that region and the cerebral cortex. The major limbic regions are the amygdala, septum, hippocampus, and limbic areas of the cortex (Figure 1.12). The behavioral functions of limbic nuclei

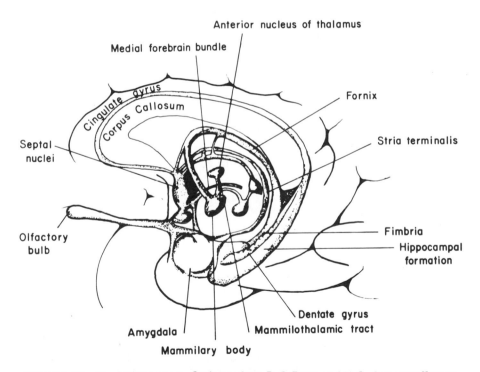

FIGURE 1.12. The limbic system. [Redrawn from F. C. Truex and M. B. Carpenter **Human Neuroanatomy,** Williams and Wilkins, 1969, reprinted by permission.]

are difficult to define. Lesion, stimulation, and recording studies indicate that they exert subtle modulatory effects on both sensory and response systems, and are involved in motivational and learning processes. Amygdala lesions in primates have been shown to affect social behavior and in human studies, hippocampal damage has been associated with memory deficits. It is possible that the true role of the limbic system does not conform to any presently defined behavioral function, but, at this point, its role in affective systems seems clear.

D. The Thalamus

Immediately dorsal to the hypothalamus is the thalamus, a group of nuclei clustered on the midline deep in the cerebrum. There are three different types of nuclei in the thalamus: relay, intrinsic, and midline. The relay nuclei are responsible for conveying information from sensory receptors lying in the periphery of the body to more central brain regions like cerebral cortex. Examples of relay nuclei are the lateral geniculate body for vision (Figure 1.13, shows the visual pathways from the retina to the cortex), the medial geniculate nucleus for audition, and the ventral nuclei for somatosensory information (visceral and skin senses). The pattern of thalamic relays for sensory information holds for all senses except taste and olfaction, which take a different route to the cortex. Intrinsic nuclei are believed to play a role in intrathalamic communication, while midline nuclei have been implicated in the nonspecific arousal of wide areas of cortex (as part of the reticular activating system). In addition, the thalamus is thought to be involved in a complex feedback circuit which regulates the appearance of highly synchronized EEG waves in the cortex (such as the alpha rhythm accompanying relaxed wakefulness).

E. The Cerebral Cortex

The vast, convoluted surface of the cerebral hemispheres consists of a six-layered cortex, approximately 2 mm thick, which overlies all the cerebral structures discussed previously. The amount and complexity of these cortical regions most clearly distinguish humans from other animals. In general, the amount of cerebral cortex in a given organism corresponds closely to the behavioral complexity and learning ability exhibited by the species. The cortical surface can be described in terms of its four lobes: frontal, parietal, occipital, and temporal (Figure 1.16). The major sensory and motor functions of the cortex are highly localized in the following regions: frontal (motor); parietal (somatosensory); occipital

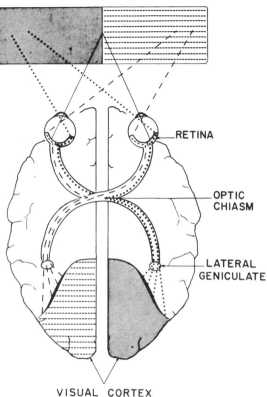

FIGURE 1.13. Visual pathways of the brain. Note that the right visual field for both eyes projects to the left visual cortex; the left field to the right side of the brain. [After R. F. Thompson **Introduction to Physiological Psychology,** Harper & Row, 1975, reprinted by permission.]

(vision); and temporal (audition). Within each of these specialized areas, a point-to-point relationship exists between a body region or receptor surface and the specific cortical region that monitors or controls it. Figure 1.14 shows, for example, the layout of body surface sensation on the surface of the somatosensory cortex. Note that not all areas of the body are equally represented—those with more complicated or essential functions (e.g., tongue and lips for speech; fingers for skilled movements) have relatively more cortical tissue devoted to them. It appears that the sensory areas generate a "model" of the environment rather than an exact representation. For example, the visual cortex is not like the focal point of a camera, receiving an inverted but exact replica of the external visual world. Rather, neurons in this area receive highly processed information and seem to respond to abstracted features of the environment—not points of light on the retina of the eye. Lines at particular angles and moving in particular directions are the preferred

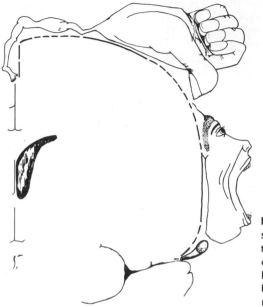

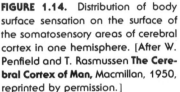

FIGURE 1.14. Distribution of body surface sensation on the surface of the somatosensory areas of cerebral cortex in one hemisphere. [After W. Penfield and T. Rasmussen **The Cerebral Cortex of Man,** Macmillan, 1950, reprinted by permission.]

stimuli for some visual cortical cells. In other words, they respond to such abstract concepts as orientation and velocity. Motor areas of the cortex also are not related as directly to movement as one might think. They appear to be involved with the initiation of movement or readjustments of movement patterns, rather than directly controlling the movement of each muscle in the body.

Areas not primarily sensory or motor have been termed "association" cortex and tend to be located in spaces between major sensory and motor areas. While the term association cortex may be a misnomer in terms of what really happens there, it is known that damage to such brain areas results in quite subtle and difficult-to-categorize disturbances of behavior that fall outside the realm of classical sensory or motor function. At such high levels of organization, though, it may be impossible to say exactly where sensory input stops and motor output begins.

While subcortical limbic and brainstem structures tend to be similar across mammals, primates (especially humans) have by far the most cortical tissue relative to brain size. In fact, the highly convoluted cortical surface is seen as an evolutionary solution to the problem of fitting more surface area (cortex) into a relatively fixed cranial volume. Figure 1.15 shows the relative amount of cortical convoluted tissue in several mam-

RAT   CAT

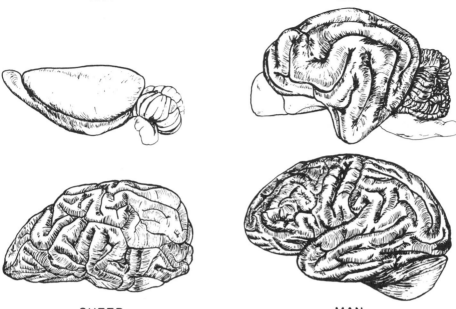

SHEEP   MAN

FIGURE 1.15. Comparison of cortical surface features in several species of mammals. (Not to scale.)

malian species. Note the smooth surface and few fissures in the rat brain; the intermediate degree in cat and sheep brains; and the large number of convolutions in primates. It is interesting to note that brain development in the ontogeny of the human embryo progresses from a primitive neural tube, through a stage with crude divisions into brainstem, midbrain, and forebrain regions, through another stage with an existing but smooth cortex, to a recognizably human, highly convoluted brain at birth. It appears, therefore, that the differentiation and elaboration of the cortical surface are relatively more recent both in evolutionary and ontogenetic terms.

F. Language and Hemispheric Specialization

Two final points in relation to the functional subdivision of cortical tissue in humans are in order. The first concerns the discovery that damage to the left side of the brain is much more likely to disturb language functions than is damage to corresponding regions in the right hemisphere. Evidence from a long series of experiments involving accidental injury has characterized different types of language impairments which correspond to selective disruption of certain regions of the left cerebral cortex. Figure 1.16 illustrates the relative positions of three regions: Broca's area, Wernicke's area, and the arcuate fasciculus. Damage to Broca's area results in severe impairment in the production of speech—other linguistic abilities are relatively intact. Injury to Wernicke's area appears to disrupt comprehension and organization of speech—although fluent but meaningless phrases can be spoken. Interruption of the arcuate fasciculus appears to separate these two important speech areas such that comprehension is good and speech is fluent, but the relationship between the two is severely impaired. Such findings seem to support the concept of language localization in the strictest sense.

We have mentioned the existence of commissures connecting similar areas of the two cerebral hemispheres. In certain cases of brain pathology, most notably epilepsy, it has been necessary to separate the hemispheres by means of severing the commissures to prevent the spread of seizure activity from one side of the brain to the other. In such cases, there is only a very slight disruption of the normal, everyday activities of the patient. However, specialized testing has shown that the two brain hemispheres tend to act in a surprisingly independent manner. Briefly,

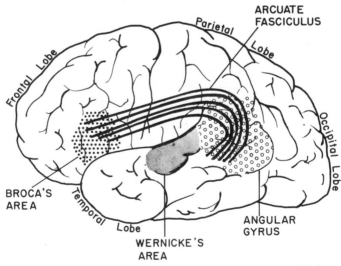

FIGURE 1.16. Primary language regions in the left cerebral cortex and delineation of the four major lobes of the brain: frontal, parietal, occipital, and temporal. [After R. F. Thompson **Introduction to Physiological Psychology,** Harper & Row, 1975, reprinted by permission.]

each cerebral hemisphere seems to be specialized for certain cognitive or perceptual functions. When this discovery was first made, cerebral dominance in language and verbal functions was ascribed to the left hemisphere since the isolated right hemisphere seemed incapable of language. However, rigorous testing of such patients indicated that "hemispheric specialization" may be a better term, since language functions appear to be present on both sides of the brain. An example may help to illustrate this point. Following surgical separation of the cerebral hemispheres, information given only to the right side of the brain elicits no verbal or linguistic responses from the subject, while the same information presented to the left side of the brain results in verbal reports of conscious experience—this fact led to the original descriptions of cerebral dominance. However, it is now known that, whereas the right side of the brain apparently cannot initiate spoken verbal responses, it can read, and respond through the left hand. Patients can match an object such as a key from a random group of items with the word "key" projected to the right hemisphere, yet verbally they are unable to report what they are doing. The right hemisphere appears to be specialized for visual–spatial tasks and creativity—but definitely not for spoken language. It should be noted that these rules hold in the case of right-handed people; cerebral specialization can be reversed in left-handers. It also appears that if injury occurs before a certain age, impaired linguistic functions can be relearned by the opposite hemisphere. Unfortunately, this rarely occurs in adults, whose brains seem to be capable of less recovery.

In summary, the human brain is an extremely complex organ, whose anatomy, physiology, and chemistry are only beginning to be understood by neuroscientists. There is, however, a great deal of concrete information available and we hope that this short review will be helpful as a preface to the following chapters.

Bibliography

Cooper, J. R., Bloom, F. E., & Roth, R. H. *The biochemical basis of neuropharmacology* (2nd ed.). New York: Oxford University Press, 1974.

Eccles, J. C. *The physiology of synapses.* New York: Springer-Verlag, 1964.

Eccles, J. C. *The understanding of the brain.* New York: McGraw-Hill, 1973.

Granit, R. *The purposive brain.* New York: Plenum, 1977.

Julien, R. M. *A primer of drug action.* San Francisco: Freeman, 1975.

Kuffler, S. W., & Nicholls, J. G. *From neuron to brain.* Sunderland, Mass.: Sinauer, 1976.

Magoun, H. W. *The Waking Brain* (2nd ed.). Springfield, Ill.: Charles C Thomas, 1963.

Noback, C. R., & Demarest, R. J. *The nervous system: Introduction and review* (2nd ed.). New York: McGraw-Hill, 1977.

Perkel, D. H., & Bullock, T. H. Neural coding. *Neurosciences Research Program Bulletin* (Vol. 6), 1968.

Pribram, K. H. *Languages of the brain: Experimental paradoxes and principles in neuropsychology.* Englewood Cliffs, N.J.: Prentice-Hall, 1971.

Thompson, R. F. *Foundations of physiological psychology.* New York: Harper & Row, 1967.

Thompson, R. F. *Introdiction to physiological psychology.* New York: Harper & Row, 1975.

Truex, R. C., & Carpenter, M. B. *Human neuroanatomy.* Baltimore: Williams & Wilkins, 1969.

Chapter II

Functional Organization of the Human Brain

COLWYN TREVARTHEN

I. Introduction: What Organizes Which Functions?

For the psychologist, the most striking feature of the mind is its ability to experience the outside world and to take up this experience, store it in memory, and use it to make acts that change the world. Most psychologists see cognitive processes as motivated at base by fairly simple inherent needs, but daily life has elaborate wishes, values, and convictions. These frequently distort or override the immediately obvious in experience. How do these more elaborate motivations arise?

Perhaps the explanation is to be found in human social existence. Humans communicate exceedingly well. It is generally supposed by all the sciences of human life that language, the main communicative activity, is an acquired skill. Obviously the vocabulary of language is acquired, as are all the techniques, rituals, rules, procedures, institutions, and constructions by which humans create and sustain their social world. But it is a strange and moving truth that similar abstract features emerge in the forms taken by these artificial creations when one compares isolated societies with quite separate histories. Humankind seems to be after common goals. The regularities in human patterns of collective action are difficult for psychologists to grasp, as are universals in highly elaborate human motives and values.

33

THE BRAIN AND PSYCHOLOGY

For the cerebral anatomist and physiologist, the clearest fact about **the** human brain is that it is elaborately organized and minutely describable. One can see this general organization in any example of **a** human brain, in spite of the unique experiences that particular brain has had. The organization of any human brain is minutely regular, conforming to the general type. Details well observed in 1879 are seen clearly in 1979. Moreover, the human brain can be compared to that of other animal forms to discover a common design and adaptive phylogenetic trends which certainly relate well to differences in ways of life. There are comforting correlates in size of brain parts with ability to perceive, act, or learn. Nevertheless, the contents of experience, the store of learning, the states or motivation or of will to act are not yet visible in brain anatomy. At best we have some gross events which wax and wane with the mental changes.

How are we to reconcile the mercurial efficiency of conscious images, intentions, and the correctness of our insights about the meaningfulness and usefulness of things with fixed regularities of brain organization, most of which appear to be present in a baby's brain when it is born, before there has been any relevant experience of either the "real" or the "imaginary" world?

The search for a scientifically valid answer to this question must take note of the extraordinary way in which this brain develops. It is a most important but much neglected fact that human brains have an elaborate and protracted embryogenesis. They are transformed in the fetus by addition of novel cortical machinery; they add vast new synaptic arrays in infancy; and they are still visibly gaining in anatomical definition all the time they are experiencing in childhood. The brain of an old man is still in process of development. This seems to be an important clue.

In the embryo, the developmental process that sorts out nerve fibers and connects nerve cells selectively depends upon intense intercellular communication in which high speed sorting is performed. The selective process is accelerated greatly by the advent of a never ceasing traffic of nerve impulses. After birth, the impulse patterns become increasingly dominated by stimuli and by correlations between stimulating events as they recur. They are also molded by the forms of actions with which the integrated brain systematically explores the field of stimulation.

In this chapter, an attempt will be made, in briefly recapitulating textbook knowledge of brain systems from spinal cord to cerebral cortex, to introduce developmental pointers. These hint at a generating of mental events that never becomes a passive image of external order. It will be suggested that the human brain has nerve cell systems that actively create motives, which are far removed from what is required for mere organic "survival." These motives balance immediate and lasting needs for such survival against a record in the brain of what the world offers as goals for many kinds of action. Gradually what was defined between nerve cells in their thousands of millions of years of development before birth becomes qualified by a memory record that adjusts the motives to external events, but the developmentally defined goals remain.

In textbooks of anatomy and physiology, the brain is represented as a maze of pathways for transmitting and processing an input of excitatory energy toward channels of motor output. Nevertheless, there is abundant evidence, which eminent brain scientists have noted throughout the past two centuries, of a vital genesis of action in the intact living brain. Most neurons in the brain have no direct contact with either stimuli or responses and most are spontaneously interacting at all times. The functional organization of the brain is the concrete result of a generative process that is perfectly capable of specifying forms of behavior and experience, as well as nuclei and tracts.

In an evolutionary perspective, the intentions which animals show in their actions and the motives that regulate the selecting and combining of intended acts are the basic adaptive constituents of brain activity. Evolution has worked upon these in the selection of efficient habits of behavior. Intentions and motives, automatic and unconscious in simpler life forms, greatly strengthened by consciousness of circumstances in the more elaborate, have anatomical formulation in brains. They must also be intimately associated with neural organs for perceiving the right goals for motor activation. This evolution of behavior works in a three-part system: a brain acting in a body within a set of environmental resources specific to each organism (Figure 2.1).

The problem of how motor coordination is represented neuroanatomically was elucidated brilliantly more than 40 years ago by Nicholas Bernstein (1967), who demonstrated that adaptive movement would be impossible unless the brain generated "motor images" in advance of the final form or goal of each desired movement. This image-guided movement has a high degree of independence of the particular muscle contractions needed to carry out the movement on any one occasion. Bernstein further showed that the central brain systems making such generative images must be integrated with other neural systems that are responsible in appropriate degree to proprioceptive feedback of error signals and progress reports picked up in the course of movement. Reafferent sensory excitation fills in a transitory "gap" prepared in the motor program. This is how the resultant activity makes the right movement: by obedience to conditions (Figure 2.2).

Bernstein went on to discuss how this control could be localized in brain anatomy. Each movement must be the outcome of activity in many hierarchically interacting or embedded brain systems converging to-

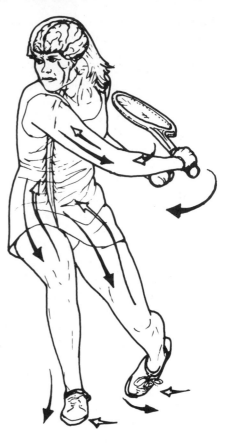

FIGURE 2.1. The brain, the body, and the environment. The brain acts on the world and receives information from it through the motor and sensory agencies of the body.

ward the final common path (Greene, 1972). Neither on the motor side nor on the sensory side can the central nerve mechanisms represent peripheral units of structure (muscles, or loci on receptor arrays) as invariant units of function. The brain cannot work as a projection screen or a keyboard. This means that to have any degree of adaptive action at all, an animal like a human possessing a body composed of complex chains of levers must have a linked set of parallel control structures in the CNS that will regulate the collective action of many equivalent or complementary peripheral elements (see Figure 2.3). Furthermore, animals would never be able to acquire a conditioned response by movements that differ greatly in detail on every occasion if the central representations were simple metrical reproductions of the peripheral events.

Perception requires a similar theory of integration by images for goals. For any outside object to become either the stimulus for an appropriate response or the object of that action, a program or formula for that

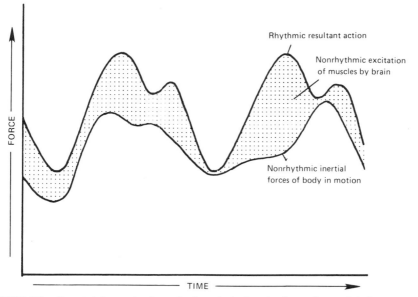

Rhythmic resultant action

Nonrhythmic excitation
of muscles by brain

Nonrhythmic inertial
forces of body in motion

FORCE

TIME

FIGURE 2.2. Bernstein's graph of cerebral control of motor force. Bernstein's force curves show how the output of the brain adapts to cooperate with forces of moving body parts.

response must exist **already** in some form in the brain, before the movement or the stimulus occurs. The potential indicators in sensory information of where that object is and of its correct identifying form, texture, color, etc., must also be indicated in the brain circuits before they are excited from outside. Accurate determination of the place and rate of any change or motion in the object must also be made before it can be oriented to and taken in or avoided. Finally, any defining feature must be recognized by some mechanism that can give that feature a functional value for the subject. In short, the amount of neural work or "computation" to be done in advance of any adaptive behavioral response, to make sense of stimuli and to make effective actions, may be far greater than that needed to transmit information from the receptors to the brain or from motor nuclei to the muscles. Many forms of brain linkage from stimulus to response must exist before either the stimulus or response occur.

In thinking about evolutionary origins of intelligence, we must remember that lives of animals are mutually adapted. They do not just compete in their behaviors because of convergent or overlapping needs with respect to common resources, but they also act on each other directly. Out of this interdependency, specialized brain processes have evolved for transmitting messages between animals. Related brain

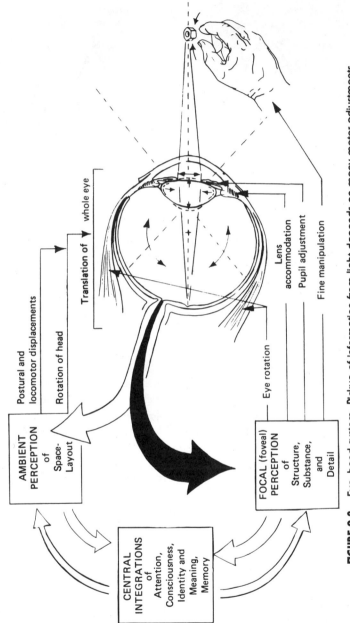

FIGURE 2.3. Eye-hand system. Pickup of information from light depends on many motor adjustments.

Postural and
locomotor displacements

Rotation of head

Translation of ▶ whole eye

AMBIENT
PERCEPTION
of
Space-
Layout

CENTRAL
INTEGRATIONS
of
Attention,
Consciousness,
Identity and
Meaning,
Memory

FOCAL (foveal)
PERCEPTION
of
Structure,
Substance,
and
Detail

Eye rotation

Lens
accommodation

Pupil adjustment

Fine manipulation

functions adjust motives to signals received from others. Evidently, as animals became increasingly active and aware of the circumstances of their actions, they became more aware of each other. The gift of being aware of the inanimate world as a rich field for advantageous use of coordinated movement (being **subjective**) automatically conferred an ability to get inside of the purposes of others and follow their interests being **intersubjective**) (see Figure 2.4). Animal communication disobeys ordinary laws of physical action and reaction because it couples the information processing and motive-generating of separate brains together; it joins understandings. Thus by linking cerebral processes, animals interact more psychologically than physically.

Bernstein's theory of how muscles are used by brain generators of movements would seem to give a good basis from which to begin the kind of classification of brain parts relating to psychological functions.

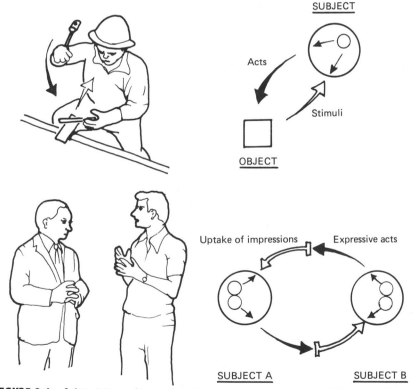

FIGURE 2.4. Subjectivity and intersubjectivity. A subject acting on an object controls movements by perception (top). Two subjects communicate by representing the other's acts as well as their own. They create an intersubjective process (bottom).

According to him, we should seek a topography of regulators of the conditions for acts. We should find nerve cell systems organized to project the body toward well-specified goals. In the end we should discover a level of representation where a living image of objects in the world may be said to be conscious, for more complex acts do not have time to discover their conditions once they are being performed. They must be "aware" of the conditions beforehand.

It seems that the greatest shortcoming of modern brain theories is an absence of even a preliminary hypothesis about how intersubjectivity is represented anatomically. How does the brain represent not only a conscious and coherent intentionality for its own person, but also the purposes and feelings of another? There is hard evidence that the brains of newborn infants perceive other people not as objects, but as partners in experience and in purpose. To begin an attack on this problem, we will try to specify certain basic features about systems of the brain that regulate communicative expression and that adjust to collective experience in society. After all, it is human cooperative awareness which has the greatest survival value in actual living, and our motives for it are strong.

II. Integrators of Body Action in the Spinal Cord

All sensory nerves of the human body behind the ears and below the neck enter the dorsal spinal cord. All muscles, excepting those of the head and throat, are activated by a few million motor cells in the ventral spinal cord. Together, these sensory and motor neurons account for no more than .2% of all neurons in the brain. The famous experiments of Charles Sherrington (Swazey, 1968) with surgically isolated spinal cords of monkeys and dogs showed that surrounding the motor cells in the spinal grey matter are longitudinal and crossing linkages with integrative power. Neurons, with beginnings and endings entirely inside the cord, are much more numerous than sensory or motor cells. They couple segment with segment and afferent endings with efferent cells into such a coherent set of coacting and reciprocating structures that individual sensory-to-motor reflex arcs are distinguished only by highly artificial analysis. Sherrington conceived of reflexes not as mechanical units to be integrated, but as dynamic integrative units relating movements to the outside world.

The nerve net of the cord makes possible smooth sequences of extension and retraction of the limbs, including withdrawals from traumatic stimuli, and it coordinates all four limbs with bending and stiffening of the trunk in standing, walking, and running. The disconnected spinal cord of a dog, separated from the brain, can motivate the same hind leg muscles as are used in walking to lift up and scratch an irritating spot near the shoulder. Treadmill experiments with spinal cats show that the different stepping cycles of walking, trotting, and galloping are "programmed" in the isolated cord. Stepping moduli persist when all sensory feedback is abolished, but they respond adaptively to changes in the sensory feedback caused by driving the limbs at different rates on the moving belt. Recent research has demonstrated how the integrator circuits of the cord, coordinated by collateral feedback from motor neurons as well as by reafferent sensory feedback, open the system to control by descending input from the brain (Grillner, 1975).

The spinal cord of a human being has less autonomy that that of other animals because it is more dependent on elaborate high level commands. Humans neither stand nor locomote without elaborate supraspinal integrations. After complete midthoracic transection of the cord, both lower extremities of a human being are totally inert (paraplegic) and all somatic and visceral responses of a human are abolished. After a few weeks this "spinal shock" clears somewhat and withdrawal from a pinprick in the foot and weak standing may be elicited.

The tissues of the body form a great receptor which reports a rich variety of discriminations about tensions and pressures back to the cord. The balance of forces in muscles is controlled by feedback from tuneable stretch detectors in tendons and muscles. Muscle spindles responding to changes of length and tension in each muscle strand are finely adjustable in sensitivity by the movements of miniature muscles activated by their own motor neurons (γ-afferents). These intrafusal (spindle) muscles permit an anticipatory scan of internal body tensions, just as oculomotor muscles permit scan of the visual array. In addition to information about forces on the inside, there are forces added by outside objects when they contact the body surface. Many different mechanical and structural characteristics of objects may be distinguished from their stimulus effects on the body. Finally, there is sensory evidence of actual or impending body injury from pain of burning, cutting, or bruising.

The spinal cord regulates essential tissue activities in the viscera. Output to the autonomic nervous system controls the regional circulation of blood through skin, muscles, and abdominal viscera, as well as secretion of sweat from the skin. These changes effect temperature control and circulation of metabolites. Related autonomic efferents regulate the gland secretions and smooth muscle activities of the gut and control urination. Sympathetic nerves regulate body defense in flight and fight, parasympathetic nerves control the conservative processes of food digestion, reproduction, and rest (Pick, 1970).

The orderly anatomy required for spinal cord functions is set down in the embryo by a sequence of intercellular negotiations that map out neural images of functional territories of the body (Trevarthen, 1973). A refined body-mapping or "somatotopy" is established (Figure 2.5). Initially quite simple in layout, it becomes much complicated by cell migrations, selective cell deaths, and the widespread interweaving of axons capable of connecting remote cell groups. Formation of selective interneuron links, visible at about the end of the first month of gestation, slows up the prior typing of neuroblasts, but contributes new interactions between cells. This advances the inductive process that determines connective affinities between cells. It gives new refinement to the somatotopy, preparing the way for formation of further integrative links. The nervous system, which in its early stages was passive to the body's architecture, comes to impose a powerful integrative force on the body, regulating growth of muscles and bones and coordinating the functions of all internal organs. Experiments with chicks in the egg and embryo rats show that alternating movements of the limbs are formed before transmission of nerve impulses from sensory nerves is possible.

In spite of its complex inherent integrative powers, any autonomous structure in the spinal cord must receive descending influences from the brain and supply the brain's afferent requirements (Nauta & Karten, 1970). Dominance of the cord by the brain is effected by numerous pathways that link the sensory fields of the body and viscera to cerebral representations of the whole subject. The brain, in return, transmits precisely selective facilitations and inhibitions down to the neuropile (synaptic network) surrounding the "final common path" motor neurons of the spinal cord. In mammals, an important descending influence is concerned with regulating the proprioceptive reafference from muscle sense organs by controlling the γ-efferent system. Thus, in addition to more-or-less direct control of the large α-motor neurons that cause contractions in powerful skeletal muscles, the spinal feedback mechanisms may be tuned and aimed by supraspinal coordinators.

III. Brainstem. Special Senses and Motor Organs of the Head. Orienting, Attending, Eating, Breathing, and Communicating

The brainstem transmits all output from the cerebral cortex and most input to it, and cortical activities depend upon integrations of its reticular core in both autonomic and exteroceptive sectors (Figure 2.6). The brainstem neuropile is also the basic motor integrator for orienting and attending and for many forms of expressive and communicative action. It regulates

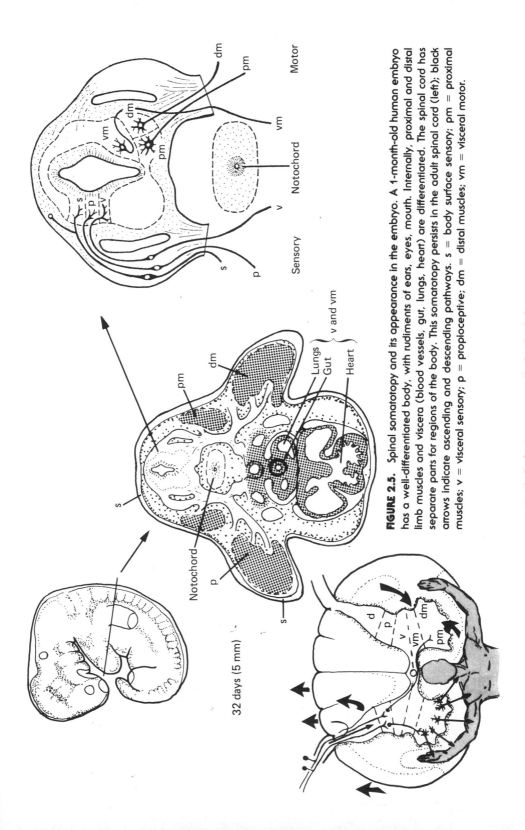

FIGURE 2.5. Spinal somatotopy and its appearance in the embryo. A 1-month-old human embryo has a well-differentiated body, with rudiments of ears, eyes, mouth. Internally, proximal and distal limb muscles and viscera (blood vessels, gut, lungs, heart) are differentiated. The spinal cord has separate parts for regions of the body. This somatotopy persists in the adult spinal cord (left): black arrows indicate ascending and descending pathways. s = body surface sensory; pm = proximal muscles; v = visceral sensory; p = proprioceptive; dm = distal muscles; vm = visceral motor.

the conservative functions of rest and sleep (Ramon-Moliner & Nauta, 1966; Scheibel & Scheibel, 1967).

A. The Hindbrain

The hindbrain contains a complex array of sensory and motor nuclei linked to cranial nerves in which functions are so interwoven as to present a nightmare to students of anatomy and neurologists alike (Figure 2.6). Because structures of the head with premium survival value and extremely varied phyolgenetic history are derived, embryogenetically, from both the anterior four body segments and the branchial arches appended to them, they confuse the classification into "somatic" and "visceral" which applied reasonably neatly to the trunk and spinal cord. The extrinsic oculomotor muscles which rotate the eye, and some muscles at the back of the neck and under the tongue are *somatic*, but most of the neck and tongue muscles and all those of the face, throat, inner ear and larynx are branchial, or *special visceral*. In addition to the special head receptors for olfaction, sight, hearing, and taste, all the afference from the skin of the face and that from the mouth, tongue, throat, and muscles of the face, enters the brainstem. Important general visceral efference from cranial nerves includes that to the blood vessels of the face (producing blanching, flushing, and blushing), the pupil and lens muscles of the eye (involved in regulating light level and the definition of the visual image), the salivary, lacrymal and nasal glands and parasympathetic innervation to the viscera of thorax and abdomen (Figure 2.6). A large output to branchial arch muscles is involved in taking in or rejecting potential food or drink, and in breathing. Changes in eating, drinking, and breathing are closely correlated with fluctuations in the metabolic condition of the body and with defence of an adaptive metabolic state against damage or stress.

In the embryo, the distribution of sensory and motor, somatic and visceral zones in the brainstem first resembles that of the spinal cord, but the plan is soon modified by the opening up of the roof of the IVth ventricle (cavity of the hindbrain) and spreading the dorsal alar laminae (sensory) to the lateral position. In the more anterior metencephalon of the hindbrain, the alar laminae give rise to cells which migrate down the side of the stem, past the basal laminae (motor) to form the nuclei of the pons. Other cells from this source move upwards to form the cerebellar cortex and deep cerebellar nuclei. In the myelencephalon (medulla) a descending migration of alar cells gives rise to the olivary nucleus (see Figure 2.7 and Figure 2.13).

In the hindbrain, the trigeminal nucleus of the face is very large, with a major portion devoted to the lower face, lips, and teeth. It extends to

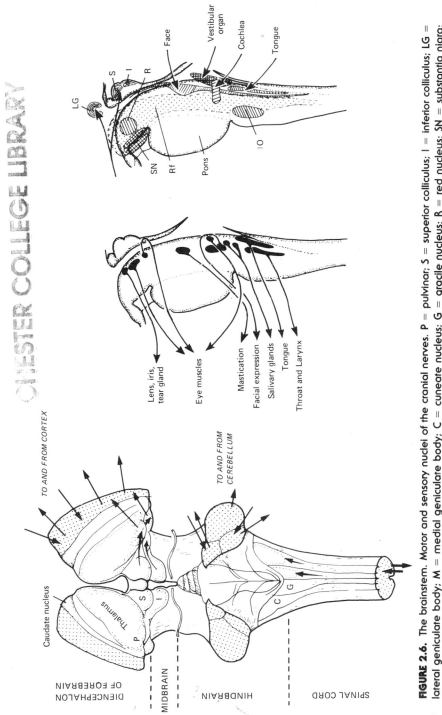

FIGURE 2.6. The brainstem. Motor and sensory nuclei of the cranial nerves. P = pulvinar; S = superior colliculus; I = inferior colliculus; LG = lateral geniculate body; M = medial geniculate body; C = cuneate nucleus; G = gracile nucleus; R = red nucleus; SN = substantia nigra; Rf = reticular formation; IO = inferior olivary nucleus.

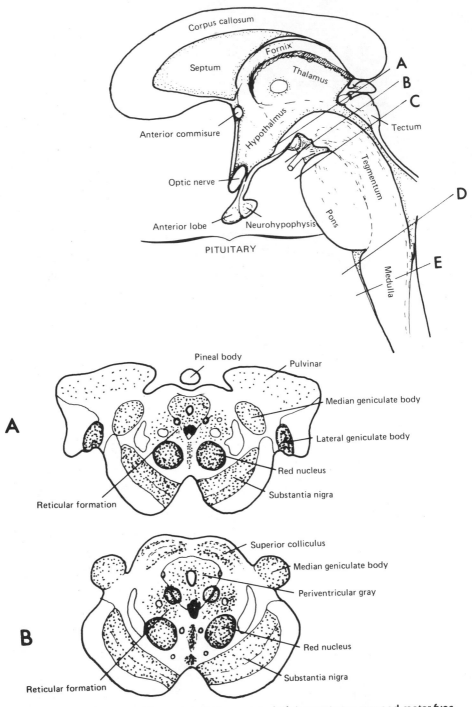

FIGURE 2.7. Brainstem. The main reticular nuclei which integrate sensory and motor functions. Fiber tracts, white. Motor nuclei, black. Letters indicate locations of cross sections.

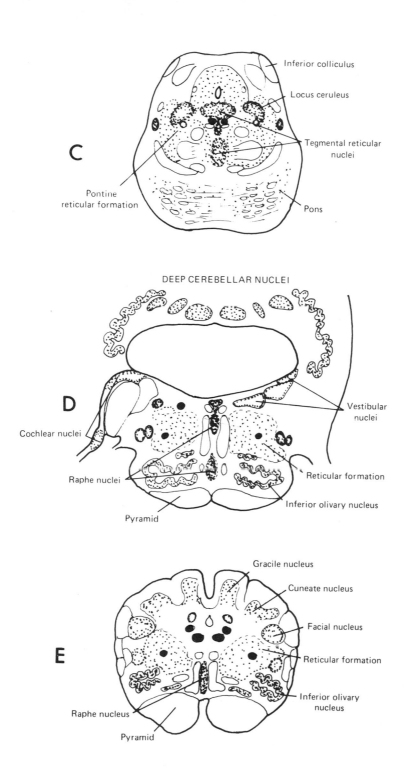

C
Inferior colliculus
Locus ceruleus
Tegmental reticular
nuclei
Pontine
reticular formation
Pons

DEEP CEREBELLAR NUCLEI

D
Vestibular
nuclei
Cochlear nuclei
Raphe nuclei
Reticular formation
Inferior olivary nucleus
Pyramid

E
Gracile nucleus
Cuneate nucleus
Facial nucleus
Reticular formation
Inferior olivary
nucleus
Raphe nucleus
Pyramid

the upper end of the cord where the gracile nuclei (leg and foot) and cuneate nuclei (arm and hand) relay and process somesthetic information from the spinal sensory nerves en route to the thalamus and cerebral cortex. Where medulla and cord meet, these three nuclei form a somatotopic array with hand, foot, and face represented disproportionately large as major sensory structures informing consciousness (Figure 2.7E).

The vestibular organs, which sense gravitational force and head accelerations, have no direct input to the cerebral cortex. The precise gyroscopic-like information they give about the displacements and rotations of the head integrates with motor control in the brainstem, cerebellum, and spinal cord. The stability of the world in consciousness, the coherence of the spatial frame for discriminations in hearing, touch, and sight, and the prediction of coherent action patterns for the body musculature, all may utilize vestibular information. There is direct and exceedingly rapid and powerful vestibular input to the oculomotor center that guides visual fixations on loci in the stable external world when the head is in motion.

The cochlear nucleus transmitting auditory input is also in the hindbrain (Figure 2.7D). The cochlea evolved in land vertebrates for picking up air vibrations caused by motion of air, water, or solids. Even where not used for sonar echo detection of energy reflected from surfaces and objects at a distance, as it most elaborately is by bats and dolphins, ears can hear the temporo-spatial arrangement of the world outside by analyzing differences in the patterning of air pressure waves transmitted to the two sides of the head, either from some other object displacing, or reflected from movements of the subject himself. The close relation of hearing one's own action to the proprioceptive functions of the vestibular organ and detectors of body vibrations or shock in muscles and joints is obvious. The precise and complex anatomy which processes data from the two ears to scan auditory space and to locate outside foci of activity is in the olivary complex and associated nuclei in the hindbrain. Auditory information for orienting is integrated in the midbrain roof: that identifying objects from their resonance, etc. and for controlling acts of manipulation that cause objects to move against one another and emit sounds, as well as for communication by speech and music, is given finer analysis in the cortex of the temporal lobe via the inferior colliculus and the auditory nucleus of the thalamus (median geniculate body).

The sensory and motor centers of the hindbrain are of supreme psychological importance because they include the core structures of communicative expression coupled to the principal regulators of bodily and emotional states. Some muscles of the head directly regulate input to olfaction, vision, hearing, and taste. They are the brain's agents for selective gating and tuning of input to perception. Nearly all of these orienting and focalizing movements enter, as well, into acts of communication. For example, flaring the nostrils, raising the eyebrows, opening the eyelids, dilation of the pupils, rotation and fixation of the eyes, cocking of the head to aid hearing, protrusion of the tongue or licking, and their opposites, all have forms modified to make them more clearly seen by persons. Indeed, such movements are often made for communication when the subject has no need of them for his own perceptions. Though profoundly modified by custom and etiquette, communicating movements are shown to be innate in general organization by their similarity across all cultures and by their clear presence in neonates and rapid incorporation into interpersonal communication in infancy. The muscles of both the upper and the lower face constitute a unique human resource, far more complex than in any other species, for transmission of rapid and exceedingly subtle information about mental activities. Above all, face movements inform a human observer about the states of motivation behind them.

Charles Darwin concluded that not just the peripheral organs of expression, but the **motive states** themselves have undergone evolutionary development by selective retention of the neural systems which regulate them to further an intricate and reliable intermental life. It is interesting to speculate on the fact that there is direct outflow of emotional information about fluctuations and levels of equilibrium in the reticular core and associated autonomic mechanisms from one brain, through the movements of muscles of expression, to these same systems in the brain of a partner. Cooperative action of brains must benefit by this direct motivational coupling.

Vocalizations form a special category of expressions. Though of no use to the originator in exploration and identification of objects (except where vocal sound is used as a sonar device), they nevertheless produce stimuli both for vocalizer and listener. Shouts, calls, and cries use larynx and throat with jaw opening and closing and little modulation of the tongue and lips. They carry subtle information about degrees of tension and force put into inhaling or exhaling air through larynx, throat, and mouth. With the addition of finely sequenced movements of lips and tongue against each other, associated with opening and closing the jaws, and large changes in the size and form of the spaces in the vocal tract, the sounds made by the vocal cords become carriers of information about expressive movements of the face.

Speech evolved out of movements of lips and tongue to grasp and perceive small objects whether to be eaten or just carried. Many primates use lips and tongue to groom one another as well as to grimace their feelings. Thus subtle communication by mouth exists without speech. Experiments on speech perception show that both appearance and sound of speech are monitored by a "listener," and that ambiguities in listening are resolved by reading the lips. Speech has huge resources for making variations in the energy distribution and temporal modulation of the sounds of voicing, and obviously the movements of larynx, throat, mouth cavity, tongue, mouth opening, and lips have been greatly adapted for this purpose.

Injuries to the brainstem produce a great variety of sensory and motor losses, but little is known about the more interesting disorders of integrative psychological activity at this level. Automatic, pathological laughter, crying, screaming or shouting, divorced from feelings of happiness, sadness, fear, or surprise, show that, as with the spinal mechanisms for locomotion and autonomic adjustments, there are highly patterned brainstem interneuronal mechanisms incorporating linkages to define combinations and sequences of movement in face, jaws, and throat and associated autonomic events. Lesions in the brainstem reticular formation can interfere with the regulation of sleep or cause coma. In the hindbrain there are vital pacemakers in the reticular formation that regulate the rate of heartbeat and breathing.

B. The Midbrain. An Ancient Visuomotor Center

Recording, stimulation, and ablation studies show that in fish and amphibia the midbrain roof (tectum) is the principal cerebral organ of sight. It performs not only the predictive and elaborately compensating integrations in command of the spinal circuits for visual orienting and visual guidance of locomotion, but it also discriminates and evaluates objects and learns visual distinctions (Herrick, 1948; Sprague, 1967; Sarnat & Netsky, 1974).

In all vertebrates, the roof of the midbrain (tectum) contains a map of visual space in the form of precisely ordered terminals of the axons from retinal ganglion cells. This eye-to-midbrain map is the most studied of all nerve circuits in experimental brain embryology (Sperry, 1965; Jacobson, 1970; Gaze, 1974; Trevarthen, 1979a). The map is oriented, in the early embryo stage, with reference to chemical markers or gradients of unknown constitution, but the final arrangement also depends upon intense interactions between terminal filaments. They do not simply follow chemical tracks. Initially, each axon projects branches to a large patch of the tectum with the contributions from many axons overlapping and mixed at each point. Then the highly mobile filaments react to each other and most are eliminated. Those that come from closely neighboring retinal cells tend to remain side by side in the tectum. Although this neighborhood selection process has been given a sound theoretical formulation, the actual mechanism is still not known. By comparing the tectal maps of forms with eyes facing in different directions in the head (e.g., a cat with forward aimed eyes and a rabbit with eyes on the side of the head), it was found (Trevarthen, 1968) that the brain's map is not oriented to give the retinal axis of symmetry a constant location. The visual field in the brain is lined up to reproduce the midplane through the body at rest, and into the external world, on the midline of the brain. I call this a body-centered map of the "behavioral field" of the subject. In it, two lateral orienting fields flank an anteromedial consummatory field in which objects are imaged when they are at the center of interest for the whole animal (i.e., when a decision may be made about their identity and how to "use" them).

The visual map could be described as somatotopic, regarding the retinae as part of the body surface. But it is the nature of eyes to form an image of the light array in a set of directions radiating from the nodal point of the optical system. This radial light field can stand for a set of directions from an "ego center" for the whole body. It could be used as a radial set of potential goal directions for movements of the mouth or hand. The distinction perhaps is made best by calling this kind of mapping with respect to the whole subject's center of action **telotopic** rather than somatotopic (telos = direction) (see Figure 2.8).

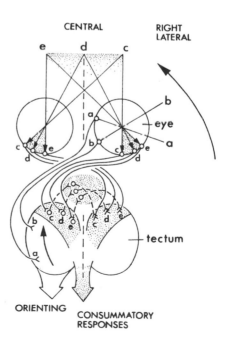

FIGURE 2.8. The telotopic map of visual space on the midbrain roof (superior colliculi or tectum) of all vertebrates.

Physiological studies with monkeys show that the superior colliculi (midbrain tectum in mammals) map not only retinal input terminals, but also a motor field of eye rotations (Robinson, 1968; Mohler & Wurtz, 1977). Stimulation of a point in deep layers on one side (say the left) causes a conjugate saccadic displacement of the two eyes through a constant angle to face a particular direction in the opposite half of the behavioral field (that would be to the right). An appropriately located stimulus from outside the body causes excitation in the surface layers in register with the eye-movement-provoking point deeper in the colliculus. When an alert monkey makes a normal spontaneous looking-movement, stepping the eyes together to face an off center direction, a flood of action potentials rises through deeper layers of the colliculus just before the movement, concentrating in the target locus to prime it so that the "expected" stimulus at that point has more excitatory effect (greater perceptual salience). This is a most interesting physiological correlate of attention related to exploratory eye movements. What the monkey is looking for becomes easier to see just before it is looked at. The colliculi certainly do not function simply to mediate foveation reflexes as they are classically held to do. In an important sense, the colliculi are part of the voluntary eye-movement apparatus.

Registration of the changed relation between the eyes and body axis after the eyes have completed an orientation step to one side must be integrated elsewhere in the brain, possibly deeper in the midbrain or even further afield in the brainstem or cerebellum. The colliculi project to the floor of the midbrain (tegmentum), to the reticular formation around the oculomotor nuclei, and also to the cerebral hemispheres (pulvinar nucleus of the thalamus and parietotemporal cortex) (Nauta & Karten, 1970; Sarnat & Netsky, 1974). They also project to the mediolateral parts of the reticular system of brainstem and cord which coordinate turning movements of the trunk and neck. The visuomotor layers of the colliculi receive a strong projection from the visual cortex as well as inputs from somesthetic and auditory systems. The vestibular afferents and cerebellum are closely integrated with the oculomotor nuclei and surrounding reticular formation. All of these circuits are likely to be involved in "compensations," so a stable visual scene is perceived while the image on the retina is being scanned by rotations of the eye (Bizzi et al., 1971).

The process of focalization, by which a sharp image of significant objects is formed on the high resolution area of the fovea, involves pupil constriction and lens accommodation. These movements are regulated in the pretectal region, where the midbrain roof meets the diencephalon just posterior to the thalamus. Of course the massive projection from the retina by way of the lateral geniculate nucleus to the striate cortex is important to the control of selective uptake of information by the fovea, and it probably plays a major role in directing conjoint action of the foveae in exploration of targets at different distances from the subject (convergence adjustments) (Robinson, 1968).

To understand the action of the various parts of midbrain, forebrain, and cortex that receive visual input, it is necessary to examine the various patterns of retinal stimulation that result from moving the eyes in different ways. The effects of collicular lesions in monkeys and human beings show that the numerous visual centers work in a tightly integrated manner performing complementary roles in the active selection of perceptual information and the formulation of movement patterns that drive visual effects in predictable ways.

The ventral half of the midbrain called the tegmentum is a key motor center (see Figure 2.7, p. 46). In the lower vertebrates it is the principal head ganglion governing coordinated turning of the whole body (Herrick, 1948). Stimulation there produces turning movements in which all muscles participate (Hess, 1958). Stimulation of the midbrain reticular formation of a sleeping monkey causes physiological arousal of the cortical EEG, waking and behavioral orientation (i.e., looking about as if to find the cause of waking) (Magoun, 1969). A core of reticular nuclei is involved in autonomic and emotional activities (Yakoulev, 1968). The central gray of the midbrain, the tegmental nuclei, and the raphé nuclei of the brainstem reticular formation have projections from the hypothalamus. Stimulation in the central gray may produce vocalizations indicative of fear, distress, or anger, and various autonomic signs (Hess, 1958).

Motor nuclei deep in the forebrain (basal ganglia) are coupled to the red nucleus and the substantia nigra of the midbrain tegmentum (see Figures 2.7, 2.9 and 2.15, pages 46, 55 and 64). The former relays a strong input from the cerebellum to the ventral lateral and anterior thalamus and prefrontal cortex, and also projects to the motor system of the precision or distal motor system of brainstem and cord (Kuypers, 1973). The nigra projects upward to the basal ganglia (caudate, globus pallidum, and putamen) and anterior ventral thalamus, receiving input from the prefrontal cortex. Nigrostriatal neurons produce dopamine as a transmitter, and disorder of this system produces the tremor of Parkinsonism.

IV. Cerebellum. Center for Motor Strategies and Skills

The cerebellum has evolved in land animals as the principal coordinator of muscle forces in a complex many-jointed body (Sarnat & Netsky, 1974). It is a powerful adjunct to the interneuronal systems of the brainstem, capable of building a coherent predictive image of the forces produced in the body by movement. Land animals move with little support or resistance from the air, their limbs suffering heavy impact against solid surfaces as they hold themselves up and propel themselves against gravitation. With the evolution of length and tension measuring devices in muscles and tendons, and of delicate rotation-detectors in joints, their bodies have become refined sensors of forces and changes of form inside themselves. The vestibular system is a central gyroscope-like detector of gravitational force and any rotational or translatory acceleration of the head. All these proprioceptors sensing body action send powerful afference to the cerebellum.

The human cerebellum has three parts which chart the long and complex evolution of body movement (Figure 2.9) (Sarnat & Netsky, 1974). The oldest part, the flocculonodular lobe (archecerebellum) responds most to the vestibular input. It has ancient links to the axial motor system and to the oculomotor nuclei. Eyes rotate together in precise coordination with locomotor changes of direction. Anticipatory step-rotations of the eyes establish the frame of visual feedback necessary to guide progression over the substrate, around obstacles, etc. This eye-direction is stabilized by the vestibular-cerebellar system which is exceedingly rapid-acting and finely tuned. Anticipatory eye rotations are not triggered by vestibular input. They require some predictive image of action (Bizzi *et al.*, 1971).

The anterior lobes of the cerebellum (paleocerebellum) have a somato-topically ordered input via the spinal cord from body mechanoreceptors, especially the stretch receptors in the muscles and the detectors of joint rotation. Its output to the basal ganglia of the forebrain, the brainstem and the cord is regulator of the support against gravity as well as controller of the dynamics of body movement. A more primitive set of nuclei, within the olivary complex of the hindbrain with input from spinal cord and midbrain reticular formation, projects these to the paleocerebellum.

The largest part of the human cerebellum consists of the hemispheres of the neocerebellum, with intimate connections to the cerebral cortex and also with the visual and auditory centers of the midbrain. The cerebellum is always large in highly agile animals. It is extremely well developed in birds and dolphins, for example (see Figure 2.10). The neocerebellum is proportionally large in the primates, which leap and use all four limbs in climbing movements that contort the whole body. The human cerebellum is involved in the delicate control of bipedal posture; the essential background for successful use of the arms and hands to manipulate objects and for their use in gestural communication. The hemispheres of the neocerebellum project to the thalamus and

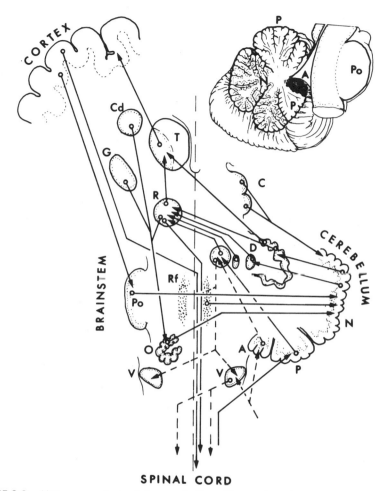

FIGURE 2.9. Main connections of the cerebellum: N = neocerebellum; P = paleocerebellum; A = archecerebellum; D = deep cerebellar nuclei; Po = pons; C = superior and inferior colliculi; O = olivary nucleus; V = vestibular nuclei; Rf = reticular formation; R = red nucleus; T = thalamus; Cd = caudate nucleus; G = globus pallidus.

MAN   DOLPHIN

FIGURE 2.10. The cerebellum of the dolphin is extremely large and elaborate. It is associated with an extremely well-developed parietal cortex, in comparison with the approximately equal-sized human brain.

thence to the motor cortex (Brodmann's areas 4 and 6) and also to the red nucleus of the midbrain motor system and to the reticular formation of the brainstem. Inputs to the neocerebellum come principally from the cerebral cortex with an additional component from the reticular formation and neoolivary nuclei of the hindbrain. The cerebral cortex projects large tracts to the neocerebellum by way of the nuclei of the pons, a conspicuous transverse mass added to the underside of the mammalian hindbrain. This circuit to and from the cortex puts the cerebellar cortex in intimate relation to the cortical and brainstem initiators of voluntary actions and it undoubtedly serves to create mechanically harmonious and economical combinations of muscle contractions to form effective acts (Eccles, 1977; McGeer, Eccles, & McGeer, 1978).

The motor activity patterns of the brain of a leaping or running animal must adjust in minimum time to perceptual predictions about the external world elaborated by the midbrain and forebrain. Experiments show that in human beings, at least, the cortical visual system may seize overriding control over the coordination of posture, standing, and walking, complementing, or even at times supplanting, the more ancient vestibulo-mechanoreceptive control (Lee, 1978). It is, therefore, important that there is physiological evidence for a strong visual input through the pons to the neocerebellum (Glickstein & Gibson, 1976). It seems certain that the anticipatory adjustments of motor excitation that Bernstein's theory requires, and the rapid coordination of excitatory patterning for guiding running, jumping, or swinging in an irregular and much cluttered three-dimensional array of solids must depend on this circuit. Its activities would seem to be at a premium in such cultivated forms of human body action as gymnastics, dance (especially balletic dance), competitive and team sports, driving wheeled motor vehicles, steering boats, flying planes, or performing music. The motor learning essential to these activities may involve widespread changes in the microstructure of the cerebellar cortex and this may mediate the unconscious efficiency with which habits of movement are stored in the brain.

Clinical studies of patients with lesions, such as the observations of Gordon Holmes on the effect of loss of one cerebellar hemisphere on execution of pointing and tracking movements (Eccles, 1977), show the cerebellar hemispheres to be essential for smooth, well-measured movements of the arms and hands, and that the cerebellum as a whole contributes to coordination of limbs and trunk in all free movements. Unfortunately, however, we have little precise knowledge of how this organ participates in complex skilled movement. It even may be of central importance in perception of movement and the appreciation of the movement-based dynamics of music and dance.

The tissues of the cerebellum have an extraordinary complexity and refinement of organization, as was revealed by the wonderful researches of the Spanish neuroanatomist, Ramón y Cajal (see Figure 2.11). The functional nerve cell connections have been subject to intensive neurophysiological analysis (Eccles, 1977). The actions of the several distinct species of cerebellar neurons have been identified. Apparently the interwoven input pathways are organized by intricate excitatory and inhibitory arrangements in axodendritic lattices which sort the influx of excitation into adaptive sequences and combinations. The entire output of the cerebellum is by way of inhibitory axons of the extraordinary fan-shaped Purkinje cells, all lined up at right angles to the folds of the cerebellar cortex and cross-connected by parallel fibers of the axons of the granule cells. Purkinje cells apply a rapid clearing influence by way of the deep cerebellar nuclei to the cerebral motor centers which are exercising competing excitatory control over spinal circuits. The speed and fine differentiation of cerebellar output is suited to shape performance of rapid and precise motor sequences, as in piano playing, as well as to timing of the successive forces that drive more massive body movements.

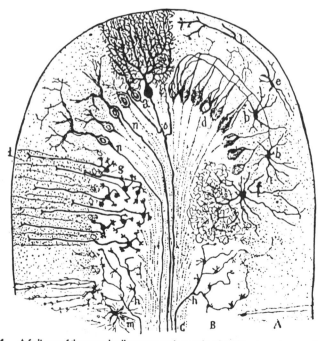

FIGURE 2.11.   A folium of the cerebellar cortex drawn by Cajal to show types of nerve cells.

Experimental anatomical studies with cats and monkeys have demonstrated that the archecerebellum projects to the cortical territories and brainstem reticular formation governing axial movements (of the trunk and neck). Other areas of the cerebellum project to the red nucleus and to more posterior parts of the motor cortex that in turn project to the zone of the spinal interneurons which governs distal movements (of the face, hands, and feet). The coupling between cerebellum, motor cortex, and brainstem reticular formation respects the somatotopic arrangements of the spinal cord with separate transmission lines and integrative territories for axial and distal musculature.

The cerebellum has an elaborate development in the life history of a human being, comparable in length with that of the cerebral hemispheres (Figures 2.12, 2.13, and 2.14) (Sidman & Rakic, 1973; Jacobson, 1970; Yakovlev & Lecours, 1967). Its cellular content is enormously

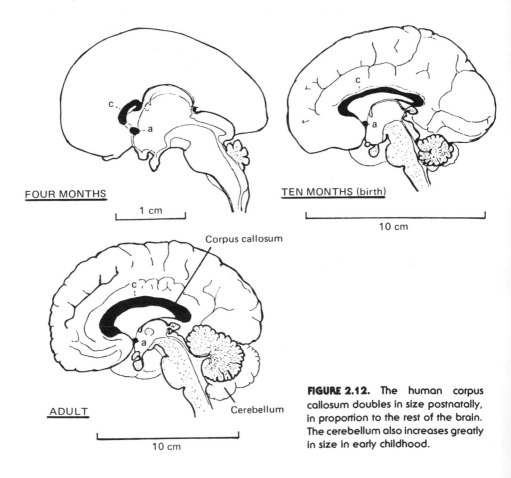

FOUR MONTHS

1 cm

TEN MONTHS (birth)

10 cm

Corpus callosum

ADULT   Cerebellum

10 cm

FIGURE 2.12. The human corpus callosum doubles in size postnatally, in proportion to the rest of the brain. The cerebellum also increases greatly in size in early childhood.

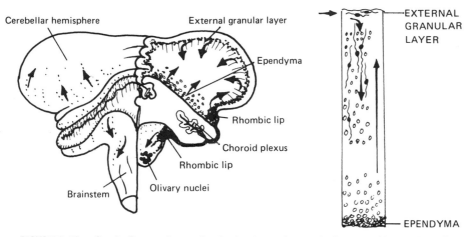

FIGURE 2.13. Cerebellum at 3 months. In the fetus, the cerebellum is added to by cells which migrate from a germinal region at the margin (Rhombic lip). This area also sends cells to form the olivary nuclei. [After Sidman and Rakic, 1973. Redrawn.]

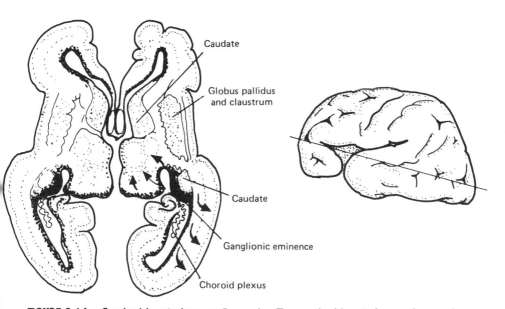

FIGURE 2.14. Cerebral hemisphere at 5 months. The cerebral hemispheres of an early fetus add cells from a germinal zone (ganglionic eminence) which injects cells at the junction of temporal and parietal cortices and the base of the frontal lobe. [After Sidman and Rakic, 1973. Redrawn.]

increased in the embryo by migration of neuroblasts from the margin of the cerebellar rudiment where they multiply. These cells spread over the surface of the rudiment, then they penetrate inwards to meet other cells migrating outward from the germinal (ependymal) layer adjacent to the ventricle of the hindbrain. The thin much-folded cerebellar cortex is thus built out of two sets of cells which approach their final positions from opposite directions. These sets remain functionally distinct after they have become mingled in the mature tissue. The first afferent connections to the cerebellum come from the vestibular nuclei and vestibular nerve in the embryo stage (second month). Then the brain stem and spinal cord contribute axons. Finally, in the fetus, the development of the connections from the cortex through the pontine nuclei couples the neocerebellum to the cerebral hemispheres. At birth the cerebellar hemispheres are still immature. Nerve cells are moving into position for long after birth, and some new cells are added. This is an exceptional condition that only the cerebral association and hippocampal cortex may match. The cerebellar cortex does not complete differentiation until well into childhood. Indeed it appears to grow with the athletic strength and agility of the child. Bernstein's studies of children walking show that efficient regulation of the forces in placing the feet on the ground is not complete until a child is more than 10 years of age (Bernstein, 1967). Cerebellar growth must provide the neuroanatomical occasions for the maturation of important aspects of the skills of moving efficiently and gracefully. The mature cerebellum is probably the site of subconscious learning of motor skills, a kind of memorizing which survives loss of memory for conscious experiences due to bilateral ablation of the hippocampus.

V. The Forebrain

In the history of the vertebrates, the forebrain has undergone great transformations. With each conquest of a new environment, with each advance in subtlety and power of behavior, and in capacity to profit from experience, the bilobed apex of the central nervous system has become larger. Hitherto insignificant and new groups of neuroblasts have burst forth to insert themselves between or to grow over older structures: These new centers, especially in the neocortex, have assumed a commanding position with respect to the integrative structures of the rest of the neuraxis (Sarnat & Netsky, 1974; Nauta & Karten, 1970).

We have seen that there are special features of the human spinal cord and brainstem. Nevertheless, it is the cerebral hemispheres of the forebrain which give a human being his superior consciousness. Indeed, the new structures at lower levels relate to the innovations arising within the cerebral hemispheres. In all mammals, the neocortex is in command of the perceptual regulation of motor activity and the learning of new responses. In the human brain new territories of neocortical tissue are asymmetrically differentiated, and this gives rise to cerebral dominance or the specialization of the left and right cerebral hemispheres for complementary modes of consciousness. These asymmetric regions are slow maturing; they develop with postnatal exercise. Their cultivated forms are transmitted from generation to generation. Thus comes about the peculiarly human trait of cultural evolution which changes entirely the forebrain: we need to explore how the evolving brain systems have achieved the awesome power of cumulating knowledge, techniques, and beliefs so that the whole of the earth becomes subservient to the needs and values of human collective imagination.

A. The Hypothalamus and Limbic System

In the amphibian forebrain described by Herrick (1948), the diencephalon is organized to regulate basic motivations. The cerebral hemispheres (telencephalon) evaluate information from the chemical olfactory sense that can decide on the quality or usefulness of goals of behavior for the whole organism. They evolve in primitive chordates from the unpaired endbrain in close proximity to the main organizer of embryo brain and body at the notochord tip (Trevarthen, 1979a).

The hypothalamus, called the "head ganglion of the autonomic system" develops from a precordal region where the pharynx and brain plate are closely opposed, and from the very early stages of chordate evolution, it is involved in regulation of states of bodily activity and changes of these to fit seasonal and diurnal fluctuations in environmental conditions. A neural protuberance from the floor of the midbrain (neurohypophysis) meets an outgrowth of the roof of the pharynx (adenohypophysis), and these two become closely coupled to form the pituitary gland which assumes a central role as overseer of the hormone-secreting glands of the body (Hamilton et al., 1962; Pick, 1970).

Just behind the hypothalamus lies the ventral neuropile or reticular tissue of the midbrain–forebrain junction. Herrick thought that this "interpeduncular neuropile" was central to the limited learning capacity of his beast, the tiger salamander. The midbrain map of the behavioral field that we have described, is lined up so that its central part is just above this integrator center that links plans for actions with evaluation of their consequences for the wellbeing of the organism. For either an embryological or a phylogenetic perspective, the cerebral hemispheres greatly augment this policymaking territory. Before the land vertebrates developed their subtle exploratory attentions to the world and the curiosity that feeds their learning powers, the ventrolateral parts of the primitive cerebral hemispheres were already an elaborate system for controlling instinctive patterns of action in conjunction with the hypothalamus (Yakovlev, 1968; Hess, 1958; Nauta & Karten, 1970).

The embryology of the human brain confirms the conclusion from comparative neurology that the hypothalamus is the apex of that component of the brain and spinal cord which has closest inductive relation to the visceral (endodermal) sector of the body. It receives input from the midline visceral nuclei of the brainstem reticular formation (central gray, tegmental nuclei, raphé), which regulate autonomic and behavioral patterns of defensive and regenerative response, as well as from the dorsomedial nucleus of the thalamus and limbic system (hippocampus, amygdala, septal nuclei and limbic cortex) (Figure 2.15). Hypothalamic output goes to the same midline reticular nuclei and related thalamic area, to the septum and cortex adjacent to it, and to the neurohypophysis of the pituitary. As central endocrine coordinator system, it controls production of many hormones vital in adjustment of coitus, birth, feeding, water balance, production of milk, blood pressure, metabolism, and bodily growth (Netter, 1958; Pick, 1970; Schally et al., 1973). Input to the hypothalamus adjusts these vital functions to external conditions and to levels of motor activity. In mammals, links of the hypothalamus with the thalamus, limbic parts of the cerebral hemispheres, and cortex involve it in the organization of pleasurable or painful feelings and in the generation of emotional states such as happiness, fear, and anger (Valenstein, 1973).

Though greatly elaborated and in intimate relationship with some of the most recently evolved neocortical regions (especially the prefrontal cortex), the limbic system of man is easily seen to be derived from ancient forebrain components that are displaced to the rim (limbus) of the cortex by the enormous expansion of the neocortex. The hippocampus is twisted out of place, by this expansion and a consequent looping of the temporal lobes through nearly a complete circle, into a ventromedial position below the thalamus and basal ganglia (see Figures 2.12, 2.13, 2.14, pp. 58–59, and Figure 2.15). Nevertheless, it retains its connections through the fornix with the mammillary bodies behind the hypothalamus, the visceral nuclei of the thalamus, the hypothalamus itself, the septal and preoptic areas, and the dorsomedial thalamus.

In both functional and anatomic relations, the limbic system is parallel to the hypothalamic visceral column. In addition to cortical connections, its main descending projection is by way of the median forebrain bundle and mammillary body to the central tegmental tract of the midbrain reticular formation. To this are related the habenular nucleus, near the base of the pineal gland, which Descartes thought was the agent of the soul in the brain, and the interpeduncular nucleus close to Herrick's more significant central integrator of the midbrain reticular formation. This midline complex of nerve centers is the core motivational system of the human brain, integrating cortical functions of consciousness with vital control of bodily state (Scheibel & Scheibel, 1967; Sprague, 1967; Magoun, 1969).

The famous studies of Hess (1958) by stimulation of the hypothalamus and neighboring structures in birds and cats showed that elaborate emotional reactions of sexual, defensive, or escape nature may be elicited from a finely differentiated mosaic of nuclei with complex interconnections. It is very difficult, however, to localize any adaptive function in a single nucleus of this region. They act together as a counterbalanced set (Valenstein, 1973). Lesions and stimulations of the human hypothalamus, amygdala, septal region, and related antero-dorsal-medial thalamic nuclei may cause moods of lust, fear, or anger with feelings of pleasure or gnawing pain; both autonomic changes and appropriate facial and other behaviors follow involuntarily. Frontal and temporal lobes of the cerebral hemispheres, which in monkeys and man are closely linked to limbic structures and to the hypothalamus, are involved in affective and motivational states, in the perceptual evaluation of objects, and in the interpersonal expression of such states in cooperative behavior.

The biochemistry of the motivational parts of the human brain is of great interest and clinical importance. Several interneuronal transmitter substances have been discovered that mediate communication in specific parts of this anatomically complex array. The psychoactive drugs, pain subduing morphines, tranquillizers, excitants, and hallucinogenic substances, seem to act by substituting for, blocking, or inactivating the natural transmitters (McGeer et al., 1978). Of these the best known are the monoamines, seratonin, dopamine, noradrenalin and adrenalin, the inhibitory transmitter gaba, acetylcholine, the autonomic and neurotransmitter, and the peptides, substance-p, enkephalins and β-endorphine.

The hippocampus, with extraordinarily specialized dendritic and synaptic arrangements that are extremely elaborate in man, is now implicated in human memory-forming processes by the finding that bilateral hippocampal removal, in an attempt to cure epilepsy, causes a drastic loss of memory for events more than a few minutes in the past (Milner, 1974; Walshe, 1978). Thus a highly specialized version of an ancient structure is organized in man as a retaining and retrieval device for integration of experiences-with-purpose in memory. Learning of motor skills, which

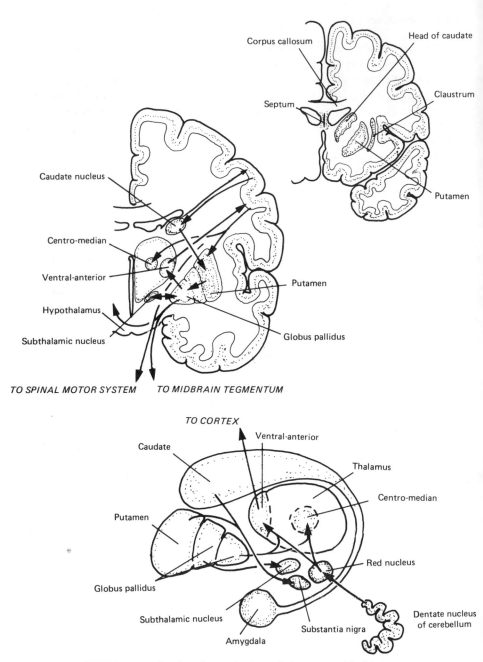

FIGURE 2.15. The basal ganglia, hypothalamus, and limbic system.

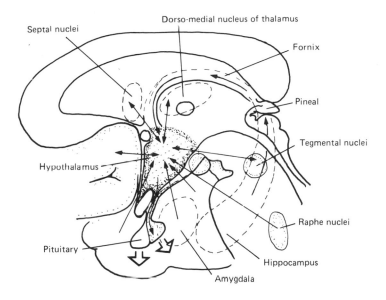

PITUITARY HORMONES INTO BLOODSTREAM

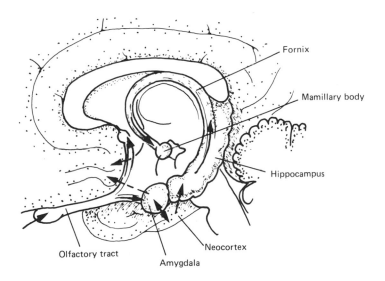

involves cerebellar circuits, and short term or perceptual memory, independent of the hippocampus, and a long term memory store of events from the presurgical period remains in some other part of the brain after both hippocampi are removed.

B. The Thalamus

When the cerebral hemispheres appear in the second month of gestation, the dorsal wall of the diencephalon develops a thickening which gains bulk in pace with the cortex throughout the fetal period. This is the thalamus. It is both the relay for all afference to the cortex and a transmitter for many recurrent corticofugal lines. Cortex and thalamus interact in perceptual and motor functions of the hemispheres and the reticular formation, and its nuclear derivatives exert a powerful influence on cortical processes via the thalamus. A considerable number of thalamic nuclei communicate with the basal ganglia and some are intermediary for a strong cerebellar input to the motor and premotor cortex. Finally, the antero- and ventrothalamic nuclei have close liaison with the hypothalamus and limbic system and with the midline reticular nuclei involved in autonomic and emotional processes (see Figures 2.9 and 2.15, pages 55 and 64).

Stimulation of the human thalamus may cause severe, poorly localized pain. Because stimulation of the cortex normally does not give rise to any painful experiences, it is traditional to regard the thalamus as the place where pain enters consciousness. This would appear to be a rather simplistic interpretation of the findings. The midline of the thalamus sometimes has an adhesion or a single fused nuclear mass (massa intermedia), but this is often absent; it is not a commissure. The thalamus on each side is functionally separate from its twin.

In the development of the thalamus, new cells are added to it from the same "ganglionic eminence" at the root of the cerebral hemisphere as gives rise to vast numbers of cortical neurons (Nauta & Karten, 1970; Sidman & Rakic, 1973) (see Figures 2.12, 2.13, and 2.14, pp. 58–59). This process, while most active in the fetal period, continues to add small stellate neurons to the cortex after birth. An addition of cells in the fetus by this route to the thalamus augments the pulvinar which is interconnected with the parietal cortex and the cortex of the parieto-temporo-occipital junction. The latter is of great importance in the late maturing asymmetric psychological functions peculiar to humans. Very likely, cells are added in a similar way to those thalamic nuclei related to the late maturing frontal lobes. Thus transformation or metamorphosis of the human cerebral hemispheres to augment the "cultural learning tissues" is accompanied by important anatomical changes in the thalamus.

C. The Basal Ganglia and Motor Initiatives

Throughout the central nervous system, the ventral half is involved in motor integrations, and in line with this, the forebrain has large nuclear masses in its ventral wall adjacent to the hypothalamus. These basal ganglia are intricately linked to each other and in close two-way communication with adjacent thalamic nuclei, the subthalamic nucleus, the hypothalamus, the brainstem reticular formation and its motor nuclei, and the cerebellum. The basal ganglia project strongly by multineuronal chains to the spinal cord. They also project up to the motor and premotor cortex, and they receive descending projections from pyramidal cells of the premotor, frontal, and parietal cortices.

The principal basal ganglia are the globus pallidus (palaeostriatum) and the caudate nucleus plus putamen (neostriatum). In the diencephalon and midbrain there are additional "extrapyramidal" motor nuclei derived from the tegmental reticular formation; the subthalamic nucleus, the substantia nigra, and the red nucleus. The latter is the major relay from the cerebellum to the motor pathways of the brainstem retucular formation, the olivary complex, and the spinal motor system. It transmit to the somatosensory cortex by way of the ventrolateral and intralaminar thalamic nuclei and receives a strong input from the motor cortex which regulates activity of the distal musculature of the opposite side of the body.

It is difficult to characterize the functions of the basal ganglia in one word. In birds, rats, and cats, they certainly have an important place in the formation and guidance of instinctual motor patterns that may be very elaborate. In man, damage to the basal ganglia interferes with the initiation and direction of voluntary movements and motor responses. Willed movements may fail to take place or be made stiffly with poor differentiation, or they may take grotesque distorted forms with wild flinging movements, erratic surges, and withdrawals. In Parkinsonism there is tremor at rest and a crippling rigidity. The face is expressionless.

The paleostriatum acts to increase activity and muscle tone—its ablation in man leads to a continuum from sleepy inactivity to the tremor of Parkinsonism. The neostriatum puts a brake on spontaneous movement; its ablation leads to forced activity or restlessness and fearlessness. Lesions of the subthalamic nucleus in men and monkeys leads to violent flinging movements of the opposite arm and jerking of the head to one side. The patterns of movement of the arm and hand and of the face with damaged neostriatal nuclei suggest that the basal ganglia are important in the organization of gestures and expressions of interpersonal communication.

It would appear that the role of the cerebral cortex in governing voluntary movement has been exaggerated in classical accounts. The motor cortex is not the sole source of volitional impulses. The basal ganglia in conjunction with the cerebellum and the brainstem tegmental reticular formation and its specialized nuclei have major responsibility for the translation of motives into motility. The corpus striatum appears also to be of vital importance in relating perception and memory of the environment to motives; thus it may play an important role in interpretive consciousness.

D. The Cerebral Cortex

The adult human cortex is a sheet of tissue 2000 cm^2 in area and about 3 mm thick. It is estimated to contain 10,000 million nerve cells (10^{10}). The cross-sectional appearance of the cortex is remarkably uniform with cells and fibers arranged in layers; variations in detail permit distinction of about 50 areas, Brodmann's scheme for these and his number system being the best known (Figure 2.16). Using classical histological methods, it requires great skill and patience to distinguish the boundaries between these areas. Nevertheless, modern neurophysiological and experimental anatomical methods confirm that there are precise boundaries between functional systems. Earlier distinctions have been upheld.

The cortex appears to be organized in columnar modules which group radial files of cells (Eccles, 1977; Szentagothai & Arbib, 1975). These arise embryologically by vertical migration of neurons along radiating strands formed of nonneural support cells (glia) connecting inner and outer surfaces of the tissue (Sidman & Rakic, 1973). A cylinder of tissue about .25 mm in diameter, corresponding in size to the disklike spread of terminal branches of a thalamic afferent axon in intermediate layers of the cortex, or to the more treelike spread of terminals from each cortico-cortical or commissural axon extending through most of the cortical depth, constitutes one module. There is a finer columnar organization within this. There are said to be 4 million modules, each with about 2500 neurons, in the cortex of one brain. Intrinsic inhibitory connections established by short axon cells of various shapes give functional contrast to these modular groups that are conceived of as acting as units and in groups, recruiting or inhibiting hundreds of their neighbors depending on the balance of interactions between them, and on their various inputs from subcortical sites. Modules may communicate over long distances in the cortex of one hemisphere, or, by the corpus callosum and anterior commissure, to the cortex of the opposite hemisphere. The modular design is confirmed by studies with radio amino-acid tracers that, when incorporated in nerve cell protein, are transported through neurons from the cell bodies down axons, or in the reverse direction from axon terminals to cells. A patch of cortex injected with such a marker is found to project to or receive input from an array of cylinders of cortex each about .25 mm in diameter (Goldman & Nauta, 1977).

The module is too fine a unit to explain how the cortex integrates psychological functions. We need to know how global anatomical and physiological organizations link modules together (Pandya & Kuypers, 1969). Cortical areas are interconnected by a vast number of precisely arranged axons that loop through the white matter under the cortical folds. The folding permits the cortical sheet to fit into the skull, but folds are also formed in relation to the functional cortico-cortical links. The pleats in the cortical sheet are equivalent in this respect to foldings of embryogenic layers in body and organ formation, and within the nervous system, to laminations of cells in subhemispheric nuclei between which functions are integrated through vertical connections. For example, the somatotopically ordered sensory and motor cortices either side of the central sulcus (which is one of the first folds to appear in the cortex of the fetus) and the many visual retinotopic or telotopic maps of the occipital lobe, are mirror images of each other over the midplan of the body or the vertical or horizontal meridians of the visual field. Interconnecting axons passing through the white matter carry the reflections.

Undoubtedly, many of the neural activity patterns of consciousness, volition, and feelings are transmitted through corticocortical links, but the cortex is regulated in all parts by precisely ordered input from subcortical sites; the thalamic nuclei, the basal ganglia, the hypothalamus and limbic structures, and the brainstem reticular formation and nuclei derived from it. Areas with input most directly from the receptors in one modality at a time, the primary sensory zones, constitute only about 5% of the cortical surface (see Figure 2.16). Other cortical regions receive sensory influences by less direct routes from several convergent modalities, including proprioceptive, vestibular, and gustatory, which have no clear primary zones.

The motor nuclei of stem and cord receive powerful efferent connections from precentral and frontal cortex (Penfield & Roberts, 1959; Eccles, 1977). Most of this outflow to motor areas is indirect, by multineuronal chains, and it is influenced by convergent effects from the basal ganglia, tegmental reticular formation, and cerebellum. However, the lower face and distal parts of the limbs, especially the hands, have more direct cortical regulation. There are even monosynaptic projections of the pyramidal cells which terminate on motor neurons for the mouth and for the fingers (distal musculature). These connections, which develop postnatally, are important in precise visual and touch guidance of manipulation as well as auditory and contact guidance of speech. Like the corticorubrospinal tract

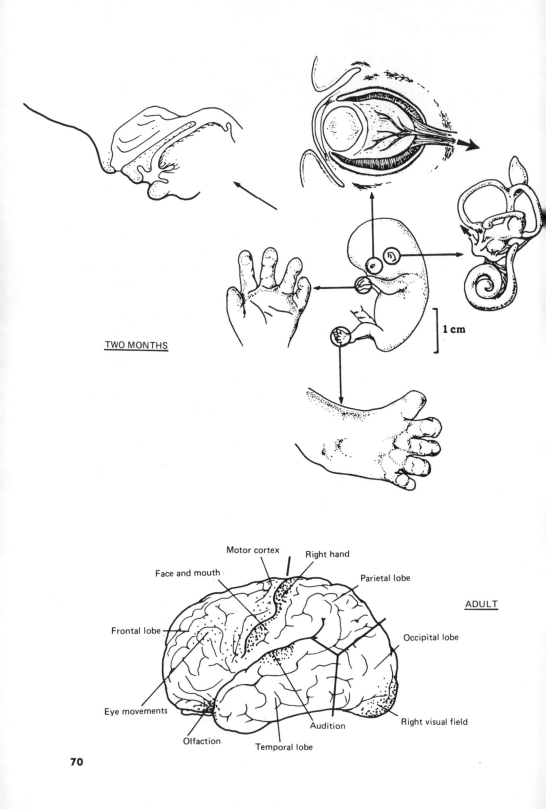

TWO MONTHS

1 cm

ADULT

Motor cortex
Right hand
Face and mouth
Parietal lobe
Frontal lobe
Occipital lobe
Eye movements
Right visual field
Olfaction
Audition
Temporal lobe

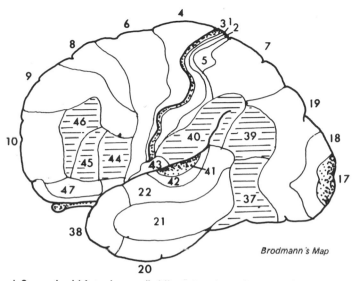

FIGURE 2.16. A 2-month-old fetus has well-differentiated nasal cavities, lips and tongue, eyes, inner ear, hands, and feet (opposite, top). These structures are represented in primary sensory and motor areas of the cerebral cortex (opposite, bottom). Brodmann's cytoarchitectonic map (above) shows histological regions at the base of the principal lobes (cross-hatched areas) which are absent from all subhuman forms.

(through the red nucleus) the direct corticomotor neuronal pathway is crossed, the left hemisphere controlling right face and right hand. A precentral pyramidal cell group or modular cluster is active immediately before a monkey performs a particular hand movement, and more widespread changes in cortical activity precede voluntary movement in monkey or man by as much as several seconds (Evarts, 1973). The cortical territory innervating the muscles of neck, trunk, and limb girdle (proximal musculature) which regulate head turning, posture, locomotion, and all powerful actions of the limbs, projects from each hemisphere to muscles of both sides of the body by way of the medial reticular formation of the midbrain and ventromedial spinal reticular zone (Kuypers, 1973). This axial system recruits strong inputs from the superior colliculus and the vestibular complex.

Eye movements are under extensive cortical regulation (Robinson, 1968; Mohler & Wurtz, 1977). They can be elicited by stimulating either the prestriate area of the occipital and parietal lobes or the "eye field" in the lateral frontal lobe. Cells in the latter region, like those in the superior colliculi, discharge when a monkey is about to look at something. Each cortex is more concerned with the contralateral half of visual space, and unilateral lesions may cause oculomotor neglect (Walshe, 1978), but intentional orientations to both left and right can be initiated from either hemisphere. Posterior parietal or frontal lesions can cause failure of oculomotor scanning at a high level of strategic planning and seriously impair visual perception. Some such failure of cognitive scanning strategy may underly the disorder of developmental dyslexia which can seriously impede the learning of reading.

Much of the cortex has no clear somatotopic or telotopic arrays, the so-called "association cortices", which are certainly not capable of mental associations on their own, lack obvious maps of the body or of space outside the body. Nevertheless, there is increasing evidence of intricate mosaic organization of modules in these areas, so that each locus has systematic relation to a particular set of modules within areas that are obviously mapped. Intermodular processes would seem to require a systematic splitting up and regrouping of somatotopic arrays in the territories to which the primary areas project. There is no reason to conclude that the association areas are "randomly" arranged.

The problem of localization of psychological functions in the cortex has a long and controversial history (Penfield & Roberts, 1959). In the late eighteenth century, the notion that a psychological aptitude could be located in a particular fold of the cortex was carried to an extreme in the phrenology of Gall and Spurtzheim. They claimed to measure differences of character, intelligence, and personality by comparing skull areas that were shaped to fit underlying brain organs. The excesses of their claims gave the notion of localization of functions a bad reputation. The brain was then described as a total system in which mental activities could not be separated. Localizationism was revived by the demonstration by Broca in the 1860s that brain damage in the left frontal convolutions could selectively impair the ability to speak. Shortly afterwards, Wernicke showed that a lesion in the dorsal temporal lobe and adjacent parietal cortex could affect comprehension of language but leave the power to articulate words intact (see Figure 2.17). At this time, Frisch and Hitzig (1870) made their exploration of the motor cortex of the dog with delicate electrical stimulation showing that it is organized as a motor image of the body. In this period also there was rapid progress by Munk, Goltz, Ferrier, Luciani and others in locating by experimental surgery the primary receptor areas for touch, vision, and hearing. By the turn of the century, when William James' textbook of psychology was published (1890), the main cortical territories of awareness and motor command had been charted, and over the years some intriguing psychic disturbances could be attributed to injuries in regions that lay between the sensory and motor areas. The remarkable case of Phineas Gage who in 1848 survived, but with a changed personality, the passage of a large

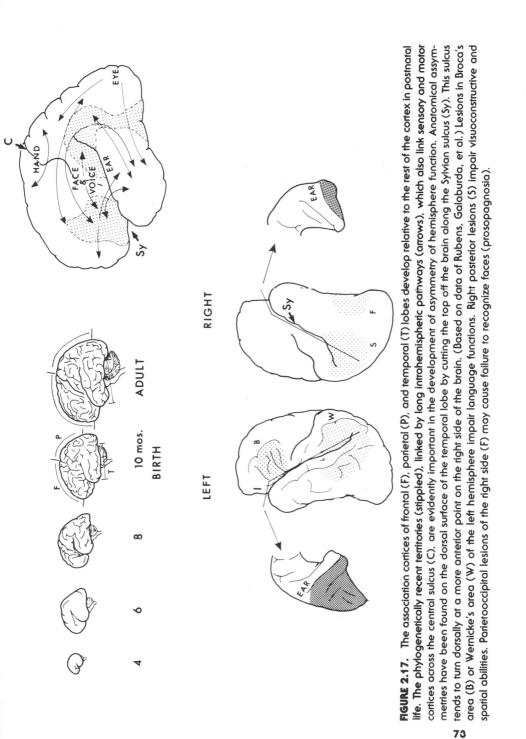

FIGURE 2.17. The association cortices of frontal (F), parietal (P), and temporal (T) lobes develop relative to the rest of the cortex in postnatal life. The phylogenetically recent territories (stippled), linked by long intrahemispheric pathways (arrows), which also link sensory and motor cortices across the central sulcus (C), are evidently important in the development of asymmetry of hemisphere function. Anatomical assymetries have been found on the dorsal surface of the temporal lobe by cutting the top off the brain along the Sylvian sulcus (Sy). This sulcus tends to turn dorsally at a more anterior point on the right side of the brain. (Based on data of Rubens, Galaburda, et al.) Lesions in Broca's area (B) or Wernicke's area (W) of the left hemisphere impair language functions. Right posterior lesions (S) impair visuoconstructive and spatial abilities. Parietooccipital lesions of the right side (F) may cause failure to recognize faces (prosopagnosia).

iron bar through his frontal lobes, had long before raised questions about the cerebral mechanisms for moral purposiveness and social responsibility.

Contemporary neuropsychology gains much from anatomical and physiological studies with animals, especially primates. The monkey cortex has been shown to have a systematic set of intracortical projections transmitting sensory information toward the motor areas and also to the temporal and prefrontal lobes (Pandya & Kuypers, 1969). It is claimed that the intricate intercellular comparisons required to visually distinguish colors, motion of objects, and their fine three-dimensional configuration may be carried out in separate cortical territories. Microelectrode recording combined with systematic presentation of simplified stimuli has revealed exceedingly elaborate microanatomy of cortical "analyzers." In the touch area for the hand, and in the visual cortex, columns of cortical cells are arranged in a precise pattern in which the cells are interconnected so that each location performs a particular operation on incoming information to layer IV from a particular receptor locus. Cortical receptor units that are sensitive to segments of boundaries where light intensity changes and to the orientation and direction of motion of these edges in the visual field, are famous. In the striate cortex (Brodmann's area 17) the terminals of lateral geniculate axons transmitting information from the two eyes are precisely segregated, then their output is recombined in graded arrangements that permit detection of interocular disparity of the images upon which binocular depth detection depends. The dimensions of the cellular array are precisely related to the acuity, texture, and motion resolving powers of the eye. The intricate anatomy on which these first steps in visual processing for perception are based is generally predetermined antenatally but refinements depend upon postnatal exposure to patterned stimulation. Large distortions in visual stimulation, artificially imposed over periods when intercellular connections are developing, may cause deformities in the cortical visual machinery (Trevarthen, 1979a).

When electrodes are placed in the inferotemporal cortex, where bilateral ablations cause failure of perceptual discrimination, more complex "real" stimuli seem to be needed, as if cells in the area categorize not stimulus dimensions but the form, etc., of objects of definite significance for the subject (Gross & Mishkin, 1977). These cells have large receptor fields extending on both sides of the vertical meridian and including the fovea; unilateral lesions in the inferotemporal cortex do not cause defects in object perception, whereas bilateral lesions do. In the monkey, prestriate visual areas receive input of visual information from area 17 and also from the superior colliculi via the pulvinar of the thalamus. There seem to be many maps there with the visual field represented in different ways, sometimes favoring the fovea, sometimes the periphery, and with cells responsive to particular stimulus features. Such observations have led to the concept of a collection of complementary stimulus analyzing regions, each with a special relationship to the behavior of the animal. Microelectrode recordings from the dorsal and anterior parietal lobe, adjacent to the postcentral map of somesthetic input (areas 5 and 7), reveal cells which are active in relation to reaching of the hands to an off center object of interest and/or orientation of the eyes to such an object. Mountcastle Lynch, Georgopolous, Sakata, and Akuna (1975), who have charted the areas, observing different combinations of activity predictive of hand or eye orientation, describe these cells as "command" units projecting actions into "extrapersonal space." These studies bridge the gap between physiological analyses of the receptor fields of visual areas 17, 18, and 19, and the somesthetic areas 1, 2, and 3.

Some years ago, with the introduction of well-controlled formal training procedures to test visual discrimination, it was found that lesions in the temporal and frontal lobes of monkeys could affect recognition of objects, learning, or memorizing of the spatial arrangements of objects recently seen. Also, ablation studies had brought to light important changes in appetite and affect from lesions in the apical area of the temporal lobe and parts of the frontal lobe linked to the limbic system, hypothalamus, and midline reticular formation.

The preceding analyses of functional organizations in the monkey brain relate well to clinical findings, and to experimental investigations with stimulation or recording of homologous regions of the human brain during brain surgery (Penfield & Roberts, 1959).

The functions of the human cerebral cortex have been investigated over more than a century by correlating functional changes with locus of lesions caused by missiles penetrating the skull and wounding the brain, collision of the head with a hard object, by diseases that destroy brain tissue, such as cancerous tumors or abscesses from infection, or by the results of bleeding or blockage of circulation in some part of the cerebral vascular supply (stroke) (Luria, 1973; Walshe, 1978). Frequently it is necessary to perform brain surgery to remove a growth or an infection likely to damage other parts, or to alleviate pressure. Damaged cortical tissue may become epileptic, generating paroxismic activity that interferes with function of other parts, and this disorder may spread. Many surgical operations on the brain are performed to remove epileptic foci.

The interpretations of clinical neurology are made difficult by the great variety and generally widespread, multiple or diffuse, location of brain damage; by transmission of abnormal activity to remote brain parts, and by the complexity, inconstancy and self-correcting nature of psychological and behavioral consequences. Traditional knowledge of the effects of brain damage is the fruit of careful descriptions of defects of behavior and mental activity in patients whose brains are seen by a surgeon or become available for postmortem inspection. Cases were observed in daily activities, usually in a hospital setting, and some were submitted to simple tests of perception in one modality at a time; of ability to handle objects and use them as instruments to do tasks, of ability to respond to requests or instructions, and of comprehension and use of language. Speech, drawing (usually with simple geometric or representational outline models for reproduction), writing, singing, musical performance, and various spatial orientation and manual construction tasks have been examined, but until the last 50 years, there was little standardization of procedures. Then psychophysical tests with highly controlled and "reduced" stimuli in vision, touch, or audition were found useful for detecting pathology in threshold of detection or elementary discrimination, and fluctuations of attention, vigilance, or concentration. But such deficits are hard to pin down. They may result from brain damage due to malnutrition, from senile degeneration, or from lesions almost anywhere in the integrative parts of the hemispheres or in the brainstem.

Advances have been made in the last 40 years by applying more critical mental tests and by use of standardized methods for quantifying performance of large groups of patients (Luria, 1973; Milner, 1971, 1974). Subgroups with lesions in different brain lobes are compared statistically. Standardized intelligence tests, validated with large populations of normal subjects to measure intellectual development in relation to training or employment and special aptitudes, have been applied to brain damaged patients with rather confusing results. There has, however, been a valuable two-way influence between methods and findings with normal subjects and the discovery of tests that are useful with neurological patients (Luria, 1973; Walshe, 1978).

As a consequence of the neuropsychological approach, combining psychological techniques with improved neuropathological and neurosurgical procedures, we have better knowledge now of the defects produced by lesions in the main lobes of the brain, and especially of the different effects lesions have in left and right hemispheres (Milner, 1971). The statistical approach has also clarified the complex variations of loss with a given lesion when subjects vary in the cause of brain malfunction, or in age, sex, education, and hand preference. The memory processes of the brain and the generative processes of consciousness, perceptual categorization, volition, and emotion have been clarified. There has been a steady gain in understanding of what are the most fruitful questions to ask about the processes of a damaged brain, and findings have increasing influence on psychology in general as well as on the treatment of patients. Neuropsychology, after a long period in which its findings were ignored by most psychologists and by many neurologists, is beginning to take a central place in comprehension of both the brain and the mind.

Present ideas on the location of high level mental processes in the human brain may be summarized as follows (Luria, 1973; Walshe, 1978). Occipital lesions invading area 17 on one side cause blindness in the opposite half of the visual field, as if the retina of both eyes had been lost in corresponding patches. There is a precise mapping of the retinal field, as was shown by Gordon Holmes in his studies of soldiers with head wounds in World War I. The foveal area is greatly magnified. This represents part of the visual system used with accurate fixation for seeing detail in good light. There is a division of left and right halves of the visual field between the hemispheres, down the vertical meridian. Area 17 is a cortical retina, necessary to inform consciousness of detail in the identification of objects, but it is not the locus of such awareness. Furthermore, there is retention of subconscious detection of the occurrence and approximate locus of events in the off-center visual field in areas where a striate lesion has produced blindness for detail and loss of conscious awareness of meaning. This extrastriate vision called "blind sight" is informed via the superior colliculi and its projection through the pulvinar nucleus of the thalamus to the more anterior occipital cortex—the second ambient visual system (Figure 2.18). Lesions extending into the parietal cortex cause disorders of visual recognition, distortions of visual space, and anomalies of visual orienting and scanning. They may cause serious deficiencies in the use of the eyes to determine how to move the hands in drawing, assembling objects, etc., and reading may be affected. A lesion low down in the parietotemporal cortex just in front of the visual area may cause failure to recognize objects by sight. Left hemisphere lesions may affect the naming of objects seen as well as defects of word recognition in reading. An extraordinary failure to recognize people by sight of their faces, called prosopagnosia, meaning psychic blindness for faces, seems to result most often from a right hemisphere parieto-temporal lesion. This disorder breaks a vital link in interpersonal communication and may interfere with perception of other people's feelings, moods, intentions, as well as their identity. Usually a prosopagnosic can identify a person immediately from the voice; it is a specifically visual disorder.

Left hemisphere lesions that do not produce blind areas in the right visual field may cause inattention to the right, which interferes with visual exploration and with reading. However, it is much more common to have neglect of the left half of space, and even of the left half of the patient's body, after a right posterior lesion. Evidently the left hemi-

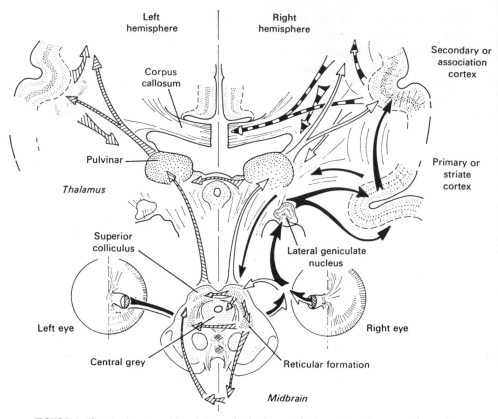

FIGURE 2.18. Ambient and focal vision. In the human brain, vision of space at large (ambient vision; white arrows) is mediated in part through the brainstem. Focal vision (black arrows) follows the classical geniculostriate route. [After Trevarthen and Sperry, 1973.]

sphere, compared to the right, contains a less complete, more one-sided representation of the body and of space outside it. There are, indeed, many indications that the right hemisphere has a stronger integration with the systems of the brain that regulate bodily action in space, including navigation relative to surroundings. Right-hemisphere-damaged patients are more frequently prone to lose their way than are left hemisphere cases. There is also evidence that the right parietal area may have stronger connections with vestibular and proprioceptive functions in which the cerebellum is greatly implicated.

The auditory representation of the world is not sharply segregated between the hemispheres into mirror halves as is the visual projection. This is related to the complex integrations of inputs from the two ears, and for both halves of space outside the body, in the brainstem.

Segregation of inputs from the two ears to the auditory cortex can be made clearer by giving different stimuli simultaneously to the two ears through earphones (Milner, 1971). This abnormal binaural conflict of stimulation (dichotic listening) forces a separation and can be used to detect unilateral temporal lobe lesions in the auditory region (area 41). Bilateral lesions of area 41 cause deafness. If cortex next to the auditory cortext of the left hemisphere is damaged, there may be severe deficiencies in the comprehension of speech. This is Wernicke's receptive aphasia, called *fluent aphasia* because people afflicted with it can talk fluently. They frequently generate nonsense or jargon and may mix up various speech sounds in highly abnormal ways. There are many forms of fluent aphasia, including inability to comprehend spoken and–or written words. Sometimes there is a selective loss of ability to recall names of objects. Usually the least common words in the language are most affected (Geschwind, 1972; Penfield & Roberts, 1959).

The extraordinary feature of this kind of disorder, as with all losses of language function, is that a lesion confined to the left side of the brain may cause a severe defect, whereas right hemisphere lesions rarely do. Progress has been made recently by Geschwind and his colleagues in identifying histologically distinct areas of cortex around the parietotemporal junction that are usually larger on the left side of the brain, even in the fetus 20 weeks before birth (Galaburda et al., 1978). The asymmetries had been seen before in adult brains, but their significance has only become apparent with examination of larger populations of brains, and with careful measurement of the size of certain histologically defined areas (see Figure 2.17, p. 73).

Brain damage just behind the central sulcus on one side causes loss of sensation of the trunk or the limbs of the opposite side of the body. Electrical stimulation of these parts results in ill-defined sensations in the corresponding parts. The hand has a very large area devoted to it and each hand is much more strongly represented in the somatosensory cortex of the opposite hemisphere. Lesions in front of the central sulcus cause paralysis and stimulation causes involuntary movements. Again, when the limbs are affected, the effect is contralateral; left hemisphere lesions resulting in hemipareses of the right arm or leg, and vice versa. Lesions in the parietal cortex next to the hand area may cause failure in object perception by the opposite hand and also failures in manipulative activity. The left hand of a right-handed person often has superior appreciation of touch information, especially about the spatial configurations of things felt; it is better at recognizing Braille signs. Visual guidance of fine finger movements is more precise for the dominant right hand. Vision is, of course, important in predicting rapid sequences of prehensile activity. Writing by the dominant hand may be regarded as a cultivated form of this lateralized ability. A posterior lesion of the left hemisphere may result in a defect in the performance of sequences of right hand movements. Kimura (1979) has shown that, where acts have to be carried out in a particular order which is arbitrarily varied, normal right-handers perform rapid sequential tasks better with their right hands. She suggests that the dominant right hand has privileged access to a center for motor sequencing in the left hemisphere.

A lesion low in the central area will cause sensory and motor losses to the face and mouth, but usually unilateral lesions in the face area of the central body maps affect only the lower face on the opposite side. The upper face, neck, and throat are bilaterally represented in each hemisphere. Damage to the large convolution in front of the motor cortex of the mouth produces the famous motor aphasia of Broca (Penfield & Roberts, 1959). The patient can speak only with difficulty, if at all, making awkward abbreviated utterances, stumbling over the act of speaking and retaining fluent pronunciation of few words, among which exclamatory words and swear words are prominent. This is called *nonfluent aphasia*. Clearly it is the motor half of a speech mechanism linking Wernicke's area (the posterior dorsal part of the temporal lobe below the Sylvian sulcus and the tempero-parieto-occipital junction area), with the lateral frontal lobe (Geschwind, 1972). As we have said, the speech mechanism is almost always more strongly developed in the left hemisphere, and at least the posterior perceptual or receptive part has visible anatomical correlates of this (see Figure 2.17, p. 73).

Since the 1940s, the classical theory that the left hemisphere is dominant in mental processes of consciousness, reasoning, etc., over an unspecialized right hemisphere lacking language has been called in question. With visuo-constructive tasks in which hand and eye work together to judge or fabricate external configurations, and for which language is not necessary, patients with right posterior lesions are more likely to be seriously impaired than those with comparable left lesions (Milner, 1971). It is now widely accepted that visual and haptic awareness of the shape and spatiotemporal organization of external phenomena may be superior in the right hemisphere. Perceptual categorization tests with brain-injured patients show that the short-term visual memory processes of the two hemispheres proceed by different strategies. Matching by appearance is evidently superior in the right hemisphere in most cases, and matching by meaning or linguistic category is superior in the left hemisphere.

Milner (1971, 1974), Kimura, and others have studied the memory functions of the temporal lobes with patients in whom parts of the lobes have been removed to eliminate epileptic foci. Verbal memory is impaired by left temporal ablations and visual and haptic shape memory is impaired with right removals. With dichotic auditory tests, words are less well perceived and retained after left temporal lesions, whereas perception of environmental sounds and aspects of musical experience is more likely to be deficient after right lesions.

Luria (1973), Milner (1974), and others have examined deficiencies of strategy in card sorting or serial ordering tasks which put demands on memory for selection or rediscovery of items from a series. These tasks, involving the making up or remembering the order of events, are sensitive to frontal lesions, and, again, tasks with words are more affected by left side lesions and those with meaningless patterns or shapes show losses with right lesions.

Asymmetries of cortical functioning are shown to have a clear but complex relationship to handedness by the differential effects of brief inactivation of one hemisphere. After the anesthetic sodium amytal has been injected into the carotid artery of one side, the related hemisphere is temporarily depressed. It is found that the usual segregation of verbal activities in the left hemisphere and nonverbal or visuo-spatial in the right does not obtain in many left-handers or in patients in whom perinatal brain injury has caused modified brain development. Language in these cases may be bilaterally distributed, or stronger on the right side. However, well over 90% of all people tested by the amytal injection procedure have speech regulated more effectively by the left hemisphere.

In attempting to categorize the cognitive functions that differentiate the hemispheres, neuropsychologists have difficulty dissociating inherent strategies of brain function from acquired asymmetries of perception, motor skills, and memory store. There seems to be a fundamental difference in the way the hemispheres regulate the uptake and the use of experience in relation to voluntary action. De Renzi and Vignolo (1962) have devised a "Token Test" using a few chips of different size, color, and shape which the patient is required to arrange in arbitrary sequences or groups specified by brief verbal instructions. This test is extremely sensitive to left hemisphere lesions, but almost unaffected by the same sized right side lesions in matching locations. It appears as if sequential specification of elements taxes the right hemisphere short-term memory, or its strategy of awareness severely. There seems to be a relationship here to Kimura's (1978) hypothesis that motor sequencing for mouth or hand movements, of discrete acts in arbitrary variations of order, is a left hemisphere function. No explanations in terms of more peripheral systems (e.g., the perceptuomotor systems for left and right hand or the motor control of the mouth and tongue), can explain the findings. Motivational formulae for communication by language or for meaningful use of objects appear to have an innate though variable asymmetry of organization.

E. Split Brains and Natural Components of the Mind

The whole question of hemispheric differences in mental processes and important aspects of the relationship between cortical and subcortical tissues in mental activities have been clarified by research with split-brain subjects (Sperry, 1970, 1974; Sperry et al., 1969). In these, all the commissural links between the hemispheres are surgically divided so that the cortical sheet on each side must integrate its functions with the other side through links to the brainstem and spinal cord and by means of receptor and motor interactions of the body with the external world. Any integrative function or process that is entirely cortical in origin must remain in one hemisphere after this operation.

Myers and Sperry showed, by cutting the corpus callosum and anterior commissure along with the optic chiasm to separate the optic nerves, that each cortex of a cat could see and learn a visual discrimination task on its own, and that each of the completely isolated and essentially normal visual memories could direct the cat as a whole to move to get a food reward. Outside special test situations the cats were indistinguishable from normal animals in awareness, motor coordination, attentiveness, and motivation. Further work in Sperry's laboratory at California Institute of Technology showed that monkeys with the same operation had the same split in psychological functioning; but the split-brain monkeys, unlike the cats, had two intentional motor systems for the hands. After surgery each eye, with input restricted by the chiasm sectioning to the hemisphere of the same side, had a much stronger control of voluntary manipulative activities of the hand on the other side. Since each eye retained vision for the contralateral visual field only, this meant that left visual field and left hand were strongly coupled in the right hemisphere, and vice versa. The operation had disengaged two eye–hand systems (Trevarthen, 1968). Later work by Brinkman and Kuypers showed that the unwillingness of split-brain monkeys to use left eye with left hand or right eye with right hand was due, not to the visual field losses caused by chiasm sectioning, nor to separation of touch discrimination by the two hands, but to division of the cortical motor control for precise differential movements of the fingers and bisection of visual input.

In 1959, Bogen and Vogel carried out a complete commissurotomy (division of the corpus callosum, anterior commissure and massa intermedia) in a man with a severe epilepsy that was sustained in considerable part by interhemispheric transmission of seizures. Tests by Gazzaniga and Sperry (1970) soon demonstrated that in humans, too, surgical division of the cortical mantle produces two conscious awarenesses. The chiasm of the optic nerves was not sectioned in the human patient, so visual input was controlled by presenting pictures, words, etc., to left and right of a fixation point on a projection screen with brief exposures to control for eye movements. The hands were tested with objects presented out of sight, and were found to have nearly completely separate experiences of the form and identity of those objects. What was seen as a picture or name in the left field could be recognized by the left hand, and similarly for the right visual field and hand, but these two combinations had no intercommunication. They were independent fields for perceiving with no common awareness (Sperry, 1970). Trevarthen and Sperry (1973) found that divided awareness only applies to detailed meaningful experiences by which the commissurotomy patient knows objects in focal vision. Less critical appreciation of visual information for awareness of space and motion of objects round the body (ambient vision) remained undivided, mediated by subhemispheric visual centers outside the geniculostriate projection.

The most dramatic finding, with no precedent in the animal studies, was that experiences shown by intermodal transfer and by appropriate voluntary use of the left hand, were consciously perceived in the right hemisphere without verbal expression. Though talking normally about experiences of the left hemisphere, the split-brain subject remained mute or spoke with random confabulation regarding what was experienced on the other side. This was impressive confirmation of left hemisphere lateralization of a mechanism governing at least the expression of language.

Soon several additional epileptic patients received treatment by commissurotomy, and within a few years a thorough survey of their mental functions had been performed. In spite of variations in detail, the findings were highly consistent, and a commissurotomy syndrome of mental functions could be confidently outlined (Sperry et al., 1969) (see Figure 2.19).

It was noted immediately after surgery that the left hand was better at copying a drawing of a cube or other shape, but that the right hand was much better at writing. Levy made a systematic examination of the perception of the three-dimensional shape by touch and vision and found the right hemisphere–left hand combination of several of the commissurotomy subjects to be definitely superior. Nebes found that perceptual synthesis of the complete experience of an object from a fragmented or partial representation of it was carried out better in the right

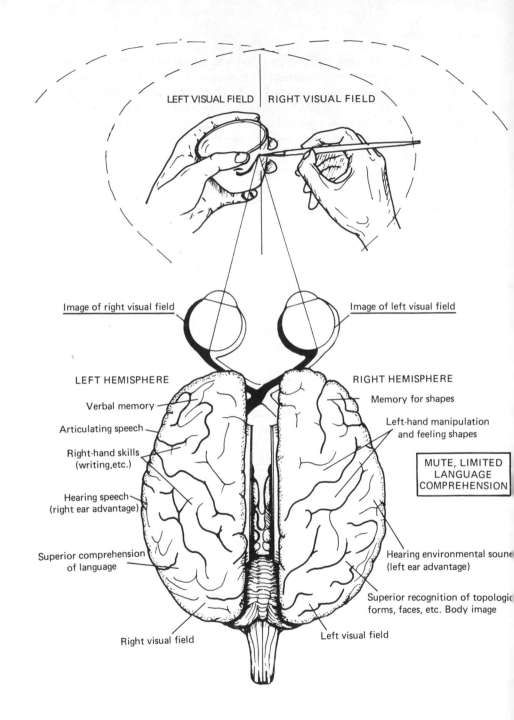

LEFT VISUAL FIELD | RIGHT VISUAL FIELD

Image of right visual field

Image of left visual field

LEFT HEMISPHERE

Verbal memory

Articulating speech

Right-hand skills
(writing, etc.)

Hearing speech
(right ear advantage)

Superior comprehension
of language

Right visual field

RIGHT HEMISPHERE

Memory for shapes

Left-hand manipulation
and feeling shapes

MUTE, LIMITED
LANGUAGE
COMPREHENSION

Hearing environmental sound
(left ear advantage)

Superior recognition of topologic
forms, faces, etc. Body image

Left visual field

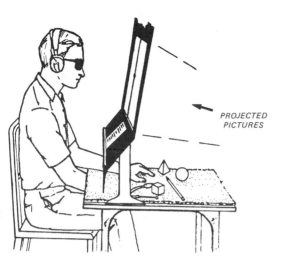

FIGURE 2.19. Split-brain studies reveal differences in psychological functions of disconnected hemispheres. The subject is tested with stimuli flashed to left or right of a fixation point on a screen, with objects felt by one or the other hand out of sight or with conflicting auditory stimuli in earphones. With chimeric stimuli, different instructions elicit either right hemisphere control (pointing to a picture of the same appearance) or left hemisphere control (giving a spoken description of the picture).

PROJECTED PICTURES

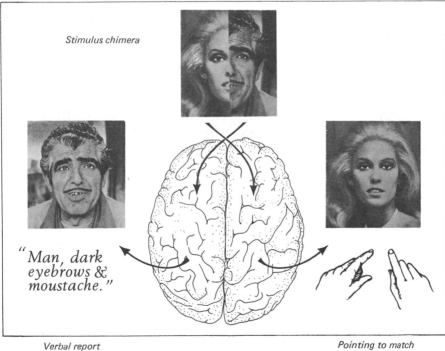

Stimulus chimera

"Man, dark eyebrows & moustache."

Verbal report

Pointing to match

hemisphere. All tests of expressive language calculation or verbal reasoning showed the isolated left hemisphere to be greatly superior. Nevertheless, there were many signs that the right hemisphere had considerable linguistic comprehension. A major result of the research on psychology of commissurotomy patients has been reformulation of the cerebral dominance hypothesis to allow for a considerable degree of linguistic comprehension in the right hemisphere as well as a definite superiority of the right hemisphere for mental processes that appreciate and use forms, spatial syntheses, or gestalts, to represent objects outside the body (Sperry, 1974). It has been proposed that the left hemisphere has a bias to analytical and serial cognitive processing while the right is synthetic and parallel, but his does not seem to be the most natural description of the undoubted complementarity in hemispheric mental modes (see Figure 2.19).

More recent work has attempted to refine the description of visual and linguistic processes and special techniques have been devised. Levy, Trevarthen and Sperry (1973) used visual stimulus chimeras. These are made by joining the left half of one picture to the right half of another. If a commissurotomy patient sees such a stimulus exposed for a brief interval (.10 sec) with the fixation point on the vertical join, then each hemisphere sees a different picture. It seems that perceptual completion occurs, each hemisphere taking information of half a picture but perceiving a whole one. The tests ask the subjects to say what they saw or to point to the matching picture in an array of possibilities (see Figure 2.19). Verbal representation of the experience causes the left hemisphere to govern the response, but direct visual matching is usually taken over by the right hemisphere. Faces and meaningless shapes are better recognized or identified by the right hemisphere and for them to be described verbally by the left hemisphere, a process of analysis into distinct namable features appears to occur. This kind of analysis seems to favor strongly the left hemisphere. Levy and Trevarthen (1977), have shown, with chimeras of simple words or pictures to which verbal descriptions are given, that both hemispheres can see and know the meaning of words, but that the right hemisphere is virtually unable to imagine the sound of the word for an object it sees. In consequence, it cannot match by rhyming with mental images of words for objects seen (such as "toes" and "rose," or "bee" and "key").

Zaidel (1980) has developed a method of attaching a miniature screen to a contact lens that fits closely to the eye of the patient and moves with the eye. With built in optics the screen appears, to the subject, to be in the plane for reading from a table top, and the screen is lined up to close off the left or right half of the visual field. By this device, and with the other eye covered completely, Zaidel can test a commissurotomy subject's perceptions and understanding with one hemisphere at a time. He can give them standardized intelligence tests taking several minutes in which they have to match words and/or pictures to indicate similarity of appearance, sound in speech, meaning, or function.

These contact screen tests confirm that the right hemisphere has considerable comprehension of spoken language and that it can read single words well. The main deficiencies appear with rare words and those with abstract reference. Metaphorical uses of symbols are understood, as are social, political, and emotive aspects. Thus the right hemisphere has a rich consciousness and considerable linguistic function, even though its total vocabulary is comparable with that of a child. The greatest difference between the hemispheres is seen, again, when the patient is required to identify a picture of an object with the picture of an object that rhymes with it. Although the right hemipshere has good auditory perception, even superior perception of musical aspects of speech, it lacks a meaning-to-sound-of-speech transformer. It also is profoundly defective in combining words into chains with well organized meaning, though it can understand spoken sentences well, especially if they are supported by a rich visual context for the understanding. Zaidel has confirmed that the right hemisphere, when disconnected from the left, is very poor at the Token Test and it is also poor at visual puzzles which require systematic isolation of elements from a confusing background or ensemble.

These remarkable research findings confirm that the cerebral cortex is the integrator of consciousness and that anatomical organizations of the two hemispheres fit them for different strategies of awareness and practice. Each cortex is integrated with the intact motivational, orienting, attentional, and motor coordinating mechanisms of the brainstem and cord, but these levels of the brain cannot transmit details of experience or memory from one side to the other when the cortical commissures have been cut.

Deconnection of the hemispheres interferes in some way with memory processes, and it reduces vigilance. Some of this kind of loss undoubtedly is due to the breakdown of cooperative partnerships of function that normally occur between the specialist functions of the two sides.

VI. Conclusions

This abbreviated account has attempted to describe the living organization of brain parts and their adaptation to acts performed by the body in relation to stimuli from the outside world. High-level brain processes of conscious awareness, intention to act, reasoning, and communication employ ancient, highly organized, and newly reconstructed mechanisms at lower levels, including special parts of the body. The top-level brain events are free of particular states in peripheral structures and able to constitute a coherent subject with a single center of experience, quick changing purposes, and a well ordered memory store because they command such effective instruments. The most interesting parts of the hemispheres stand in relation to the brainstem structures of motivation and dynamic coordination, and by this they integrate the functions of the better understood specialist receptor or motor regions of the cortex in representations of goals, meaning, and values for the whole person.

It is extremely important that the human cerebral cortex has special regions, unique to it, which have a tendency to develop elaborate asymmetry. The halves of the forebrain grow through childhood into progressively more specialized complementary mental systems. The basis for this is innate but it requires rich **cultural** (i.e., cooperatively and historically transmitted experience) to mature. The special human zones of frontal and parietotemporal cortex, which are both associative and motivational, appear late in the fetal cycle of hemisphere neurogenesis. In these cortices, dendrites, synaptic arrays, and myelinated interconnections mature late in fetal life and on into infancy and childhood. They are involved in the creation of processes of cultural importance—such as language and technical mastery of manual constructions which also take the whole of childhood to reach maturity. They are deformed when the life of a child lacks human care. These are, therefore, the organs of human cooperative awareness. They use the primate adaptations of visual and manual exploitation of the world and primate social aptitudes plus a greatly enriched facial and vocal mechanism for interpersonal transmission of feelings, motives, knowledge, and purposes. Understanding these cooperative functions, which make and use cultural artifacts and transmit them from generation to generation, is the most interesting, most urgent, and most baffling task confronting those who believe that mental events and brain organization both must conform to one set of principles adapted to human life (Trevarthen, 1979b,c).

Bibliography

Bernstein, N. *The coordination and regulation of movements.* Oxford: Pergamon, 1967.
Bizzi, E., Kalil, R. E., & Tagliasco, V. Eye–head coordination in monkeys: Evidence for centrally patterned organization. *Science*, 1971, *173*,452–454.

DeRenzi, E., and Vignolo, L. The token test: A sensitive test to detect disturbancies in aphasics. *Brain*, 1962, *85*, 665–678.

Eccles, J. C. *The understanding of the brain*. New York: McGraw-Hill, 1977.

Evarts, E. V. Brain mechanisms in movement. *Scientific American*, 1973, *229*, 96–103.

Frisch, G., and Hitzig, E., Uber die electrische erregbarkeitdes grosshirns. *Archiv für Amatomie Physiologie und Wissenschaftdishe Medecin*, 1870, *37*, 300–332.

Galaburda, A. M., Le May, M., Kemper, T. L., & Geschwind, N. Right-left asymmetries in the brain. *Science*, 1978, *199*, 852–856.

Gaze, R. M. Neuronal specificity. *British Medical Bulletin*, 1974, *30*, 116–121.

Geschwind, N. Language and the brain. *Scientific American*, 1972, *226*, 76–83.

Glickstein, M., & Gibson, A. R. Visual cells in the pons of the brain. *Scientific American*, 1976, *234*, 90–98.

Goldman, P. S., & Nauta, W. J. H. Columnar distribution of cortico-cortical fibers in the frontal association, limbic and motor cortex of the developing rhesus monkey. *Brain Research*, 1977, *122*, 393–413.

Greene, P. H. Problems of organization of motor systems. In R. Rosen & F. M. Snell (Eds.), *Progress in theoretical biology* (Vol 2). New York: Academic Press, 1972.

Grillner, S. Locomotion in vertebrates: Central mechanisms and reflex interaction. *Physiological Reviews*, 1975, *55*, 247–304.

Gross, C. G., & Mishkin, M. The neural basis of stimulus equivalence across retinal translation. In S. R. Harnad (Ed.), *Lateralization in the nervous system*. New York: Academic Press, 1977.

Hamilton, W. J., Boyd, J. D., & Mossman, H. W. *Human embryology* (3rd ed.). Cambridge: Heffer, 1962.

Hécaen, H. Acquired aphasia in children and the ontogenesis of hemispheric functional specification. *Brain Language*. 1976, *3*, 114–134.

Herrick, C. J. *The brain of the tiger salamander*. Chicago: University of Chicago Press, 1948.

Hess, W. R. *The functional organization of the diencephalon*. New York: Grune and Stratton, Inc., 1958.

Jacobson, M. *Developmental neurobiology*. New York: Holt, 1970.

James, W. *The principles of psychology* (2 Vols.). New York: Holt, 1890.

Kimura, D. Neuromotor mechanisms in the evolution of human communication. In H. D. Steklis and M. J. Raleigh (Eds.), *Neurobiology of social communication in primates: An evolutionary perspective*. New York: Academic Press, 1979.

Kuypers, H. G. J. M. The anatomical organisation of the descending pathways and their contributions of motor control, especially in primates. In T. E. Desmedt (Ed.), *New developments in E.M.G. and clinical neurophysiology* (Vol. 3). Basel: Karger, 1973.

Lee, D. N. The functions of vision. In H. L. Pick & E. Saltzman (Eds.) *Modes of perceiving and processing information*. Hillsdale, N.J.: Erlbaum, 1978. pp. 170–195.

Levy, J. & Trevarthen, C. Perceptual, semantic and phonetic aspects of elementary language processes in split-brain patients. *Brain*, 1977, *100*, 105–118.

Levy, J., Trevarthen, C., & Sperry, R. W. Perception of bilateral chimeric figures following hemispheric deconnection. *Brain*, 1972, *95*, 61–78.

Luria, A. R. *The working brain*. Harmondsworth: Penguin, 1973.

McGeer, P. L., Eccles, J. C., & McGeer, E. G. *Molecular neurobiology of the mammalian brain*. New York: Plenum, 1978.

Magoun, H. W. *The waking brain* (2nd ed.). Springfield, Ill: Charles C. Thomas, 1969.

Milner B. Interhemispheric differences in the localization of psychological processes in man. *British Medical Bulletin*, 1971, *27*, 272–277.

Milner, B. Hemispheric specialization: Scope and limits. In F. G. Worden & F. O. Schmitt

(Eds.) *The neurosciences: Third study program*. Cambridge, Mass.: M.I.T. Press, 1974. Pp. 75–89.

Mohler, C. W., & Wurtz, R. H. Role of striate cortex and superior colliculus in visual guidance of saccade eye movements in monkeys. *Journal of Neurophysiology*, 1977, *40*, 74–94.

Mountcastle, V. B., Lynch, J. C., Georgopolous, A., Sakata, H., & Acuna, C. Posterior parietal association cortex of the rhesus monkey: Command functions for operations within extrapersonal space. *Journal of Neurophysiology*, 1975, *38*, 871–908.

Nauta, W. J. H., & Karten, H. J. A general profile of the vertebrate brain, with sidelights on the ancestry of cerebral cortex. In F. O. Schmitt, G. C. Quarton, T. Melnechuk, & G. Adelman (Eds.), *The neurosciences* (Vol. 2). New York: The Rockefeller University Press, 1970.

Netter, F. H. *Nervous system*. Summit, N.J.: Ciba Pharmaceutical Products, 1958.

Noback, C. R. & Demarest, R. J. *The human nervous system: Basic principles of neurobiology* (2nd ed.). New York: McGraw-Hill, 1975.

Pandya, D. N. & Kuypers, H. G. J. M. Cortico-cortical connections in the rhesus monkey. *Brain Research*, 1969, *13*, 13–36.

Penfield, W. & Roberts, L. *Speech and brain mechanisms*. Princeton: Princeton University Press, 1959.

Pick, J. *Autonomic nervous system: Morphological, comparative, clinical, and surgical aspects*. Philadelphia: J. B. Lippincott Co., 1970.

Ramon-Moliner, E., & Nauta, W. J. H. The isodendritic core of the brain stem. *Journal of Comparative Neurology*, 1966, *126*, 311–336.

Robinson, D. A. Eye movement control in primates. *Science*, 1968, *161*, 1219–1224.

Sarnat, H. B., & Netsky, M. G. *Evolution of the nervous system*. Oxford: Tavistock, 1974.

Schally, A. V., Arimura, A., & Kastin, A. J. Hypothalamis regulatory hormones. *Science*, 1973, *179*, 341–350.

Scheibel, M. E., & Scheibel, A. B. Anatomical basis of attention mechanisms in vertebrate brains. In G. C. Quarton, T. Melnechuk, & F. O. Schmitt (Eds.), *The neurosciences* (Vol. 1). New York: The Rockefeller University Press, 1967.

Sidman, R. L. & Rakic, P. Neuronal migration, with special reference to developing human brain: A review. *Brain Research*, 1973, *62*, 1–35.

Sperry, R. W. Neurology and the mind-brain problem. *American Scientist*, 1952, *40*, 291–312.

Sperry, R. W. Embryogenesis of behavioral nerve nets. In R. L. De Haan & H. Ursprung (Eds.), *Organogenesis*. New York: Holt, 1965.

Sperry, R. W. Perception in the absence of the neocortical commissures. *Research Publications for the Association for Research in Nervous and Mental Diseases*, 1970, *48*, 123–138.

Sperry, R. W. Lateral specialization in the surgically separated hemispheres. In F. O. Schmitt, & F. G. Worden (Eds.), *The neurosciences* (Vol. 3). Cambridge, Mass.: MIT Press, 1974.

Sperry, R. W., Gazzaniga, M. S., & Bogen, J. E. Interhemispheric relationships: the neocortical commissures; syndromes of hemispheric deconnection. In P. J. Vinkin, & G. W. Bruyn (Eds.), *Handbook of clinical neurology* (Vol. 4). Amsterdam: North Holland, 1969.

Sprague, J. M. The effects of chronic brainstem lesions on wakefulness, sleep and behavior. *Research Publications for the Association for Research in Nervous and Mental Diseases*, 1967, *45*, 148–194.

Szentagothai, M. J., & Arbib, M. A. The module concept in cerebral cortex architecture. *Brain Research*, 1975, *95*, 475–496.

Swazey, J. P. Sherrington's concept of integrative action. *Journal of the History of Biology,* 1968, *1,* 57–89.

Trevarthen, C. Two mechanisms of vision in primates. *Psychologische Forschung,* 1968, *31,* 299–337.

Trevarthen, C. Behavioral embryology. In E. C. Carterette & M. P. Friedman (Eds.), *Handbook of perception* (Vol. 3), New York: Academic Press, 1973.

Trevarthen, C. Modes of perceiving and modes of acting. In H. Pick, & E. Saltzman (Eds.), *Modes of perceiving and processing information.* Hillsdale, N.J.: Erlbaum, 1978. Pp. 99–136.

Trevarthen, C. Neuroembryology and the development of perception. In F. Falkner, & J. M. Tanner (Eds.), *Human growth: A comprehensive treatise* (Vol. 3). New York: Plenum, 1979. (a)

Trevarthen, C. Instincts for human understanding and for cultural cooperation: Their development in infancy. In M. von Cranach, K. Foppa, W. Lepenies, & D. Ploog (Eds.), *Human ethology.* Cambridge: Cambridge University Press, 1979. (b)

Trevarthen, C. The tasks of consciousness: How could the brain do them? In M. O'Connor (Ed.), *Brain and mind.* London: Churchill: Ciba Foundation Symposium, 1979 (c). Pp. 187–215.

Trevarthen, C., & Sperry, R. W. Perceptual unity of the ambient visual field in human commissurotomy patients. *Brain,* 1973, *96,* 547–570.

Valenstein, E. S. *Brain stimulation and motivation.* Chicago: Scott, Foresman, & Co., 1973.

Walshe, E. W. *Neuropsychology: A clinical approach.* Edinburgh: Churchill Livingstone, 1978.

Wurtz, R. M. and Mohler, C. W. Organization of monkey superior colliculus: Enhanced visual response of superficial layer cells. *Journal of Neurophysiology,* 1976, *39,* 745–765.

Yakovlev, P. I. Telencephalon "impar," "semi-par" and "totopar:" Morphogenetic, tectogenetic and architectonic definitions. *International Journal of Neurology,* 1968, *6,* 245–265.

Yakovlev, P. I. and Lecours, A. R. The myelogenetic cycles of regional maturation of the brain. In A. Minkowski (Ed.), *Regional development of the brain in early life.* Oxford: Blackwell, 1967. Pp. 3–70.

Zaidel, E. Man's elusive right hemisphere. *Scientific American.* 1980. In press.

PART II

INFORMATION PROCESSING IN THE BRAIN

After the discussions in Part I of the organization of the structures and the cognitive processes of the brain, we now analyze in greater detail several of the major cognitive processes or information processing systems of the brain, including individual differences among some of them. Part II of the volume discusses the cognitive processes of attention, perception, encoding, memory, and language. These important processes encompass much of the recent research on the human brain conducted by psychologists and by neuroscientists. Although in the future, some new categories, perhaps a new organization, may emerge from the joint findings in these two areas to represent better the many subtle and complicated cognitive processes and functions of the brain. The topics discussed in Part II provide a useful, familiar way to organize the current state of research in the different but complementary fields of cognitive psychology and neuroscience.

Chapter III

The Neuropsychology of Attention: Emotional and Motivational Controls

DIANE McGUINNESS
KARL PRIBRAM

I. Introduction

Everyone knows what attention is. It is the taking possession by the mind, in clear and vivid form, of one out of what seem several simultaneously possible objects or trains of thought.
        —W. James (1890)

William James, in *The Principles of Psychology* (1890), began his discourse on attention with this straightforward description of what is now called selective attention. He then went further in the chapters on attention and the will, to outline at least 12 attentional modes of operation. His analysis anticipated most of the current theory, as well as describing certain phenomena that have yet to be considered or studied. Thus, anyone willing to dip into *The Principles of Psychology* will find a clear statement of the ranges of behavioral manifestations of "paying attention." However, James was unable to solve the problem of **how** attention is paid, and had no evidence available to him concerning the mechanisms involved in the control of attention, the problems which form the content of this paper. Before outlining the current evidence on control mechanisms in attention, it is of interest to follow the historical

95

THE BRAIN AND PSYCHOLOGY

events that led to the rebirth of attention as a valid concept in psychology. Attention has returned through the backdoor, as it were, and has appeared in different guises depending upon the specific orientations of the various investigators.

Experimenters measuring animal behavior were forced to admit the importance of "attention" when animals were found to notice some stimuli and ignore others in studies on cue sampling and discrimination learning (Trabasso & Bower, 1968; Honig, 1970). These experimenters explained their data in terms of cue salience, assuming that certain stimulus parameters were more noticeable or meaningful to the animals. Human experimental research has focused exclusively on selective attention. Studies were initiated in an attempt to answer the question posed by Miller (1956) and Broadbent (1958) concerning how a limited central processor reduces the flow of information received from the senses. The impetus to this line of inquiry stemmed from information theory. Selective attention research has spawned subsets of inquiry such as "divided attention" research utilizing dichotic listening techniques (Treisman, 1969; Kahneman, 1973). Speed or efficiency of the selective process, measured in reaction time, has also been of considerable interest to experimenters using visual and auditory search tasks (Kornblum, 1973). Neisser (1967) in his book on cognitive psychology attempted to frame categories of attention by suggesting that attention operated selectively in two primary modes. One was broad, unfocused, and extracted global information; the other was narrowly focused and permitted detailed analysis. In either case, memory traces of previous perceptual events feed out (MacKay, 1956; Pribram, 1971) to operate upon the incoming stimuli, a process he called "analysis-by-syntheses" His definition is synonymous with what James had described in 1890 as "preperception," a process concomitant with paying attention. Thus, the behavioral sciences have begun to map a range of phenomena which are subsumed under the headings of selective attention and discrimination.

Meanwhile, investigators in the brain sciences and in human psychophysiology have been converging, through quite disparate experimental techniques, on the concept that attention varies as a function of arousal or activation, terms often used interchangeably to describe a continuum from wakefulness to sleep. Because arousal and activation are central to the theoretical framework developed in this paper, we will pursue the historical course of this discovery in some detail.

In the 1920s Berger reported that during changes in wakefulness, brain waves recorded from the scalp (EEG) could range between fast, low voltage activity and the slow, high amplitude wave forms characteristic of deep sleep. The physiological correlates of these shifts of activity remained a mystery until the discovery by Lindsley, Bowden, and Magoun (1949) and by Moruzzi and Magoun (1949) that the reticular formation, a collection of short-fibered, many branched neurons in the brainstem, is essential for maintaining an alert organism. Lesions to portions of this system caused somnolence, coma, and death, whereas electrical stimulation of these same regions produced an alert organism with fast brain wave activity.

These results, along with others, served to initiate a conceptualization of the brain as "aroused" or "activated." Allying these discoveries to the behavioral data on performance efficiency during different intensities of stimulation, researchers began to view both brain and behavior as complying with the Yerkes–Dodson law (1908), which postulates an inverted U-shaped function of efficiency depending upon the degree of "arousal" of the organism. Under or overaroused subjects perform poorly; optimal efficiency occurs in a moderately aroused state (Hebb, 1955). The activity of the reticular formation was assumed to parallel these states. Thus far, no EEG correlates of "overarousal" have been demonstrated.

The notion of brain activation or arousal as existing on a continuum has led to a considerable amount of confusion in the light of subsequent investigations. This confusion has been particularly evident in human psychophysiology in studies of emotion where changes in autonomic nervous system (ANS) activity have been produced by psychically arousing events. Paradoxes soon became evident. The desynchronization of the EEG corresponded to many of the peripheral changes, yet gross EEG does not habituate readily to stimulus repetition, whereas autonomic responses do so reliably. Critical experiments by Lacey (1967); Lacey and Lacey (1970) challenged the notion of a unified arousal mechanism by demonstrating a fractionation in responding between physiological systems. When a subject looks or listens to external events, heart rate slows and skin resistance decreases. However, when a subject attempts to solve a difficult problem, heart rate accelerates rapidly, while skin resistance still decreases. (This same phenomenon was observed by Feré in 1899.)

Additional problems for a unified arousal theory were produced by the concurrent endeavors of Sharpless and Jasper (1956) in the United States and Sokolov (1960, 1963) in Russia. These researchers originally discovered that when arousal to a novel event produced a change in the activity of the CNS and ANS, habituation of the response will ensue if the event is recurrent. Sokolov went a step further, however, by showing that changing **any** parameter of the stimulus causes a reappearance of the arousal response, or in the Russian term, the orienting reflex. This suggests that the arousal reaction may reflect a mismatch of novel input to a brain representation of prior inputs—a "neuronal model." Sharpless and Jasper also noticed that the CNS response separated into a *phasic* component which habituated readily and a *tonic* component which habituated more slowly. Studies have demonstrated that the phasic portion is almost always on the order of 1–3 sec, depending upon the intensity of the stimulus, and is essentially reflexive. It is most commonly produced by a mismatch to a previously encoded input (a memory trace). In other words, it suggests that the phasic portion of the orienting reflex is sensitive to stimulus information. The balance between the phasic (orienting) and the tonic portions can be brought under voluntary control and depends upon the interest or intentions of the individual. Note that arousal seems to split into two parts, one of which is partly outside the control of the subject, and one which is not.

A final blow to the unified arousal concept came from the results of lesion studies on humans and on monkeys by Pribram (e.g., Bagshaw, Kimble, & Pribram, 1965; Kimble, Bagshaw, & Pribram, 1965; Luria, Pribram, & Homskaya, 1964). It was found, contrary to expectation, that the behavioral correlates of orienting (head turning, ear flicking, focusing, etc.) could be dissociated from the autonomic responses of skin resistance and heart rate. The critical finding was that if the organism failed to produce autonomic responses to stimulation because of specific lesions, behavioral orienting was observed, but the behavior failed to habituate. The brain structures involved in this dissociation were the frontal cortex, and the amygdala (a system of basal nuclei found in the forebrain).

It will be apparent from these studies that a unitary arousal concept is too simplistic, forcing the conclusion that more than one process is involved. The hope of arriving at principles relating arousal to attention seems at first glance even more elusive. Already we have touched upon a vast range of processes: arousal, activation, and habituation; stimulus facilitation, cue salience, etc. How can these possibly relate to selectivity, discrimination, analysis-by-synthesis, and global and focused attention?

The distinction noted by Sharpless and Jasper between phasic and tonic arousal provides the key to a possible solution. James initially drew a similar distinction when he referred to two major categories of attention. He noted that certain classes of biologically relevant stimuli which are novel, salient, or intense impinge upon awareness regardless of ongoing activity. Further, he observed that there are modes of attending in which the subject determines the contents of his own awareness and the duration of each episode. He called the former involuntary or **reflex** attention, and the latter voluntary attention, or the **will.**

ii. Arousal, Activation, and Effort—A Model of Attention

In our review on animal and human neuropsychology and psycho-physiology (Pribram & McGuinness, 1975), this division became the cornerstone of a model of attention. At present, we find the edifice intact and the model strengthened and amplified by new data, especially from recent biochemical evidence on brain systems. We wish to restate our original model, to elaborate our rationale, and to include new data which provide an unequivocal basis for our original suggestion of three major systems that operate as controls on attention.

The distinction between involuntary and voluntary attention identifies two aspects of attentional control. To bring these concepts into line with the evidence and the terminology from physiological studies, the involuntary modes have been redesignated as *arousal*, a phasic short-lived and reflex response to input, and *activation*, a tonic long-lasting and involuntary readiness to respond. A third system coordinates arousal and activation. The operation of this system results in voluntary control and is experienced as *effort*.

Note that the model refers exclusively to **process** and not to the **content** of awareness. Much of the difficulty in establishing a viable framework for the categories of attention has been caused by the confusion between state, process, and content. This confusion is amplified by the resurgence of interest in consciousness. Consciousness has been used interchangeably with awareness, and with attention. Because of this confusion, we wish to draw careful distinctions between the way we intend to use psychological language.

Consciousness, which will not be a topic for discussion in this chapter, infers a *state*. The state of consciousness results from the sum or interaction of all possible neurochemical events affecting it. (For a more detailed account of consciousness, see Pribram, 1976). We accept for purposes of this paper that the controls on attention operate concurrently during a state of consciousness best described as normal wakefulness.

Further, these mechanisms controlling attentional set are independent of the perceptual and ideational contents of awareness (the "one of several possible objects" James described). A more formal description of this interaction is that each state of consciousness can invoke several modes of attention, each of which requires a particular configuration of the arousal, activation, and effort systems. These modes operate on the contents of awareness to define a bounded set, one of a number of possible sets. What is selected is determined either by sudden or intense

stimuli, or by previous perceptual and motor experiences and their associational memories. The sensitivity of discrimination or the speed of
selectivity in a reaction time task may be constrained less by attentional
control than by the efficiency of the perceptuo-motor apparatus.

Our model thus deals with the physiological systems that operate the
attentional controls on perceptual events and not with perceptual events
themselves or transformations (cognitive operations) on these events.
These distinctions must be kept clear because different brain systems are
involved in attention, perception, and cognition. The interaction between these systems is another problem for the study of attention and
one that will be touched upon only briefly in this presentation.

A. Arousal

It has been noted that the ubiquity of the arousal concept has obscured
more than it has enlightened. Here we restrict the use of the term to be
synonymous with the orienting reaction.

Arousal is said to occur when an input change produces a measurable
phasic change in a physiological (e.g., GSR) or behavioral (e.g., head
turning) indicator over a baseline. The types of input change that produce arousal have been studied extensively and have been labelled by
Berlyne (1969) as collative (defined as, to collect and compare carefully in
order to arrange into informative order) variables. These include sudden
changes in intensity to which the organism is unaccustomed, changes in
the timing of inputs, and changes in the ground in which a stimulus
figure appears. In short, arousal results when, in the history of the
organism's experience, an input is surprising, complex, or novel. Such
collative characteristics also define the concept "information" as it is
used in the study of communication systems (e.g., Brillouin, 1962); thus
it has become customary to treat organisms subject to arousal as "information processing systems." Inherent in such treatment is the assumption that the input is matched against some residual of past experience in
the organism, or some competence (Bruner, 1957; Miller, 1960; Pribram,
1971). Without such matching, there could be no novelty or information,
nor even a measure of change in intensity.

It was noted previously that the waning or habituation of the arousal
response must be due to the establishment of such a residual neuronal
model of that event—since any small change in one parameter of the
signal will reconstitute the arousal reaction (Sokolov, 1960, 1963). Further, certain salient stimuli, such as one's name, produce facilitation and
not habituation, at least in a relevant context, suggesting that a high-

level overide is involved. We note therefore that there are two consequences of the orienting reaction; reflex behavioral and neural changes
over baseline, and mnemic "registration" which ensues with stimulus
repetition.

B. Activation

The interaction between behaving organisms and their environment is
not one-sided. The organism is not a switchboard for incoming stimulation. Rather, behaving organisms are spontaneously active, generating
changes in the environment often by way of highly programmed (i.e.,
serially ordered) responses (Miller et al., 1960; Pribram 1960, 1962, 1963,
1971). These organizations of behavior must involve the construction of
neuronal models in at least two ways: (a) control of the somatomotor
system which effects the responses and (b) feedback from the outcomes
(reinforcing consequences) of the behavior. Sherrington (1955), in dis-
cussing central representations, framed the question: "Is the organism
intending to *do* something about the stimulus variables in the situation?" Germana (1968, 1969) in a review of the evidence, suggested that
any central representation or neuronal model must include such "demand" characteristics. Thus he proposes that Pavlov's "What is it?"
reaction (which we have called arousal and the registration of input in
awareness and memory) may not occur in isolation from a "What's to be
done?" reaction. As we shall see, our analysis suggests that both reactions occur and that they can be distinguished: arousal and the registration of input indicating "What is it?" and readiness signaling "What's
to be done?"

Activation differs from arousal therefore in maintaining a set to continue ongoing behavior. Maintaining a tonic readiness is reflected in an
increase in cortical negativity (CNV) (e.g., Walter, Cooper, Aldridge,
McCallum, & Winter, 1964; Donchin, Otto, Gerbrandt, & Pribram, 1971)
and tonic heart rate deceleration (Lacey & Lacey, 1970). Studies of readiness have shown that with development an additional component
comes into play. This component is "vigilance" and is addressed to
overcoming habituation in situations in which the maintenance of a set
is no longer automatic.

C. Effort

Thus the systems involved in arousal and activation can be distinguished; arousal defined as a phasic reaction to input; activation, as a

tonic readiness to respond. Yet, under many circumstances, the two reactions appear to be yoked. In such situations they share the function of reflex coupling input to output, stimulus to response. In the absence of controlled arousal and activation, behaving organisms would be constantly aroused by their movements and moved by arousing inputs. There must be some control process that involves both arousal and activation and allows the uncoupling to take place. Manifestations of this process are registration and its consequent habituation and the overrides on habituation, such as facilitation and vigilance. As a rule, action generated inputs (the outcomes of actions—their reinforcing consequences) appear to generate more complexly structured neuronal models than repetitions of simple inputs. This complexity is largely the result of participation of the central motor systems in generating input. Thus it takes longer to form a habit in, than to habituate to, the same situation. Such a process, requiring flexible shifts from a change in primitive through-put states, appears to be experienced as effort.

Effort is reflected centrally (see last section) and peripherally where muscular contraction shifts to an anaerobic metabolic cycle (Berdina, Kolenko, Kotz, Kuzetxov, Rodinov, Savtechencko, & Thorevsky, 1970). This is particularly noticeable during problem solving and is accompanied by chronic accelerations of heart rate (Lacey & Lacey, 1970).

Effort is thus defined as an expenditure of energy (metabolic output) due to a change of state in central control systems. This definition is in keeping with a physical definition of energy (e.g., McFarland, 1971) as the capacity for doing work, that is, for changing the state of a system. Effort then, is a measure of the **rate** of changing the state of a system (or maintaining a state in the face of changes in external parameters).

III. Human Psychophysiology and Autonomic Correlates of Attention

A. Arousal

A major departure from the concept of a unified arousal model initially stemmed from Sharpless and Jasper's (1956) designation of phasic and tonic arousal. Once the implications of this division became clear, a host of human psychophysiological data fell into place. The notion of effort further clarified the significance of heart rate elevation.

In studies measuring changes in autonomic activity (skin conductance or GSR, blood pressure, heart rate, etc.) while the subject is paying attention, the sympathetic nervous system measures (GSR or blood volume) often mirror stimulus parameters of novelty and complexity, whereas the parasympathetic division controlling the vagal regulation of heart rate, reflects the parameters of the somatomotor readiness and response mechanisms—which in turn reflect the incentives and response biases developed as the reinforcing consequences of behavior. This distinction has been clearly demonstrated in studies by Elliott (1969), Elliott, Bonkart, and Light (1970), by Dahl and Spence (1971), and by Hare (1972).

Experimenters appear to use the term arousal defined by the amount of information in the stimulus, and studies of selective attention in which input must be categorized by the subject before he can respond appropriately have shown consistently that sympathetically innervated phasic responses distinguish between variations in task largely on the basis of their novelty, surprisingness, or complexity (Blaylock, 1972; Hare, 1972; Kilpatrick, 1972; Lacey & Lacey, 1970; McGuinness, 1973). A typical experiment (Hare, 1972) in which subjects viewed slides without discriminating between them were less aroused (showed fewer skin conductance changes) than those who had to categorize. Differences in phasic skin conductance amplitudes and these phasic responses returned to baseline (habituated) over trials. Difficulty due to changes required in response operations were reflected in tonic skin conductance; most precisely by tonic heart rate changes.

A precise relationship between tonic levels of skin conductance and response output variables has not been demonstrated. To date, skin conductance has not been implicated in any metabolic function (Venables & Christie, 1973), but data by Bohlin (1976) suggest that either readiness (state of activation) or effort produces a elevation in tonic skin conductance. In her study, subjects were asked to perform difficult mental arithmetic tasks interspersed with habituation trials to a series of tones. Skin conductance was continuously and significantly elevated in both shock-threat and no-shock-threat groups compared to controls who relaxed throughout the experiment. Bohlin describes these groups as exhibiting tonic "arousal." We would suggest that the experimental groups were maintaining readiness to respond to the arithmetic problems and that this required effort. However, more information is needed to understand how tonic skin conductance levels relate to the parasympathetic activity that produces tonic heart rate changes. Current data show that the involvement of somatomotor responses during activation or readiness affect tonic cardiovascular changes, and this relationship provides one clue to unraveling the controversial and apparently disparate views of the psychophysiological mechanisms involved in attention. We therefore focus on the relationship between heart rate, the somato-motor readiness system, and effort.

B. Readiness and Execution

Two prevailing theories concerning the meaning of cardiovascular processes during attention appear diametrically opposed. On one hand, there is the baroceptor feedback theory of Lacey (1967); Lacey and Lacey (1970) which, simplified, states that increased heart rate will directly affect stimulus intake or rejection through a process of feedback to the bulbar inhibitory centers in the brainstem, reducing arousal of the central nervous system (Bonvallet & Allen, 1963). On the other hand, Obrist and his colleagues (Obrist, Webb, Sutterer, & Howard, 1970a,b) propose that heart rate is regulated by the motor demands of the organism that are controlled centrally. Findings by Jennings, Averill, Opton, and Lazarus (1971) have challenged the adequacy of either of these explanations and have produced results in line with an "amount of attention" hypothesis. They argue that as demands on attention increase, heart rate will **fall** in proportion to the number of the categorizations demanded by the task, unless metabolic activity is engaged. This is somewhat in line with the view of this article, but their suggestions are still incomplete. As they note, this hypothesis does not explain the functional significance of cardiac deceleration during attention. Nor, we might add, does it explain why heart rate always **increases** during problem solving.

To resolve these conceptual difficulties, the physiological processes will be examined in more detail. The assumption of a majority of theories is that there is a unitary relationship between cardiovascular and somatic processes, whereas evidence shows that the situation is far more complex (Lawler, Obrist, & Lawler, 1976; McCanne & Sandman, 1976).

Any registered orienting response produces a dual sympathetic–parasympathetic effect. The cardiovascular reflex in orienting results in sympathetically controlled and cholingerically mediated gross blood flow shifts which are sometimes accompanied by an initial phasic heart rate acceleration. This will vary in magnitude with stimulus intensity (Graham & Clifton, 1966), and an initial respiratory block will often combine to elevate the acceleratory effect (Jennings et al., 1971; Petro, Holland, & Bouman, 1970; Wood & Obrist, 1964), although the effect of intensity is not entirely predictable (Bull & Lang, 1972). We now know that this is due to parasympathetic inhibition, and that all attentional (as opposed to movement-produced) heart rate changes are under vagal regulation (Eckberg, Fletcher, & Braunwald, 1972; Forsyth, 1970; Obrist, Howard, Lawler, Sutterer, Smithson, & Martin, 1972).

The initial arousal phase is followed immediately by a heart rate change in the direction of deceleration, which is due to the vagus restablizing the system. If the prepared somatic systems become mobilized to initiate an appropriate consummatory or defense pattern—eating, drinking, withdrawal, flight, or attack (Abrahams, Hilton, & Zbrozyna, 1964)—heart rate will then come under the control of the somatomotor system and a chronic increase in rate occurs to meet the demands of the activity. The processes occur in fixed order: Stimulus → blood flow shift → heart rate acceleration → heart rate deceleration, until the motor response determines tonic heart rate acceleration and the system ultimately restabilizes.

During a vigilance or categorization task involving the prolonged intake of information (Lacey & Lacey, 1970), the vagal restabilization phase is extended as part of a tonic activation—the vigilant readiness process. Lewis and Wilson (1970) examined cardiac responses to a picture-matching task in young children. In all children, a marked deceleration occurred which lasted until the choice was made. The most interesting finding was that the greatest deceleration was related to **correct** responses—if a subject was asked to guess again, heart rate did not return to baseline until the final choice. Correct responses occurred with longer response times and greater cardiac deceleration, which supports the suggestion that the vigilant readiness phase of the control processes has been extended.

Correlation with IQ demonstrated that there was a relationship to both deceleration and error score for girls only. The sex difference finding could possibly be due to the greater amount of movement found in boys, which would cause a heart rate acceleration and less attention to the task. This explanation is made more tenable by the recent finding of Obrist, Howard, Sutterer, Hennis, and Murrell (1973) that children's reaction times are slower in proportion to the amount of uncontrolled movement they produce. The relationship between motor control and reaction time was linear with age. As reaction times increased, motor responses and heart rate decreased. We therefore suggest, in line with Obrist et al. (1970a,b), that when activation must be maintained, heart rate deceleration occurs as an accompaniment of somatomotor readiness.

This then partially accounts for the sequence of physiological events occurring when the organism prolongs attention while categorizing external events. During this intake episode, he reduces extraneous noise by eliminating random movements. Heart rate adjusts to the reduced demands of the system, reflecting characteristics of the somatomotor system in which overt movements regularly precede blood flow changes and heart rate acceleration. For example, Petro et al. (1970) found that after a voluntary contraction of the biceps muscle, heart rate increased with a latency of approximately 500 msec. However, when problem solving, with its emphasis on which response to produce when, and the actual trial-and-error making of overt or covert responses is initiated, the cardiovascular and somatomotor response relationship is reversed.

C. Muscular Effort and Problem Solving

The locus of the demand for effort is different in categorizing and in problem solving or reasoning, and this raises the question of (a) the relationship between the various forms of attention and effort, and (b) of the nature of effort itself. Could it be that the muscular contractions involved in making responses are totally responsible for the effort necessary in problem solving? A change in actual movement as during categorizing and reasoning would obviously be accompanied by a decrease (categorizing) or an increase (reasoning) in isotonic contraction, but, activation of the readiness mechanism may also be due to change to a special sort of metabolism, usually thought to be largely anaerobic, which has been shown to be active during concentration and problem solving, and which involves isometric contraction.

An understanding of this special metabolic process during attention has been provided by Berdina et al. (1972). Until this study there was no functional explanation for the finding that sympathetically innervated blood flow shifts actually reduce oxygen uptake by the muscle, whereas somatic activation increases it (Rosell & Uvnas, 1962). The study of Berdina et al. (1972) suggests the possibility that this special sort of metabolism of muscle fibers is due to cholinergic mediators. Berdina et al. were interested in the effect of problem solving on blood flow and muscle contraction. They were the first to establish any precise relationship between electromyogram (EMG) recording and problem solving due to the small amount of amplification produced by the technique, which often results in unreliable values (Jennings et al., 1971; Lader, 1965; Matthews & Lader, 1971; see also McCanne & Sandman, 1976). To avoid this difficulty, they introduced a condition of partial muscular contraction: Subjects had to grip a hand dynamometer which they were pretrained to maintain at 30% of their maximum grip. Then, during the problem-solving experiment, subjects were asked to grip the dynamoneter for as long as possible.

Both contraction alone and problem solving (arithmetic) alone caused significant blood flow changes. However, a combination of contraction plus arithmetic produced no greater changes in blood flow than either condition alone. On the other hand, the contraction **duration** was significantly increased by arithmetic from 181 to 235 sec ($p < .001$). To disentangle voluntary effects from purely reflex effects, they induced a forearm contraction by electrical stimulation. The results were the same even when the subject had no voluntary control over his muscles. An injection of atropine significantly decreased blood flow during arithmetic, and during contraction plus arithmetic, but not during contraction alone. Atropine also reduced contraction duration during the combined task, showing that the increased contraction during problem solving was **not** a somatic effect since small amounts of circulating atropine do not affect the neuromuscular junction. It was concluded therefore that some form of sympathetically controlled metabolism was causing muscle force to increase, making muscles "work" under the special conditions of isometric contraction.

Apart from other considerations, this experiment demonstrated conclusively that muscular effects do occur during problem-solving tasks and that they involve gross changes in tonicity which cannot always be observed by EMG recording. Equally relevant is the fact that as heart rate correlates so precisely with blood flow changes (Matthews & Lader, 1971), an increase in blood flow during problem solving automatically implies a corresponding increase in heart rate. The Berdina experiment thus explained the functional significance of heart rate changes during problem solving and reasoning: Maintaining attention while problem solving is effortful and involves hard work and hard work is accompanied by metabolic changes. The results of this study appear to establish the outlines of the metabolic processes operating during intense concentration.

In summary, the discovery that two types of muscle activation (isotonic and isometric) and two metabolic functions (aerobic and anaerobic) are involved in both voluntary (effortful) attention and action makes it easier to understand why some confusion has arisen in the study of the psychophysiology of attention. Returning briefly to the Lacey hypothesis, physiological responding during stimulus intake will depend entirely upon how a task is constructed and whether it is primarily a categorizing or reasoning problem. We agree with Lacey that during a state of behavior characterized by heart rate deceleration, we are most open to environmental cues (Lacey & Lacey, 1970) but not necessarily for the reasons he suggests (see also a critique by Hahn, 1973). Lacey's theory also requires acceleration when decisions are made.

How then could one interpret what is occurring during the acquisition of a perceptual or motor skill? When the coordination of arousal and activation is demanded, heart rate acceleration reflects the amount of effort involved in registering, adjusting, and changing the central representation to the requirements of the task. In accord with Lacey's assumptions, intake of information may alternate with concentration. A process ensues that must constantly shift among relevant stimuli in order to overcome the rapid decrementing of the system (just as continuous eye movements overcome the rapid adaptation of retinal receptors). When one plays tennis, for example, heart rate is elevated, but the player must flexibly attend (be aroused by) such cues as the angle and velocity of the approaching ball, the ground lines, the height of the net, and the position and angle of the opponent's body and racket. The intricacy of the series of highly refined changes in response and the transformational calculations based on this evidence could elevate heart rate, even without the behavioral activity of playing tennis (e.g., in a spectator). This is brought out clearly in a study by Johansson and Frankenhaeuser (1973) in which high heart rate accompanied the complex transformations required during an intake task.

In reasoning tasks, activation precedes arousal. For instance, in playing a game of chess or engaging in any similar pursuit requiring transformational calculations, reasoning must occur before the effective response. Once the "move" has been made, it may arouse an "aha" reaction: The move was successful, or, "Oh dear, why didn't I see that!" Again, the physiological changes that occur are those that have been shown in the Berdina experiments, although the theories of Jennings et al. (1971) and Obrist et al. (1970a,b) would predict the opposite.

Some of the task variables which affect arousal and activation and the effort required to overcome resistance to extinction of a prior set during categorizing and reasoning have also been investigated by Dahl and Spence (1971). They propose an activation theory which adopts Bergum's (1966) technique of taxonomic analysis of performance, in which tasks are evaluated according to complexity and activation of response. Task demands were rated by independent judges, and the amount of heart rate change was correlated to each task. Heart rate increased with response demand, and all correlations were significant. A subsequent factor analysis revealed a major factor which they designated "density," or degree of concentration required; in other words, the total amount of cognitive **effort** involved in the task. The other factor which accounted for the greatest amount of variance in task performance was information content of relevant stimuli. Thus, again, collative variables were distinguished from the amount of transformational effort or "work" required in problem solution.

In summary, the autonomic changes that take place during processing of external and internal events appear to be consistently or lawfully related to certain attentional modes. Any sudden or informative input triggers an arousal response which is reflected most precisely by phasic responses of the sympathetic nervous system. When an organism is maintaining a set to respond to externally produced events, heart rate deceleration is generally observed. Conversely, when problem solving takes place, typified by what Lacey describes as a stimulus rejection episode, heart rate acceleration reflects the amount of effort required by the task in uncoupling the involuntary arousal–activation systems.

IV. The Delineation of Brain Systems in Attention

A. The Control of Arousal in Reflex Attention: The Corebrain Arousal System and the Amygdala Circuits

Just as arousal produces a phasic response of the sympathetic nervous system, studies of the behavior of neural systems during arousal in animals have revealed that phasic responses to sudden changes in stimulus events are a ubiquitous property of certain portions of the central nervous system. In an extensive series of experiments (reviewed by Groves & Thompson, 1970) these authors distinguished a system of arousal neurons in the medial portions of the spinal cord. This system of neurons in turn converges with another more laterally placed set of decrementing neurons onto a final common path that habituates and dishabituates much as does the motor behavior in which these neural systems are involved. There is every reason to believe that the rostral extension into the mesencephalic brainstem of this column of medially placed cells accounts for the well-documented arousal effects of stimulations of the reticular formation (see Lindsley, 1961; Magoun, 1958 for review). Such effects are obtained even more rostrally in the diencephalon in a continuation of this neuron system into the hypothalamus where episodes of fighting and fleeing are produced by electrical or chemical stimulation of the so-called "defense" region of the hypothalamus.

These behaviors have been shown to be related to the orienting reaction. Abrahams and Hilton (1958) and Abrahams et al. (1964) found that in attempting to produce a defense response by stimulation of the hypothalamus, at first a low degree of arousal occurred, indicated by pupil dilation and postural alerting. Only when the level of stimulation was increased and maintained for a few seconds, did hissing, snarling, running, and piloerection occur. In the later study, alerting behaviors were measured in greater detail, and during mild stimulation the authors observed changes in pupil dilation, head movements, pricking the ears, respiration, and blood flow. These same changes were also recorded during responses to simple auditory, visual, or cutaneous stimuli, in the absence of hypothalamic stimulation. Since these physiological changes are the same as those observed in all orienting responses, the defense reaction could therefore be considered in part to be due to an increase in arousal.

Converging on these hypothalamic structures are two reciprocally acting circuits regulating arousal. These circuits center on the amygdala (see the more extensive review by Pribram & McGuinness, 1975). One of these circuits involves the dorsolateral frontal cortex and is excitatory since resections of this structure **invariably** eliminate visceral autonomic orienting responses. The other, opposite in function, is more likely related to the orbitofrontal cortex which has been shown to be the rostral pole of an extensive inhibitory pathway (Kaada, Pribram, & Epstein, 1949; Wall & Davis, 1951; Pribram, 1961; Skinner & Lindsley, 1973; Sauerland & Clemente, 1973). These data relate to the descriptions of the behavior of amygdalectomized animals (Pribram & Bagshaw, 1953) which focused on the fact that they were tame, unresponsive to threat, and nonaggressive. However, the opposite finding was occasionally observed (e.g., Rosvold, Mirsky, & Pribram, 1954) and more recent behavioral studies by Ursin and Kaada (1960) using restricted lesions and electrical stimulations have confirmed the suggestion that at least two more or less reciprocal systems can be identified in the amygdala.

Such reciprocal innervation allows sensitive modulation (tuning) of the arousal mechanism. This is in accord with evidence on other control functions of the amygdala and related structures. Thus, injections of carbachol into the appropriate hypothalamic site will initiate drinking; such injections into the amygdala have no effect unless the animal is already drinking, in which case the amount of drinking becomes proportional to the amount of carbachol injected in an exquisitely accurate relationship (Russell, Singer, Flanagan, Stone, & Russell, 1968). Extrapolating to the issue before us, the frontoamygdala influence can be conceived as a finely tuned determinant controlling visceroautonomic arousal initiated by the hypothalamic mechanism during orienting. It is as if in the absence of the frontoamygdala systems, the animal would fail to control its drinking behavior: Once started it would drink under circumstances in which others would stop. This is exactly what happens —and more. Both eating and drinking are controlled in this fashion— and not only their cessation, but also their initiation (Fuller, Rosvold, & Pribram, 1957).

A clue to what these controls on arousal accomplish comes from the finding that despite an essentially normal reactivity to shock, the amygdalectomized subjects have fewer spontaneous GSRs during the shock sessions, suggesting a change in base level (Bagshaw & Pribram, 1968). That baseline changes do occur after amygdala lesions was demonstrated directly in sustained chronic changes in the response measures (Pribram, Reitz, McNeil, & Spevack, 1979) and indirectly by various studies which showed that although behavioral and some electrocortical responses appeared to be normal during orienting (Schwartzbaum, Wilson, & Morrissette, 1961; Bagshaw & Benzies, 1968) the background level of these responses is lower than for controls. Ear flicking is practically absent during interstimulus intervals, and it takes less time for the lesioned animals to attain a criterion of slow wave activity in the EEG (Bagshaw & Benzies, 1968) in the preparatory phase of the experiment. Electromyographic responses occur with normal latency, although their amplitude is considerably reduced (Pribram, Reitz, McNeil, & Spevack, 1979). These results indicate that at the forebrain level, just as at the spinal level in Groves and Thompson's experiments (1970), arousal and decrementing systems converge to produce orienting, habituation, and dishabituation.

Perhaps the most striking chronic psychophysiological change to follow amygdalectomy was the finding of a paradoxically elevated basal heart rate (Bagshaw & Benzies, 1968; Pribram et al., 1979). This puzzled us considerably and made data analysis difficult, since operated and control monkeys had to be matched for basal rate, and it had to be shown that no ceiling effect was operating. We wondered whether arousal as a concept was in fact untenable in the face of a lack of evidence for orienting coupled with an elevated heart rate. Experimental results obtained by Elliott et al. (1970) and his analysis clarified the issues. He expected an elevated tonic heart rate to accompany arousal (defined as a response to collative variables such as surprise, uncertainty, novelty, and complexity of input much as we have defined them here) but as he was recording tonic rather than phasic changes he found the opposite: "These collative variables either had no effect on tonic heart rate or they had an effect (deceleratory) opposite to expectations; but response factors and incentive factors (reinforcing consequences) had strong accelerating effects [p. 185]." Thus, arousal as noted earlier is accompanied primarily by no change or immediately followed by tonic heart rate deceleration, which is indicative of activation. In short, our monkeys with absent arousal reactions showing an elevated chronic heart rate appeared to be working with considerable effort. In accord with the psychophysiological data on humans, such elevated tonic heart rate is manifest when the situation demands effort on the part of the organism. Our observations suggest that without such expenditure of effort the amygdalectomized monkeys tend readily to fall asleep.

We therefore interpret the effects of amygdalectomy as follows: Because the specific controls on arousal are removed, arousal results not in the registration of the situation by altering the neuronal model, but in immediate reflexive distraction. This increased distractibility evokes a defensive effort to cope with the situation. The defense reaction is characterized by an attempt to shut off further input (Pribram, 1969), an effect inferred from neurophysiological evidence of control over input. The effort is reflected in an elevated heart rate and other changes in chronic variables indicative of a continuing defense against impending breakdown in the coordination involved in maintaining a set in the face of distraction. This interpretation is borne out by the results of an experiment in which infant kittens were raised in isolation; when examined at the age of six months, their visceroautonomic and endocrine reactivity in orienting experiments was similar to that of amygdalectomized subjects. They had not learned to cope with situations and thus showed the "defensive" syndrome suggestive of considerable **effort** (Konrad & Bagshaw, 1970).

In summary, studies relating brain function and the orienting reaction to sensory input have pointed to the presence of a system of neurons responding to the amount of input by maintaining or incrementing their activity. This core system of neurons extends from the spinal cord through the brainstem reticular formation, including hypothalamic sites, and lies in close proximity to those responsible for the engenderment of visceroautonomic responses. By way of its diffuse connections, this system is responsible for the ubiquitous arousal responses recorded throughout the brain concomitant with orienting. Forebrain control over this corebrain arousal system is exerted by reciprocal facilitatory and inhibitory circuits centered on the amygdala. These circuits control the onset and duration of neural arousal much as they control the onset and duration of visceroautonomic and appetitive responses.

Our interpretation of the relationship between the lack of visceroautonomic responses to orienting and the failure to habituate behaviorally has led us to suggest that a deficiency is produced in the ubiquitous central mechanism by which organisms register input. When such failure in registration occurs, the organism's nervous system is temporarily swamped by the arousing input and reacts defensively to shut out all further input. This leads to automatisms. Our interpretation fits the clinical picture of the amnestic states (*deja* and *jamais vue*) and the automatisms occurring during psychomotor seizures produced by epileptic lesions in the region of the amygdala. There is also considerable congruity between this interpretation and those of Mednick and Schulsinger (1968) and of Venables (Gruzelier & Venables, 1972) in their report of two classes (GSR responders and nonresponders) of patients diagnosed as schizophrenics. However, the interpretation also suffers from the difficulties that plague understanding of these clinical syndromes: How do disturbances of registration in immediate awareness influence subsequent retrieval? More of this in the following sections.

B. Activation and the Control of Attention: The Contingent Negative Variation and Transcortical Negative Variations

As noted earlier, activation is marked by a period of delay between either (a) an arousal to input and the performance of an act, or (b) action sequences. As the animal (or human) is intending to do something about the current situation his behavior is arrested.

The simplest situation demanding serially organized responses is one in which two successive input signals are separated by an interval. The first input signals the organism to become ready to make a response to the second, which determines the outcome. As noted above, a large body of data has been gathered in this situation, using slow changes in brain electrical activity such as the *contingent negative variation* (CNV) (Walter, Cooper, Aldridge, McCallum, & Winter, 1964) and tonic changes in heart rate (Lacey & Lacey, 1970).

The CNV was originally proposed to reflect an expectancy developed when a specific response was contingent on awaiting the second of two stimuli. This would suggest that the CNV reflects another central event indicating that an input is about to be matched to the organism's neuronal model. However, other workers suggested that the negative shift in potential reflected intended motor activity (e.g., Kornhuber & Deecke, 1965; Vaughan, Costa, & Ritter, 1968). Still others (Weinberg, 1972; Donchin, Gerbrandt, Leifer, & Tucker, 1972) demonstrated that a CNV occurs whether or not an overt motor or even a discriminative response is required, provided some set or expectancy is built into the situation. Such sets do, of course, demand postural motor readiness. Weinberg (1972), for instance, has shown that in man the CNV continues until feedback from the consequences of reinforcement of the response occurs. Similar evidence has been obtained in monkeys (Pribram, Spinelli, & Kamback, 1967).

In a review of the CNV literature, Tecce (1972) suggests that three types of negative potentials interact depending upon the demands of the experiment: (*a*) CNV due to expectant attentional processes; (*b*) the motor readiness potential signaling intention to act; and (*c*) more or less spontaneous shifts whose occurrence cannot be attributed to specific task situations. This classification, though consonant with results from a series of animal studies (Donchin, Otto, Gerbrandt, & Pribram, 1971, 1973), does not indicate the full diversity of the CNV. Recordings were made from several cortical locations under a variety of vigilance conditions. These studies showed that sites which produced *transcortical negative variations* (TNVs) depended upon the type of vigilance task. Thus, frontal TNVs are recorded only early in a task and when the task is changed; motor negative potentials are recorded only in anticipation of the necessity to make an overt response; postcentral negative potentials are largest when the organism must hold a response (continuously depress a lever) until a signal to release it occurs; and special sensory systems respond to their specific inputs (Pribram, 1971). The TNV appears to be an indication of either arousal or activation of the brain tissue from which it is recorded.

These data are amply confirmed by a recent study on humans (Gaillard, 1977) in which preparation was compared to expectancy in three detection tasks, one involving speed, another accuracy, and the third, detection, but no response. The frontal leads mirrored the task expectancy, whereas the posterior leads were affected by the task demands. The speed condition produced maximal CNV shifts in the parietal leads, whereas no parietal CNV occurred in the no response condition.

Sustained, tonic changes in potential have also been noted in subcortical negative potential shifts recorded in animals by Rebert (1972, 1973a,b) and in man by Grey Walter (1967) and by Haider (1970). It is yet too early to characterize the meaning of such shifts for every location, but in general, it appears that negativity develops whenever a portion of brain tissue is maintaining a readiness for processing. This conclusion has also been reached by Hillyard (1973) in an analysis of the CNV and human behavior. Hillyard also noted, in line with our analysis, that brainstem controls on overall cerebral negativity exist. We therefore will distinguish between the term TNV (multiple local readiness of cerebral tissues) and CNV (controls on these local potential shifts).

At the end of the negativity, if and when the organism actually begins to **do** something, a sharp positive deflection is usually observed, and this positivity has been related to consummatory behavior (Clemente, Sterman, & Wyrwicke, 1964) and to a sharp increase in power both in the alpha (8–12 Hz) and theta (4–8 Hz) ranges (Grandstaff, 1969) in the visual cortex.

Preliminary evidence (Rebert, 1972; Walter, 1967) suggests that a source controlling CNVs indicative of activation may be located somewhere in the region of the dorsal thalamus and basal ganglia of the forebrain because the polarity of slow variations in brain potential is similar in hypothalamic and cortical leads but shows a reversal in the depths of the brain. There is a mechanism which converges onto the far-lateral hypothalamic region which is not composed of cells but of fiber tracts such as the median forebrain bundle and others perpendicular to it. The data, from the studies recording deep-lying CNVs, suggest the hypothesis that we look for the control of the activation process in the basal ganglia which give rise to many of the fiber tracts that make up the far lateral hypothalamic crossroads. Recently completed studies substantially support this hypothesis.

In a series of studies employing multiple small stereotactic lesions in the globus pallidus, putamen and caudate nucleus, Denny–Brown and Yanagisawa (1976) report their findings with the following summary: "What, then, is absent? It would appear to be the activating 'set' or 'pump primer' for a certain act, the preparation of the mechanism preparatory to a motor performance oriented to the environment [p. 41]." They also note a particular type of ramp discharge in electrical activity in putamen neurons (DeLong & Strick, 1974) which precedes the motor performance at every stage. They suggest this operates as a facilitatory discharge which establishes a "climate" for performance.

They further suggest "the basal ganglia have all the aspects of a 'clearing house' that accumulates samples of ongoing cortical projected activity and, on a competitive basis, can facilitate any one and suppress all others [p. 45]." This indicates that part of this system relates to an ability to transfer attention from one type of stimulus to another and maintain that attentional set.

In addition, studies on animal and human patients with basal ganglia lesions (Bowen, 1976) could be interpreted as indicating an inability to maintain attention. Patients showed deficits in a range of perceptual and cognitive tasks, including orientation for both internal and external space, concept formation tasks, formation of a set to respond, and short-term memory in all modalities. As these tasks are unrelated to one another in the cognitive domain, we suggest the deficit is due to problems of maintaining readiness (or set) to complete a task.

C. Effort in the Integration of Arousal and Activation

The data on animal behavior following hippocampectomy strongly imply that this structure is critical in the regulation of the arousal and activation modes. Subjects with bilateral hippocampectomy tend to show a percentage of reactivity and amplitude of the GSR opposite to that observed in the nonresponding amygdalectomized monkeys (Figures 3.1 and 3.2) in the ordinary orienting paradigm. In addition, the phasic skin response terminates considerably more rapidly in hippocampectomized subjects than in controls (Figure 3.3). It appears from this that hippocampectomized monkeys (and amygdalectomized hyperresponders) reequilibrate more rapidly than normal subjects whose slower GSR recovery may indicate a more prolonged processing time. As we shall see, this finding is consistent with other data that show impaired processing of the disequilibration produced by a mismatch of input to the neuronal model as a result of hippocampectomy.

A further change is that such subjects show delayed or absent orienting reactions when thoroughly occupied in performing some other task

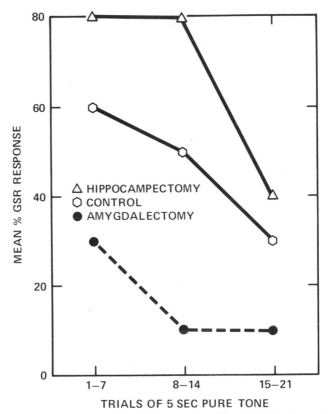

FIGURE 3.1. Curves for a more detailed analysis of the first 21 trials (split into 7-trial blocks) or percentage of galvanic skin response (GSR) to a 5-sec tone for the amygdalectomized, hippocampectomized, and unoperated monkeys.

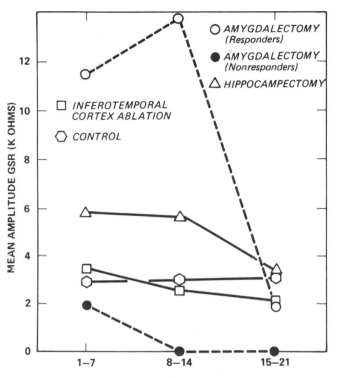

FIGURE 3.2. Group mean amplitude for galvanic skin response (GSR) to tone on the first 21 trials showing the bimodal distribution of the amygdalectomized monkeys when compared with normal (control) and with two other brain-lesioned groups of monkeys: inferotemporal cortex resection and hippocampectomy.

(Crowne & Riddell, 1969; Kimble, Bagshaw, & Pribram, 1965; Raphelson, Isaacson, & Douglas, 1965; Riddell, Rothblat, & Wilson, 1969; Wicklegren & Isaacson, 1963). In short, these animals appear to be abnormally indistractible.

But in some situations this appearance of indistractibility is restricted to the overt **responses** of the organism, not to orienting per se. Douglas and Pribram (1969) used distractors in a task in which responses were required to each of two successive signals. Hippocampectomized monkeys initially responded much as controls did by overtly manipulating the distractors, which were presented between the two signals, increasing the time between the two required responses. In contrast to the behavior of the controls, who habituated manipulation of the distractors and the interresponse time, the hippocampectomized group showed

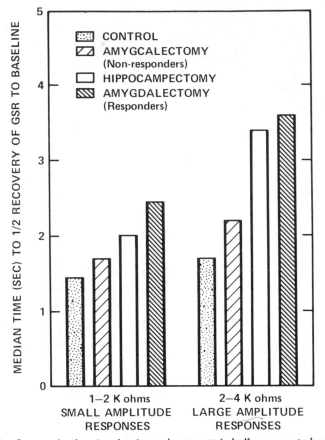

FIGURE 3.3. Bar graphs showing the time taken to attain half recovery to baseline of the visceroautonomic perturbation measured as an electrodermal response (galvanic skin response, GSR). Small, 1–2 Kohms, and large, 2–4 Kohms, perturbations are treated separately since amplitude of response has an obvious effect on recovery time.

decrementing only of the manipulations—their interresponse time failed to habituate at all. In this situation, hippocampectomized monkeys continue to be **perceptually** distractible while becoming behaviorally habituated and indistractible (Figure 3.4). This result is identical to that obtained in man with medial temporal lesions: Instrumental behavior can to a considerable extent be shaped by task experience, but verbal reports of the subjective aspects of experience fail to indicate prior acquaintance with the situation (Milner, 1958).

The dissociation between habituation of perceptual responses and habituation involving somatomotor performance appears to be part of a

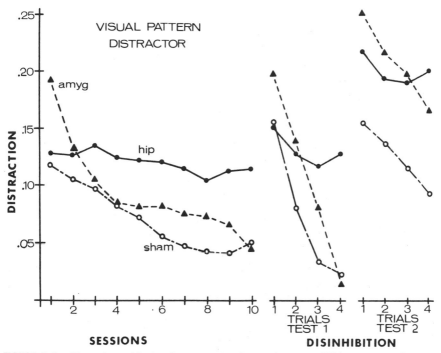

FIGURE 3.4. Distraction with visual pattern stimulus as distractor. (Abbreviations: sham = sham-operated subjects; amyg = amygdalectomized monkeys; hip = hippocampectomized animals.)

more general effect of hippocampal lesions, as it is manifest in other situations in which hippocampectomized monkeys are tested. In a discrimination reversal situation, extinction of previously learned behavior and acquisition of new responses were observed. In contrast to their controls, however, the monkeys with the hippocampal lesions remained at a chance level of performance for an inordinately long time (Pribram, Douglas, & Pribram, 1969). This effect was due to the "capture" of the behavior by a position bias during the 50% schedule of reinforcement—a bias hardly manifest in unoperated monkeys (Figure 3.5 and 3.6; Spevak & Pribram, 1973). This result suggested that a hierarchy of response sets was operative in the situation such that "observing" responses (indicative of attention) were relinquished when the probabilities of reinforcement ranged around the chance level.

Taken together, these experimental results suggest that interference with the hippocampal circuit reduces the organism to a state in which effort-demanding relationships between perception and action, between observing and instrumental responses, and between stimulus and re-

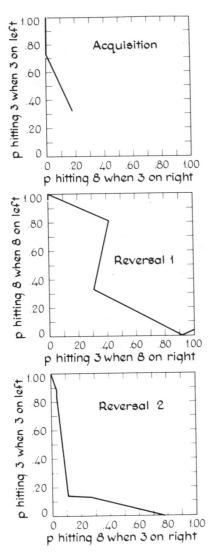

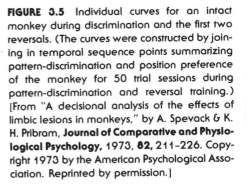

FIGURE 3.5 Individual curves for an intact monkey during discrimination and the first two reversals. (The curves were constructed by joining in temporal sequence points summarizing pattern-discrimination and position preference of the monkey for 50 trial sessions during pattern-discrimination and reversal training.) [From "A decisional analysis of the effects of limbic lesions in monkeys," by A. Spevack & K. H. Pribram, **Journal of Comparative and Physiological Psychology,** 1973, **82,** 211–226. Copyright 1973 by the American Psychological Association. Reprinted by permission.]

sponse, are relinquished for more primitive relationships in which either input or output captures an aspect of the behavior of the organism without the coordinating intervention of central control operations. The mechanism by which the hippocampal circuit accomplishes this relationship has been elucidated to some extent by recordings of electrical activity from the hippocampus, both with micro- and macroelectrodes, and by precise electrical stimulations of selected parts of the hippocampal circuit.

The hippocampus with its three-layered cortex provides the best opportunity for observing unit activity responsible for the changes observed in gross electrical activity in repetitive situations. Vinogradova (1970) found that **all** neurons of the hippocampus habituate to repetition of a stimulus and dishabituate to any change in the stimulus configuration. But she distinguished two types of neurons, A and I: those activated (30–40%) and those inhibited (60%) by a stimulus, respectively.

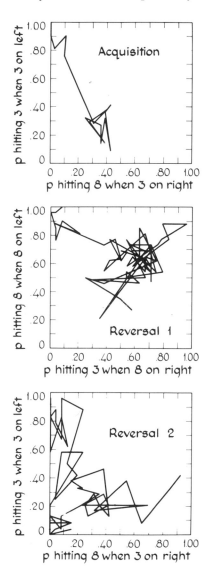

FIGURE 3.6. Individual curves for a hippocampectomized monkey during discrimination and the first two reversals (The curves were constructed by joining in temporal sequence points summarizing pattern-discrimination and position preference for the monkey for 50 trial sessions during pattern discrimination and reversal training.) [From "A Decisional Analysis of the effects of limbic lesions in monkeys," by A. Speveck & K. H. Pribram, **Journal of Comparative and Physiological Psychology,** 1973, **82,** 211–226. Copyright 1973 by the American Psychological Association. Reprinted by permission.]

Habituation occurs by a progressively shortening response in the course of 16–20 repeated presentations. The averaged poststimulus histograms of the two classes are "mirror images of each other."

Some important characteristics of hippocampal units are (a) the latencies of response to a stimulus do not change; (b) they are of the order of 100–1000 msec even initially; (c) in the ventral hippocampus (the only part present in primates, including man) stimuli must be of a minimum duration of from .5 to 1 sec to produce any noticeable change in the background activity; and (d) such facilitation persists up to 1 min after the cessation of the stimulus. These characteristics indicate a necessity for a long period of summation to precede hippocampal facilitation. Vinogradova (1970) interprets her findings as follows: "The duration of reactions in hippocampal neurones shows that the processes continue here long after the information processing is finished in all specific sensory structures, and in primary and secondary areas of the cortex as well. . . . As Gloor (1961) indicated, the quality of sensory information is almost erased in hippocampal neurones [pp. 114–115]."

These results are in accord with proposals previously put forward by Douglas and Pribram (1966). They suggested that the hippocampus constitutes part of an error (mismatch) evaluating mechanism which was conceived to process only the perturbations resulting from the mismatch among inputs (including those consequent on responses) (Pribram, 1971). Vinogradova is in agreement, therefore, in suggesting that precise sensory information is not involved. Further, she suggests a mechanism by which such processing can be achieved: "The hippocampus exerts a tonic inhibitory influence upon the reticular formation, blocking activatory processes through the tonic discharge of its I-neurones when novelty is absent and registration is not needed. But when a stimulus which is not registered in the memory system appears, this inhibitory control is blocked (I-neurones become silent), arousal occurs, and the process of registration starts [p. 114]."

Lindsley has recently elaborated the nechanism by which the hippocampally controlled reticular formation can effect these changes in registration. Lindsley (Macadar, Chalupa, & Lindsley, 1974) in keeping with many other recent publications (e.g., Fibiger et al., 1973; Ungerstedt, 1974) has dissociated two systems of neurons that influence the hippocampal circuit. One system originates in the median raphé and associated structures of the mesencephalic reticular formation, the other originates more laterally in the locus coeruleus and other portions of the periaqueductal gray. Lindsley's findings were obtained by electrical stimulations of the appropriate structures in the mesencephalic reticular formation. Stimulations of the raphé mechanisms produced hippocampal desynchronization and at the same time a synchronization of the amygdala circuits. Taken together with Vinogradova's evidence, this suggests a reciprocal process by which the controls on arousal are maintained as long as hippocampal inhibition of the reticular formation is in progress—much as Vinogradova suggests. Only when a mismatch from the neuronal model is signaled to the reticular formation does this inhibitory control become loosened, producing hippocampal desynchronization and concomitant relaxation (synchronization) of the arousal functions of the amygdala circuits. Lindsley has found that often, though not always, such hippocampal desynchronization is accompanied by desynchronization of the sensorimotor projection systems, suggesting that registration, an alteration of the neuronal model of the cortical representation, is occurring. Note that in this formulation the term "registration" refers to a change in the neuronal model, thus a "registration in memory," a process that, as we shall see, requires effort. This use of the term registration must be distinguished from "registration in awareness" which, as noted earlier, is disrupted by interference with the amygdala circuits.

The second mechanism discerned by the Lindsley studies is the locus coeruleus system. This mechanism makes possible the "What is to be done?" reaction, the processing of response-produced inputs. When electrically stimulated, the mesencephalic portions of this mechanism initiate hippocampal rhythmic activity in the theta range of frequencies. Early studies (Green & Arduini, 1954) had uncovered the paradox that the desynchronization of the EEG recorded from the brain's convexity during activation was accompanied by synchronization in the recordings obtained from the hippocampus. Though such synchronization is not as obvious in records obtained in monkey and man, computer analysis has shown that it does occur and that it can be studied in the primate (Crowne, Konow, Drake, & Pribram, 1972). This synchronous rhythm is in the theta range (4–8 Hz) and has become the focus of a long series of studies.

Theta frequencies were first recorded from the hippocampus by Jung and Kornmuller in 1938. Since this discovery, theta has been implicated in orienting behavior (Green and Arduini, 1954; Grastyan, 1959, Grastyan, Lissak, Madarsz, & Donhoffer, 1959) and in intended movement, even when tested under curare (Dalton & Black, 1968; Black & Young, 1972; Black, Young, & Batenchuck, 1970). Vanderwolf and his associates (Bland & Vanderwolf, 1972a,b; Vanderwolf, 1969, 1971; Whishaw, Bland, & Vanderwolf, 1972) noted that theta activity occurred almost exclusively when animals (rats) were making voluntary movements.

Brenner (1970) analyzed the changes in theta activity along three dimensions: (*a*) an increase or decrease in the total amount of power (amplitude in millivolts) in the theta range; (*b*) a narrowing or broadening of the range of energy or power around a particular frequency; (*c*) the specific peak frequency. An increase in power of the whole theta range relates to visceroautonomic arousal and a decrease in power to somatomotor readiness. The changes in bandwidth seem to be dependent upon whether the animal is performing in an intake (categorization) or a rejection (problem solving) mode; and thus relate to **effort** and the contents of awareness.

V. Neurochemical Mechanisms in Attention

Currently, a body of data has accumulated relating a variety of brain peptides, many of them derivatives of adrenocorticotropic hormone (ACTH), to a variety of behaviors. Interestingly, the behaviors that have become involved in brain peptide research are to a large extent the same as those involved initially in amygdala research and then shown to be dependent on hypothalamic, basal ganglia, and hippocampal function as well. Thus the neural organization of the mechanisms of arousal, activation, and effort delineated by neurobehavioral and psychophysiological techniques may well be relevant to the analysis of the relationship between neurochemical and behavioral processes.

A. Brain Amines in Arousal and Activation

Perhaps the easiest place to start is the by now well established and dramatic finding of a dopaminergic nigrostriatal system (Fibiger, Phillips, & Clouston, 1973; Ungerstedt, 1974) which has already been discussed. The evidence has repeatedly been reviewed to the effect that dopamine is involved in the maintenance of postural readiness and motivational activation (Matthysse, 1974; Snyder, 1974). It is also known (e.g., King & Hoebel, 1968) that assertive behavior such as predatory aggression depends on the activation of a cholinergic mechanism. Thus, it is likely that the dopamine fibers interdigitate a cholinergic matrix (Fuxe, 1977) to determine the activation level of the nervous system and the readiness of the organism.

Two other by now well known neurochemical systems are those involving serotonin and norepinephrine. A large amount of research (e.g., reviews by Jouvet, 1974; Barchas, Ciaranello, Stoke, Brodie, & Hamburg, 1972) has related these substances to the phases of sleep: serotonin to ordinary (slow-wave) sleep and norephinephrine to paradoxical (rapid-eye-movement, or REM) sleep during which much dreaming occurs. The relationship between serotonergic and norepinephrinergic mechanisms and the amygdala, seems to be similar to that between acetylcholine (ACh) and dopamine, and the striatum of the basal ganglia. Serotonergic and norepinephrinergic systems of fibers densely innervate the amygdala, the norepinephrinergic systems interdigitating a serotonergic matrix (see Pribram and Isaacson, 1976, for review).

The regulation of sleep by the amygdala has not been quantitatively documented but sleep disturbances are commonplace immediately following amygdalectomy, the animals often falling into a torpor from which they are difficult to rouse for several days to several weeks.

However, norepinephrine has been related to a behavioral function in which the amygdala is thoroughly implicated—the effects of reinforcing events (Stein, 1968). Norepinephrine has also been related to orienting and affective agonistic reactions. Once again a phasic response to novelty —sensed against a background of familiarity—is norepinephrinergic, whereas "familiarity" in the guise of "territoriality" and "isolation" has been shown to some extent to be dependent on a serotonergic mechanism (see reviews by Reis, 1974; and Goldstein, 1974).

These data suggest that norepinephrine acts by modulating a serotonergic substrate (which is determining one or another basic condition of the organism) to produce paradoxical sleep, reinforcement, orienting to novelty, and perhaps other behaviorally relevant neural events that interrupt an ongoing state. The data are not as clearly supportive of this suggestion as those that relate acetylcholine to an assertive state that is modulated by the activity of dopamine to produce specific readinesses. Nonetheless, as a first approximation to the data at hand, let us hold these possible neurochemical relations in mind as a tentative model with which to analyze the mass of evidence on the behavioral neurochemistry of the polypeptides.

B. Neuropeptides and the Effort—Comfort Mechanism

The neurochemical evidence on ACTH-related peptides leads directly to the hypothesis that they are involved in the hippocampal mechanism. To begin with, Bohus (1976) and McEwen, Gerlach, and Micco (1976) have shown that the hippocampal circuit (hippocampus and septum) is the brain site most involved in the selective uptake of adrenal cortical steroids. As McEwen states:

> It is only quite recently that we have come to appreciate the role of the entire limbic brain, and not just the hypothalamus, in these endocrine-brain interactions.
>
> Our own involvement in this revelation arose from studies of the fate of injected radioactive adrenal steroids, particularly corticosterone, when they

entered the brain from the blood. These studies were begun, under the impetus of recent advances in molecular biology of steroid hormone action, to look for intracellular hormone receptors in brain tissue. We expected to find such putative receptors in the hypothalamus, where effects of adrenal steroids on ACTH secretion have been demonstrated (Davidson *et al.* 1968; Grimm & Kendall, 1968). Much to our surprise, the brain region which binds the most corticosterone is not the hypothalamus but the hippocampus [McEwen et al., 1976, p. 285].

Thus the receptors of adrenal cortical hormones can set the neural state which becomes modulated by ACTH-related peptides. Evidence that such modulation of a corticosterone determined state involves the hippocampus has been presented by van Wimersma, Greidanus, and de Wied (1977).

Second, as previously noted, the hippocampal circuit functions to coordinate arousal (phasic response to input) and activation (tonic readiness to respond). Thus, in any complex behavioral situation, coordination would be influenced by manipulations of this circuit—and a host of apparently conflicting results might be obtained with very slight changes in the conditions of the experiment. (The best known of such slight changes is the one-way versus two-way conditioned avoidance task, see Pribram, Poppen, & Bagshaw, 1966; and van Wimersma et al., 1977.)

Further, effects on phasic and tonic processes (arousal and activation) as well as on their coordination (effort) would be expected. This expectation is borne out in the catalogue of effects of manipulations of ACTH related peptides: extinction of two-way but not one-way avoidance (de Wied, 1974); interference with passive avoidance (Levine & Jones, 1965); interference with learned taste avoidance (the Garcia effect—Levine, 1977); interference with discrimination reversal (Sandman, George, Walker, Nolan, & Kastin, 1977); facilitation of memory consolidation (van Wimersma et al., 1977); facilitation of exploratory behavior and conditioning (Endroczi, 1972, 1977).

Just as in the case of manipulations of hippocampal activity, **ongoing** behavioral activity (memory consolidation, exploratory behavior) is facilitated while any **change** in behavior (two-way shuttle, passive avoidance, learned taste aversion, discrimination reversal) is interfered with. This appears initially as tilting the bias toward readiness. But as Pribram and Isaacson (1976) show for hippocampal function, and Sandman's group conclude (see Miller, Sandman, & Kastin, 1977), such an interpretation does not hold up. In the case of hippocampal research, the initial formulation stated that after hippocampal resections, animals could not inhibit their responses (McCleary, 1961). This interpretation foundered when such animals were shown to perform well in go–no–go alternation tasks (Pribram & Isaacson, 1976; Mahut, 1972) and that they could withhold behavioral responses despite an increase in reaction time when distractors were presented (Douglas & Pribram, 1969).

The most cogent analysis has been performed on discrimination reversals. Isaacson, Nonneman, & Schwartz (1968) and Nonneman and Isaacson (1973) have shown that reversal learning encompasses three stages: Extinction of the previously correct response, reversion to a position habit, and acquisition of the currently correct response. Pribram, Douglas, and Pribram (1969) and Spevak and Pribram (1973) have shown that hippocampally lesioned monkeys are intact with regard to both the extinction and the new acquisition phases of the reversal training experience. However, such monkeys seem to become "stuck" in the 50% reinforcement phase or in position response patterns. In short, the monkeys' behavior seems to be taken over by a relatively low variable interval schedule of reinforcement and they fail to "make the effort" to "pay attention" to the cues which would gain them a higher rate of reward. Champney, Sahley, and Sandeman (1977) have shown ACTH-related peptides to operate on just this aspect of the reversal experience—and, in fact, have shown interactions with sex differences.

Finally, we note that the ACTH-related peptides, the enkephalins, are endorphins—endogenous hormones that have morphinelike effects and in fact act as ligands on morphine receptors. These neuropeptides, and the hippocampal circuit in which they are operative, function therefore to modulate an effort–comfort dimension of experience and behavior

Evidence such as this makes highly plausible the hypothesis that ACTH-related peptides operate on the hippocampal circuit and therefore the "effort" process. But there is more. Strand, Cayer, Gonzales, and Stoboy (1977) present direct evidence that muscle fatigue is reduced by ACTH-related neuropeptides and that this effect must be central. Until this study, the only evidence available on metabolic shifts due to the effort of paying attention came from the Berdina et al. (1972) study reviewed in the preceding section. It now appears that these peripheral anaerobic shifts affecting muscle tonicity may be a reflection of central processing modulated by ACTH neuropeptides.

V. Conclusion: Emotion and Motivation in Attention

Beginning with the work of Claude Bernard (1858), Karplus and Kreidel (1909) and Cannon (1929), the corebrain stem has been known to contain the major control mechanisms for visceroautonomic (homeostatic) regulations. As reviewed in Section IV, it became evident that these controls often involved reciprocally operating processes: those that stop behavior because satiety has been achieved and those that maintain appetitive behavior (see e.g., Grossman, 1966; and Pribram, 1971, for summaries). Feeding, for instance, is maintained during activity record-ed from electrodes placed in the far lateral region of the hypothalamus whereas satiety is signaled by excitation of cells in its ventromedial nucleus. These go and stop mechanisms are multiply interlinked both centrally and by their peripheral effects; thus the homeostatic regulations in their totality are complex (Brobeck, 1948). Nontheless, the reciprocal mechanisms can be determined to be at the root of the process. Further-more, as noted earlier, electrical excitation of the satiety mechanisms has been shown to produce not only cessation of behavior but, at some-what higher intensity, phasic arousal, and with even higher intensities, emotional behavior such as rage (Abrahams & Hilton, 1958; Abrahams et al., 1964). As we noted in Section IV these psychophysiological and behavioral manifestations characterize an entire brain system with con-nections to the medial hypothalamus. This system involves the amygdala and frontal cortex.

Further, we also noted that the far lateral system has interesting ramifications. At the hypothalamic level it is essentially devoid of cells and is mainly a crossroads of fiber tracts. The behavioral correlates of the system must therefore stem from the cells of origin of these fiber tracts. Recent cytochemical evidence (Ungerstedt, 1974) showed that the largest of the tracts in the crossroads was the nigrostriatial path-way which composes the prime dopaminergic system in the brain. Psychopharmacalogical studies (Fibiger, Phillips, & Clouston, 1973; Teitelbaum & Epstein, 1962) then demonstrated that antidopaminergic drugs would almost completely replicate the syndrome (aphagia which can be overcome under special conditions) produced by lesions of the far-lateral hypothalamic region. These results indicate that the appeti-tive behavior characterizing the functions of the far lateral system is largely due to involvement of the basal ganglia, structures known from clinical observation and other experiments to be also involved in the maintenance of postural and perceptual sets (Denny-Brown & Yana-gisawa, 1976).

Taken together, these various experimental results have distinguished two neural systems, one clearly related to phasic arousal and emotional reactivity and the other to readiness and the maintenance of set and appetitive behaviors. As we reviewed in Section IV, there is further evidence that the readiness system is the substrate of psychophysiologi-cal tonic activation as defined in this chapter.

In short, these studies and the additional neurochemical evidence reviewed in Section V define separate brain systems to operate in emotional and motivational processes. Emotion is thus related to a phasic arousal system and motivation to a readiness, tonic activation system. The foregoing analysis and review of evidence indicates that these are systems in which neurochemical events determine to a large extent the behavioral functions that are regulated by these structures.

Regulation is in part affected by the establishment, through central receptor sensitivities, of neural representations of peripheral endocrine processes, and by direct influences on these representations of centrally active neurochemical substances. Among the many relationships between endocrines and central sensitivities, some were singled out as providing sufficient evidence that a systemization might be attempted. Others, such as the possible central effect of insulin, or the special sensitivity of the amygdala to sex hormones, have not been included, although they cannot be ignored in any future attempt at synthesis.

At the moment three classes of systems are discernible. One class determines specific neuromuscular and neurosensory readinesses. A second deals with the momentary cessations of ongoing behavior, cessations due to interrupting distractors, the intervention of satiety, or the recurrence of reinforcing events. The third class of systems coordinates the readinesses of the organism with the processes that lead to their momentary suspension.

The proposal was made that states of specific readiness were due to a cholingergic mechanism operated upon (i.e., modulated by), dopaminergic systems. The basal ganglia are the major gross forebrain embodiments of a readiness mechanism.

The amygdala is the gross forebrain locus upon which the systems that deal with momentary cessation of behavior and the concomitant emotional reactions, such as arousal (interest) and upset, converge. Neurochemically, these systems are posited to be basically serotonergic with norepinephrinergic operators modulating the basic serotonergic state.

Finally, a coordinating effort–comfort determining mechanism was discerned whose forebrain extension lies within the hippocampal circuit. The neurochemical constitution of this class of systems is hormonal with neuropeptides operating on the hormonally induced neural state to regulate behavior. Corticosteroids and ACTH-related neuropeptides are examples of the functions of this third class of systems.

We have identified emotional processes as rooted in the phasic arousal mechanisms discussed here and distinguished them from motivational processes rooted in the readiness mechanisms. Thus the neurochemical

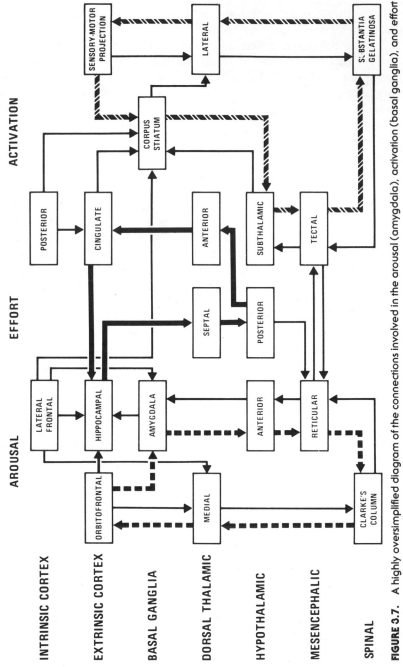

FIGURE 3.7. A highly oversimplified diagram of the connections involved in the arousal (amygdala), activation (basal ganglia), and effort (hippocampal) circuits.

analysis undertaken here is relevant to both emotion and motivation. The analysis would predict that neuropeptides would be only indirectly involved in the regulation of emotion (affect) and motivation. Only when emotional and motivational processes need to be coordinated would neuropeptide manipulations show an effect. Emotion and affect are found to be minimally influenced by ACTH-related compounds in man (Ehrensing & Kastin, 1977). Conflict producing tasks such as passive avoidance (Levine & Jones, 1970), learned taste aversion (Levine, 1977), two-way shuttles (de Wied, 1974, 1977), and frustrative nonreward (Grey, 1977) are the instruments of choice for demonstrating the effects of neuropeptides. One-way shuttles and simple punishments show either no effect or a mild facilitation of the reinforcing process.

A summary diagram of the three systems is presented in Figure 3.7. Thus, emotional and motivational controls on attention have been found to operate via three neuroanatomical, neurophysiological, and neurochemical systems. One such system deals with arousal defined as a phasic response to input. The second system deals with activation, a readiness to respond. The third system coordinates arousal and activation along an effort–comfort dimension. Neurophysiological and neurobehavioral evidence has been reviewed which link these systems to emotion and motivation and delineate their influence on attention. Psychophysiological evidence was adduced to show how these attentional processes operate during categorizing and reasoning. Attention thus becomes the central process that links emotion and motivation to cognitive operations.

Bibliography

Abrahams, V. C., & Hilton, S. M. Active muscle vasodilation and its relation to the "fight and flight reactions" in the conscious animal. *Journal of Physiology*, 1958, *140*, 16–17.

Abrahams, V. C., Hilton, S. M., & Zbrozyna, A. W. The role of active muscle vasodilation in the alerting stage of the defense reaction. *Journal of Physiology*, 1964, *171*, 189–202.

Bagshaw, M. H., & Benzies, S. Multiple measures of the orienting reaction and their dissociation after amygdalectomy in monkeys. *Experimental Neurology*, 1968, *20*, 175–187.

Bagshaw, M. H., Kimble, D. P., & Pribram, K. H. The GSR of monkeys during orienting and habituation and after ablation of the amygdala, hippocampus, and inferotemporal cortex. *Neuropsychologia*, 1965, *3*, 111–119.

Bagshaw, M. H., & Pribram, J. D. Effect of amygdalectomy on stimulus threshold of the monkey. *Experimental Neurology*, 1968, *20*, 197–202.

Barchas, J. D., Ciaranello, R. D., Stolk, J. M., Brodie, H. H., & Hamburg, D. A. Biogenic amines and behavior. In S. Levine (Ed.), *Hormones and behavior*. New York: Academic Press, 1972.

Berdina, N. A., Kolenko, O. L., Kotz, I. M., Kuzetxov, A. P., Rodinov, I. M., Savtechencko, A. P., & Thorevsky, V. I. Increase in skeletal muscle performance during emotional stress in man. *Circulation Research*, 1972, *6*, 642–650.

Bergum, B. O. A taxonomic analysis of continuous performance. *Perceptual and Motor Skills*, 1966, *23*, 47–54.

Berlyne, D. E. The development of the concept of attention in psychology. In C. R. Evans & T. B. Mulholland (Eds.), *Attention in neurophysiology*. New York: Appleton-Century-Crofts, 1969.

Bernard, C. Leçons sur la physiologie et la pathologie du système nerveus. (Lecture 16, Vol. 2). Paris: Ballière, 1858.

Black, A. H., & Young, G. A. Electrical activity of the hippocampus and cortex in dogs operantly trained to move and to hold still. *Journal of Comparative and Physiological Psychology*, 1972, *79*, 128–141.

Black, A. H., Young, G. A., & Batenchuck, C. The avoidance training of hippocampal theta waves in flaxedized dogs and its relation to skeletal movement. *Journal of Comparative and Physiological Psychology*, 1970, *70*, 15–24.

Bland, B. H., & Vanderwolf, C. H. Diencephalic and hippocampal mechanisms of motor activity in the rat: Effect of posterior hypothalamic stimulation on behavior and hippocampal slow wave activity. *Brain Research*, 1972, *43*, 67–88.

Bland, B. H., & Vanderwolf, C. H. Electrical stimulation of the hippocampal formation: Behavioral and bioelectrical effects. *Brain Research*, 1972, *43*, 89–106.

Blaylock, B. Some antecedents of directional fractionation: Effects of "intake-rejection", verbalization requirements, and threat of shock on heart rate and skin conductance. *Psychophysiology*, 1972, *9*, 40–52.

Bohlin, G. Delayed habituation of the electrodermal orienting response as a function of increased level of arousal. *Psychophysiology*, 1976, *13*, 345–351.

Bohus, B. The hippocampus and the pituitary adrenal system hormones. In R. L. Isaacson & K. H. Pribram (Eds.), *The hippocampus*. New York: Plenum Press, 1976.

Bonvallet, M., & Allen, M. B. Prolonged spontaneous and evoked reticular activation following discrete bulbar lesions. *Electroencephalography and Clinical Neurophysiology*, 1963, *15*, 969–988.

Bowen, F. P. Behavioral alterations in patients with basal ganglia lesions. In M. D. Yahr (Ed.), *The basal ganglia*. New York: Raven Press, 1976.

Brenner, F. J. The effect of habituation and conditioning trials on hippocampal EEG. *Psychonomic Science*, 1970, *18*, 181–183.

Brillouin, L. *Science and information theory*. New York: Academic Press, 1962.

Broadbent, D. E. *Perception and communication*. New York: Pergamon Press, 1958.

Brobeck, J. R. Review and synthesis. In M. A. B. Brazier (Ed.), *Brain and behavior*, (Vol. II). Washington: American Institute of Biological Sciences, 1963.

Bruner, J. S. On perceptual readiness. *Psychylogical Review*, 1957, *64*, 123–152.

Bull, K., & Lang, P. J. Intensity judgments and physiological response amplitudes. *Psychophysiology*, 1972, *9*, 428–436.

Cannon, W. B. *Bodily changes in pain, hunger, fear and rage*. New York: D. Appleton & Co., 1929.

Champney, T. F., Sahley, T. L., & Sandman, C. A. Effects of neonatal cerebral ventricular injection of ACTH 4-9 and subsequent adult injections on learning in male and female albino rats. *Pharmacology and Biochemical Behavior* (Suppl.), 1976, *5*, 3–10.

Clemente, C. C., Sterman, M. B., & Wyrwicke, W. Post-reinforcement EEG synchronization during alimentary behavior. *Electroencephalography and Clinical Neurophysiology*. 1964, *16*, 355–365.

Crowne, D. P., Konow, A., Drake, K. J., & Pribram, K. H. Hippocampal electrical activity in the monkey during delayed alternation problems. *Electroencephalography and Clinical Neurophysiology*, 1972, 33, 567–577.

Crowne, D. P., & Riddell, W. I. Hippocampal lesions and the cardiac component of the orienting response in the rat. *Journal of Comparative and Physiological Psychology*, 1969, 69, 748–755.

Dahl, H., & Spence, D. P. Mean heart rate predicted by task demand characteristics. *Psychophysiology*, 1971, 7, 369–376.

Dalton, A., & Black, A. H. Hippocampal electrical activity during the operant conditioning of movement and refraining from movement. *Communications in Behavioral Biology*, 1968, 2, 267–273.

De Long, M. R., & Strick, P. L. Relation of basal ganglia, cerebellum and motor cortex to romp and ballistic limb movements. *Brain Research*, 1974, 71, 327–335.

Denny-Brown, D. & Hanagisawa, N. The role of the basal ganglia in the initiation of movement. In M. D. Yahr (Ed.), *The basal ganglia*. New York: Raven Press, 1976.

de Wied, D. Pituitary-adrenal system hormones and behavior. In F. O. Schmitt & E. G. Worden (Eds.), *The neurosciences* (Vol. 3). Cambridge, Mass.: MIT Press, 1974, pp. 653–660.

Donchin, E., Gerbrandt, L. A., Leifer, L., & Tucker, L. Is the contingent negative variation contingent on a motor response? *Psychophysiology*, 1972, 9, 178–188.

Donchin, E., Otto, D., Gerbrandt, L. K., & Pribram, K. H. While a monkey waits: Electrocortical events recorded during the foreperiod of a reaction time study. *Electroencephalography and Clinical Neurophysiology*, 1971, 31, 115–127.

Donchin, E., Otto, D., Gerbrandt, L. K., & Pribram, K. H. While a monkey waits. In K. H. Pribram & A. R. Luria (Eds.), *Psychophysiology of the frontal lobes*. New York: Academic Press, 1973.

Douglas, R. J., & Pribram, K. H. Learning and limbic lesions. *Neuropsychologia*, 1966, 4, 197–220.

Douglas, R. J., & Pribram, K. H. Distraction and habituation in monkeys with limbic lesions. *Journal of Comparative and Physiological Psychology*, 1969, 69, 473–480.

Eckberg, D. L., Fletcher, G. F., & Braunwald, E. Mechanisms of prolongation of the R-R interval with electrical stimulation of the carotid sinus nerves in man. *Circulation Research*, 1972, 30, 131–138.

Ehrensing, R. H., & Kastin, A. J. Clinical investigations for emotional effects of neuropeptide hormones. *Pharmacology and Biochemical Behavior (Suppl.)*, 1976, 5, 89–94.

Elliott, R. Tonic heart rate: Experiments on the effects of collative variables lead to a hypothesis about its motivational significance. *Journal of Personality and Social Psychology*, 1969, 12, 211–228.

Elliott, R., Bankart, B., & Light, T. Differences in the motivational significance of heart rate and palmar conductance: Two tests of a hypothesis. *Journal of Personality and Social Psychology*, 1970, 14, 166–172.

Endröczi, E. Brain mechanisms involved in ACTH-induced changes of exploratory activity and conditioned avoidance behavior. In L. H. Miller, C. A. Sandman, & A. J. Kastin (Eds.), *Neuropeptide influences on the brain and behavior*. New York: Raven Press, 1977.

Fibiger, H. C., Phillips, A. G., & Clouston, R. A. Regulatory deficits after unilateral electrolytic or 6-OHDA lesions of the substantia nigra. *American Journal of Physiology*, 1973, 225, 1282–1287.

Forsyth, R. P. Hypothalamic control of the distribution of cardiac output in the unanesthetized Rhesus monkey. *Circulation Research*, 1970, 26, 783–794.

Freré, Ch. *The pathology of emotions*. London: The University Press, 1899.

Fuller, J. L., Rosvold, H. E., & Pribram, K. H. The effect on affective and cognitive behavior in the dog of lesions of the pyriform-amygdala-hippocampal complex. *Journal of Comparative and Physiological Psychology*, 1957, *50*, 89–96.

Fuxe, E. The dopaminergic pathways. In *Proceedings of the American Neuropathological Association*, in press.

Gaillard, A. W. K. The late CNV wave: Preparation versus expectancy. *Psychophysiology*, 1977, *14*, 563–568.

Germana, J. Response characteristics and the orienting reflex. *Journal of Experimental Psychology*, 1968, *78*, 610–616.

Germana, J. Autonomic-behavioral integration. *Psychophysiology*, 1969, *6*, 78–90.

Goldstein, M. Brain research and violent behavior. *Archives of Neurology*, 1974, *30*, 1–35.

Graham, F. K., & Clifton, R. K. Heart rate changes as a component of the orienting response. *Psychological Bulletin*, 1966, *65*, 305–320.

Grandstaff, N. W. Frequency analysis of EEG during milk drinking. *Electroencephalography and Clinical Neurophysiology*, 1969, *27*, 55–57.

Grastyan, E. The hippocampus and higher nervous activity. In M. A. B. Brazier (Ed.), *The central nervous system and behavior*. New York: Josiah Macy, Jr. Foundation, 1959.

Grastyan, E., Lissak, K., Madarasz, I., & Donhoffer, H. Hippocampal electrical activity during the development of conditioned reflexes. *Electroencephalography and Clinical Neurophysiology*, 1959, *11*, 409–430.

Gray, J. A. & Garrud, P. Adrenopituitary hormones and frustrative nonreward. In L. H. Miller, C. A. Sandman, & A. J. Kastin (Eds.), *Neuropeptide influences on the brain and behavior*. New York: Raven Press, 1977.

Green, J. F., & Arduini, A. Hippocampal electrical activity in arousal. *Journal of Neurophysiology*, 1954, *17*, 533–557.

Grossman, S. P. The VMH: A center for affective reactions, satiety, or both? *Physiology and Behavior*, 1966, *1*, 1–10.

Groves, P. M., & Thompson, R. F. Habituation: A dual-purpose theory. *Psychological Review*, 1970, *77*, 419–450.

Gruzelier, J. H., & Venables, P. H. Skin conductance orienting activity in a heterogeneous sample of schizophrenics. *Journal of Nervous and Mental Diseases*, 1972, *155*, 277–287.

Hahn, W. W. Attention and heart rate: A critical appraisal of the hypothesis of Lacey and Lacey. *Psychological Bulletin*, 1973, *79*, 59–70.

Haider, M. Neuropsychology of attention, expectation and vigilance. In D. I. Mostofsky (Ed.), *Attention: Contemporary theory and analysis*. New York: Appleton-Centry-Crofts, 1970.

Hare, R. D. Response requirements and directional fractionation of autonomic responses. *Psychophysiology*, 1972, *9*, 419–427.

Hebb, D. O. Drives and the CNS (conceptual nervous system). *Psychological Review*, 1955, *62*, 243–254.

Hillyard, S. A. The CNV and human behavior: A review. In W. C. McCallum & J. R. Knott (Eds.), *Event related slow potentials of the brain: Their relation to behavior*. Amsterdam: Elsevier, 1973.

Honig, W. K. Attention and the modulation of stimulus control. In D. I. Mostofsky (Ed.), *Attention: Contemporary theory and analysis*. New York: Appleton-Century-Crofts, 1970.

Isaacson, R. L., Nonneman, A. J., & Schwartz, L. W. Behavioral and anatomical sequelae of the infant limbic system. In *The Neuropsychology of Development, A Symposium*. New York: John Wiley & Sons, 1968.

James, W. *The principles of psychology* (2 Vols.). New York: Holt, 1890.

Jennings, J. R., Averill, J. R., Opton, E. M., & Lazarus, R. S. Some parameters of heart rate change: Perceptual versus motor task requirements, noxiousness, and uncertainty. *Psychophysiology*, 1971, 7, 194–212.

Johansson, G., & Frankenhauser, M. Temporal factors in sympatho-adrenomedullary activity following acute behavioral activation. *Biological Psychology*, 1973, 1, 63–73.

Jouvet, M. Monoaminergic regulation of the sleep-waking cycle in the cat. In F. O. Schmitt & E. G. Worden (Eds.), *The neurosciences* (Vol. 3). Cambridge, Mass.: MIT Press, 1974.

Jung, R., & Kornmueller, A. E. Eine methodik der Ableitung lokalisierter Potentialschwankungen aus subcorticalen Hirngebieten. *Archiv für Psychiatrie und Nervenkrankheiten*, 1938, 109, 1–30.

Kaada, B. R., Pribram, K. H. & Epstein, J. A. Respiratory and vascular responses in monkeys from temporal pole, insula, orbital surface and cingulate gyrus: A preliminary report. *Journal of Neurophysiology*, 1949, 12, 347–356.

Kahneman, D. *Attention and effort*. Englewood Cliffs, N.J.: Prentice-Hall, 1973.

Karplus, J. P., & Kreidl, A. Gehirn und Sympathicus. I. Zwischenhirnbasis und halssympathicus. *Archiv ges. Physiologische Pflügers*, 1909, 129, 138–144.

Kilpatrick, D. G. Differential responsiveness of two electrodermal indices to psychological stress and performance of a complex cognitive task. *Psychophysiology*, 1972, 9, 218–226.

Kimble, D. P., Bagshaw, M. H., & Pribram, K. H. The GSR of monkeys during orienting and habituation after selective partial ablations of the cingulate and frontal cortex. *Neuropsychologia*, 1965, 3, 121–128.

King, M. B., & Hoebel, B. G. Killing elicited by brain stimulation in rats. *Community Behavioral Biology* (Part A), 1968, 2, 173–177.

Konrad, K. W., & Bagshaw, M. H. Effect of novel stimuli on cats reared in a restricted environment. *Journal of Comparative and Physiological Psychology*, 1970, 70, 157–164.

Kornblum, S. *Attention and performance* (Vol. 4). New York: Academic Press, 1973.

Kornhuber, H. H., & Deecke, L. Hirnpotentialaenderungen bei Willkurbewegungen und passiven Bewegungen des Menschen: Bereitschaftspotential und reafferente Potentiale. *Pflügers Archiv für die gesante Physiologie des Menschen und der Tiere*, 1965, 284, 1–17.

Lacey, J. I. Somatic response patterning and stress: Some revisions of activation theory. In M. H. Appley & R. Trumball (Eds.), *Psychological stress: Issues in research*. New York: Appleton-Century-Crofts, 1967.

Lacey, J. I., & Lacey, B. C. Some autonomic central nervous system interrelationships. In P. Black (Ed.), *Physiological correlates of emotion*. New York: Academic Press, 1970.

Lader, M. H. The effects of cyclobarbitone on the pulse volume, pulse rate and electromyogram. *Journal of Psychosomatic Research*, 1965, 8, 385–398.

Lawler, K. A., Obrist, P. A., & Lawler, J. E. Cardiac and somatic response patterns during a reaction time task in children and adults. *Psychophysiology*, 1976, 13, 448–455.

Levine, S., & Jones, L. E. Adrenocorticotropic hormone (ACTH) and passive avoidance in two inbred strains of mice. *Hormones and Behavior*, 1970, 1, 105–110.

Levine, S., Smotherman, W. P., & Hennessy, J. W. Pituitary-adrenal hormones and learned taste aversion. In L. H. Miller, C. A. Sandman, & A. J. Kastin (Eds.), *Neuropeptide influences on the brain and behavior*. New York: Raven Press, 1977.

Lewis, M., & Wilson, C. D. The cardiac response to a perceptual-cognitive task in the young child. *Psychophysiology*, 1970, 6, 411–420.

Lindsley, D. B. The reticular activating system and perceptual integration. In D. E. Sheer (Ed.), *Electrical stimulations of the brain*. Austin: University of Texas Press, 1961.

Lindsley, D. B., Bowden, J., & Magoun, H. W. Effect upon the EEG of acute injury to the brain stem activating system. *EEG Clinical Neurophysiology*, 1949, 475–486.

Luria, A. R., Pribram, K. H., & Homskaya, E. D. An experimental analysis of the behavioral disturbance produced by a left frontal arachnoidal endothelloma (menin-
gioma). *Neuropsychologia*, 1964, *2*, 257–280.

Macadar, A. W., Chalupa, L. M., & Lindsley, D. B. Differentiation of brain stem loci which
affect hippocampal and neocortical electrical activity. *Experimental Neurology*, 1974, *43*,
499–514.

MacKay, D. M. The epistemological problem for automata. In C. E. Shannon & J. McCar-
thy (Eds.), *Automata studies*. Princeton: Princeton University Press, 1956.

Magoun, H. W. *The waking brain*. Springfield, Ill.: Charles C Thomas, 1958.

Mahut, H. Spatial and object reversal learning in monkeys with partial temporal lobe
ablations. *Neuropsychologia*, 1971, *9*, 409–424.

Mandler, G. The interruption of behavior. In D. Levine (Ed.) *Nebraska Symposium on
Motivation*, (Vol. 12). Lincoln: University of Nebraska Press, 1964.

Matthews, A, M., & Lader, M. H. An evaluation of forearm blood flow as a psychophysiological measure. *Psychophysiology*, 1971, *8*, 509–524.

Matthysse, S. Schizophrenia: Relationship to dopamine transmission, motor control, and
feature extraction. In F. O. Schmitt & E. G. Worden (Eds.), *The neurosciences* (Vol. 3).
Cambridge, Mass.: MIT Press, 1974.

McCanne, T. R., & Sandman, C. A. Human operant heart rate conditioning: The importance of individual differences. *Psychological Bulletin*, 1976, *83*(4) 587–601.

McCleary, R. A. Response specificity in the behavioral effects of limbic system lesions in
the cat. *Journal of Comparative and Physiological Psychology*, 1961, *54*, 605–613.

McEwen, B. S., Gerlach, J. L., & Micco, D. J. Putative glucocorticoid receptors in hippocampus and other regions of the rat brain. In R. L. Isaacson & K. H. Pribram (Eds.)
The hippocampus (Vol. I). New York: Plenum Press, 1976.

McFarland, D. J. *Feedback mechanisms in animal behavior*. New York: Academic Press, 1971.

McGuinness, D. Cardiovascular responses during habituation and mental activity in anxious men and women. *Biological Psychology*, 1973, *1*, 115–123.

Mednick, S. A., & Schulsinger, F. Some premorbid characteristics related to breakdown in
children with schizophrenic mothers. In D. Rosenthal & S. S. Kety (Eds.), *The transmission of schizophrenia*. New York: Pergamon Press, 1968.

Miller, G. A. The magical number seven, plus or minus two, or, some limits on our
capacity for processing information. *Psychological Review*, 1956, *63*(2), 81–97.

Milner, B. Psychological defects produced by temporal lobe excision. In H. C. Solomon, S.
Cobb, & W. Penfield (Eds.), *The brain and human behavior*. Baltimore: Williams & Wilkins, 1958.

Neisser, U. *Cognitive psychology*. New York: Appleton-Century-Crofts, 1967.

Nonneman, A. J., & Isaacson, R. L. Task dependent recovery after early brain damage.
Behavioral Biology, 1973, *8*, 143–172.

Obrist, P. A., Howard, J. L., Hennis, H. S., & Murrell, D. J. Cardiac-somatic changes
during simple reaction time tasks: A developmental study. *Journal of Experimental Child
Psychology*, 1973, *16*(2), 346–362.

Obrist, P. A., Howard, J. L., Lawler, J. E., Sutterer, J. R., Smithson, W. W., & Martin, P.
L. Alternations in cardiac contractibility during classical aversive conditioning in dogs:
Methodological and theoretical implications. *Psychophysiology*, 1972, *9*, 246–261.

Obrist, P. A., Webb, R. A., Sutterer, J. R., & Howard, J. L. Cardiac deceleration and
reaction time: An evaluation of two hypotheses. *Psychophysiology*, 1970, *6*, 695–706.

Obrist, P. A., Webb, R. A., Sutterer, J. R., & Howard, J. L. The cardiac-somatic relationship; Some reformulations. *Psychophysiology*, 1970, *6*, 569–587.

Petro, J. K., Holland, A. P., & Bouman, L. N. Instantaneous cardiac acceleration in man induced by a voluntary muscle contraction. *Journal of Applied Physiology*, 1970, *24*, 794–798.

Pribram, K. H. The intrinsic systems of the forebrain. In J. Field, H. W. Magoun, & V. E. Hall (Eds.), *Handbook of physiology, neurophysiology* (Vol. 2). Washington, D.C.: American Physiological Society, 1960.

Pribram, K. H. Limbic system. In D. E. Sheer (Ed.), *Electrical stimulation of the brain*. Austin: University of Texas Press, 1961.

Pribram, K. H. Interrelations of psychology and the neurological disciplines. In S. Koch (Ed.) *Psychology: A study of science* (Vol. 4). *Biologically oriented fields: Their place in psychology and in biological sciences*. New York: McGraw-Hill, 1962.

Pribram, K. H. Reinforcement revisited: A structural view. In M. Jones (Ed.), *Nebraska Symposium on Motivation* (Vol. 2). Lincoln: University of Nebraska Press, 1963.

Pribram, K. H. Neural servosystems and the structure of personality. *Journal of Nervous and Mental Diseases*, 1969, *140*, 30–39.

Pribram, K. H. *Languages of the brain: Experimental paradoxes and principles in neuropsychology*. Englewood Cliffs, N.J.: Prentice-Hall, 1971.

Pribram, K. H. Problems concerning the structure of consciousness. In G. Globus, G. Maxwell, & I. Savodnick (Eds.), *Science and the Mind-Brain Puzzle*. New York: Plenum Press, 1976.

Pribram, K. H., & Bagshaw, M. H. Further analysis of the temporal lobe syndrome utilizing frontotemporal ablations in monkeys. *Journal of Comparative Neurology*, 1953, *99*, 347–375.

Pribram, K. H., Douglas, R. J., & Pribram, B. J. The nature of nonlimbic learning. *Journal of Comparative and Physiological Psychology*, 1969, *69*, 765–772.

Pribram, K. H., & Isaacson, R. L. *The hippocampus*, (Vol. 2). New York: Plenum Press, 1976, pp. 429–441.

Pribram, K. H., Lim, H., Poppen, R., & Bagshaw, M. H. Limbic lesions and the temporal structure of redundancy. *Journal of Comparative and Physiological Psychology*, 1966, *61*, 365–373.

Pribram, K. H., & McGuinness, D. Arousal, activation and effort in the control of attention. *Psychological Review*, 1975, *82*(2), 116–149.

Pribram, K. H., Reitz, S., McNeil, M., & Spevack, A. A. The effect of amygdalectomy on orienting and classical conditioning. *Pavlovian Journal of Biological Science*, Oct./Dec., 1979.

Pribram, K. H., Spinelli, D. N., & Kamback, M. C. Electrocortical correlates of stimulus response and reinforcement. *Science*, 1967, *157*, 94–96.

Raphaelson, A. C., Isaacson, R. L., & Douglas, R. J. The effect of distracting stimuli on the runway performance of limbic damaged rats. *Psychonomic Science*, 1965, *3*, 483–484.

Rebert, C. S. Cortical and subcortical slow potentials in the monkey's brain during a preparatory interval. *Electroencephalography and Clinical Neurophysiology*, 1972, *33*, 389–402.

Rebert, C. S. Elements of a general cerebral system related to CNV genesis. In W. C. McCallum & J. R. Knott (Eds.), *Event related slow potentials of the brain: Their relationships to behavior*. Amsterdam: Elsevier, 1973 (a).

Rebert, C. S. Slow potential changes in the monkey's brain during reaction time foreperiod. In C. W. McCallum & J. R. Knott (Eds.), *Event related slow potentials of the brain: Their relationships to behavior*. (Vol. 2). Amsterdam: Elsevier, 1973 (b).

Riddell, W. L., Rothblat, L. A., & Wilson, W. A., Jr. Auditory and visual distraction in hippocampectomized rats. *Journal of Comparative and Physiological Psychology*, 1969, *67*, 216–219.

Reis, D. J. The chemical coding of aggression in brain. In R. D. Myers & R. R. Drucker-Colin (Eds.), *Neurohumeral coding of brain function*, 1974, pp. 125–150.

Rosell, S., & Uvnäs, B. Vasomotor activity and oxygen uptake in skeletal muscle of the anesthetized cat. *Acta Physiologica Scandinavica*, 1962, *54*, 209–222.

Rosvold, H. E., Mirsky, A. F., & Pribram, K. H. Influence of amygdalectomy on social interaction in a monkey group. *Journal of Comparative and Physiological Psychology*, 1954, *47*, 1973–1978.

Russell, R. W., Singer, G., Flanagan, F., Stone, M., & Russell, J. W. Quantitative relations in amygdala modulation of drinking. *Physiology and Behavior*, 1968, *3*, 871–875.

Sandman, C. A., George, J., Walker, B., Nolan, J. D., & Kastin, A. J. Neuropeptide MSH/ACTH 4–10 enhances attention in the mentally retarded. *Pharmacology and Biochemical Behavior* (Suppl.), 1976, *5*, 23–28.

Sauerland, E. K., & Clemente, C. D. The role of the brain stem in orbital cortex induced inhibition of somatic reflexes. In K. H. Pribram & A. R. Luria (Eds.), *Psychophysiology of the frontal lobes*. New York: Academic Press, 1973.

Schwartzbaum, J. S., Wilson, W. A., Jr., & Morrissette, J. R. The effects of amygdalectomy on locomotor activity in monkeys. *Journal of Comparative and Physiological Psychology*, 1961, *54*, 334–336.

Sharpless, S., & Jasper, H. Habituation of the arousal reaction. *Brain*, 1956, *79*, 655–680.

Sherrington, C. *Man on his nature*. Garden City, N.Y.: Doubleday, 1955.

Skinner, J. E., & Lindsley, D. B. The nonspecific medio-thalamic-fronto-cortical system: Its influence on electrocortical activity and behavior. In K. H. Pribram & A. R. Luria (Eds.), *Psychophysiology of the frontal lobes*. New York: Academic Press, 1973.

Snyder, S. H. Catecholamines as mediators of drug effects in schizophrenia. In F. O. Schmitt & E. G. Worden (Eds.), *The neurosciences* (Vol. 3). Cambridge, Mass.: MIT Press, 1974.

Sokolov, E. N. Neuronal models and the orienting reflex. In M. A. B. Brazier (Ed.), *The central nervous system and behavior*. New York: Josiah Macy, Jr. Foundation, 1960.

Sokolov, E. N. *Perception and the conditioned reflex*. New York: Macmillan, 1963.

Spevack, A., & Pribram, K. H. A decisional analysis of the effects of limbric lesions in monkeys. *Journal of Comparative and Physiological Psychology*, 1973, *82*, 211–226.

Stein, L. Chemistry of reward and punishment. In E. H. Effron (Ed.) *A review of progress 1957–1967*. (Public Service Publication No. 1836), Washington, D. C.: U.S. Government Printing Office, 1966.

Strand, F. L., Cayer, A., Gonzales, E., & Stoboy, H. Peptide enhancement of neuromuscular function: animal and clinical studies. *Pharmacology and Biochemical Behavior* (Suppl.), 1976, *5*, 179–188.

Tecce, J. J. Contingent negative variation (CNV) and psychological process in man. *Psychological Bulletin*, 1972, *77*, 73–108.

Teitelbaum, P., & Epstein, A. N. The lateral hypothalamus syndrome: Recovery of feeding and drinking after lateral hypothalamic lesions. *Psychological Review*, 1962, *69*, 74–90.

Treisman, A. M. Strategies and models of selective attention. *Psychological Review*, 1969, *76*, 282–299.

Ungerstedt, U. Brain dopamine neurons and behavior. In F. O. Schmitt & F. G. Worden (Eds.), *The neurosciences* (Vol. 3). Cambridge, Mass.: MIT Press, 1974.

Ursin, H. & Kaada, B. R. Functional localization within the amygdala complex within the cat. *Electroencephalography and Clinical Neurophysiology*, 1960, *12*, 120.

van Wimersma Greidanus, Tj.B., & de Wied, D. The dorsal hippocampus: a site of action of neuropeptides on avoidance behavior? *Pharmacology and Biochemical Behavior* (Suppl.) 1976, *5*, 29–34.

Vanderwolf, C. H. Hippocampal electrical activity and voluntary movement in the rat. *Electroencephalography and Clinical Neurophysiology*, 1969, *26*, 407–418.

Vanderwolf, C. H. Limbic-diencephalic mechanisms of voluntary movement. *Psychological Review*, 1971, *78*, 83–113.

Vaughan, H. G., Costa, L. D., & Ritter, W. Topography of the human motor potential. *Electroencephalography and Clinical Neurophysiology*, 1968, *25*, 1–10.

Venables, P. H. & Christie, M. J. Mechanisms, instrumentation, recording techniques and quantification of response. In W. F. Prokasy & D. C. Raskin (Eds.), *Electrodermal activity in psychological research*. New York: Academic Press, 1973.

Vinogradova, O. Registration of information and the limbic system. In G. Horn & R. A. Hinde (Eds.), *Short-term changes in neural activity and behavior*. Cambridge: Cambridge University Press, 1970.

Wall, P. D., & Davis, G. D. Three cerebral cortical systems affecting autonomic function. *Journal of Neurophysiology*, 1951, *14*, 507–517.

Walter, W. G. Electrical signs of association, expectancy and decision in the human brain. *Electroencephalography and Clinical Neurophysiology*, 1967, *25*, 258–263.

Walter, W. G., Cooper, R., Aldridge, V. J., McCallum, W. C., & Winter, A. L. Contingent negative variation: An electric sign of sensorimotor association and expectancy in the human brain. *Nature*, 1964, *23*, 380–384.

Weinberg, H. The contingent negative variation: Its relation to feedback and expectant attention. *Neuropsychologia*, 1972, *10*, 299–306.

Whishaw, I. Q., Bland, B. H., & Vanderwolf, C. H. Hippocampal activity, behavior, self-stimulation, and heart rate during electrical stimulation of the lateral hypothalamus. *Journal of Comparative and Physiological Psychology*, 1972, *79*, 115–127.

Wicklegren, W. O., & Isaacson, R. L. Effect of the introduction of an irrelevant stimulus on runway performance of the hippocampectomized rat. *Nature*, 1963, *200*, 48–50.

Wood, R. A. & Obrist, P. A. Effects of controlled and uncontrolled respiration on the conditioned heart rate response in humans. *Journal of Experimental Psychology*, 1964, *68*, 221.

Chapter IV

Visual Perception and Memory

DAVID J. MADDEN
ROBERT D. NEBES

I. Introduction

It has been over 100 years since the discovery that in man the right and left cerebral hemispheres are not identical with respect to the higher cognitive functions they subserve. Until fairly recently, investigations into the nature of this hemispheric specialization of function have relied solely on examination of the behavioral deficits which follow unilateral cortical injuries such as strokes or surgical excisions. The experimental approach most frequently adopted has been to compare, on a given task, the performance of two groups of individuals: one composed of patients with brain damage restricted to the right hemisphere, the other composed of patients with damage restricted to the left hemisphere. Any difference in performance between these two groups has been typically seen as an indication that there is an underlying difference in the relative contribution of the right and left hemispheres to the accomplishment of the same task in normal individuals. That is, if persons with a lesion in one hemisphere do worse on a task than do persons with a lesion in the other hemisphere, the inference is drawn that the first hemisphere must have a more crucial role in the performance of the task, by virtue of the possession of some unique capacity. For example, since a lesion in the right hemisphere is more likely to produce severe deficits in the com-

141

THE BRAIN AND PSYCHOLOGY

prehension and drawing of maps than is a lesion in the left hemisphere (Benton, 1969), it is assumed that whatever spatial ability is required in these map tasks is organized primarily in the right hemisphere.

While the above approach has generated much of the experimental evidence indicating that the right and left hemispheres are specialized for different cognitive functions, there are a number of methodological and conceptual limitations to this paradigm which have led to studies of normal individuals as a way of confirming and extending the results obtained from brain-damaged subjects. This work with normal subjects has significantly revised our understanding of hemispheric functioning, and will be the focus of the present chapter. First, however, in order to indicate why it is necessary to have additional evidence for hemispheric specialization from normal individuals, we will review some of the factors which compel caution in accepting uncritically the results of unilateral brain damage studies. This is not done in an attempt to discredit these results, but rather to show why it is important to obtain confirmation from a different population.

Most of the methodological problems in the brain damage literature arise from the population studied. It is very difficult to assemble two groups of patients having unilateral cortical injuries which are equated on all those personal variables, such as age, intelligence, and education, which are known to influence cognitive performance. Even more difficult and crucial is the matching of the two groups with regard to the size and location of the lesion. There is substantial evidence suggesting that various cortical areas **within** a given hemisphere have very different functions, and unless the loci of the damage in the right and left lesion groups are matched, there is a potential confounding of **intra**hemispheric with **inter**hemispheric differences. Similarly, a spurious indication of hemispheric differentiation of function can result if the size of the lesions in the two groups is not matched. For example, both hemispheres may contain cortical areas which are in fact equally important for the successful execution of some mental operation. When the performances of two groups of patients possessing unilateral lesions of different average extent are compared, a decrement may well be exhibited by the group with the more extensive damage. This difference would be based not on any unequal representation of function by the two sides of the brain, however, but solely on the fact that the more extensive the lesion, the greater the probability that it will involve the critical cortical region. This criticism has been often raised with respect to studies in which right-lesioned individuals show a greater decrement than do left-lesioned individuals. It has been pointed out that patients with large lesions on the left tend to be excluded from studies because they have language comprehension problems which are not seen in patients with large right-sided lesions; thus the right lesion group is likely to contain individuals with more widespread damage than is the left lesion group (Bogen, 1969). One other problem which complicates localizing function on the basis of brain injury is that no matter how restricted a lesion may be, it often has widespread effects due to vascular spasm, edema, and deafferentation, which can influence the performance of the intact hemisphere as well (Smith, 1975).

Difficult as these methodological problems are, interpretation of the cognitive deficits which follow brain injury is even more perilous. In such interpretations, the relative competence of the two hemispheres to carry out a certain mental operation must be inferred from a comparison of the severity of the performance deficits displayed by the two patient groups on a task requiring that operation. The danger in this situation is that performing a particular cognitive task rarely involves a unitary, clearly definable mental operation. All our tests require a variety of mental skills, and patients can therefore fail them for a variety of reasons. Earlier attempts to localize cognitive abilities to different cortical regions foundered on just this problem. It was found that functions such as "reading" could be disrupted by lesions in widely different areas, including even the right hemisphere (Kinsbourne & Warrington, 1962a). As the number of disparate centers for reading, writing, and other skills (as inferred from lesion-produced deficits) multiplied, many investigators rejected the assumption that defects in performance could be used to infer the cerebral localization of normal function (Goldstein, 1948, Ch. 3). A good deal of this controversy can now be seen to result from attempts to localize unitary or "fundamental" mental functions which were not fundamental at all, but rather were complexes of different operations. The final product of these operations, such as reading competence, was thus capable of being disrupted in a variety of ways by a variety of lesions. While the definition of basic mental operations is a problem in any attempt to anatomically localize cognitive abilities, even just to one or the other hemisphere, it is especially crucial in the interpretation of brain damage, where the researcher must deduce from the pattern of the patient's deficits the nature of the basic functions(s) disrupted by that lesion. The interpretation of brain damage is complicated even further by the fact that a lesion is rarely small and limited to just one anatomical region. Thus a number of different functions may be simultaneously affected, producing not only additive but also interactive effects on cognition and behavior.

Another possible source of inferential error in the unilateral brain damage paradigm has been pointed out by Semmes (1968). It is possible that both hemispheres are equally involved in the execution of a particular cognitive operation, but that the anatomical organization of this ability differs in the two hemispheres, being focally represented in one hemisphere and diffusely represented in the other. As a result, lesion studies could produce evidence which would lead one to infer, incorrectly, that one hemisphere is more important than the other for this operation. A lesion in the diffusely organized hemisphere would be apt to produce a mild deficit, one perhaps not detectable by our crude behavioral measures, while a critically placed lesion in the focally organized hemisphere would cause a dramatic deficit, leading to the inference that this hemisphere was more essential for the operation in question.

Whereas investigations of other patient populations, such as those in whom the cerebral commissures have been severed, or those in whom one hemisphere has been temporarily inactivated chemically, avoid some of these problems (Nebes, 1978), confirmation of the phenomena of hemispheric specialization in a normal population is still essential. Recently, techniques which allow separate assessment of some of the normal operations of the right and left hemispheres have been developed. The initial focus of the work in this area was to confirm the main conceptualization of hemispheric differences contributed by brain damage studies: that the left hemisphere is the neural substrate for verbal skills, the right for spatial skills. However, the paradigms and theoretical constructs of experimental psychology have been. increasingly used in an attempt to develop a more explicit and comprehensive account of these functional differences between the right and left sides of the brain. In this chapter we will review this burgeoning field of research within the context of the set of theoretical constructs prevailing in the human perception and memory literature today—"information processing." We will briefly review current thinking on how visual information is registered, selected, coded, and manipulated, and will relate these operations to present work on the functioning of the two hemispheres.

In the investigation of the normal functioning of the right and left hemispheres in subjects without brain injury, researchers have taken advantage of the anatomy of the visual system. When an individual's gaze is fixated on a point in space, stimuli appearing to the left of that point project onto the right side of the retina in both eyes. From here, the visual fibers travel through several relays to the visual cortex in the right hemisphere. Stimuli appearing to the right of fixation fall on the left side of the retina in both eyes and from there, information is projected to the left hemisphere. This anatomical arrangement makes it possible to present material selectively to one hemisphere by restricting the stimulus to one half of the visual field. Since a subject will immediately attempt to turn his eyes toward any stimulus appearing peripheral to his center of gaze, the presentation must be kept shorter than the time needed to initiate a lateral eye movement. Stimulus durations are therefore usually less than 200 msec.

In studies of hemispheric differences in normal individuals, the ability of a person to carry out some cognitive operations on a stimulus presented to his left visual half-field (LVF) is compared to his ability to process a stimulus presented to his right visual half-field (RVF). Any discrepancy in performance between the two fields is assumed to reflect a difference in capacity between the subject's right and left hemispheres to carry out the task. Performance is measured in terms of either accuracy or reaction time (RT), that is, the time required to make some decision about the stimulus.

As with any experimental paradigm, there are some methodological and conceptual complications inherent in this approach. First, the selective **presentation** of visual information to one hemisphere is no guarantee that the **processing** of the information is restricted to that hemisphere. In normal individuals, considerable sharing of information between the hemispheres is likely to occur, and as noted previously, even simple tasks may require a variety of component skills. It is thus important to determine which aspects or stages of processing are contributing to the visual field (VF) differences that may appear. Harcum (1978) has recently reviewed many of the task-related variables that may be critical in this regard. Secondly, the brief duration for which the stimulus can be shown greatly limits the amount and complexity of the material which can be presented. This limitation is accentuated by the fact that the stimuli are shown several degrees to one or the other side of fixation. Since the subject has centered the fixation point on his fovea, the stimuli are falling outside that region of the retina which has the greatest resolving power. The limitation of the stimulus duration is not a serious experimental obstacle, however, since information processing tasks often employ familar and easily recognizable stimuli. A final problem, at least with those studies using RT as a dependent variable, is that the traditional responses by which the subjects signal their decisions are all controlled by just one hemisphere—vocalization and right hand movement by the left hemisphere, and left hand movement by the right hemisphere. Consequently, interpretation of differences in the time needed to process information selectively presented to the right and left hemispheres is complicated by the presence of differences in response speed, which are in turn a function of which hemisphere is controlling the response. Moscovitch (1973), however, has developed a method for using these hemisphere–response relationships as a way of evaluating hemispheric differences in processing (See Section V, B).

In spite of the problems mentioned, a number of theoretical accounts of hemispheric differences in normal individuals have been developed. Although VF differences in tachistoscopic recognition had been obtained by earlier researchers investigating the "span of apprehension" (e.g., Crosland, 1931), it was the report of Mishkin and Forgays (1952) that introduced the concept of hemispheric specialization into explanations of VF effects. Mishkin and Forgays obtained a RVF advantage for English words presented unilaterally, and also obtained a nonsignificant tendency toward a LVF superiority for the identification of Yiddish words by bilingual subjects. Their explanation combined the notions of reading habits and cerebral dominance; the claim was that since, when reading English text, each successive word appears first in the RVF, the left hemiretina (onto which the RVF projects) becomes relatively more sensitive to verbal material. The development of this retinal sensitivity during years of reading, in turn, contributes (in some unspecified fashion) to the specialization of the left hemisphere for language functions. The elimination of this RVF identification advantage when Yiddish words were presented would be expected, since reading this language involves the appearance of new information to the left of successive fixations.

Subsequent reports based on a variety of different verbal stimuli, such as single letters (Bryden & Rainey, 1963) and words of different orders of approximation to English (Dornbush & Winnick, 1965) confirmed the fact that unilateral presentation to the RVF leads to more accurate recognition than does LVF presentation (see also White, 1969, 1972). However, Mishkin and Forgay's theory relating VF differences to the hemispheric processes involved in reading was gradually replaced by the belief that VF effects were instead related to the more general functional hemispheric asymmetries suggested by studies of unilateral brain injury. Perhaps the most influential approach of this type was that of Kimura (1966, 1973), who claimed that the RVF and LVF advantages in the recognition of some types of verbal and nonverbal stimuli, respectively, resulted from the more direct access provided by the contralateral visual pathways to the left and right hemispheres. That is, verbal information presented to the RVF reaches the left hemisphere through a direct projection system, while LVF information projects first to the right hemisphere and must then be transmitted across the corpus callosum to the left hemisphere. This more recent interpretation of VF differences has made use of the fact that right-handedness in adults is highly correlated with left hemisphere control of linguistic functions, and that left-handedness is not a reliable predictor of this control. Milner (1974), for example, has reported her observations on over 200 patients for whom it was necessary (for neurological reasons) to determine the cerebral representation of speech by means of the Wada technique. This technique involves injecting sodium amytal into a single cerebral hemisphere through the ipsilateral carotid artery; the patient will demonstrate aphasic symptoms when the hemisphere primarily contributing to linguistic functioning is injected. Milner found that 92% of her right-handed patients possessed speech functions represented by the left hemisphere. Sixty-nine percent of the left-handers who had not undergone early childhood damage to the left hemisphere also possessed left hemisphere speech representation. In addition, approximately 15% of left-handers, but only 1% of right-handers, showed aphasic deficits after the injection of amytal into **either** hemisphere. It thus appears that while right-handedness is strongly associated with left hemispheric speech functioning, left-handedness can be associated with left, right, or even bilateral representation of speech. A relationship between VF differences and cerebral dominance for speech is suggested by the fact that a RVF advantage for the recognition of verbal material is typically obtained with right-handed subjects, but is either markedly reduced or absent for left-handed subjects (Bryden, 1965; Zurif & Bryden, 1969; McKeever & Gill, 1972a; McKeever, Gill, & Van Deventer, 1975).

Tachistoscopic research has also lent some support to the theory that left hemisphere specialization for verbal functions is complemented by right hemisphere specialization for the apprehension of spatial relationships, although the results have not been as consistent as when verbal stimuli are used. The findings of the initial studies of nonverbal stimuli, for example, were negative. Heron (1957) found no significant differences between the VFs in the identification accuracy of familiar forms (such as stars and circles) presented unilaterally; Bryden and Rainey (1963) used a similar paradigm and even obtained slight RVF advantages for these stimuli. Some of the first evidence regarding right hemispheric processing of spatial forms was provided by Kimura (1966), who found that subjects required to report how many dots were present during a tachistoscopic exposure were more accurate in enumerating dots presented to the LVF. However, when required to select which of a group of nonsense figures had been presented on a trial, subjects demonstrated no VF differences. When, in another experiment in this series, Kimura required subjects to report how many nonsense figures were present, she again obtained a LVF superiority. Kimura (1969) found that subjects' postexposure location judgments of tachistoscopically presented dots demonstrated a LVF superiority, although there were no VF differences in the exposure duration necessary for the detection of dots. A related result has been obtained by Robertshaw and Sheldon (1976), whose subjects judged whether a particular position within a 12–celled matrix, cued after each presentation, had contained a letter. A signal-detection analysis showed that sensitivity to the position information was greater for matrices presented to the LVF. Durnford and Kimura (1971) asked subjects to judge whether a laterally presented vertical rod was nearer or farther than a central one, and found that more accurate judgments resulted from LVF presentation. This result was only obtained when subjects viewed the display with both eyes, and not when viewing was monocular, however, and the authors suggest that the use of binocular disparity was a critical factor. The trend of the above research is that right hemisphere specialization may be more closely related to the recognition of such spatial information as the number and position of stimuli, as opposed to their identities. This conclusion is still tentative, however, since Bryden (1976) has reported that in dot localization tasks, an apparent superiority for LVF presentation may actually be the product of response bias. In addition, later researchers have been somewhat more successful in obtaining VF differences for the recognition of the form, rather than just the number or position, of nonverbal figures. Fontenot (1973), for example, presented the randomly shaped Vanderplas figures unilaterally, and found that subsequent selection of the target from a group of items was more accurate for LVF forms. This was only true for figures of relatively high complexity (12 point), however; low complexity (6 point) items did not produce any VF differences, and perhaps was a factor in the negative findings of previous researchers. Right hemisphere advantages have also been observed for the recognition of a number of different types of nonverbal stimuli in the information processing tasks to be discussed. The VF differences exhibited by normal subjects are thus consistent with the clinical finding that unilateral lesions can selectively impair the recognition of verbal and spatial events, although it is not always clear which aspects of the recognition tasks are contributing to the VF differences obtained.

Although it is evident that recent accounts of VF differences differ significantly from Mishkin and Forgays' (1952) proposal, an underlying assumption has been that VF effects do actually reflect some form of hemispheric specialization of function. An alternative to this assumption, and in fact, one of the first explanations for VF differences was the "postperceptual scan" model (Heron, 1957). As already noted, early experiments had found that when verbal materials were presented to just one side of fixation, those presented to the RVF were recognized more accurately than those presented to the LVF. Some researchers attributed this result to an "attentional" scanning of visual material in the same direction as it would normally be read by successive eye movements. The direction in which this attentional scanning is carried out is the result of extensive experience with reading, which in our culture proceeds from left to right. Bryden (1960) and White (1969) have discussed how such attentional shifts after tachistoscopic exposure could account for VF differences. When verbal material is presented to the right of the fixation point, the learned tendency to start at the left end of the material, and the tendency to scan from left to right are in accord, allowing the scan to begin immediately. When material is presented to the LVF, however, the subject would have to first shift his attention to the left before beginning the rightward scan, and during the time needed for this shift the trace of the stimulus would deteriorate. Another variable which would favor a rightward scan is the fact that the initial letter of a word is the most crucial one for recognition (Eriksen & Eriksen, 1974). With unilateral presentation the initial letter of a word in the RVF lies closer to fixation, and thus to the fovea, than does the first letter of a word presented in the LVF. This difference in retinal sensitivity, in conjunction with scanning tendencies, could play a significant role in determining the recognition advantage for RVF words (Mackavey, Curcio, & Rosen, 1975). The main point which distinguishes this type of explanation from the cerebral dominance models is that the postexposure scan theory views VF differences as being essentially a peripheral artifact of acquired reading habits, a learned visual search strategy, rather than the result of an inherent specialization of the two cerebral hemispheres for different cognitive abilities.

The postexposure scan model was the prevailing explanation for VF differences for many years, as it could handle several phenomena which the cerebral dominance models could not. First, when verbal material was presented simultaneously in both VFs, a LVF superiority for recognition was found (Crosland, 1931; Heron, 1957; Bryden, 1960; Bryden & Rainey, 1963). Since with these bilateral stimuli, subjects would always first orient to the left, in order to reach the beginning of the line, the scanning model would predict an advantage to LVF presentation. The cerebral dominance models, on the other hand, would still predict greater accuracy for RVF items. Second, the recognition of stimulus materials which we have not been taught to scan in any particular direction (e.g., geometric forms) often showed no VF differences (Heron, 1957; Terrace, 1959; Bryden, 1960; Bryden & Rainey, 1963). Third, when tachistoscopic experiments included subjects from cultures which read from right to left (e.g., readers of Hebrew), unilateral presentation of words led either to no field differences (Mishkin & Forgays, 1952) or to the LVF superiority predicted by a scanning model (Orbach, 1953).

In recent years, however, more evidence has accumulated which favors hemispheric specialization models. McKeever and Huling (1971a) made a number of criticisms of studies which had demonstrated a LVF superioity when words were presented bilaterally. While admitting that scanning might affect the size of VF differences, they carried out a series of experiments showing that when scanning possibilities were reduced or eliminated, VF effects still existed, and in a form consistent with a cerebral specialization model. McKeever and Huling used meaningful words, rather than strings of unrelated letters, and employed a shorter exposure duration (20 msec) than previous studies. More importantly, they attempted to control subjects' fixation by requiring them to report a centrally presented digit which appeared at the same time as the bilateral words. McKeever and Huling felt this last control to be vital, since when bilateral stimuli are used, subjects know that a word will always be presented on the left. Subjects in this situation may thus bias their attention, if not their gaze, toward the LVF. With a central fixation stimulus, the subject's attention and eyes would be held centrally, and field differences independent of scanning tendencies would be revealed. When these techniques were used with bilateral words, a very strong RVF superiority for word recognition was found. A variety of other studies using similar techniques (Hines, 1972, 1975; McKeever & Huling, 1971b; Mackavey et al., 1975) have yielded the same result. Other techniques used to minimize the effect of scanning, as well as of the spatial location of the first letter of the word, such as (a) arranging the letters of the word vertically in the field rather than horizontally (Fudin, 1976; McKeever & Gill, 1972a; Bryden, 1970; Mackavey et al., 1975; Barton, Goodglass, & Shai, 1965); (b) presenting single letters as stimuli (McKeever & Gill, 1972a; Rizzolatti, Umiltà, & Berlucchi, 1971; Carmon, Nachshon, Isseroff, & Kleiner, 1972); and (c) presenting mirror image letters or words (Isseroff, Carmon, & Nachshon, 1974; Bryden, 1966); have all shown that verbal material is processed faster and more accurately when presented to the RVF.

Recent studies with readers of Hebrew have also shown that learned reading habits cannot be the sole determinant of VF differences. When fixation is controlled by requiring the report of a central digit (Barton et al., 1965), when the stimuli are single Hebrew letters (Carmon et al., 1972), or when only right-handers are considered (Orbach, 1967), a substantial RVF superiority for the recognition of verbal material is exhibited even by individuals who read from right to left. The presence of a complementary LVF superiority for the processing of various nonverbal materials such as faces (Rizzolatti et al., 1971; Ellis & Shepherd, 1975), line orientations (Umiltà, Rizzolatti, Marzi, Zamboni, Franzini, Camarda, & Berlucchi, 1974), and nonsense shapes (Fontenot, 1973), as well as the correlation between VF differences and handedness (Zurif & Bryden, 1969), are also hard to explain on the basis of a scanning theory. Thus, a postexposure scan may contribute to VF differences, especially in situations where verbal material is presented bilaterally and fixation is not controlled, but scanning is probably not the major cause of these differences.

In addition to theories based on cerebral dominance and scanning tendencies, a model has recently been advanced by Kinsbourne (1970, 1973) which explains VF differences in terms of attention. This model accepts the fact that, in man, certain cognitive operations are carried out predominantly by one or the other cerebral hemisphere. Kinsbourne, however, suggests that it is not the directness of the anatomical connections which produces VF differences in normals, but rather the subject's expectancy as to the nature of the mental operation required by the task. If, for example, a subject knows that verbal stimuli are to be presented, his left hemisphere is assumed to become more active, and his right hemisphere less active, in anticipation of processing this material. Such shifts in the interhemispheric balance of activation have been related to changes in EEG pattern (McLeod & Peacock, 1977). According to Kinsbourne, this inequality of hemispheric activation is directly related to the spatial distribution of the subject's attention. It is known that lateral orientation movements of the head and eyes are controlled by the opposite hemisphere; the left hemisphere controls orientation to the right, the right hemisphere, orientation to the left (Crosby, 1953). Kinsbourne suggests that this is true also of shifts in the center of visual attention, even when the eyes and head are still. In this model, the spatial location of a person's center of attention is determined by the state of the dynamic balance which exists between the opposing lateral orientation tendencies programmed by the right and left hemispheres. When one hemisphere becomes relatively more active, as the left hemisphere does when the subject expects a verbal stimulus, this activation influences the attention-directing system, producing a biasing of attention toward the right side of space. (This attentional bias is not seen by Kinsbourne as an adaptive maneuver, but rather as an epiphenomenon due to the superimposition in man of hemispheric specialization onto a mammalian brain having a symmetrically organized attention-directing system.) If a stimulus is then tachistoscopically presented to the RVF, the required decision can be made quickly and accurately, since the subject's attention is already centered there. If, however, the stimulus is flashed in the LVF, attention must be shifted, which takes time. During this time, the stimulus trace has deteriorated, leading to slower and less accurate responses.

This attentional model has at least two testable predictions. First, by behaviorally "activating" one hemisphere, it should be possible to produce field differences in tasks in which they normally do not occur. This could be done by requiring the subject to perform, concurrently with the visual task of interest, a nonvisual task calculated to selectively engage the abilities of one hemisphere. Using this technique, it should also be possible to enhance or reduce the size of a visual field difference typically associated with a certain task. The second prediction of the attentional model is that if the subject is uninformed about the nature of the stimulus material or cognitive operation required on the next trial, then VF differences should either be absent, or constant for all stimuli, according to the type of set adopted.

Kinsbourne (1970) has produced evidence supporting the first of these predictions. Subjects were shown outline squares which extended either to the left or right of fixation, although one edge always passed through the fixation point; the task was to determine whether or not a small gap was present in any edge. In the absence of any concurrent task, decisions regarding the outer edges of the RVF and LVF squares were equally accurate, although detection was better for the edge passing through the central fixation point. When, however, prior to each trial the subjects were given six words to remember, detection accuracy increased for the RVF edges but decreased for the LVF lines, suggesting an effect of left hemisphere activation. Kinsbourne (1973) replicated this finding and also reported that with concurrent verbal activity there was a nonsignificant tendency for "central" gaps to be detected more accurately when they occurred in the right edge of a square. That is, the shift in accuracy was not a function of the stimulus's absolute position in space, but its relative position. The left hemisphere activation resulting from concurrent verbal activity tended to improve gap detection on the right side of the objects, regardless of where in the VF they appeared.

Unfortunately, other researchers investigating this attentional theory have not obtained such clear results. Gardner and Branski (1976), for example, used the methods of signal detection theory to analyze the results obtained in a gap detection study. They found that any selective changes in accuracy which did result from concurrent activity were due not to increased visual discrimination ability for one VF, but rather to a change in criterion (i.e., an increased tendency of subjects to say that a gap was present in the half-field opposite the hemisphere engaged in a concurrent task). Klein, Moscovitch, and Vigna (1976) attempted to reduce the size of field differences that exist under normal conditions. They investigated both the recognition of faces (typically more accurately recognized in the LVF) and of words (typically more accurately recognized in the RVF) and examined how the order in which subjects performed these two tasks affected VF differences. Klein et al. found that when the face recognition task was performed first, LVF accuracy on the subsequent word recognition task was selectively improved, and that performing the word recognition tests first selectively improved RVF accuracy in subsequent face recognition. That is, subjects who had just finished a set of face recognition trials showed better LVF word recognition than did subjects without this prior priming, although performance on RVF trials was not affected. The opposite was true when the face recognition task followed a set of word trials: Recognition was more accurate in the RVF than was the case in subjects without prior priming with a word recognition task, although the LVF scores were unaffected. While such results are consistent with an attentional theory of VF differences, the Klein et al. findings may be more closely related to response variables than to perceptual ones, since the interaction between the type of prior test material and the size of the VF difference disappeared when the output in the word recognition task was switched from a vocal (naming) to a manual (pointing) response. A final qualification of the Klein et al. results is that although prior cognitive priming did selectively increase performance accuracy for one VF, accuracy for the other VF did not show the decrease which would be expected from a shift in the spatial locus of the center of attention, a decrease which Kinsbourne (1970, 1973) did find.

The second prediction which follows from Kinsbourne's model of attentional bias is that under conditions where the subject cannot anticipate the nature of the stimulus material which will occur on a given trial, VF differences in speed or accuracy will not be present, or will be the same for all types of stimuli. Cohen (1975) did find that when digits, words, and dot patterns occurred randomly over trials, VF differences in speed of response were either absent or very slight. When, however, prior to each trial, subjects were told the nature of the upcoming stimulus, they were faster in recognizing words and numbers in the RVF than in the LVF, whereas with the dot patterns they were faster for LVF presentation. Only the field difference for the words was significant, however. Hellige (1978, Experiment 1) has reported that a LVF advantage in the accuracy of recognizing a series of forms actually shifts to a RVF advantage when the forms are intermixed with a series of word recognition trials, suggesting a selective left hemisphere activation. On the other hand, Berlucchi, Brizzolara, Marzi, Rizzolatti, and Umiltà

(1974) mixed trials presenting letter pairs with those presenting faces, and found that subjects recognized faces faster in the LVF and words faster in the RVF. These are the same results as had been found in an earlier study with the same material in which the stimuli had not been mixed (Rizzolatti et al., 1971). Geffen, Bradshaw, and Nettleton (1972) have also found that RVF and LVF superiorities can be obtained for the appropriate trials of a randomly mixed sequence. Finally, Pirozzolo and Rayner (1977, Experiment 1) have shown that when words and faces are paired and presented bilaterally, trials on which a RVF word is paired with a LVF face lead to greater recognition accuracy than trials possessing the reverse arrangement. If attentional biasing were responsible for VF effects, however, no difference between these two types of bilateral presentation should occur; the amount and type of biasing material is constant, only the stimulus type/hemisphere of presentation relationship is different.

In its strongest form, Kinsbourne's theory offers a complete explanation of VF differences in normal subjects on the basis of a lateral shift in the center of the subject's visual attention. This explanation is challenged by studies showing that field differences can be obtained even when the subject has no way of anticipating which type of stimulus will occur next, and thus has no basis for selectively activating one hemisphere. A weaker version of the theory, and one which is consistent with the results of studies using concurrent activity or priming effects, is that VF differences represent the interaction of hemispheric specialization with a number of performance variables, one of which is attentional bias. In order to discuss this interaction in more detail, however, we need to introduce some of the concepts presently being used in descriptions of visual information processing.

II. Visual Processing

Three assumptions fundamental to the current information processing approach to visual perception have been discussed by Haber (1969a). The first, and most important one, is that perceptual experience is not an immediate consequence of visual stimulation, but is the end result of a series of analyzing processes or stages. A central theoretical goal thus becomes the description of the types of analyses performed, the order in which they occur, and the duration of each. While possessing considerable intuitive appeal, this proposal provides a sharp contrast between the information processing approach and the perceptual theory of Gestalt psychology, the most influential approach to perception in the early decades of the twentieth century. In this latter theory, the immediate apprehension of the configurational properties of objects, and not temporally extended processing, was emphasized (Hochberg, 1974). The information processing approach is thus an indirect descendant of the work of Helmholtz (1911/1925), who claimed that the richness of perceptual experience is due to processes of "unconscious inference" applied subsequent to retinal stimulation. An additional link to Helmholtz can be seen in the recent resurgence of interest in the method of Donders (1869/1969) for estimating the duration of mental operations. Donders sought to estimate the time needed for certain decisions by the application of a "subtractive method"; he reasoned that if two tasks can be assumed to differ only in a particular decision or stage of analysis, then the difference in the time necessary to perform these tasks is an estimate of the duration of the stage of interest. Elaborations of this method devised by Posner (1969) and Sternberg (1969) have been useful in the study of visual memory. As noted by Massaro (1975, p. 44), Donders fashioned his method on the procedure used by Helmholtz to measure the speed of the nervous impulse; a result was that a hundred years later information processing theory would describe perceiving as temporally successive stages of analysis.

A second assumption of the information processing approach is that there are limits to the amount of processing that can be completed. The paradigmatic demonstrations of such limitations come from the study of auditory perception: Cherry's (1953) and Broadbent's (1954) demonstrations that humans are not efficient at understanding two simultaneously presented verbal messages. Consequently, information processing theorists were led to consider the role of selective attention in the total course of processing. If humans cannot make use of all of the information that is potentially available at a particular point in time, the theoretical questions are then the location of selection within the processing sequence and the similarity of the selection process of vision and audition (Kahneman, 1973; Garner, 1974; Shriffrin & Schneider, 1977). This assumption of limitations on processing also underlies the distinction between short-term and long-term memory (STM–LTM) championed by information processing researchers. The limitations on the "span of immediate memory" discussed by Miller (1956), as well as the rapid forgetting of recently presented items that occurs when rehearsal is prevented (Peterson & Peterson, 1959), led many theorists (e.g., Atkinson & Shiffrin, 1968) to propose that human memory is composed of both a STM of

limited capacity and duration, and a LTM which is apparently permanent and of unbounded capacity. The STM–LTM distinction has proved
to be as controversial as it is fundamental, and the major differences
separating many information processing models involve claims about
the storage capacity, resistance to forgetting, and coding processes
which characterize the two memory systems (Postman, 1975). There is
even a movement inspired by the suggestion of Craik and Lockhart
(1972) to essentially abandon the STM–LTM distinction, and to concentrate instead on the "levels of processing" required by particular tasks.
Yet this controversial distinction goes back at least as far as James's
(1890/1950) equating "primary memory" with awareness of the immediate present, and it is probably this difference between the retention
of items in consciousness versus those long out of awareness which
most theorists, even Craik and Lockhart (1972, p. 676) would accept.

The final theoretical assumption mentioned by Haber (1969a) is that of
the commonality of perception and memory. Haber emphasizes that
visual stimulation produces not only a percept but also a memory of the
stimulation, and that these are difficult to distinguish experimentally.
This is particularly true when, as in most experimental situations, a
visual stimulus is presented extremely briefly. Does the subject's subsequent response then represent what is **seen** or what is **remembered?**
From an information processing perspective this is always a relative
rather than an absolute distinction, since visual processing is extended
over time. Within the whole processing sequence, it is difficult to describe any events that are exclusively "perceptual," in the sense of being
isolated from any memory process. More importantly, it may not be
conceptually helpful to propose any absolute distinction between perception and memory. One consequence of the limitations on processing
capacity, for example, is that the retention of visually presented events
will depend on how these events are **encoded** (i.e., how the stimulus
dimensions of an external object are perceptually organized in an internal representation). Conversely, the identification of an object always
involves a perceiver's bringing past experience to bear on the present
stimulation. Current theories of pattern recognition (e.g., Reed, 1973;
Palmer, 1975; Lindsay & Norman, 1977) are thus concerned with the
nature of the stored information that can successfully guide this interpretation of sensory phenomena. In the information processing approach, perceptual and memory processes both contribute to the identification of visual events.

There is more agreement among information processing researchers
in their use of these assumptions of temporally extended processing,

capacity limitations, and the commonality of perception and memory, than in their descriptions of the particular types of analyses involved in visual processing. Substantial reviews of the issues and experiments in this area are presented by Neisser (1967), Haber and Hershenson (1973), Massaro (1975), and Lindsay and Norman (1977). Many of the original articles from which the information processing approach emerged can be found in the collections edited by Haber (1968, 1969b). As these collections demonstrate, information processing has been extremely influential in guiding contemporary perceptual research, but this does not necessarily mean that it is the most theoretically productive form of guidance. We remarked earlier on the methodological links between information processing theory and the subtractive method which Donders derived from Helmholtz. Turvey (1977) has recently drawn attention to some theoretical assumptions of Helmholtz's perceptual theory which persist in information processing theory as well. Perhaps the most important of these assumptions is that visual stimulation is essentially impoverished with respect to perceptual experience. Helmholtz had adopted Berkeley's hypothesis that perceivers have access only to the two-dimensional retinal image adequately defined by geometrical optics. The perception of the three-dimensional properties of the world must consequently be the result of supplementing this image (by unconscious inference) with information obtained from other modalities, especially touch (Pastore, 1971). While theories of perception have certainly become more sophisticated in the last century, Turvey notes that many information processing appeals to coding strategies and perceptual-memory interactions, like Helmholtz's proposals, arise from the assumption that perceptual experience must involve the supplementation of a two-dimensional retinal image. A theoretical alternative to information processing, favored by Turvey, is the framework developed by J. J. Gibson (1966, in press). Gibson proposes that a perceiver's visual world is composed of surfaces, objects, and events, not the points of light forming a retinal image. As a result, perceptual theory should begin from a description of the light available to the eye, a description which Gibson has termed "ecological optics." Rather than assume that veridical perception involves the supplementation of a two-dimensional retinal mosaic, Gibson proposes an investigation of the information available in the "optic array," the series of nested solid angles of light converging at a particular point of observation. A thorough characterization of this array, especially as it changes over time and observation point, reveals that there are a variety of "higher-order variables of stimulation" which specify environmental objects and their properties. Perception may therefore be more accurately described in terms of the picking up of this information in the optic array than in terms of the processing of a retinal image.

Gibson's emphasis on the need for a theory of the perceptual information that is **available** to perceivers rather than **provided** by them is an intriguing alternative to the information processing approach, an alternative being considered by an increasing number of perceptual theorists (Shaw & Bransford, 1977). While we have adopted the concepts of information processing for the present discussion, it is possible that these concepts will undergo substantial revision as a result of ecological theorizing. With this *caveat* in mind, the present focus will be on three types of concepts that are central to a theory of visual processing: (*a*) the registration and selection of information; (*b*) encoding and retention; and (*c*) the identification of patterns. In each case, our concern will be with using these concepts as a context for understanding the differences in hemispheric functioning exhibited by the human brain.

III. Registration and Selection

An important discovery associated with the information processing approach is that even the initial registration of a visual event is a process which continues after the stimulus itself has been terminated. This first stage of visual processing provides the raw material for STM, and apparently involves the representation of a pattern in a manner rich in visual detail but subject to decay within a fraction of a second. The term *iconic memory* was offered by Neisser (1967) as a name for this process of visual registration; its properties have been revealed chiefly by studies of visual masking and the development of partial-report techniques.

Visual masking, the interference with the recognition of one stimulus by the presentation of another in close temporal contiguity, has been investigated since the nineteenth century (Raab, 1963). Masking and target stimuli are usually each presented at the same spatial location, for a duration less than that needed to complete an eye movement, approximately 100 msec. Situations in which target and mask do not spatially overlap are technically known as *metacontrast* (Kahneman, 1968; Weisstein, 1972) and both metacontrast and masking by visual patterns have provided evidence supporting the information processing assumption that visual perception is extended over time. One early indication of the significance of metacontrast, for example, was the observation by Werner (1935) that a tachistoscopically presented ring could perceptually "erase" a previously presented disk, if the outer diameter of the disk were aligned with the inner diameter of the ring. Werner claimed that the perception of an object required time and depended on the integrity of the contour of the object. When this integrity was radically disturbed, as when the outer contour of the disk became identified with the formation of the interior of the ring, perception became impossible, and the disk was erased. More recent work with metacontrast and visual masking suggests that this erasure phenomenon is actually a form of disruption, during a critical period, of an extremely brief, centrally located form of visual storage, iconic memory. For example, investigations of metacontrast in which a ring surrounds one target item in a letter array (Averbach & Coriell, 1961; Weisstein & Haber, 1965) have found that recognition of the target letter is relatively unimpaired if the letter and ring are presented simultaneously. However, the target is perceptually erased if the ring is delayed for 50–100 msec after the termination of the array, with recognition improving at longer letter–ring intervals. Masking by means of a visual pattern also impairs target recognition if the mask is presented within a critical period, although in this situation masking occurs with simultaneous target–mask presentation as well. Another feature of pattern masking is that it can be obtained when the target and mask are presented to opposite eyes (i.e., dichoptically), suggesting that iconic storage is not solely the result of retinal processes (Schiller & Wiener, 1963; Schiller, 1965). Estimates of the duration of iconic memory vary, depending on such factors as the luminance of the target and pre- and postexposure fields, but masking phenomena are typically less robust as the interval between the target and mask begins to exceed 250 msec. Masks coming after the critical period are not disruptive because the transfer from iconic memory to STM has occurred.

The above account of iconic memory has often been referred to as an *interruption theory*, because it assumes that the target array appears instantaneously in iconic memory, the effect of the mask being to interrupt the serial transfer of items from this representation into STM. Other theorists have pointed out that masking may influence recognition by altering the quality of this representation, rather than terminating it (Kinsbourne & Warrington, 1962b,c; Eriksen & Hoffman, 1963; Eriksen, 1966). According to this *integration theory*, the target and mask are subject to a simple process of energy summation by the visual system, with the result that the figure–ground contrast of the target is substantially reduced. Turvey (1973) has investigated this possibility in a series of nineteen experiments on the identification of letters masked by random bits of visual noise and by patterns composed of letterlike elements; he concluded that both the interruption and integration theories are relevant to the concept of iconic memory. Turvey found that masking by visual noise resembled masking by flashes of light: Dichoptic effects were not present, and target energy was reciprocal with the minimal interstimulus interval (ISI) necessary to identify the target. In other words, this type of masking is essentially a peripheral process in which a "bright" target can compensate for a brief exposure duration, as the integration theory would predict. Masking by patterns similar to the target letters, on the other hand, did produce dichoptic (i.e., central) effects, and in this situation target energy was not reciprocal with critical ISI. Instead, as the interruption theory would predict, the amount of time for which the stimulus is available proved to be the critical feature, and exposure duration plus critical ISI equaled a constant. Turvey concluded that iconic memory is composed of both these peripheral and central processes, although the composition is complex. The output of the peripheral processes is a set of context-independent, fundamental features of visual objects (Hubel & Wiesel, 1962). The output of the central processes is a decision regarding the relational properties of these features (size, general shape, etc.), though the identity of the object is not ascertained. According to Turvey, these peripheral and central processes proceed concurrently, with the central decisions being contingent upon the outcome of the peripheral events.

Studies of visual masking have demonstrated the central nature and rapid decay of iconic memory. The development of a partial-report technique has helped determine the capacity and type of information registered. Since the nineteenth century, it has been known that subjects can typically report only about four to six items from a briefly exposed display. But since in this situation subjects are attempting to report the whole array, it is not clear where the limitation occurs, whether in the recognition process or in the retention of the items during report. Reporting the array takes time, and thus perceptual information regarding some of the items could be lost during the report of others. Sperling (1960) attempted to reduce any limitations imposed by the retention of the array by requiring the report of only a partial number of items presented on each trial. In his paradigm, three rows of four letters appeared simultaneously for 50 msec. After a variable delay, a tonal signal of either high, medium, or low pitch indicated which single row the subjects were to report. Since subjects do not know which row to report until after the display has been turned off, the percentage of items correctly reported from a single row is an estimate of the percentage of items available from the whole array. Sperling found that subjects could "see" more than they could "remember"; approximately three items could be correctly reported from a single four-item row when the tone immediately followed the offset of the array. This meant that about nine of the twelve items in the whole array were actually available for report, some of which were lost when subjects had attempted to recall the whole array. When the tonal cue was delayed for one second after array offset, however, the partial-report estimate of the number of available items approximated the four-item level obtained when report of the whole array was required. As do studies of visual masking, these results suggest the presence of an information-rich iconic memory which decays within a fraction of a second. Peripheral processes are also involved to some extent in these partial-report results. Sperling found that the advantage of partial report over whole report could be extended to cue delays of well over a second when the pre- and postexposure fields were dark, permitting afterimages.

The type of information preserved in iconic memory seems to be the physical features of items rather than their names. For example, cuing by row essentially requires report based on the spatial location of items. Sperling (1960) also performed an experiment in which each row in the array contained half consonants and half digits, randomly mixed. When subjects were required to selectively report either the consonants or the digits, there was no superiority of partial report over whole report. Apparently the use of iconic memory depends on the presence of some physical features by which items can be grouped together for report. The letter–digit classification must be determined for each item individually, and during this classification the image decays. Similar advantages of partial report over whole report for brief cue delays have been obtained for classification based on shape (Turvey & Kravetz, 1970), color (Clark, 1969), and size (von Wright, 1968, 1970).

The difference between the partial and whole report of briefly presented arrays has suggested a distinction between an information-rich but rapidly fading iconic memory, in which physical features rather than object identities are present, and a short-term memory of more limited capacity, whose contents are available for report. How does the selection of information from iconic memory occur? Following Broadbent's (1958) lead, most information processing theorists have formed this question in terms of locating a selective "filter" in the processing sequence. Descriptions of this selection process have differed, primarily depending on whether the paradigms employed required the report or the detection of visual information. Sperling (1963) asked subjects to name as many items as they could from an array which ranged between two and six letters in size, and was immediately followed by a visual noise mask after a variable delay. He found that subjects could report approximately one additional letter from an array for each 10-msec delay of the mask, up to a limit of about four letters, regardless of array size. This implied that an extremely fast, 10 msec per item, selection from iconic memory to

STM was occurring. In addition, this selection apparently proceeded on an item-by-item basis (i.e., in a "serial" fashion). If items in the array could be processed simultaneously and independently of each other (i.e., in "parallel"), then the number of items available for report per unit time would have increased with array size. An additional form of evidence for a serial selection out of iconic memory was reported by Harris and Haber (1963). These authors presented subjects with a series of cards, on each of which was a set of geometrical objects which varied along the dimensions of number, shape, and color. After an exposure duration of 100 msec, subjects were instructed to report the contents of a card. The most interesting results were obtained for the "dimension coders," subjects whom Harris and Haber trained to report the different dimensions of the objects separately. That is, when one red triangle and three green circles appeared on a card, these subjects learned to report "red–green; triangle–circle; one–three." On some trials, Harris and Haber emphasized to their subjects that a particular dimension was much more important than the others. In addition, the order of report of the dimensions was varied, and signaled to the subject after stimulus presentation. Harris and Haber found that emphasized dimensions were reported more accurately than unemphasized ones, even at the first report position, suggesting that the emphasized dimension was first selected from iconic memory.

Since the studies discussed above relied on subjects' verbal report of the array, the selection involved may actually intervene between recognition and report, rather than between iconic memory and recognition. As Haber and Hershenson (1973, p. 238) note, it is possible that iconic information is encoded in a parallel fashion into a more stable visual format within STM, and that serial selection only becomes necessary for the report of the features of this image. In fact, Eriksen and Spencer (1969) have obtained results suggesting that when the detection rather than the report of items is required, items are encoded simultaneously and independently of each other, in parallel. In the Eriksen and Spencer paradigm, a succession of between one and nine single letters was presented to equally sensitive foveal areas for 2 msec each; at the end of the sequence subjects decided whether or not a single target letter had been presented. The most important result was that subjects were just as accurate when there was only 5 *msec* between letters as when there was 3 *sec* intervening. Apparently subjects were able to encode the letters in a parallel fashion, with the result that nine letters could be scanned as efficiently in 50 msec as in 25 sec. Subsequent results supporting this conclusion were obtained by Shiffrin and Gardner (1972). In their experiments, the display consisted of four locations arranged as the corners of a square: The four locations were presented either simultaneously for 50 msec or in a known clockwise sequence of four individual displays of 50 msec each. The task was to decide whether any of the locations contained one of two target letters. Shiffrin and Gardner found that subjects were no more accurate in the sequential condition, where they knew the location of a potential target, than they were in the simultaneous condition, where all four locations required attention. In other words, the opportunity to selectively allocate processing to a single location did not improve accuracy relative to the condition in which all four locations had to be monitored simultaneously. The results of the simultaneous and sequential conditions were also similar, in that accuracy was reduced by the presence of distractors in other locations that visually resembled the targets, but not by visually dissimilar distractors. This equivalence of the simultaneous and sequential conditions was present even when Shiffrin and Gardner modified the paradigm to allow 500 msec between successive displays. Shiffrin and Geisler (1973) report a similar pattern of results for the detection of simple dot patterns: The visual similarity of the distractor items lowered performance, but there was no difference between simultaneous and sequential presentation. This suggests that the recognition of the items in the array was established in a parallel fashion, since subjects were not aided by the opportunity to selectively attend in the sequential condition. In addition, the detrimental effect of the visually confusable distractors found by Shiffrin and Gardner was apparently due to decision processes in STM. Gardner (1973) has shown that, in the simultaneous condition, target detection decreases with array size in the presence of visually similar distractors, but that detection is constant over array size when distractors not resembling the target are present.

Studies of visual masking, metacontrast, and partial report have made an important contribution by defining a distinct stage of visual recognition, iconic memory, which preserves the physical features, rather than the identities, of items subsequently available for report in STM. Items registered in iconic memory are apparently transferred to STM simultaneously and independently of each other (i.e., in parallel), as studies of letter detection have shown, while the verbal report of such items seems to require a serial selection. Although only a few studies investigating hemispheric differences in iconic storage have been reported, there is evidence that such differences do exist, at least for the registration of verbal material. McKeever and Gill (1972b), for example, reported some VF differences in the effects of backward masking. In their paradigm, one pair of letters was presented bilaterally for 30 msec followed by a second pair appearing at the same spatial location. McKeever and Gill found that when there was 100 msec between the two pairs of items, right-handed subjects were significantly more accurate in reporting the RVF items of the initial pair. At a .1 msec interval this RVF advantage was also present, though not statistically significant. Left-handed subjects, however, were significantly more accurate in reporting the LVF items of the initial letter pair at both retention intervals. It is difficult to determine whether McKeever and Gill's results are actually associated with iconic storage, since their shorter retention interval is virtually zero, and the longer delay may be close to the upper limit of iconic persistence. Their findings do suggest, though, that in a backward masking paradigm verbal items presented to the "language hemisphere" are less vulnerable to disruption by the masking stimuli. This conclusion was also reached by Oscar-Berman, Goodglass, and Cherlow (1973), who investigated the effects of backward masking on the recognition of vertically oriented, unilaterally presented words. Oscar-Berman *et al.* first obtained a recognition threshold for these stimuli for each subject, and then presented the words at just above threshold duration, as targets to be identified in a backward masking paradigm. The interval between the target and mask was increased in 5 msec steps until the words could be successfully identified, that is, until masking of the iconic persistence was no longer effective. This estimate of the processing time necessary to escape backward masking was shorter for words presented to the RVF, suggesting that these items were more rapidly transferred from iconic to STM than were words presented in the LVF. Ward and Ross (1977) have also reported that the time required to escape backward masking is less for RVF than for LVF presentation of single letters, although in their experiments this was true only for the first of three testing sessions. Finally, McKeever and Suberi (1974) found that the time required to escape backward masking was shorter for RVF items presented in a metacontrast paradigm. They required subjects to identify individual letters which were followed after a varying delay by a surrounding ring (cf. Averbach & Coriell, 1961). Like previous investigators of metacontrast, McKeever and Suberi found that the improvement of letter identification over the letter–ring interval was not monotonic. Specifically, identification declined between intervals of 0 and 30 msec, and them improved steadily. The shape of the identification function was similar for LVF and RVF presentation, except that the LVF function was displaced approximately 13 msec from the RVF curve. Accuracy was higher for RVF than for LVF items at letter–ring intervals between 30 and 90 msec, where the greatest improvement in identification occurred.

The experiments on backward masking discussed above have suggested that the persistence of verbal information in iconic memory is relatively briefer for items presented to the RVF–left hemisphere, that is, these items are more rapidly encoded into STM. A related left hemisphere advantage has also been observed for the selection of information in iconic memory, using the partial report paradigm developed by Sperling (1960). Cohen (1976) presented six-letter arrays unilaterally for 100 msec, and investigated the effects of masking and of partial report based on physical features. She found that a masking stimulus appearing 20 msec after the offset of the array significantly impaired the identification of letters presented to the LVF, but not those presented to the RVF. Partial report was cued either by color (red versus black letters) or by location (inner versus outer column); partial report based on either physical cue was superior to whole report, but only when the cue preceded the letter array, and not when it followed the array. That is, the cues could only be used to selectively attend to the array rather than to report from the iconic trace. In addition, this advantage of partial over whole report was significant for RVF but not for LVF presentation. Cohen also devised estimates of the time that subjects needed to select the letters on the basis of color and location, and found that both forms of selection were significantly faster for RVF presentation. Analogous estimates of the persistence of the array in iconic memory, and of the rate of encoding items from iconic into STM, were significantly shorter for the RVF– left hemisphere.

Cohen's results are interesting because they represent a situation in which the perceptual **use** of the physical features of a display, color and location, is more efficient for left hemisphere presentation. That is, although processing of such physical stimulus dimensions is usually attributed to the right hemisphere, the use of such dimensions as the basis for verbal report from iconic memory leads to a left hemisphere advantage. A related finding was obtained by Oscar-Berman et al. (1973), who reported that the processing time required to escape backward masking in the identification of nonsense shapes was (albeit nonsignificantly) shorter for the RVF. Such results imply that encoding of all types of information from iconic memory is more efficient for left hemisphere presentation. Oscar-Berman, Blumstein, and DeLuca (1976), however, found that an advantage to LVF presentation in the iconic storage of a nonverbal stimulus could be obtained when identification was signaled by a manual response. Using trained musicians as subjects, these authors investigated the identification of visually presented musical notes in a backward masking paradigm, and discovered that the time required to escape masking was shorter for LVF presentation. Unfortunately, this particular right hemisphere advantage is apparently not consistent across different sets of nonverbal stimuli. Moscovitch, Scullion, and Christie (1976), for example, investigated hemispheric differences and backward masking in the identification of drawings of faces. In Experiment 3 of the series reported, a single drawing was presented to the central visual field (CVF), followed after a variable delay by a face presented to either the RVF or LVF; subjects responded only if the second face was the same as the first. Moscovitch *et al.* report that at retention intervals of 100 msec and 1 sec, manual RT was significantly faster for LVF presentation, indicating that the processing was performed primarily by the right hemisphere. No consistent VF differences were present at intervals of 5 and 50 msec, however, which suggests that at these intervals the two hemispheres have equal access to the iconic trace of the central stimulus. In Experiment 4 the authors employed the same paradigm but added a masking pattern during the retention interval. In this situation, RT was consistently faster for the LVF faces at all delays. In other words, when the iconic trace of the initial stimulus is masked, and subjects must make their decisions on the basis of relatively more complex analyses of the CVF face, a right hemisphere superiority is revealed. Although the results of Cohen and others mentioned earlier show that verbal material presented to the RVF is vulnerable to backward masking for a shorter period of time, and thus is more rapidly encoded from iconic memory to STM than LVF items, hemispheric differences in the iconic storage of nonverbal material are apparently related to a number of variables which have not yet been adequately characterized.

IV. Encoding and Retention

We consider encoding to be the perceptual organization of stimulus dimensions into an internal representation, a representation which is related in complex ways to external stimuli (Kintsch, 1977, Ch. 3; Melton & Martin, 1972). While studies of visual registration have addressed questions regarding the time course of the **formation** of this internal representation, studies of encoding are concerned with the consequences of different **forms,** or types, of perceptual representation. These questions have been most frequently posed experimentally in terms of the processing of verbal versus nonverbal information.

A. Dual Coding Theory

Differences in the retention of visually presented words and pictures have often been reported. For example, Shepard (1967) wondered if the capacity limitations stressed by information processing theory might be exceeded when recognition rather than recall was used as a measure of retention. He tested three groups of subjects, each of which was shown approximately 600 of a particular type of visual stimuli: single words, sentences, or pictures. He found that in an immediate forced-choice recognition test, subjects could correctly identify 98% of the "old" pictures previously seen. Recognition performance with words (90%) and sentences (88%) was also surprisingly good, though less than that of the pictures. Standing (1973) examined the difference between verbal and pictorial recognition for stimulus sets of up to 1000 items; in addition, he placed pictorial stimuli which were judged to have interesting subject matter into a "vivid" category. Standing found that the recognition of vivid pictures was superior to that of the "normal" ones, which in turn was more accurate than word recognition. The three types of stimuli were similar, though, in that the estimate of the number of items retained increased with the size of the stimulus set. For words and both types of pictures, this increase possessed the same mathematical form, a power function. In an attempt to define the limits of this recognition capacity, Standing persuaded five of his subjects to view 10,000 pictures over a 5-day period. The results provided by these subjects were still in agreement with the power function obtained from subjects viewing the smaller set sizes; performance showed no sign of diminishing. The estimated number of retained items was 6600, demonstrating a remarkable property of human visual processing.

The apparently superior retention of pictorial stimuli is not limited to the use of recognition procedures. Standing (1973) also presented different groups of subjects with a set of 200 stimuli, either pictures or words, and instructed them to prepare for a memory test of an unspecified form. A forced-choice recognition test of 40 pairs of items was then given, followed by a recall task in which the "picture" subjects wrote descriptions of as many slides as they could remember. Surprisingly, both the recall and recognition of the pictures was more accurate than that of the words, although for both types of stimuli the level of performance was lower in the recall than in the recognition condition. A similar result has been obtained by Paivio and Csapo (1973). In Experiment 4 of the series reported, an incidental learning paradigm was used; subjects were presented with a series of pictures and single concrete words in a random sequence, and their task was to predict whether each succeeding item would be a picture or a word. In a standard free recall condition, other subjects were told to learn a similar list of pictures and words for later recall. Paivio and Csapo found that while recall was significantly poorer in the incidental than in the standard condition, both situations evidenced superior recall of the pictures over the words.

In Experiment 5, these authors examined the effects of repeating items in the lists during the incidental and standard recall conditions. That is, some items appeared twice as a picture, twice as a word, or once as a picture and once as a word. Again, for items appearing only once, picture recall was superior to verbal recall for both conditions. In addition, it was found that items appearing as both a picture and as a word were correctly recalled significantly more often than items appearing twice as a word. In fact, alternating the repetition format had an approximately additive effect in the standard recall condition, while retaining either format had a less than additive effect. Paivio and Csapo claim that these results do more than represent the fact that pictorial stimuli may lead to more accessible memory representations. A series of correlations showed that various measures of the "memorability" of both words (e.g., printed frequency) and pictures (e.g., rated imagery value) were unsuccessful in predicting recall scores in the incidental condition, where these attributes should have been most salient. Rather, the additive effect of picture–word repetition in the standard recall condition suggests the use of independent imaginal and verbal memory codes.

The differences in the retention of visually presented words and pictures mentioned above, as well as the sizable facilitation that imagery can provide in certain verbal learning paradigms, have led Paivio (1971, 1974, 1977) to develop a *dual coding* theory of cognition. Paivio (1977) proposes that two assumptions are fundamental to this theory: "The most general assumption is that verbal and nonverbal information are represented and processed in independent but interconnected symbolic systems. A second general assumption is that the nature of the symbolic information differs qualitatively in the two systems [p. 60]." The results obtained by Paivio and Csapo (1973) are clearly supportive of this approach. The additivity of picture–word repetition suggests the use of two different codes, and yet the codes must be interconnected in some way for there to be any recall facilitation in the "alternating" condition. Additional findings will be discussed below which suggest that humans are capable of using nonverbal coding in a variety of visual comparison tasks. Paivio's theory has been often implicitly adopted by researchers investigating VF effects, since there is an obvious resemblance between the functions of the proposed nonverbal and verbal systems and the hemispheric differences obtained in visual recognition tasks. In fact, Paivio (1977, p. 62) views the effects of unilateral lesions in brain-damaged subjects, and the VF differences obtained in normal individuals, as evidence supporting the dual coding theory. However, as Neisser (1972, p. 244) has cautioned, the assumption that nonverbal and verbal coding systems exist may oversimplify the types of cognitive events we wish to characterize. One problem, for example, is the ambiguity inherent in the term "system." What Paivio seems to have in mind by this term is something like "form of knowledge." The primary assumption of the dual coding theory, as quoted, referred to the systems as "representing" (as well as "processing") information. A consequence of the different ways in which information is represented in the two systems is that: "my knowledge of the world includes information that has never been expressed verbally to me or by me, such as the appearance of my home or my office, and a good deal that is impossible or difficult to describe [Paivio, 1977, p. 61]." The claim here is apparently that there is a nonverbal form of knowledge which differs from its verbal counterpart by virtue of being ineffable, incapable of description. Yet just because we can be said to know how something looks, this does not necessarily mean that there is a distinct system of nonverbal knowledge. What it does mean to know how something looks was examined by Perkins (1971). Perkins contrasted theoretical understanding, exemplified by the type of understanding possessed by someone who has mastered a set of scientific concepts, with "whatlike understanding," one version of which depends on the acquaintance with the **appearance** of particular objects or events. A person who has actually seen and heard blue jays, for example, possesses (when he remembers and discusses these experiences) an understanding of "what blue jay behavior is like" that differs from the understanding of an individual lacking the relevant experiences. According to Perkins, perceptual experiences can contribute to the meaning of the words that would be used to describe blue jay behavior; these words would thus have a slightly different meaning for the individual who has perceived blue jays than they would for an individual perceptually unacquainted with blue jays. Understanding "what X is like," however, does not depend on understanding "what X resembles." The person who has observed blue jay behavior may claim that it does not resemble anything else that he knows, but this would not reduce our confidence that he does understand what the behavior is like. This understanding of resemblances is an example of knowledge proper, the placing of concepts or experiences within a structure of relationships (cf. Natsoulas, 1978, p. 274). Perkins emphasizes that whatlike understanding does not entail the possession of any knowledge that would be unavailable without the relevant perceptual experience. That is, lacking the observation of blue jays would not prevent an individual from developing a **complete** theoretical understanding of blue jay behavior. There would be no additional facts for him to discover, he would simply not possess a concrete personal memory of these creatures' appearance. Information acquired firsthand about the visual appearance of objects and events in the world may thus play some role in the meaning of the words we use to express what we know about these objects. The mere presence of this visual information, though, is not the apprehension of relationships that constitutes knowledge. Simply having visual information available (e.g., as a visual memory, or as a visual image) about the appearance of one's home or office is not equivalent to knowing something about this appearance, just as having a photograph in one's pocket does not entail knowing anything about the object pictured (cf. Pylyshyn, 1973, p. 6; Natsoulas, 1977, p. 80). Thus, having information about visual appearances does not require the dual coding assumption of a separate system of nonverbal knowledge.

What motivated the hypothesis of independent verbal and nonverbal "symbolic systems," though, was perhaps not a consideration of the content or objects of **knowledge,** but rather the way in which such contents **appear.** The second assumption of the dual coding theory is more closely related to the concept of appearance. This assumption proposes that the nature of the information is qualitatively different in the two systems.

> Specifically, one system is specialized for representing and processing information concerning nonverbal objects and events in a rather direct, analog fashion. Since imagery is a unique expression of its functioning, it is convenient to refer to it as the imagery system. The other is specialized for dealing with linguistic units and generating speech, so let us call it the verbal system. The qualitative distinctions extend to the way information is organized in the two systems. The imagery system organizes elementary images into higher-order structures so that the informational output of the system has a synchronous or spatial character, whereas the verbal system organizes linguistic units into higher-order sequential structures [Paivio, 1977, p. 60].

It is important to note that this qualitative difference, while quite valid, refers to what individuals can **do** with nonverbal and verbal information, rather than what they can **know** about it. As a consequence of having a visual image of one's office, one might be able to verify the fact that a desk is to the left of a window; but this fact can also be determined, though perhaps less rapidly, from a verbal description of the room. Even this functional difference in the use of these two types of information is probably not absolute. Standing's (1973) results point to the similarity of verbal and pictorial systems: In both cases recall is worse than recognition, capacity is apparently unlimited, and the power function accurately describes the increase in recognition performance over set size. Pellegrino, Rosinski, Chiesi, and Siegel (1977) have reported that the pattern of RTs in a category decision task was more consistent with the predictions of a "unitary" model of semantic memory than with those based on a dual coding model. One finding was that stimulus pairs that referred to the same category (e.g., animals) but involved common subcategories (e.g., duck–chicken) elicited faster RTs than those involving different subcategories (e.g., trout–goat), and this was true of both word–word and picture–picture decisions. A related finding is that of Pezdek (1977), who performed a signal-detection analysis of the delayed comparison of sentence and picture pairs. For both stimulus "modalities," detectability was lowered by the presence of a semantically related intervening item, compared to the presence of an unrelated item, even though these intervening stimuli were in a different "modality" than the items to be compared. Thus there is evidence that the processing characteristics of the proposed verbal and nonverbal systems overlap considerably. The key aspect of the qualitative difference proposed in the Paivio quote is the "synchronous or spatial character." When using visual imagery, or otherwise engaging the nonverbal system, the contents of the processing have a spatial quality; that is, these contents are arrayed before us (or in the "mind's eye") as a visual scene. However, as we remarked above, the use of a visual format or code is not sufficient to justify the assumption of a separate form of knowledge. The use of nonverbal and verbal codes has been shown to contribute to the speed and accuracy of judgments in many experimental tasks, and these coding differences do have a central role in information processing theory (e.g., Kosslyn & Pomerantz, 1977). The important point is that such differences do not necessarily imply the existence of two independent systems of perceiving. Rather than equate the two cerebral hemispheres with verbal and nonverbal systems, it may be theoretically more profitable to attempt to define the complex and interrelated stages involved in the recognition of verbal and nonverbal events, and to determine whatever hemispheric specialization may exist for each of these aspects of perceptual function.

B. Analog Processing

Research involving a task developed by Posner has provided a significant amount of evidence that visual coding can be used in making same–different judgments (e.g., Posner & Keele, 1967; Posner & Mitchell, 1967; Posner, Boies, Eichelman, & Taylor, 1969). In this task, the stimuli to be compared are typically two letters of the alphabet separated by a variable delay. At the appearance of the second letter, subjects respond yes or no as rapidly as possible to the implicit question, "Do these items have the same name?" Yes judgments are equally appropriate for pairs which are physically identical (e.g., A–A) as for those which are identical in name only (e.g., A–a), yet subjects are able to complete the physical matches approximately 70 msec before the name matches. This RT difference is often referred to as the Posner effect, and has suggested the existence of two codes in letter recognition: one relatively visual, relying on the shape of the letter, and one verbal, employing the letter's name. Much of the original evidence indicating the differences between these two codes is summarized by Posner (1969). The codes are apparently independent, since when subjects are instructed to consider only physically identical letters to be "same," RT for "different" letters having the same name (e.g., A–a) is no longer than for those with different names (e.g., A–b). In other words, in this situation, the deeply ingrained knowledge that A–a have the same name does not interfere with the task based on physical matching. In addition, RT for the physical and name matches can be manipulated independently. When the first of the two letters to be compared was flanked by visually similar letters (e.g., OGQ), RT for the physical matches, but not for the name matches, was increased. Conversely, requiring subjects to hold eight items in memory until the end of a trial elevated RT on name identity trials but not on the physical identity trials.

Using the visual code is an example of what Posner (1969) called an "analog" operation: "The idea is that analog matching depends upon operations like size variation or rotation, which can be performed within the visual system and need not require contact with past experience [p. 57]." "The analog processes involve operations on the input information only, while the name matches depend upon stored information [p. 59]." One form of evidence for analog processing is the fact that name matches between visually dissimilar letters, such as A–a, were slower than between visually similar letters, such as C–c, which in turn were slower than between physically identical letters. The selective interference with the physical and name matches discussed above suggests that subjects perform the analog and name operations in parallel, rather than finishing the analog match before searching for the name of the stimulus. Additional evidence for this conclusion is the fact that the name matches were no faster in a series of trials that contained all name matches than in a series composed of both name and physical matches. If subjects usually spend time performing the analog operation first, they should have been able to use the absence of physical matches in the "pure" list to speed their decisions. Analog operations can be applied to nonalphabetic stimuli as well. Posner trained subjects to respond "same" to pairs of dot patterns of various degrees of similarity, and found that (at least up to a certain level of complexity) the RT of these judgments was a linear function of the degree of visual similarity between the patterns. One problem with Posner's (1969) account of analog operations, however, is that it is probably not the restriction of processing to "input information only" which is the defining characteristic; even in Posner's paradigm, the delayed comparison must involve the stored representation of the first letter. Rather, it is the **type** of comparison which is important. As suggested by Shepard (1975), analog processes apply the types of procedures appropriate to the external, physical object to internal representations.

The results of more recent experiments investigating both the mental rotation of visually presented items and the use of information stored in LTM also suggest the presence of analog operations. The use of mental rotation as a visual comparison process was first demonstrated by Shepard and Metzler (1971), who presented subjects with two simultaneous perspective drawings of geometrical objects, and asked them to decide as quickly as possible if the drawings were of the same object. Some of the "same" pairs contained objects which differed in perspective, specifically rotation, either in the picture plane or in depth. Shepard and Metzler found that the RT of the "same" decisions for these pairs was a remarkably linear function of the angular separation between the objects, for both depth- and picture-plane rotations. This result indicated that subjects were mentally rotating one of the objects at a constant rate in order to make the comparison, a conclusion consistent with subjects' introspective reports. Similar results have been obtained by Cooper and Shepard (1973), who required subjects to decide if individual letters or digits, tilted to varying degrees, were in the normal or a reversed orientation. In addition, Cooper and Shepard (1973) obtained some evidence that when given information about the identity and orientation of the test item to be presented, subjects could generate and rotate a mental image of it as the basis for the normal–reversed decision. Cooper (1975) has proposed that these two types of mental rotation, occurring before and after stimulus presentation, proceed at approximately the same rate. She first trained subjects to discriminate between "standard" and "reflected" versions of randomly shaped figures at a particular orientation. In later testing sessions, during which a presented form could appear rotated between 60° and 300° from its training position, the expected linear relationship between the standard–reflected decision RT and degree of test form rotation was found. Cooper then performed an experiment in which advance information about the identity and rotation of the test stimulus was provided to the subject. On each trial, an outline drawing of the particular test stimulus in the training orientation was followed by an arrow indicating the orientation of the test stimulus to be presented. Subjects terminated the

appearance of the arrow with a manual response when they felt prepared for the test stimulus; the standard–reflected discrimination was
indicated at the presentation of the test form by a vocal response. The
time subjects used to prepare for the upcoming test stimulus could thus
be measured independently of the time needed to perform the discrimination, and in fact the relation of these RTs to test form rotation was
quite different. The preparation RT was linearly related to the angle of
departure of the test form from the learned orientation; the discrimination RT, on the other hand, was constant over angle of rotation. In other
words, subjects were generating a mental image of the designated form
in a learned orientation, rotating it, and using the result to decide about
the test form which followed. The slope of the prestimulus (preparation)
RT function obtained in the second experiment was similar to the poststimulus slope obtained in the first experiment, leading Cooper to conclude that "both sorts of mental rotation are carried out at comparable
rates [p. 41]."

The studies of mental rotation described above are important not only
because they suggest the use of analog operations in visual comparison,
but also because they indicate that information from LTM can be used
in these operations. That is, the prestimulus rotation generated by
Cooper's (1975) subjects refers to a standard orientation which they have
already learned, and this rotation proceeds at about the same rate
as the poststimulus rotation, which uses information just presented.
Additional information concerning the use of visual properties of LTM
has come from a paradigm developed by Moyer (1973). In this paradigm,
subjects were visually presented with two animal names, and required
to throw a switch under the name referring to the larger animal. Before
the experiment, subjects were shown a list of the animal names appropriately ranked in size, and at the end of the experiment subjects as-
signed numerical values representing their size estimates of each animal. Moyer found that the larger the difference between the actual
sizes of the animals named, the faster subjects could make the required
choice. While this result might be intuitively expected, the important
point is that the form of this RT function is the same as that describing
the speed of perceptual decisions regarding which of two simultaneously presented lines is longer (Johnson, 1939). The retrieval from LTM
of information regarding the sizes of the referents of animal names was
thus an analog operation, one having the same properties as would be
present in the actual perceiving of the objects named. Moyer's findings
have been replicated and extended by Paivio (1975) who attempted to
clarify the visual nature of the judgments involved in this particular task.
Paivio found that when pictures of objects and animals, rather than their

names, were presented in Moyer's paradigm, the size relationship between the presented stimuli could influence the speed of the decision about the actual object. Specifically, when two pictures referred to objects of different sizes, but the sizes of the pictures themselves were incongruent with this relationship (e.g., a picture of a lamp being larger than that of a zebra) the subjects' decisions were significantly slowed, compared to a condition in which stimulus size was congruent with real size. When pairs of object names were the stimuli, however, the congruence between stimulus size and referent size was unrelated to the decision RT. Finally, Paivio discovered that he could reverse the effect of the stimulus size by asking for a different type of judgment: Rather than choosing the larger real object, subjects decided which object was farther away. In this instance, the size incongruent stimuli actually led to faster RTs. Since the larger of a pair of objects will appear to be relatively smaller when distant, subjects could use stimulus size incongruence as a cue to relative distance. When the size relationship of the stimuli was congruent with actual sizes, however, the relative distance was more difficult to discern, resulting in increased RT. Again, the important characteristic of the analog operation is not its failure to make use of stored information, but the similarity between this operation and perceptual processing.

The superiority of pictorial recognition obtained by Standing (1973) and by Paivio and Csapo (1973) suggests that verbal and visual encoding can have different consequences for retention; the visual comparison tasks developed by Posner (1969), Shepard and Metzler (1971), and Moyer (1973) have shown that judgments involving both recent and long-term memory can be analog in nature, that is, similar to perceptual processing. While Paivio has proposed that such results represent the products of independent verbal and nonverbal cognitive systems, we have preferred to consider such findings in the context of different codes that subjects use to perform certain tasks, codes which do not constitute clearly dichotomous forms of knowledge. Evidence has in fact appeared which suggests that the difference between nonverbal and verbal representation is far from absolute. Neisser and Kerr (1973), for example, have shown that visual images containing "concealed" objects (i.e., a cradle resting inside the beak of a pelican) can be just as effective mnemonic aids as more traditionally pictorial images. A related finding is that of Marmor and Zaback (1976), who discovered that individuals blind from birth, as well as sighted subjects, demonstrated analog processing: a linear increase in comparison time as a function of the angular separation of tactilely presented forms. Much remains to be accomplished, both theoretically and experimentally, before a satisfactory characterization of perceptual representation is available. The distinction between verbal and visual encoding has been useful in describing how subjects performing information processing tasks make use of the specifically visual aspects of the stimuli. However, the studies by Neisser and Kerr, and by Marmor and Zaback, demonstrate that neither the use of information in a visual image nor even the rotation of an internal representation will typically involve just the use of these visual aspects. Rather, the noticing and use of relational information probably is involved. This information may be more accurately characterized as spatial than as visual, and as we noted above (Section IV, A) it is this noticing of relationships that characterizes knowledge, regardless of whether or not the object of knowing is represented in a visual manner.

C. Identification

Studies of analog processing have suggested that there are many tasks in which the use of internal representations resembles the procedures applied to visually perceived objects. These studies have predominantly assumed that the **identification** of the different stimuli is successful. That is, theories about how subjects decide whether a particular form is in a normal or reflected orientation, or whether one animal is larger than another, assume that the form and the animals have been correctly identified. An important question for theories of visual processing is just how this identification occurs.

Information processing theory would appear to be a good candidate for a framework in which to specify the stages of analysis leading to object identification. Especially in view of the fact that the type of information represented in iconic memory is apparently more closely related to the physical properties of items than to their identities (Turvey, 1973), it should be theoretically possible to "follow the stimulus inward" until its internal representation somehow links up with the perceiver's knowledge of its name. Unfortunately, this appealing account is not tenable; there is evidence that some semantic analysis of a visual event occurs quite early in processing, and may even precede the analysis of some physical features. Reicher (1969), for example, has obtained results suggesting that subjects possess information about whether a letter array is a word or nonword before they have identified the individual letters of the array. In Reicher's experiment, the stimuli were words, anagram sequences, and individual letters; the task was letter recognition. On each trial, a single type of array would be tachistoscopically presented and immediately followed by a visual noise mask. A pair of letters appeared along with the mask above one of the letter-positions of the array, and subjects chose one of these letters as having just been presented in that array position. Each of the recognition letters were appropriate choices for the word arrays. Thus, stimuli such as "WORD," "OWRD," and "D" would be followed by a mask and the test pair "D–K" immediately above the fourth letter position. Subjects did not know which array position would be tested until after the array was turned off. Reicher found that subjects were more accurate in choosing the correct letter from the test pair when the array was a word; performance was equivalent for the anagram and single letter arrays. That is, the fact that an array was a word rather than an anagram led to improved recognition of the individual letters of the array. The problem is to understand how subjects could make use of the word–anagram distinction without having **already identified** the individual letters. Coltheart (1972) suggests that in order to make sense of Reicher's results it may be necessary to distinguish the concepts of (a) having information about an item's meaning (e.g., whether it is a word or an anagram); and (b) being able to identify an item (e.g., report individual letters). Whatever context is developed for understanding Reicher's results, his findings provide intriguing evidence against the notion that pattern identification is simply a matter of performing more complex analyses at successive stages of processing.

One attempt to include the contributions of both sensory phenomena and knowledge in an information processing theory of visual identification is that of Lindsay and Norman (1977), who discuss the difference between "data driven" and "conceptually driven" processing.

> We call this system of analysis *data driven*, because all activity in the system is started by the arrival of sensory data. Data-driven processing starts with sensory data and systematically works its way through successive stages of analysis . . . Conceptually driven processing starts with general knowledge of the events that are being experienced and with the specific expectations generated by this knowledge. The expectations are really simple theories or hypotheses about the nature of the sensory signals that are expected to occur. These expectations guide the stages of analysis at all levels. . . . [pp. 278–279].

In the identification of a visual object both data driven and conceptually driven processing would be involved; the former determining what types of analyses are performed, the latter determining the nature of the expected and achieved results of the analyses. When the visual object is a sentence, for example, data driven processing contributes analyses of such features as the length and shape of each word, as well as the features of individual letters. Conceptually driven processing, on the other hand, uses rules of grammar and meaning to narrow the range of possible words which would be compatible with the sensory analysis. As more context becomes available, the importance of the data driven processing diminishes, and decisions regarding the identities of some words can then be made on the basis of incomplete sensory evidence.

Current theories of pattern recognition (e.g., Reed, 1973) have primarily focused on the data driven processing, the ways in which the analysis of the specifically visual properties of objects leads to identification. The two most widely discussed models of data driven processing are those of template matching and feature analysis. Template matching arises as a logical possibility, though it is without much psychological support. According to this possibility, a particular pattern is identified as belonging to a certain category because at the presentation of the pattern some internal representation of that category (i.e., a template) is activated. A particular letter of the alphabet, such as an *A*, would be identified as a result of the coupling between the pattern of retinal events occurring at the appearance of the *A* and some CNS representation. Template matching fails as a model of identification for the same reasons that identification poses an interesting psychological problem; we can recognize a variety of different types of *A*s: printed, handwritten, in different typefaces, appearing at different places and in different orientations on the retina. Postulating a new template for each successful identification of an *A* does not constitute much of an explanation. On the other hand, while all capital *A*s do not look exactly alike, as a template matching process would require, they do share many features in common, such as a horizontal bar and three acute angles. It may be the case that the recognition of the presence of these features is an important part of the identification of an *A*, since many of these features could remain constant over different instances of the letter. In fact, features have been found to play an important role in many types of visual processing. Neisser (1964), for example, investigated a visual search task in which subjects scanned down a column of letters for the presence of one or more target letters. If some version of template matching were involved in the scanning of the list, then the rate of scan should depend on the number of targets to be detected (i.e., on the number of templates to be compared against the list items). Neisser found, instead, that practiced subjects could search for ten target letters as rapidly as for one. In addition, the rate of scan was affected by the context of the list; search for a Z was much more difficult in a list primarily composed of lines such as *VMXWE* than in a series of lines like *ODUGQ*. Finally, subjects reported that they did not "see" individual letters during their scan of the list at all, but that the list was a blur from which a target stood out. This pattern of results led Neisser to conclude that the use of a small set of critical features, rather than individual letter templates, was being employed in the search of the list. The importance of feature analysis has also been stressed by E. Gibson (1969), who has collected substantial evidence suggesting the presence of two trends in the child's development of perceptual skills: the abstraction of distinctive features differentiating individual items, and the abstraction of invariant relations among features which characterize a class of items. The role of feature analysis as a data driven form of processing has been suggested by physiological evidence as well. Riggs, Ratliff, Cornsweet, and Cornsweet (1953) developed a "stabilized image" technique, in which a pattern is projected to the retina in a way that maintains a constant retinal location in spite of eye movement. Images stabilized in this manner begin to fade after a few seconds, presumably because of receptor adaptation. Interestingly, complex patterns do not fade in a random manner; meaningful segments disappear separately (Pritchard, 1961). This suggests that at some level of the CNS, visual patterns are represented as a combination of elementary units, such as lines, angles, and edges. Receptor adaptation would thus lead to the disappearance of configurations formed of these basic features, rather than to a randomly distributed fading of the image. In fact, adaptation effects can be obtained (with human perceivers) which are restricted to quite specific aspects of visual stimuli, such as a particular combination of line orientation and color (McCollough, 1965). The results of these adaptation studies are consistent with the substantial evidence indicating that some cells of the mammalian visual system are specifically responsive to certain environmental features (Robson, 1975), but the actual role of such cells in human visual processing is still an open question (Dodwell, 1975).

An influential account of how the analysis of individual features might functionally contribute to pattern recognition was the "Pandemonium" model offered by Selfridge (1959). In this model, patterns are recognized in a series of stages of increasing complexity, each stage being governed by a set of hypothetical CNS events called "demons." That is, the individual members of a particular class of patterns (e.g., letters of the alphabet) are assumed to be uniquely specified by a set of features (e.g., horizontal lines, acute angles, etc.). "Cognitive demons" represent the combinations of features distinguishing the patterns (e.g., letters), and at the appearance of a particular pattern each cognitive demon responds in proportion to the number of "its" features that have been detected. A "decision demon" signals the identification of the presented pattern, depending on which cognitive demon is responding most actively. Pandemonium-type computer programs have actually enjoyed some success at tasks such as recognizing hand-printed letters (Selfridge & Neisser, 1960), and modified versions of the Pandemonium model are included in both the Lindsay and Norman (1977) and Shiffrin and Schneider (1977) accounts of pattern recognition by humans. A central question for theories involving feature analysis has been whether this analysis is applied in parallel to many features simultaneously, or sequentially to one feature at a time. No simple answer to this question exists. Evidence favoring the notion of serial analysis was obtained by Egeth (1966) and Nickerson (1967). In the Egeth experiment, subjects performed same–different judgments of pairs of stimuli which could vary along three dimensions: color, shape, and the orientation of a centrally placed line. The speed of the "different" decisions was inversely related to the number of dimensions distinguishing the stimuli, indicating that the comparison was serial and self-terminating. In other words, subjects examined one dimension at a time and responded as soon as a difference between the stimuli was detected. Nickerson used a similar paradigm and also found that "different" RT decreased with the number of dimensions separating stimulus pairs, even when the items were separated by a retention interval of 2 sec. Bradshaw and Wallace (1971) investigated same–different judgments of pairs of drawings of faces which could differ in two, four, or seven features. Subjects searched for five identical pairs of faces in a list which also contained 40 pairs differing in a fixed number of features. List scanning time was inversely related to the number of features distinguishing the "different" pairs, again suggesting a serial, self-terminating comparison of the features of each stimulus pair.

Other results of these experiments, however, have not been consistent with the notion of serial analysis. For example, if a serial comparison alone were responsible for the results, then the "same" RTs should be longer than the "different" RTs, since identity decisions would always require comparison of all dimensions. Yet neither Egeth (1966) nor Nickerson (1967) obtained this result, and in fact, Nickerson found that subjects comparing sequentially presented pairs demonstrated "same" RTs that were as fast as the most rapid "different" decision. Bamber (1969) proposed that the relationship between the speed of the "same" and "different" decisions can be understood if it is assumed that stimuli are processed simultaneously by (a) a relatively fast "identity reporter," which (presumably) operates in parallel, responding only if the stimuli are identical; and (b) a slower "serial processor" which must analyze one feature at a time. The presence of these two types of analyses would lead to rapid "same" decisions regarding identical stimuli, and to "different" RTs which decrease linearly with the number of dimensions distinguishing the items. An additional qualification of a purely serial comparison is the effect of retention interval. Smith and Nielsen (1970) required subjects to make same–different decisions on pairs of schematic faces separated by 1, 4, or 10 sec. "Different" RTs were inversely related to the number of different features between the members of a pair, at all retention intervals, again suggesting serial processing. "Same" decisions were independent of the number of relevant features, consistent with the presence of a parallel identity match, but only at the 1 sec interval. "Same" RT increased with the number of relevant dimensions at the longer retention intervals. Thus Bamber's identity reporter may in fact be responsible for the relatively fast "same" responses, but depend on the presence of some visual representation which is subject to decay after 1 sec. The loss of this apparently parallel matching over the retention interval corresponds to a similar decline in the use of the analog match in the Posner paradigm (Posner & Keele, 1967). Finally, the amount of practice in the type of decision required is also an important determinant of the type of analysis carried out. Grill (1971) has examined the effect of practice on the comparison of pairs of geometrical stimuli presented either simultaneously or after a 4.4 sec retention interval. Like Smith and Nielsen (1970), Grill found that both "same" and "different" RTs to successive presentation were consistent with a serial, self-terminating analysis; she additionally discovered that this pattern was consistent over nine sessions of practice. The simultaneously presented stimuli elicited a different pattern of results, however, in which a shift from serial to parallel processing occurred over the nine sessions. This shift is conceivably related to the development of "automatic" processing with practice described by Shiffrin and Schneider (1977).

Current studies of feature analysis have thus presented a very complex account of visual identification. While some version of the Pandemonium model is probably an appropriate context for understanding the role of feature analysis in identification, it is not yet clear which aspects of this model are best described as a serial or parallel comparison. Making an absolute distinction between these alternatives may be impossible, however, since as Corcoran (1971) and Townsend (1971) have noted, some mathematical formalizations of parallel processing predict the same pattern of results as a serial processing model. In cases where they are distinguishable, serial and parallel comparison are likely to be different aspects of the recognition process which change as a function of such variables as practice and the retention interval. It must also be kept in mind that these studies have only been concerned with data driven processing. Sutherland (1968) argued that recognition of a pattern involves more than isolating a list of features; some description of the relationship between features is probably employed as well. Reicher's (1969) results, discussed earlier, remind us that semantic information can appear in the initial stages of visual processing. In other words, the role of conceptually driven processing in identification also needs to be considered.

Information processing theory has only recently begun to develop questions regarding conceptually driven processing. Since the identification of events typically involves the use of some previously stored knowledge, such as a name, it will be important to develop ways of asking how the organization of this knowledge is related to the act of identification. While methods for describing this relationship in depth are not currently available, experimental interest in the relation between knowledge and perception has recently increased. One example of this interest, an elegant demonstration of the perceptual use of the rules of chess, has been reported by Chase and Simon (1973). These authors were interested in the previous finding (de Groot, 1965) that chess players of master ranking were more accurate than weaker players in reconstructing an actual chess position from memory after a 5 sec exposure, even though there was no difference between these players in the memory for randomly arranged pieces. Chase and Simon hypothesized that the master players were subject to the same memory limitations as the weaker players, but that the masters were able to use their knowledge of chess to encode more information into memory when viewing the actual game positions. In an attempt to characterize the structure of this encoding and the relation between perceptual and memory processing, Chase and Simon videotaped the performance of a master, a class A, and a beginning chess player in two types of tasks. In the memory task, the players were shown a board position for 5 sec, and then required to reconstruct it with an actual board and chess pieces. The perceptual task was similar, except that the position to be reconstructed was left in the player's view. Chase and Simon replicated de Groot's finding that the relationship between playing ability and memory for board position was restricted to positions that could have occurred in actual play. In addition, both the perceptual and memory tasks revealed differences in the placement of successive pieces within 2 sec of each other as compared to those whose placement was separated by more than 2 sec. For all three players, pieces placed within 2 sec of each other tended to share tactical relationships such as pawn structure or attack and defense relations over small spatial distances. This clustering of related pieces was apparently separated by visual glances between the two chess boards in the perceptual task. That is, pieces successively placed while a player looked at the board he was working on shared tactical structure, while the placement of pieces separated by a glance back at the model position did not have this relationship. It thus seemed to be the case that in the perceptual task, the players glanced at the board to encode a single meaningful "chunk" (Miller, 1956) of the board position into STM, an event which takes about 2 sec. Reconstruction of this chunk on the adjacent board can then be performed without hesitation between successive pieces. This chunking procedure was also used when attempting to recall the positions of the briefly exposed pieces from memory, resulting in the appearance of a 2 sec boundary between chunks. The advantage of the master player was in being able to include more pieces in the perceptual chunk, although there was evidence of his using a larger number of chunks as well. Yet this advantage did not represent a departure from the strategy used by all three players: perceptually grouping the overall board position into a sequence of tactically related sets of pieces.

The Chase and Simon study is a successful demonstration of the relation between knowledge and perception because the structure of the knowledge of interest, the rules of chess, can be adequately specified. This specification is much more difficult where the everyday perception of objects is concerned, although an interesting approach to this problem has been offered by Palmer (1975). The approach taken by Palmer is to develop a formal description of visual representation, and to investigate the relation between data- and conceptually driven processing within this description. Specifically, Palmer proposes that visual information is best characterized as a set of propositions, a proposition being defined as "an assertion about the relation between informational entities [p. 281]." Thus **color** would be a relation holding between an object or part of an object, and some values on the dimensions of hue, saturation, and brightness. Similarly, **part** relations hold between a square and its component lines and angles, where the latter possess some values of location, length, and angular size. Palmer claims this approach can be generalized to the representation of three-dimensional, real-world objects, in which parts of an object can be specified relative to a reference frame established by the whole object. The propositional representation of a human face, for example, would be a structural description including values of location, orientation, and size of subparts, such as eyes, specified in relation to the location, orientation, and size of the head. The processing which makes use of this propositional information would be data driven and conceptually driven at the same time. That is, the visual presence of global properties of an object, such as the size and orientation of the human head, would activate the entire structural description of a head, thus generating expectations for the additional presence of the subparts of the object. The final identification would depend on the consistence between the structural descriptions "activated" by sensory data, and the actual features "discovered" on the basis of the expectations deriving from the descriptions.

Although none of the paradigms discussed is both comprehensive and specific enough to account for visual identification, Lindsay and Norman's (1977) distinction between data driven and conceptually driven processing has provided a way of characterizing two aspects of identification that have traditionally been investigated independently. The type of data driven processing most frequently studied has been feature analysis, and the results of recognition tasks such as those devised by Egeth (1966) and Nickerson (1967) have suggested that both serial and parallel procedures may be involved in this analysis. Serial feature comparison is more closely associated with "different" decisions at all retention intervals, and with both "same" and "different" decisions at longer intervals. At shorter retention intervals, and after extensive practice, however, the parallel analysis of features may be possible (see also Shiffrin & Schneider, 1977). Yet the analysis of elementary units is also conceptually driven, guided by what the perceiver knows, as Reicher's (1969) results demonstrate. What remain to be developed are experiments which clarify how the organization of perceptual knowledge (e.g., Palmer, 1975) interfaces with the processing of features.

V. Hemispheric Differences in Encoding

Although information processing theory has not provided a complete account of the relations among the processing stages leading to visual identification, the experiments on visual encoding previously discussed demonstrate considerable agreement as to the types of concepts relevant to the development of this account. Our knowledge of the hemispheric differences involved in the complex processing sequence following stimulus presentation is more tentative, however. Most of the original studies of VF differences had assumed that these effects, like the cognitive deficits resulting from brain damage, were the expression of hemispheric specialization for dealing with distinct categories of stimuli. As Kimura and Durnford (1974) stated, "the verbal or nonverbal nature of the material is a ubiquitous factor in the occurrence of field differences [p. 27]." However, current approaches have been focused more often on the nature of the subjects' decisions than on just the category of the stimuli, and have involved the attempt to relate VF differences to the theoretical constructs devised by information processing researchers.

This approach, in turn, has been associated with an increase in the use of RT, rather than just accuracy, as a dependent measure of VF effects. Reaction time studies had been undertaken in the past primarily as a way of measuring the neural transmission times associated with various combinations of stimulus and response pathways (Poffenberger, 1912; Smith, 1947). The development of Donders' subtractive method by information processing theory (see Section II; Sternberg, 1969) meant that RT could also be used to investigate the VF differences associated with the different stages composing a single perceptual task. While the use of RT is accompanied by its own methodological problems (Pachella, 1974), this approach has begun to reveal some of the complex relations between hemispheric differences and visual identification in humans. Three types of results arising from this recent approach are relevant to the present discussion. First, research suggests that although the left and right hemispheres may, in general terms, be said to be specialized for verbal and spatial recognition, in the case of visual identification this specialization is more closely related to the encoding of stimuli than to their category membership. Second, what is usually described as verbal recognition includes a number of different functions, which may differ in the degree to which they are lateralized. Third, the hemispheric differences involved in a particular type of decision also depend on concurrent memory and attentional demands placed on the subject.

A. Categories versus Codes

Some of the first RT studies of hemispheric differences in visual processing were essentially extensions of conclusions previously based on identification accuracy. Rizzolatti et al. (1971), for example, found that opposite VF differences could be obtained for verbal and nonverbal stimuli in a visual discrimination task. Subjects in this experiment memorized either two faces or two letters belonging to a "positive" set; they responded manually only when a member of the positive set was presented, and not when other items appeared. Rizzolatti et al. found that responses to a series of single letters were more rapid for RVF presentation, presumably reflecting a left hemisphere dominance for verbal recognition. Faces were more rapidly identified when presented to the LVF–right hemisphere, however. The results of Geffen, Bradshaw, and Wallace (1971) were also consistent with the notion that verbal and nonverbal recognition is selectively carried out by the left and right hemispheres. In the first of five experiments reported, subjects memorized a single photograph of a face, and performed a series of yes–no discriminations of test faces presented unilaterally. Subjects in this paradigm also demonstrated a RT advantage to LVF stimuli, and this was true both of "same" and "different" decisions. Experiment 2 showed that no VF differences were present for the same task with vocal RT substituted for manual RT, suggesting that the right hemisphere processing advantage shown by Experiment 1 could be outweighted by the requirement to make a vocal response presumably controlled by the left hemisphere. Yet it also seemed to be the case that vocal responses that are identificatory are more subject to left hemisphere control than nonidentificatory ones. Experiment 3 showed that a vocal RT advantage to RVF presentation existed when subjects were required to name un-ilaterally presented digits; but no VF differences were present when a single response ("bonk") was given at the appearance of any digit (Ex-periment 4). Finally, a manual response was also shown to be associated with a RVF advantage when the decision depended upon the identity of a unilaterally presented digit (Experiment 5).

The above studies substantiated the assumption that RT measures of visual processing could be applied to questions of hemispheric speciali-zation, and also provided the first demonstrations of a right hemisphere superiority for the identification of nonverbal stimuli by normal subjects; Kimura's (1966, 1969) studies had involved judgments of the number and location of dots. Subsequent studies of RT have been successful in eliciting right hemisphere processing for decisions regarding line orien-tation (Atkinson & Egeth, 1973; Umiltà et al., 1974), curvature (Longden, Ellis, & Iverson, 1976), and randomly shaped polygons (Hellige, 1975, Experiment 2). Two reports appearing in 1972, however, provided some of the initial reasons for developing "encoding" accounts of hemispheric specialization for the recognition of verbal and spatial items. Cohen (1972) noted that the experimenter's classification of stimuli as verbal or nonverbal may not accurately represent the strategies actually used by subjects in performing an identification. In order to examine verbal and spatial processing independently of stimulus type, Cohen employed the Posner task (see Section IV, B), in which comparisons for a single type of stimulus (e.g., letters) can be made either on the basis of name identity (e.g., A–a) or physical identity (e.g., A–A). As discussed earlier, the possibility of using an analog process gives an approximately 70 msec edge to decisions involving the physically identical items. On each trial of Cohen's study, subjects decided whether or not two unilaterally pre-sented letters possessed the same name; the letters always appeared simultaneously and in the same VF. Cohen found that RVF presentation was associated with a smaller RT difference between name and physical identity trials than was LVF presentation. That is, a significant RVF advantage for the name-match trials, combined with a LVF advantage for the physically identical (i.e., analog) pairs, led to a relatively smaller Posner effect for RVF presentation. Since all the decisions referred to verbal stimuli, Cohen proposed that the VF effects obtained would be best described in terms of hemispheric specialization for verbal and spatial processing rather than for different types of stimuli. A similar pattern of results was obtained by Geffen et al. (1972). These authors also used a Posner paradigm with unilateral presentation, although they additionally investigated the effect of presenting the name and analog matches in separate blocks of trials. Like Cohen, they found that name matches were associated with a RVF advantage, and analog matches with a LVF advantage. This pattern was constant over different blocks of trials in which the "same" pairs were either just analog matches, just name matches, or a randomized mixture of the two. In fact, the LVF advantage for the analog matches was slightly greater when analog and name matches were randomized within the same block. The pattern was also constant across conditions in which the pairs were presented to each VF in either a blocked or randomized manner. Since giving subjects advance knowledge about either the type or the location of the stimuli did not alter the pattern of VF effects, biases resulting from subjects' expectancies (Kinsbourne, 1970, 1973) could not be responsible for the results. As do Cohen's results, the Geffen et al. findings suggest that hemispheric differences in visual identification are determined to a greater extent by whether an internal representation is encoded into a relatively verbal or spatial format, than by the nature of the presented stimuli. This is the type of conclusion that raises more questions than it answers, however; the challenge is to determine more precisely what is entailed by the concepts of verbal and spatial encoding and how this contributes to subjects' decisions in different perceptual situations.

B. Right Hemisphere Verbal Processing

An important implication of the Cohen (1972) and Geffen et al. (1972) results is that the right hemisphere may make some contribution to verbal recognition, even if only at the analog level. In fact, evidence from a variety of sources, recently reviewed by Searleman (1977), has long pointed to the conclusion that the right hemisphere is capable of at least some of the many different skills composing linguistic function. For example, right-handed patients who become aphasic following damage to the left hemisphere have on occasion recovered some measure of speech function. When such a patient subsequently becomes aphasic following right hemispheric damage, the conclusion must be that the right hemisphere had developed the compensatory linguistic function

(Nielsen, 1946). Similarly, Kinsbourne (1971) has reported that in two right-handed patients who had become aphasic as a result of left hemisphere damage, subsequent amytal testing revealed that the right hemisphere was responsible for the aphasic speech. Even the commissurotomy patients, from whom so much of our current knowledge of hemispheric specialization is derived, have demonstrated some right hemisphere linguistic ability (Nebes, 1978). Although the level of this ability is clearly inferior to that of the left hemisphere (Zaidel, 1976), some syntactic and semantic comprehension is certainly involved. A commissurotomy patient may be successful at selecting a magnifying glass with the left hand (i.e., right hemisphere), among other objects hidden from view, in response to instructions to find find the object that "makes things look bigger" (Nebes & Sperry, 1971). The right hemisphere of the commissurotomy patient is not adept at the phonological recoding required for judging whether the names of two visually presented objects rhyme, however (Levy, Trevarthen, & Sperry, 1972), or at controlling the vocal musculature for speech production. These are the types of findings which have led Moscovitch (1973) to contrast "strict localization" with "split-brain" models of cerebral dominance for language in normal individuals. That is, in the vast majority of cases aphasia in right-handers results from a left-sided lesion, and this fact has been responsible for many researchers assuming that verbal functions are localized strictly in the left hemisphere. Studies of the commissurotomy patients, on the other hand, are more consistent with the notion that speech, or at least speech comprehension, is represented by both hemispheres, though more strongly by the left. Reaction time studies of VF differences in normal individuals can help decide between these alternatives, claims Moscovitch, since if the right hemisphere in the normal brain plays any significant role in a particular tachistoscopic task, then an interaction between VF of presentation and responding hand should appear. Each hemisphere controls the fine motor movement of the contralateral hand; for tasks such as simple visual detection, RT is faster for the VF that is ipsilateral to the responding hand, and thus contralateral to the responding hemisphere (Bradshaw & Perriment, 1970; Berlucchi, Heron, Hyman, Rizzolatti, & Umiltà, 1971). If the right hemisphere is involved in a verbal task, its more direct involvement in the LVF–left hand pathway would serve to offset the left hemisphere advantage in processing speed, when the left hand was responding, leading to a smaller RVF advantage. If verbal functions were strictly left hemisphere events, however, advantages to RVF presentation should be constant over response hand. That is, according to the strict localization model, information presented to the LVF–right hemisphere will be at a perceptual disadvantage, even when the left hand responds, since with a LVF presentation two callosal relays are necessary: the first when visual information arriving in the right hemisphere from the LVF is relayed to the left hemisphere for processing, the second when the proper response is relayed back to the right hemisphere for execution by the left hand. Right field information, of course, only requires the second type of transfer in this situation, and no transfer at all when the right hand responds, with the result that RT would be relatively faster to RVF presentation when either hand was responding. A version of the split-brain model, however, proposes that if the right hemisphere alone can identify the LVF stimulus and direct the left hand response, then the size of the field difference will be determined solely by the amount of time by which right hemisphere identification exceeds the time needed for the left hemisphere to reach a decision about RVF stimuli and to transfer the decision across the callosum for the left hand response. When the right hand is responding, however, a RVF advantage will be more apparent, since to the relatively longer right hemisphere identification time will be added the time necessary to transfer the right hemisphere decision across the callosum for a right hand response. Moscovitch (1973) gives a comprehensive explanation of this rationale; the important point for the present discussion is that the strict localization theory predicts a RT advantage for the RVF that is independent of response hand, while the split-brain model predicts a VF by response hand interaction.

Moscovitch (1973) attempted to distinguish the two models of hemispheric specialization discussed in these studies, by auditorily presenting subjects with a single letter of the alphabet, followed after 2 sec by a single probe letter presented visually to one VF for a same–different judgment. A significant RT advantage for LVF presentation was present in this task for subjects responding with their left hands, although only for the "same" judgments; a group of subjects responding with their right hands exhibited a slight RVF advantage for the "same" trials. Whereas both the left and right hemispheres could apparently match the visual to the auditory letter (i.e., the VF differences present depended on the response hand being used), the nature of the right hemisphere contribution to this verbal task is still unclear. The "same" decision could be reached on the basis of an analog match between the test letter and visual representation of the auditory letter, as well as on the basis of a name match. Moscovitch pursued this possibility in a second experiment by increasing the number of auditory letters to six, making it unlikely that subjects could develop a visual representation for all of the letters in the memory set. A RVF advantage for "same" decisions of the test letter, independent of response hand, appeared in this experiment, suggesting that the LVF effect obtained in the earlier study was the product of a visual matching strategy. These findings were replicated in a third study in which the same subjects were tested in both the one and six letter memory set conditions. It thus seemed that the strict localization model was a more accurate description of normal hemispheric function than the split-brain model. The right hemisphere participation in this verbal task was either limited to the phonemic analysis of a single letter, or to a strategy based on visual matching.

In a more recent attempt to distinguish the strict localization and split-brain models experimentally, Moscovitch (1976, Experiment 1) used the same paradigm as previously, but divided the "different" trials of the single memory-letter condition between visually similar pairs (e.g., E–F) and acoustically similar pairs (e.g., E–D). The rationale here was that if the right hemisphere were forming an analog representation to which it matched the probe, it would have greater difficulty with visually similar letters than with acoustically similar letters. For the "same" RTs, a significant VF by response hand interaction appeared, confirming the previous finding that either hemisphere could perform this type of single letter comparison. Decisions regarding the "different" trials were significantly longer for visually similar pairs, and this effect did not interact with VF or response hand. Thus both hemispheres seemed to be using a visual representation to compare to the probe and arrive at a decision; the question remained whether the identification of the auditorily presented memory letter and the generation of its visual representation were performed just by the left, or by both hemispheres. In a second experiment, Moscovitch simultaneously presented the auditory and visual letters to be compared, reasoning that if the right hemisphere does linguistically identify the auditory letter, the effect of acoustic similarity should be accentuated in this situation, in which the trace of the acoustic stimulus does not have time to fade before the appearance of the visual test letter. Under these conditions, a significant VF by similarity interaction appeared, with the difference between the acoustically and visually similar pairs being larger for LVF presentation, regardless of response hand. That is, the right hemisphere's use of a visual representation selectively increased the RT to visually similar pairs, but apparently only the left hemisphere is responsible for translating the auditory letter into this representation, and thus **both** visual and acoustic similarity will influence RVF recognition. This strict localization account was also supported by the results of a third experiment, in which subjects were instructed to respond "same" to auditory–visual letter pairs (separated by a 2 sec interval) that ended with the same vowel sound (e.g., B–G). When this type of phonemic analysis was required, subjects demonstrated a significant RVF advantage for the end-alike pairs, independently of response hand.

In all of his experiments, Moscovitch found that a strict localization theory of cerebral dominance for language provides a more accurate description of the results than does the split-brain model. Yet this localization model is still a much more sophisticated approach than that developed from the original studies of VF differences. In Moscovitch's studies, the aspect of language that is considered to be localized is the encoding of letters along a phonological dimension, the type of analysis necessary for deciding whether a visual and auditory letter are identical, or end in the same sound. This is a different type of operation than that studied by Cohen (1972) and Geffen et al. (1972), who obtained RVF–left hemisphere advantages for decisions regarding whether different case letters possessed the same name. Yet in each instance, the hemispheric differences involved depended upon the way in which the stimuli were encoded rather than on the presence of verbal items alone. In addition, Moscovitch's (1976) investigations of visual similarity showed that both hemispheres can analyze the visual features of the test items, even though the items themselves are verbal in nature. Besides the ability to make an analog match, however, the right hemisphere of normal individuals did not seem to possess the linguistic abilities which would have been expected on the basis of the earlier split-brain patients. In an attempt to reconcile these differences, Moscovitch (1973, 1976) described a "functional localization" model of cerebral dominance for language, in which he claims that the right hemisphere of normal persons does possess the linguistic competence demonstrated by the commissurotomy patients, but that this competence is inhibited or suppressed by the dominant left hemisphere which controls speech production. This is a model that accounts for both the normal and split-brain data, since the inhibition of the verbal functions of the right hemisphere by the left would be removed once the interhemispheric pathways were severed (cf. Selnes, 1976). This model can also incorporate phenomena which contradict a strict localization model, such as the preservation of language comprehension and some speech production after the removal of the dominant hemisphere during adulthood (Smith, 1966).

Evidence has appeared recently, though, which suggests that right hemisphere involvement in linguistic tasks can be demonstrated for normal individuals, although the presentation of words rather than letters may be critical. Ellis and Shepherd (1974) noted that VF differences in the accuracy of identifying bilateral pairs of nouns depended upon whether the words were concrete or abstract. Specifically, they found that concrete nouns were more accurately reported than the abstract nouns for LVF presentation, but that recognition was equivalent for the two types of items for RVF presentation. In other words, the RVF recognition advantage was larger for abstract than for concrete items. Hines (1976) also reported that a RVF advantage in identification accuracy was larger for abstract than for concrete nouns, although this was only true for "familiar" nouns, those with a relatively high frequency of occurrence. Orenstein and Meighan (1976) were not able to replicate Ellis and Shepherd's findings, however, and even obtained LVF report advantages for both types of nouns. Hines (1977) has recently replicated the larger RVF advantage for abstract nouns, and in this study did not obtain an interaction with word frequency. There is obviously considerable variability associated with these data, yet they are potentially important, since they suggest that in normal individuals the right hemisphere is not limited to the pictorial matching strategy of Moscovitch's experiments, but instead, has access to the storage of "concrete" lexical items. In order to investigate this possibility, Day (1977) performed a series of three RT experiments which applied Moscovitch's methodological rationale to the question raised by Ellis and Shepherd. In the first experiment, Day used unilateral presentation, and on each trial subjects were shown a vertically oriented lexical item which could either be a concrete noun, an abstract noun, or a pronounceable nonword. The task was to decide as rapidly as possible whether each lexical string was an acceptable English word and to respond only when a word had actually been presented. In this task, subjects demonstrated a significant RT advantage to abstract words appearing in the RVF, regardless of responding hand, and no VF or hand effect for concrete words. In line with the Ellis and Shepherd findings, then, this experiment showed that concrete nouns could be accessed equally efficiently from either hemisphere, but that abstract nouns were retrieved more efficiently from the left hemisphere. Day then questioned whether the right hemisphere had access to some semantic relations among the words it apparently "knows." Gross (1972, Experiment 1) had previously found that the speed of decisions regarding category membership for concrete nouns was associated with a RVF advantage that was constant over response hand. Her stimuli were horizontally oriented word pairs presented unilaterally, however, and thus scanning biases favoring the RVF cannot be ruled out. In Day's second experiment, a single word, always a category name, was presented to the central VF, followed after 1 sec by a vertically oriented word in the LVF or RVF. In this situation, subjects responded whenever the second word was a member of the category named by the first item. For categories of abstract words, a RVF RT advantage, independent of response hand, was again present. Similarly, for concrete categories, no VF or hand effects were evident, suggesting that both hemispheres are able to recognize this type of verbal association. The possibility remained, though, that the right hempshere's lexical memory was activated not as a direct result of the presentation of the category name, but rather by left hemisphere processing occurring during the retention interval. In a third experiment, Day tested this explanation by presenting the category name and instance simultaneously. The results of Experiment 2 were still obtained, however: a RVF advantage for the abstract categories, independent of hand, and no VF differences for the concrete categories. The lexical memory of the right hemisphere apparently contributing to decisions regarding membership in the concrete categories could thus not be attributed to a left hemisphere function.

Day's findings suggest that when meaningful stimuli are used, the split-brain model of cerebral dominance for language in normal individuals is a more accurate account than the functional localization model. Day also notes that the development of the functional localization model may not even have been necessary. Moscovitch (1973, 1976) proposed the model in order to reconcile the fact that the commissurotomy patients' ability to recognize words presented to the right hemisphere contrasts markedly with normal individuals' inability to use phonemic information presented to the LVF. Yet this approach assumes that the use of the meaning of words must be based on an earlier analysis of their phonological features, and this assumption may not be warranted (Baron, 1973). In addition, even the right hemispheres of the commissurotomy patients were not successful at decisions requiring the use of the specifically phonological aspects of stimuli, such as judging whether the names of two objects rhymed (Levy et al., 1972). When one thus uses meaningful words, rather than individual letters, as stimuli, the linguistic competence of the normal right hemisphere is more apparent. What Day's experiments do not explain, though, is why the right hemisphere should be competent at decisions about whether a particular concrete noun is an instance of a certain category, but relatively inefficient at deciding whether "A" and "a" belong to the same category (Cohen, 1972; Geffen et al., 1972). Is the type of decision different, or is perhaps the use of lexical strings critical? Hopefully, this question will be resolved once that more is known about the **functional** differences between stimuli that are related to hemispheric effects. While demonstrating differences that depend on the rated concreteness of nouns is a good beginning, how the subjects are making use of this dimension of concreteness is still an open question. The presence of some form of pictorial strategy associated with the recognition of concrete nouns is the most obvious possibility, although Day does not speculate along these lines. However these questions are resolved, our accounts of hemispheric specialization have been improved by the above experiments. It is not only the encoding of visually presented items into a verbal representation, but also the type of verbal representation (i.e., phonemic versus lexical; concrete versus abstract) which are critical variables. Yet the type of processing involved in even the relatively simple perceptual decisions discussed above probably contains a number of other factors contributing to hemispheric differences. For example, research also has been directed at how retention, the amount of information retained, and subjects' recognition strategies influence visual laterality patterns.

C. Memory, Activation, and Strategy

Although the results of the previously discussed studies were interpreted in terms of hemispheric differences in perception, the subjects' task often involved some demand upon memory. In the Rizzolatti et al. (1971) and Geffen et al. (1971) experiments, for example, subjects memorized the set of positive stimuli before beginning the experiment, so that on each trial a same–different comparison involved a presented stimulus and an item from LTM. Given the close relationship between memory and perceptual variables in information processing tasks it would be expected that retention does contribute to VF effects, and in fact this is the case. The Moscovitch et al. (1976) studies discussed earlier (Section III), in which a consistent RT advantage to LVF presentation of faces was only obtained after the iconic trace of the stimuli had been disrupted, imply that right hemispheric processing is more closely associated with the later stages of the recognition of nonverbal events. A related finding is that of Dee and Fontenot (1973) who presented subjects with 12 point Vanderplas polygons unilaterally; after 0, 5, 10, or 20 sec a response card was shown, from which the target was to be chosen. In addition, half of the subjects performed an "interfering" task during the retention interval, attempting to remember a series of briefly presented polygons, while for half the subjects the interval was unfilled. Dee and Fontenot found that significant LVF advantages were present in identifying the unilateral targets at the 10 and 20 sec retention intervals, but not at the shorter delays, suggesting that the retention of the nonverbal material, rather than identification per se, is an important component of recognition accuracy advantages for right hemisphere presentation. The authors report that no significant differences between the interference groups emerged, but since it was not mentioned whether recall for the interfering polygons was actually tested, it is possible that the subjects were not attending to these stimuli.

Visual field differences for verbal material are also influenced by retention. Hines and his associates (Hines, Satz, Schell, & Schmidlin, 1969; Hines & Satz, 1971; Hines, Satz, & Clementino, 1973) have reported that when a series of bilateral pairs of letters or digits are presented on each trial, RVF advantages in the accuracy of report are greater for the earlier serial positions, those more remote in time and subject to interference from following items. Hannay and Malone (1976) investigated the retention of nonsense trigrams in a paradigm similar to that of Dee and Fontenot (1973). On each trial a vertically oriented nonsense trigram was presented unilaterally, and after an unfilled interval of 0, 5, or 10 sec, subjects attempted to identify the target item on a response card. Significant recognition advantages for trigrams presented to the RVF were associated with the 5 and 10 sec delays, but not with the zero delay, again implicating the role of memory in VF differences. This interaction was present only for the male subjects, however; female subjects did not demonstrate any significant VF differences. In addition, the main effect of delay was not significant, suggesting that the decrease in recognition accuracy that did occur over the retention interval was relatively slight. Like studies of verbal encoding, experiments demonstrating the influence of retention on VF differences have helped revise our theories of hemispheric specialization. Yet just as more information needs to be obtained about the **types** of encoding contributing to VF effects, the ways in which such retention-related variables as interference, rehearsal, and recall–recognition differences are related to VF effects still need to be determined.

A recent investigation by Hellige and Cox (1976, Experiment 1) has clarified the way in which different types of retention demands and hemispheric specialization interact in determining VF differences. Hellige and Cox employed a form recognition task in which a randomly shaped polygon was presented unilaterally on each trial; subjects then attempted to choose the target from five alternatives on a response card. Without any additional memory load, accuracy was significantly higher for forms presented to the LVF. For subjects required to remember either two or four nouns on each form recognition trial, however, recognition of RVF forms improved, and a significant RVF advantage appeared. That is, the concurrent verbal memory load selectively activated the left hemisphere sufficiently to shift the recognition advantage away from the right hemisphere. The authors noted that their results support Kinsbourne's (1970, 1973) proposal that VF differences are the result of shifts in perceptual orientation. The pattern of selective activation obtained by Hellige and Cox differs from Kinsbourne's conception of attention, though, since there was no significant effect of memory load on the LVF trials, and such an effect would be expected from a change in just the distribution of attention. That is, if attention were being shifted rightward due to left hemisphere activation, the improvement in RVF performance would be associated with a decline in the identification of LVF items. In addition, a different result was obtained when subjects were given a concurrent load of six nouns. In this situation, performance on the RVF trials declined markedly, producing a LVF advantage. As the authors mention, this apparent overloading of the left hemisphere by a concurrent verbal retention task would not be predicted from the concept of perceptual orientation alone. The same concurrent task can provide either activation or interference depending on the level of difficulty imposed. Hellige and Cox proposed instead that VF differences in experimental tasks represent the interaction of such factors as selective interference and perceptual orientation with hemispheric specialization for verbal and spatial processing.

A perceptual orientation theory might reply to Hellige and Cox's account of VF differences by noting that hemispheric specialization for the perceptual aspects of their task may be minimal, since presenting a series of form-recognition trials would be expected to selectively activate the right hemisphere, thus biasing attention to the LVF. However, Hellige and Cox obtained slightly different laterality patterns, in the absence of a concurrent verbal memory load, for forms of different levels of complexity, and this argues against a purely orientational explanation. Specifically, they obtained a slightly larger LVF advantage for 12-point forms than for 16-point forms, even though these stimuli were distributed randomly in the trial sequence: In addition, the effect of memory load was equivalent for the two types of forms, suggesting that the effect of stimulus complexity was independent of that of activation. What the difference in form complexity does represent is difficult to determine. Even though the forms were equated for overall verbal association value, Hellige and Cox note that more verbal associations to "specific objects or situations" were given to the 16-point forms. There may thus be a difference in verbal codability for the two types of forms, independent of hemispheric activation, which leads to a reduced right hemisphere advantage for the 16-point forms. Hellige (1978) has also demonstrated that the effects of stimulus complexity are independent of activation in form recognition. In the first experiment reported, Hellige found that in the recognition of a randomly mixed series of 12-point and 16-point polygons, a LVF advantage was only associated with the 12-point forms. For a group of subjects whose form recognition trials were interspersed with a series of word-recognition trials, though, the only VF difference was a RVF effect for the 16-point forms. That is, the presence of word-recognition trials shifted the form-recognition laterality pattern in the direction of a RVF–left hemisphere advantage. Again, the degree of this shift was equivalent for the two types of forms, independent of their differences in the pure form list. This effect of the word recognition trials presumably reflects left hemisphere activation, and in fact, Hellige (Experiment 3) found that adding a two-noun concurrent memory load also altered the laterality pattern for a pure list of forms in the same manner as Experiment 1. However, adding both a series of word recognition trials and a two-noun memory load did not shift the pattern of VF differences to a greater extent than did either of these variables individually (Experiment 4). Thus, while selective activation of the left hemisphere does have a consistent effect on form recognition, a complete theory of VF differences must also include a description of the hemispheric specialization responsible for the independent effects of form complexity.

As was the case with Day's (1977) studies of different laterality patterns for concrete versus abstract nouns, the type of encoding leading to the differences between Hellige's 12-point and 16-point forms is still undefined. While Hellige (1978) claims that the effect of form complexity represents "stimulus codability," the support for this claim primarily comes from Hellige and Cox's (1976) finding that subjects gave slightly more specific object associations to the 16-point stimuli. This finding is consistent with the results of Clark (1965) and Kelly and Martin (1974), who found that subjects were more likely to verbally code complex forms than simple forms during a recognition task. Fontenot (1973), however, found that Vanderplas polygons which were either high or low in verbal association value did not produce different visual laterality patterns. Fontenot also discussed codability, in terms of the ease with which a verbal label could be ascribed to a given shape, and claimed that his more complex (12-point) forms were less codable, in this sense, than his less complex (6-point) forms (i.e., the more complex shapes require a longer verbal description). From Fontenot's perspective, Hellige's 16-point forms should be **less** verbally codable than the 12-point forms, and thus show a relatively greater LVF recognition advantage, which is not what Hellige has found. It is possible that subjects are using a different type of visual recognition strategy, rather than using a difference in verbal coding, in their identification of these two types of forms. As noted earlier (Section IV, C), two fundamental types of data driven processing are the serial and parallel analyses of features. Since the 16-point forms are relatively more complex, they may require a serial, feature–by–feature, encoding or comparison with the test items more often than the 12-point forms.

Some evidence has appeared suggesting that serial and parallel analyses are characteristic processing strategies of the left and right hemispheres, respectively, although such evidence is not consistent across different types of stimuli and tasks, and should be interpreted extremely cautiously. Cohen (1973, Experiment 1) presented clusters of 2, 3, or 4 letters unilaterally, in which the letters were either all the same or one differed. "Same" RT increased with set size for RVF but not for LVF presentation, suggesting that serial processing was being carried out by the left hemisphere. Cohen also presented clusters of typographical characters (i.e., [, <,), and /), rather than letters (Experiment 2), and found that there was no consistent increase of RT with set size for the "same" decisions in either VF, even though an overall RVF advantage was present. When the letters and symbols were intermixed in a series of trials (Experiment 3) an increase in "same" RT was again restricted to the letters presented to the RVF. It appears that although serial processing is associated with left hemisphere presentation, it is also restricted to verbal stimuli. It is difficult to draw unequivocal conclusions from Cohen's data, though, since in the first experiment "same" RT to the letters was fairly constant over set size for LVF presentation, suggesting parallel processing, while the comparable condition in the third experiment yielded RTs which decreased significantly with an increase in set size. In addition, as Cohen mentions, "same" responses were always made with the right hand, thus giving RVF items a response advantage. A different pattern of results was obtained by Gross (1972, Experiment 2), whose subjects decided whether two unilaterally presented 16-cell matrices (containing three blackened cells) were the same or different. In this task a significant LVF RT advantage was present, which was independent both of decision type and hand of response. Gross also found that "different" RTs decreased as the number of blackened cells "out of register" increased, the same result that Egeth (1966) and Nickerson (1967) felt reflected a serial comparison. This RT function in Gross's experiment was linear for both LVF and RVF matrices; the rate of decrease was also similar, the LVF advantage being constant over the number of differing cells. In other words, both hemispheres could be characterized as employing a serial strategy in this task, although the right hemisphere was relatively more efficient in developing the spatial representations required. Patterson and Bradshaw (1975) suggested that it is only in tasks of a certain level of difficulty that the "serial–analytic" processing advantage of the left hemisphere is evident. These authors found that in same–different comparisons of sequentially presented pairs of schematic faces, there was a RT advantage to the LVF faces when the task was relatively easy; "same" pairs always being identical, and "different" pairs always differing in three features. This result held when there was a 1 sec interval between the items of a pair, as well as when a single "target" face was memorized for a block of 64 trials; the LVF advantage was more consistent across paradigms for the "same" decisions, however. In a more difficult task, in which the targets were again memorized, but "different" test faces were only distinguishable by **one** feature, a RVF advantage for both decision types was evident. This shift from a right to a left hemisphere advantage as more features of a pattern must be consulted in reaching a decision is consistent with Hellige's finding of a smaller LVF advantage for more complex polygons. Yet even here there are conflicting results: Bradshaw, Gates, and Patterson (1976, Experiment 3) could not replicate the Patterson and Bradshaw (1975) findings using a different type of stimuli; Moscovitch *et al.* (1976, Experiment 5) suggest that the use of "higher order pictorial features," even when the task is difficult (as in comparing a caricature with a photograph) is an important aspect of right hemisphere processing. It is thus apparent that no single difference in visual processing strategy, at least as currently conceived, can invariably characterize hemispheric differences. While serial and parallel strategies are almost certainly related to hemispheric effects, it will be difficult to make any more precise statements about this relationship until more information is acquired about how the hemispheric interaction with these strategies may change as a function of such variables as the type of stimuli subjects are given, whether immediate or delayed recognition is involved, and the level of performance reached through practice.

VI. Conclusions

The experiments reviewed in this chapter provide substantial evidence that hemispheric differences in normal subjects can be investigated within the context of contemporary perceptual theory, although as Cohen (1975) has cautioned, "Clinical observations and experimental results suggest that where hemispheric specialization does exist, it is not absolute, not constant, and not simple [p. 366]." This caution is necessary in interpreting investigations of hemispheric differences, since the nature of these differences must be inferred from the subject's performance with material presented to the left and right visual fields. The inference itself is reasonable, since procedures for monitoring subjects' fixation, LVF advantages for nonverbal recognition, and the demonstrated relationship between handedness and VF differences, rule out scanning tendencies as the sole determinant of VF effects. In addition, the recommendation of Moscovitch (1973), that VF differences be assessed in relation to the effects of response hand, allows hemispheric effects to be distinguished from a more peripheral advantage of the VF ipsilateral to the responding hand. Yet the interpretation of these effects must also take into account the host of interrelated task- and subject-specific variables contributing to observed performance. It is apparent that no single theory of VF differences currently includes all of these relevant variables. The strength of the information processing approach, however, is its concern with the isolation of the series of stages composing perceptual identification, and the use of information processing concepts in tachistoscopic research promises at least to make available a more complete theory of VF differences. For example, the assumption that visual processing is extended over time was associated with investigations of the concept of iconic storage, the earliest stage of visual recognition. The use of partial-report and backward-masking techniques in VF experiments has led to the demonstration of a fairly consistent left hemisphere advantage in the processing of verbal material in iconic memory, although contradictory results have appeared for the iconic recognition of nonverbal stimuli. The information processing notion that visual events are endoded into a relatively visual or verbal internal representation has also influenced theories of VF effects. While it was initially assumed that VF differences represented hemispheric specialization for the recognition of verbal and nonverbal stimuli, VF researchers are currently paying more attention to the coding strategies of subjects than to the category of the experimental stimuli. One result of this change in perspective is that better accounts are becoming available of the specific forms of verbal processing contributed by the normal right hemisphere. Finally, the interdependence between perceptual and memory variables in information processing tasks has led to VF theories which include information about the effects of these different types of retention demands. The presence of a brief retention interval between presentation and recognition or report has been found to increase VF differences in accuracy for both verbal and nonverbal material; the presence of a concurrent verbal memory task, however, can either increase or decrease a LVF advantage in form recognition, depending on the number of items retained.

In spite of the assistance that information processing concepts have provided in the interpretation of VF differences, there is a danger that the stimulus–category dichotomy previously employed to describe these differences can reappear as a "processing" dichotomy. That is, the assumption that the left and right hemispheres are specialized for the recognition of verbal and nonverbal material has a tendency to persist under the guise of alleged processing dichotomies such as "analytic–holistic" or "serial–parallel." These processing strategies do represent different types of identification procedures, and are relevant concepts in interpreting VF differences. Yet the difference between serial and parallel processing in any experiment is rarely absolute, but is relative to the type of decision being made, the retention interval involved, and other variables. In using information processing concepts to characterize hemispheric specialization, therefore, it will be necessary to work with sets of closely related concepts rather than just individual dichotomies. In addition, different types of feature analysis have been traditionally discussed only as data driven forms of processing. As more information is acquired about the ways in which conceptually driven and data driven processing interact, theories of hemispheric specialization will also need revision. Our accounts of hemispheric differences will thus be likely to increase in complexity as a result of the experiments reviewed here, yet so will our theories of visual perception, and in each case we believe they will become more accurate as well.

Acknowledgments

Preparation of this chapter was supported by NIH Training Grant No. AG00029 from the National Institute on Aging and by NINDS Grant No. 06233. We are grateful to Thomas Natsoulas for his helpful comments on earlier versions of the manuscript.

Bibliography

Atkinson, J., & Egeth, H. Right hemisphere superiority in visual orientation matching. *Canadian Journal of Psychology*, 1973, *27*, 152–158.

Atkinson, R. C., & Shiffrin, R. M. Human memory: A proposed system and its control processes. In K. W. Spence & J. T. Spence (Eds.), *The psychology of learning and motivation* (Vol. 2). New York: Academic Press, 1968.

Averbach, E., & Coriell, A. S. Short-term memory in vision. *Bell System Technical Journal*, 1961, *40*, 309–328.

Bamber, D. Reaction time and error rates for "same–different" judgments of multidimensional stimuli. *Perception & Psychophysics*, 1969, *6*, 169–174.

Baron, J. Phonemic stage not necessary for reading. *Quarterly Journal of Experimental Psychology*, 1973, *25*, 241–246.

Barton, M. I., Goodglass, H., & Shai, A. Differential recognition of tachistoscopically presented English and Hebrew words in right and left visual fields. *Perceptual and Motor Skills*, 1965, *21*, 431–437.

Benton, A. L. Disorders of spatial orientation. In P. J. Vinken & G. W. Bruyn (Eds.), *Handbook of clinical neurology* (Vol. 3): *Disorders of higher nervous activity.* Amsterdam: North-Holland Publishing Company, 1969.

Berlucchi, G., Brizzolara, D., Marzi, C., Rizzolatti, G., & Umiltà, C. Can lateral asymmetries in attention explain interfield differences in visual perception? *Cortex,* 1974, *10,* 177–185.

Berlucchi, G., Heron, W., Hyman, R., Rizzolatti, G., & Umiltà, C. Simple reaction times of ipsilateral and contralateral hand to lateralized visual stimuli. *Brain,* 1971, *94,* 419–430.

Bogen, J. E. The other side of the brain. II: An appositional mind. *Bulletin of the Los Angeles Neurological Societies,* 1969, *34,* 135–162.

Bradshaw, J. L., Gates, A., & Patterson, K. Hemispheric differences in processing visual patterns. *Quarterly Journal of Experimental Psychology,* 1976, *28,* 667–681.

Bradshaw, J. L., & Perriment, A. D. Laterality effects and choice reaction time in a unimanual two-finger task. *Perception & Psychophysics,* 1970, *7,* 185–188.

Bradshaw, J. L., & Wallace, G. Models for the processing and identification of faces. *Perception & Psychophysics,* 1971, *9,* 443–448.

Broadbent, D. E. The role of auditory localization and attention in memory span. *Journal of Experimental Psychology,* 1954, *47,* 191–196.

Broadbent, D. E. *Perception and communication.* New York: Pergamon, 1958.

Bryden, M. P. Tachistoscopic recognition of nonalphabetic material. *Canadian Journal of Psychology,* 1960, *14,* 78–86.

Bryden, M. P. Tachistoscopic recognition, handedness, and cerebral dominance. *Neuropsychologia,* 1965, *3,* 1–8.

Bryden, M. P. Left–right differences in tachistoscopic recognition: Directional scanning or cerebral dominance? *Perceptual and Motor Skills,* 1966, *23,* 1127–1134.

Bryden, M. P. Left–right differences in tachistoscopic recognition as a function of familiarity and pattern orientation. *Journal of Experimental Psychology,* 1970, *84,* 120–122.

Bryden, M. P. Response bias and hemispheric differences in dot localization. *Perception & Psychophysics,* 1976, *19,* 23–28.

Bryden, M. P., & Rainey, C. A. Left–right differences in tachistoscopic recognition. *Journal of Experimental Psychology,* 1963, *66,* 568–571.

Carmon, A. Nachshon, I., Isseroff, A., & Kleiner, M. Visual field differences in reaction times to Hebrew letters. *Psychonomic Science,* 1972, *28,* 222–224.

Chase, W. G., & Simon, H. A. Perception in chess. *Cognitive Psychology,* 1973, *4,* 55–81.

Cherry, E. C. Some experiments on the recognition of speech, with one and with two ears. *Journal of the Acoustical Society of America,* 1953, *25,* 975–979.

Clark, H. J. Recognition memory for random shapes as a function of complexity, association value, and delay. *Journal of Experimental Psychology,* 1965, *69,* 590–595.

Clark, S. E. Retrieval of color information from the preperceptual storage system. *Journal of Experimental Psychology,* 1969, *82,* 263–266.

Cohen, G. Hemispheric differences in a letter classification task. *Perception & Psychophysics,* 1972, *11,* 139–142.

Cohen, G. Hemispheric differences in serial versus parallel processing. *Journal of Experimental Psychology,* 1973, *97,* 349–356.

Cohen, G. Hemispheric differences in the effects of cuing in visual recognition tasks. *Journal of Experimental Psychology: Human Perception and Performance,* 1975, *1,* 366–373.

Cohen, G. Components of the laterality effect in letter recognition: Asymmetries in iconic storage. *Quarterly Journal of Experimental Psychology,* 1976, *28,* 105–114.

Coltheart, M. Visual information-processing. In P. C. Dodwell (Ed.), *New horizons in psychology* (Vol. 2). Baltimore: Penguin, 1972.

Cooper, L. A. Mental rotation of random two-dimensional shapes. *Cognitive Psychology,* 1975, *7,* 20–43.

Cooper, L. A., & Shepard, R. N. Chronometric studies of the rotation of mental images. In W. G. Chase (Ed.), *Visual information processing.* New York: Academic Press, 1973.

Corcoran, D. W. J. *Pattern recognition.* Baltimore: Penguin, 1971.

Craik, F. I. M., & Lockhart, R. S. Levels of processing: A framework for memory research. *Journal of Verbal Learning and Verbal Behavior,* 1972, *11,* 671–684.

Crosby, E. C. Relations of brain centers to normal and abnormal eye movements in the horizontal plane. *Journal of Comparative Neurology,* 1953, *99,* 437–479.

Crosland, H. R. Letter-position effects, in the range of attention experiment, as affected by the number of letters in each exposure. *Journal of Experimental Psychology,* 1931, *14,* 477–507.

Day, J. Right-hemisphere language processing in normal right-handers. *Journal of Experimental Psychology: Human Perception and Performance,* 1977, *3,* 518–528.

de Groot, A. D. *Thought and choice in chess.* The Hague: Mouton, 1965.

Dee, H. L., & Fontenot, D. J. Cerebral dominance and lateral differences in perception and memory. *Neuropsychologia,* 1973, *11,* 167–173.

Dodwell, P. C. Contemporary theoretical problems in seeing. In E. C. Carterette & M. P. Friedman (Eds.), *Handbook of perception* (Vol. 5): *Seeing.* New York: Academic Press, 1975.

Donders, F. C. On the speed of mental processes. (W. G. Koster, Trans.). *Acta Psychologica,* 1969, *30,* 412–431. (Originally published, 1869.)

Dornbush, R., L. & Winnick, W. A. Right–left differences in tachistoscopic identification of paralogs as a function of order of approximation to English letter sequences. *Perceptual and Motor Skills,* 1965, *20,* 1222–1224.

Durnford, M., & Kimura, D. Right hemisphere specialization for depth perception reflected in visual field differences. *Nature,* 1971, *231,* 394–395.

Egeth, H. Parallel versus serial processes in multidimensional stimulus discrimination. *Perception & Psychophysics,* 1966, *1,* 245–252.

Ellis, H. D. & Sheperd, J. W. Recognition of abstract and concrete words presented in left and right visual fields. *Journal of Experimental Psychology,* 1974, *103,* 1035–1036.

Ellis, H. D., & Shepherd, J. W. Recognition of upright and inverted faces presented in the left and right visual fields. *Cortex,* 1975, *11,* 3–7.

Eriksen, B. A., & Eriksen, C. W. The importance of being first: A tachistoscopic study of the contribution of each letter to the recognition of four letter words. *Perception & Psychophysics,* 1974, *15,* 66–72.

Eriksen, C. W. Temporal luminance summation effects in backward and forward masking. *Perception & Psychophysics,* 1966, *1,* 87–92.

Eriksen, C. W., & Hoffman, M. Form recognition at brief duration as a function of adaptation field and interval between stimulations. *Journal of Experimental Psychology,* 1963, *66,* 485–499.

Eriksen, C. W., & Spencer, T. Rate of information processing in perception: Some results and methodological considerations. *Journal of Experimental Psychology Monograph,* 1969, *79* (2, Pt. 2).

Fontenot, D. J. Visual field differences in the recognition of verbal and nonverbal stimuli in man. *Journal of Comparative and Physiological Psychology,* 1973, *85,* 564–569.

Fudin, R. Analysis of superiority of the right visual field in bilateral tachistoscopic word-recognition. *Perceptual and Motor Skills,* 1976, *43,* 683–688.

Gardner, E. B., & Branski, D. M. Unilateral cerebral activation and perception of gaps: A signal detection analysis. *Neuropsychologia,* 1976, *14,* 43–53.

Gardner, G. T. Evidence for independent parallel channels in tachistoscopic perception. *Cognitive Psychology*, 1973, *4*, 130–155.

Garner, W. R. Attention: The processing of multiple sources of information. In E. C. Carterette & M. P. Friedman (Eds.), *Handbook of perception* (Vol. 2): *Psychophysical judgment and measurement*. New York: Academic Press, 1974.

Geffen, G., Bradshaw, J. L., & Nettleton, N. C. Hemispheric asymmetry: Verbal and spatial encoding of visual stimuli. *Journal of Experimental Psychology*, 1972, *95*, 25–31.

Geffen, G., Bradshaw, J. L., & Wallace, G. Interhemispheric effects on reaction time to verbal and nonverbal visual stimuli. *Journal of Experimental Psychology*, 1971, *87*, 415–422.

Gibson, E. J. *Principles of perceptual learning and development*. New York: Appleton-Century-Crofts, 1969.

Gibson, J. J. *The senses considered as perceptual systems*. Boston: Houghton-Mifflin, 1966.

Gibson, J. J. *An ecological approach to visual perception*. Boston: Houghton-Mifflin, in press.

Goldstein, K. *Language and language disturbances: Aphasic symptom complexes and their significance for medicine and theory of language*. New York: Grune & Stratton, 1948.

Grill, D. P. Variables influencing the mode of processing of complex stimuli. *Perception & Psychophysics*, 1971, *10*, 51–57.

Gross, M. M. Hemispheric specialization for processing of visually presented verbal and spatial stimuli. *Perception & Psychophysics*, 1972, *12*, 357–363.

Haber, R. N. (Ed.). *Contemporary theory and research in visual perception*. New York: Holt, Rinehart, & Winston, 1968.

Haber, R. N. Introduction. In R. N. Haber (Ed.), *Information-processing approaches to visual perception*. New York: Holt, Rinehart, & Winston, 1969. (a)

Haber, R. N. (Ed.). *Information-processing approaches to visual perception*. New York: Holt, Rinehart, & Winston, 1969. (b)

Haber, R. N., & Hershenson, M. *The psychology of visual perception*. New York: Holt, Rinehart, & Winston, 1973.

Hannay, H. J., & Malone, D. R. Visual field effects and short-term memory for verbal material. *Neuropsychologia*, 1976, *14*, 203–209.

Harcum, E. R. Lateral dominance as a determinant of temporal order of responding. In M. Kinsbourne (Ed.), *Asymmetrical function of the brain*. New York: Cambridge University Press, 1978.

Harris, C. S., & Haber, R. N. Selective attention and coding in visual perception. *Journal of Experimental Psychology*, 1963, *65*, 328–333.

Hellige, J. B. Information processing differences revealed by differential conditioning and reaction time performance. *Journal of Experimental Psychology: General*, 1975, *104*, 309–326.

Hellige, J. B. Visual laterality patterns for pure- versus mixed-list presentation. *Journal of Experimental Psychology: Human Perception and Performance*, 1978, *4*, 121–131.

Hellige, J. B., & Cox, P. J. Effects of concurrent verbal memory on recognition of stimuli from the left and right visual fields. *Journal of Experimental Psychology: Human Perception and Performance*, 1976, *2*, 210–221.

Helmholtz, H. von *Treatise on physiological optics* (J. P. C. Southall, Ed. and trans.). Rochester, New York: Optical Society of America, 1925. (Originally published, 1911.)

Heron, W. Perception as a function of retinal locus and attention. *American Journal of Psychology*, 1957, *70*, 38–48.

Hines, D. Bilateral tachistoscopic recognition of verbal and nonverbal stimuli. *Cortex*, 1972, *8*, 315–322.

Hines, D. Independent functioning of the two cerebral hemispheres for recognizing bilaterally presented tachistoscopic visual half-field stimuli. *Cortex*, 1975, *11*, 132–143.

Hines, D. Recognition of verbs, abstract nouns, and concrete nouns from the left and right visual half-fields. *Neuropsychologia*, 1976, *14*, 211–216.

Hines, D. Differences in tachistoscopic recognition between abstract and concrete words as a function of visual half-field and frequency. *Cortex*, 1977, *13*, 66–73.

Hines, D., & Satz, P. Superiority of right visual half-fields in right-handers for recall of digits presented at varying rates. *Neuropsychologia*, 1971, *7*, 21–25.

Hines, D., Satz, P., & Clementino, T. Perceptual and memory components of the superior recall of letters from the right visual half-fields. *Neuropsychologia*, 1973, *11*, 175–180.

Hines, D., Satz, P., Schell, B., & Schmidlin, S. Differential recall of digits in the left and right visual half-fields under free and fixed order of recall. *Neuropsychologia*, 1969, *7*, 13–22.

Hochberg, J. Organization and the Gestalt tradition. In E. C. Carterette & M. P. Friedman (Eds.), *Handbook of perception* (Vol. 1): *Historical and philosophical roots of perception*. New York: Academic Press, 1974.

Hubel, D. H., & Wiesel, T. N. Receptive fields, binocular interaction and functional architecture in the cat's visual cortex. *Journal of Physiology*, 1962, *160*, 106–154.

Isseroff, A , Carmon, A., & Nachshon, I. Dissociation of hemifield RT differences from verbal stimulus directionality. *Journal of Experimental Psychology*, 1974, *103*, 145–149.

James, W. *The principles of psychology* (Vol. 1). New York: Dover, 1950. (Originally published, 1890.)

Johnson, D. M. Confidence and speed in the two-category judgment. *Archives of Psychology*, 1939, *34* (Serial No. 241).

Kahneman, D. Method, findings, and theory in studies of visual masking. *Psychological Bulletin*, 1968, *70*, 404–426.

Kahneman, D. *Attention and effort*. Englewood Cliffs, N. J.: Prentice-Hall, 1973.

Kelly, R. T., & Martin, D. W. Memory for random shapes. *Journal of Experimental Psychology*, 1974, *103*, 224–229.

Kimura, D. Dual functional asymmetry of the brain in visual perception. *Neuropsychologia*, 1966, *4*, 275–285.

Kimura, D. Spatial localization in the left and right visual fields. *Canadian Journal of Psychology*, 1969, *23*, 445–458.

Kimura, D. The asymmetry of the human brain. *Scientific American*, 1973, *228*, 70–78.

Kimura, D., & Durnford, M. Normal studies on the function of the right hemisphere in vision. In S. J. Dimond & J. G. Beaumont (Eds.), *Hemisphere function in the human brain*. New York: Wiley, 1974.

Kinsbourne, M. The cerebral basis of lateral asymmetries in attention. *Acta Psychologica*, 1970, *33*, 193–201.

Kinsbourne, M. The minor cerebral hemisphere as a source of aphasic speech. *Archives of Neurology*, 1971, *25*, 302–306.

Kinsbourne, M. The control of attention by interaction between the cerebral hemispheres. In S. Kornblum (Ed.), *Attention and performance IV*. New York: Academic Press, 1973.

Kinsbourne, M., & Warrington, E. K. A variety of reading disability associated with right hemisphere lesions. *Journal of Neurology, Neurosurgery, and Psychiatry*, 1962, *25*, 339–344. (a)

Kinsbourne, M., & Warrington, E. K. The effect of an aftercoming random pattern on the perception of brief visual stimuli. *Quarterly Journal of Experimental Psychology*, 1962, *14*, 223–224. (b)

Kinsbourne, M., & Warrington, E. K. Further studies on the masking of brief visual stimuli by a random pattern. *Quarterly Journal of Experimental Psychology*, 1962, *14*, 235–245. (c)

Kintsch, W. *Memory and cognition*. New York: Wiley, 1977.

Klein, D., Moscovitch, M., & Vigna, C. Attentional mechanisms and perceptual asymmetries in tachistoscopic recognition of words and faces. *Neuropsychologia*, 1976, *14*, 55–66.

Kosslyn, S. M., & Pomerantz, J. R. Imagery, propositions, and the form of internal representations. *Cognitive Psychology*, 1977, *9*, 52–76.

Levy, J., Trevarthern, C., & Sperry, R. W. Perception of bilateral chimerical figures following hemispheric deconnection. *Brain*, 1972, *95*, 61–78.

Lindsay, P. H., & Norman, D. A. *Human information processing: An introduction to psychology* (2nd ed.). New York: Academic Press, 1977.

Longden, K., Ellis, C., & Iverson, S. D. Hemispheric differences in the discrimination of curvature. *Neuropsychologia*, 1976, *14*, 195–202.

Mackavey, W., Curcio, F., & Rosen, J. Tachistoscopic word recognition performance under conditions of simultaneous bilateral presentation. *Neuropsychologia*, 1975, *13*, 27–33.

Marmor, G. S., & Zaback, L. A. Mental imagery by the blind: Does mental rotation depend on visual imagery? *Journal of Experimental Psychology: Human Perception and Performance*, 1976, *2*, 515–521.

Massaro, D. W. *Experimental psychology and information processing*. Chicago: Rand McNally, 1975.

McCollough, C. Color adaptation of edge-detectors in the human visual system. *Science*, 1965, *149*, 115–116.

McKeever, W. F., & Gill, K. M. Visual half-field differences in the recognition of bilaterally presented single letters and vertically spelled words. *Perceptual and Motor Skills*, 1972, *34*, 815–818. (a)

McKeever, W. F., & Gill, K. M. Visual half-field differences in masking effects for sequential letter stimuli in the right and left-handed. *Neuropsychologia*, 1972, *10*, 111–117. (b)

McKeever, W. F., Gill, K. M., & Van Deventer, A. D. Letter versus dot stimuli as tools for "splitting the normal brain with reaction time." *Quarterly Journal of Experimental Psychology*, 1975, *27*, 363–373.

McKeever, W. F., & Huling, M. D. Lateral dominance in tachistoscopic word recognition performances obtained with simultaneous bilateral input. *Neuropsychologia*, 1971, *9*, 15–20. (a)

McKeever, W. F., & Huling, M. D. Bilateral tachistoscopic word recognition as a function of hemisphere stimulated and interhemispheric transfer time. *Neuropsychologia*, 1971, *9*, 281–288. (b)

McKeever, W. F., & Suberi, M. Parallel but temporally displaced visual half-field metacontrast functions. *Quarterly Journal of Experimental Psychology*, 1974, *26*, 258–265.

McLeod, S. S., & Peacock, L. J. Task-related EEG asymmetry: Effects of age and ability. *Psychophysiology*, 1977, *14*, 308–311.

Melton, A. W., & Martin, E. (Eds.). *Coding processes in human memory*. Washington, D. C.: Winston, 1972.

Miller, G. A. The magical number seven, plus or minus two: Some limits on our capacity for processing information. *Psychological Review*, 1956, *63*, 81–97.

Milner, B. Hemispheric specialization: Scope and limits. In F. O. Schmitt & F. G. Worden (Eds.), *The neurosciences: Third study program*. Cambridge, Mass.: M.I.T. Press, 1974.

Mishkin, M., & Forgays, D. G. Word recognition as a function of retinal locus. *Journal of Experimental Psychology*, 1952, *43*, 43–48.

Moscovitch, M. Language and the cerebral hemispheres: Reaction-time studies and their implications for models of cerebral dominance. In P. Pliner, T. Alloway, & L. Krames

(Eds.), *Communication and affect: Language and thought.* New York: Academic Press, 1973.

Moscovitch, M. On the representation of language in the right hemisphere of right-handed people. *Brain and Language,* 1976, *3,* 47–71.

Moscovitch, M., Scullion, D., & Christie, D. Early versus late stages of processing and their relation to functional hemispheric asymmetries in face recognition. *Journal of Experimental Psychology: Human Perception and Performance,* 1976, *2,* 401–416.

Moyer, R. S. Comparing objects of memory: Evidence suggesting an internal psychophysics. *Perception & Psychophysics,* 1973, *13,* 180–184.

Natsoulas, T. On perceptual aboutness. *Behaviorism,* 1977, *5,* 75–97.

Natsoulas, T. Residual subjectivity. *American Psychologist,* 1978, *33,* 269–283.

Nebes, R. D. Direct examination of cognitive function in the right and left hemispheres. In M. Kinsbourne (Ed.), *Asymmetrical function of the brain.* New York: Cambridge University Press, 1978.

Nebes, R. D., & Sperry, R. W. Hemispheric deconnection syndrome with cerebral birth injury in the dominant arm area. *Neuropsychologia,* 1971, *9,* 247–259.

Neisser, U. Visual search. *Scientific American,* 1964, *210,* 94–102.

Neisser, U. *Cognitive psychology.* New York: Appleton-Century-Crofts, 1967.

Neisser, U. Changing conceptions of imagery. In P. W. Sheehan (Ed.), *The function and nature of imagery.* New York: Academic Press, 1972.

Neisser, U., & Kerr, N. Spatial and mnemonic properties of visual images. *Cognitive Psychology,* 1973, *5,* 138–150.

Nickerson, R. S. Same–different reaction times with multi-attribute stimulus differences. *Perceptual and Motor Skills,* 1967, *24,* 543–554.

Nielsen, J. M. *Agnosia, apraxia, aphasia: Their value in cerebral localization.* New York: Hoeber, 1946.

Orbach, J. Retinal locus as a factor in recognition of visually perceived words. *American Journal of Psychology,* 1953, *65,* 555–562.

Orbach, J. Differential recognition of Hebrew and English words in right and left visual fields as a function of cerebral dominance and reading habits. *Neuropsychologia,* 1967, *5,* 127–134.

Orenstein, H. B., & Meighan, W. B. Recognition of bilaterally presented words varying in concreteness and frequency: Lateral dominance or sequential processing? *Bulletin of the Psychonomic Society,* 1976, *7,* 179–180.

Oscar-Berman, M., Blumstein, S., & DeLuca, D. Iconic recognition of musical symbols in the lateral visual fields. *Cortex,* 1976, *12,* 241–248.

Oscar-Berman, M., Goodglass, H., & Cherlow, D. G. Perceptual laterality and iconic recognition of visual materials by Korsakoff patients and normal adults. *Journal of Comparative and Psysiological Psychology,* 1973, *82,* 316–321.

Pachella, R. G. The interpretation of reaction time in information processing research. In B. H. Kantowitz (Ed.), *Human information processing: Tutorials in performance and cognition.* Hillsdale, N. J.: Erlbaum, 1974.

Paivio, A. *Imagery and verbal processes.* New York: Holt, Rinehart, & Winston, 1971.

Paivio, A. Language and knowledge of the world. *Educational Researcher,* 1974, *3,* 5–12.

Paivio, A. Perceptual comparisons through the mind's eye. *Memory & Cognition,* 1975, *3,* 635–647.

Paivio, A. Images, propositions, and knowledge. In J. M. Nicholas (Ed.), *Images, perception, and knowledge.* Dordrecht, Holland: D. Reidel, 1977.

Paivio, A., & Csapo, K. Picture superiority in free recall: Imagery or dual coding? *Cognitive Psychology,* 1973, *5,* 176–206.

Palmer, S. E. Visual perception and world knowledge: Notes on a model of sensory–

cognitive interaction. In D. A. Norman & D. E. Rumelhart (Eds.), *Explorations in cognition*. San Francisco: Freeman, 1975.

Pastore, N. *Selective history of theories of visual perception: 1650–1950*. New York: Oxford University Press, 1971.

Patterson, K., & Bradshaw, J. L. Differential hemispheric mediation of nonverbal visual stimuli. *Journal of Experimental Psychology: Human Perception and Performance*, 1975, *1*, 246–252.

Pellegrino, J. W., Rosinski, R. R., Chiesi, H. L., & Siegel, A. Picture–word differences in decision latency: An analysis of single and dual memory models. *Memory & Cognition*, 1977, *5*, 383–396.

Perkins, M. Matter, sensation, and understanding. *American Philosophical Quarterly*, 1971, *8*, 1–12.

Peterson, L. R., & Peterson, M. J. Short-term retention of individual verbal items. *Journal of Experimental Psychology*, 1959, *58*, 193–198.

Pezdek, K. Cross-modality semantic integration of sentence and picture memory. *Journal of Experimental Psychology: Human Learning and Memory*, 1977, *3*, 515–524.

Pirozzolo, F. J., & Rayner, K. Hemispheric specialization in reading and word recognition. *Brain and Language*, 1977, *4*, 248–261.

Poffenberger, A. T. Reaction time to retinal stimulation with special reference to the time lost in conduction through nerve centres. *Archives of Psychology*, 1912, *3* (Serial No. 23).

Posner, M. I. Abstraction and the process of recognition. In G. H. Bower & J. T. Spence (Eds.), *The psychology of learning and motivation* (Vol. 3). New York: Academic Press, 1969.

Posner, M. I., Boies, S. I., Eichelman, W. H., & Taylor, R. I. Retention of visual and name codes of single letters. *Journal of Experimental Psychology Monograph*, 1969, *79* (1, Pt. 2).

Posner, M. I., & Keele, S. W. Decay of visual information from a single letter. *Science*, 1967, *158*, 137–139.

Posner, M. I., & Mitchell, R. F. Chronometric analysis of classification. *Psychological Review*, 1967, *74*, 392–409.

Postman, L. Verbal learning and memory. In M. R. Rosenzweig & L. W. Porter (Eds.), *Annual review of psychology* (Vol. 26). Palo Alto: Annual Reviews, Inc., 1975.

Pritchard, R. M. Stabilized images on the retina. *Scientific American*, 1961, *204*, 72–78.

Pylyshyn, Z. W. What the mind's eye tells the mind's brain: A critique of mental imagery. *Psychological Bulletin*, 1973, *80*, 1–24.

Raab, D. H. Backward masking. *Psychological Bulletin*, 1963, *60*, 118–129.

Reed, S. K. *Psychological processes in pattern recognition*. New York: Academic Press, 1973.

Reicher, G. M. Perceptual recognition as a function of the meaningfulness of the material. *Journal of Experimental Psychology*, 1969, *81*, 275–280.

Riggs, L. A., Ratliff, F., Cornsweet, J. C., & Cornsweet, T. N. The disappearance of steadily fixated objects. *Journal of the Optical Society of America*, 1953, *43*, 495–501.

Rizzolatti, G., Umiltà, C., & Berlucchi, G. Opposite superiorities of the left and right cerebral hemispheres in discriminative reaction time to physiognomic and alphabetic material. *Brain*, 1971, *94*, 431–442.

Robertshaw, S., & Sheldon, M. Laterality effects in judgment of the identity and position of letters: A signal detection analysis. *Quarterly Journal of Experimental Psychology*, 1976, *28*, 115–121.

Robson, J. G. Receptive fields: Neural representation of the spatial and intensive attributes of the visual image. In E. C. Carterette & M. P. Friedman (Eds.), *Handbook of perception* (Vol. 5): *Seeing*. New York: Academic Press, 1975.

Schiller, P. H. Monoptic and dichoptic visual masking by patterns and flashes. *Journal of Experimental Psychology*, 1965, *69*, 193–199.

Schiller, P. H., & Wiener, M. Monoptic and dichoptic visual masking. *Journal of Experimental Psychology*, 1963, *66*, 386–393.

Searleman, A. A review of right hemisphere linguistic capabilities. *Psychological Bulletin*, 1977, *84*, 503–528.

Selfridge, O. G. Pandemonium: A paradigm for learning. In *The mechanization of thought processes*. London: Her Majesty's Stationery Office, 1959.

Selfridge, O. G., & Neisser, U. Pattern recognition by machine. *Scientific American*, 1960, *203*, 60–68.

Selnes, O. A. A note on "On the representation of language in the right hemisphere of right-handed people." *Brain and Language*, 1976, *3*, 583–589.

Semmes, J. Hemispheric specialization: A possible clue to mechanism. *Neuropsychologia*, 1968, *6*, 11–26.

Shaw, R., & Bransford, J. (Eds.). *Perceiving, acting, and knowing: Toward an ecological psychology*. Hillsdale, N. J.: Erlbaum, 1977.

Shepard, R. N. Recognition memory for words, sentences, and pictures. *Journal of Verbal Learning and Verbal Behavior*, 1967, *6*, 156–163.

Shepard, R. N. Form, formation, and transformation of internal representations. In R. L. Solso (Ed.), *Information processing and cognition: The Loyola symposium*. Hillsdale, N. J.: Erlbaum, 1975.

Shepard, R. N., & Metzler, J. Mental rotation of three-dimensional objects. *Science*, 1971, *171*, 701–703.

Shiffrin, R. M., & Gardner, G. T. Visual processing capacity and attentional control. *Journal of Experimental Psychology*, 1972, *93*, 72–82.

Shiffrin, R. M., & Geisler, W. S. Visual recognition in a theory of information processing. In R. L. Solso (Ed.), *Contemporary issues in cognitive psychology: The Loyola symposium*. Washington, D. C.: Winston, 1973.

Shiffrin, R. M. & Schneider, W. Controlled and automatic human information processing: II. Perceptual learning, automatic attending, and a general theory. *Psychological Review*, 1977, *84*, 127–190.

Smith, A. Speech and other functions after left (dominant) hemispherectomy. *Journal of Neurology, Neurosurgery, and Psychiatry*, 1966, *29*, 467–471.

Smith, A. Neuropsychological testing in neurological disorders. In W. J. Friedlander (Ed.), *Advances in neurology* (Vol. 7): *Current reviews of higher nervous system dysfunction*. New York: Raven Press, 1975.

Smith, E. E., & Nielsen, G. D. Representations and retrieval processes in short-term memory: Recognition and recall of faces. *Journal of Experimental Psychology*, 1970, *85*, 397–405.

Smith, K. Y. Bilateral integrative action of the cerebral cortex in man in verbal association and sensory motor coordination. *Journal of Experimental Psychology*, 1947, *37*, 367–376.

Sperling, G. The information available in brief visual presentations. *Psychological Monographs*, 1960, *74* (11, Whole No. 498).

Sperling, G. A model for visual memory tasks. *Human Factors*, 1963, *5*, 19–31.

Standing, L. Learning 10,000 pictures. *Quarterly Journal of Experimental Psychology*, 1973, *25*, 207–222.

Sternberg, S. The discovery of processing stages: Extensions of Donders' method. *Acta Psychologica*, 1969, *30*, 276–315.

Sutherland, N. S. Outlines of a general theory of visual pattern recognition in animals and man. *Proceedings of the Royal Society of London* (Series B), 1968, *171*, 297–317.

Terrace, H. The effects of retinal locus and attention on the perception of words. *Journal of Experimental Psychology*, 1959, *58*, 382–385.

Townsend, J. T. A note on the identifiability of parallel and serial processes. *Perception & Psychophysics*, 1971, *10*, 161–163.

Turvey, M. T. On peripheral and central processes in vision: Inferences from an information-processing analysis of masking with patterned stimuli. *Psychological Review*, 1973, *80*, 1–52.

Turvey, M. T. Contrasting orientations to the theory of visual processing. *Psychological Review*, 1977, *84*, 67–88.

Turvey, M. T., & Kravetz, S. Retrieval time from iconic memory with shape as the selection criterion. *Perception & Psychophysics*, 1970, *8*, 171–172.

Umiltà, C., Rizzolatti, G., Marzi, C. A., Zamboni, G., Franzini, C., Camarda, R., & Berlucchi, G. Hemispheric differences in the discrimination of line orientation. *Neuropsychologia*, 1974, *12*, 165–174.

von Wright, J. M. Selection in immediate memory. *Quarterly Journal of Experimental Psychology*, 1968, *20*, 62–68.

von Wright, J. M. On selection in visual immediate memory. *Acta Psychologica*, 1970, *33*, 280–292.

Ward T. B., & Ross, L. E. Laterality differences and practice effects under central backward masking conditions. *Memory & Cognition*, 1977, *5*, 221–226.

Weisstein, N. Metacontrast. In D. Jameson & L. M. Hurvich (Eds.), *Handbook of sensory physiology* (Vol. 7, pt. 4): *Visual psychophysics*. Berlin: Springer-Verlag, 1972.

Weisstein, N., & Haber, R. N. A U-shaped backward masking function in vision. *Psychonomic Science*, 1965, *2*, 75–76.

Werner, H. Studies on contour: I. Qualitative analyses. *American Journal of Psychology*, 1935, *47*, 40–64.

White, M. J. Laterality differences in perception: A review. *Psychological Bulletin*, 1969, *72*, 387–405.

White, M. J. Hemispheric differences in tachistoscopic information processing. *British Journal of Psychology*, 1972, *63*, 497–508.

Zaidel, E. Auditory vocabulary of the right hemisphere following brain bisection or hemidecortication. *Cortex*, 1976, *12*, 191–211.

Zurif, E. B., & Bryden, M. P. Familial handedness and left-right differences in auditory and visual perception. *Neuropsychologia*, 1969, *7*, 179–187.

Chapter V

Language and Verbal Processes

DANIEL BUB
HARRY A. WHITAKER

Perhaps the simplest model of the language structures of the brain that has been proposed follows the division of the brain into sensory and motor areas. It assumes that areas in the frontal cortex subserve the production of language, whereas areas in the sensory cortex subserve the reception of language. Since these two aspects of language interact with each other, the model includes a connection between the sensory and motor language areas. This model is essentially the classical one proposed by Wernicke in 1874.

In Wernicke's model the frontal lobes contain the mechanism for directing the movements necessary to produce speech sounds. The first temporal gyrus, a sensory language area, was presumed to contain the auditory traces of word images. These two centers were connected directly and also were linked indirectly to perceptual centers of various kinds—visual, tactile, etc. Both sound and sensory images functioned together in normal brains in the production of language.

Wernicke's model proved to be surprisingly powerful in predicting a variety of aphasic symptoms. For example, damage to language areas in the frontal cortex impairs the mechanisms for organization and execution of language (*Broca's aphasia*). Damage to the language areas in the temporoparietal cortex impairs the mechanisms of comprehension (*Wernicke's aphasia*). Damage to the pathways connecting the posterior

211

THE BRAIN AND PSYCHOLOGY

and anterior areas for speech and language results in relatively intact comprehension and production but poor repetition (conduction aphasia).

Since Wernicke's time, the classical model of aphasia has been refined, although it is still basically a localization–disconnection theory of brain structure. The basic clinical symptomatology in the refined model is presented in Table 5.1. The syndromes listed in Table 5.1 represent relatively special cases of lesions located primarily in the identified brain areas. These special cases do occur, although not frequently. The syndromes are described in terms of global language functions, such as expressive speech, writing, and comprehension, and in terms of generalized linguistic structures such as phonemes, function words, and content words. Both descriptions are simplifications that are considered appropriate from a clinical perspective rather than from a research perspective. Contemporary observations of aphasia have made it quite clear that the classical model just discussed cannot do justice to the great variety and complexity of the language disorders. Wernicke himself questioned aspects of his own classification, noting that he was no longer of the opinion that, in pure motor aphasia, the ability to understand speech always remains unimpaired. In addition to the blurring of the distinction between a motor aphasia and a sensory aphasia, we note that there are important individual differences in cortical morphology (Whitaker & Selnes, 1976), and that the lateralization of language functions varies as a function of handedness (Hécaen & Sauguet, 1971; Shankweiler & Studdert-Kennedy, 1975; McKeever, Vandeventer, & Sabiri 1973), and age (Brown, 1976; Brown & Jaffe, 1976). These findings make the task of extracting generalizations about structure and function rather difficult. Nevertheless, brain damage may impair selectively discrete aspects of language, such that it is possible to separate out linguistic processes that are highly interactive in the normal adult. On occasion these processes may be referred to particular cortical structures.

Some of the language functions identified by linguistics in the study of semantics, syntax, lexical organization, and phonology have also been isolated in psychological studies of aphasia. Each of these language functions may be relatively selectively disrupted following brain lesions. Language processing appears to follow definite stages. It may be impaired at either peripheral or central levels. Although the early work of Marie, Charcot, Dejerine, Jackson, Trousseau, Wernicke, Freud, Bastian and others still exercises a considerable influence on our current thinking, simple localizationist models have been superseded by more sophisticated analyses in terms of functional systems which perform a role in language processing (Hécaen, 1969; Luria, 1964, 1970; Whitaker, 1971).

I. Disorders in Phonological Processing

Dysarthria is an articulatory impairment caused by a faulty innervation of the muscles of the vocal tract, either singly or in neural groupings. It most frequently follows lesions of the subcortical (including cerebellar) speech systems (Whitaker, in press). Dysarthria is not a true aphasia, per se, in that it is neuromuscular rather than symbolic in nature. Errors in speech and in voluntary and reflexive motor acts involving the vocal tract musculature are relatively uniform in nature (Darley, Aronson, & Brown, 1975) in comparison with the relatively inconsistent nature of errors in *apraxia* of speech produced only during voluntary speaking (Lebrun, 1976; Johns & LaPointe, 1976). The initial syndrome described by Broca in 1861 was considered by him to be an apraxia of speech, a loss of the coordinated movements of articulated speech. Broca noted that patients with this impairment can carry out all movements except speech-articulatory ones with the tongue and lips; the nonarticulatory movements remain intact.

Sasanuma and Fujimura (1971) studied two groups of aphasics, with and without speech apraxia in a visual recognition and writing task requiring the processing of ideograms (kanjis) and phonograms (kanas). Patients with apraxia of speech were selectively impaired in the processing of phonological stimuli; both groups were impaired in the processing of ideograms relative to a control group. Rosenbeck, Wertz and Darley (1973) found that patients with apraxia of speech were impaired on an oral–sensory perceptual task relative to a group without apraxia of speech but that errors were not qualitatively different. This suggests that apraxic patients have an oral–sensory perceptual deficit the errors not being due to artifacts such as confusion or perseveration.

Shankweiler and Harris (1966), investigating some of the factors causing errors in the speech of patients presenting "phonetic disintegration" associated with motor aphasia found that subjects made more errors in articulation at the beginning of words. Shankweiler and Harris (1966) concluded from their study that the frequency of errors seemed to indicate a disturbance of coordinated sequencing of several articulators rather than a disorder of a particular articulatory structure since the errors were not confined to any particular feature such as *voicing* or *place*.

Many studies employing phonemic discrimination in brain damaged patients have aimed at demonstrating a relationship between the speech errors of patients and their perceptual errors. Alajouanine and Lhermitte (1964) investigated the relationship between the sensitivity of conduction aphasics to the encoding of speech sounds and phonological difficulties experienced in a repetition task. Conduction aphasics showed a

Table 5.1
Aphasic Syndromes and Symptomatology

Clinical syndrome	Locus of lesion	Speech output	Written output	Auditory comprehension	Reading input
Broca's aphasia	Inferior posterior frontal	Phonemic paraphasias; agrammatic deletions; word order OK; meaning OK	Same as verbal	Limited understanding of function words; otherwise OK	Same as auditory comprehension
Wernicke's aphasia	Superior mid- and posterior temporal	normal to jargon; word order may be normal to very impaired; meaning may be irrelevant, vague or nonsensical;	Same as verbal	Can distinguish speech from non-speech; auditory comprehension is mildly to severely impaired	Impaired to degree of auditory comprehension
Conduction aphasia	Parietal operculum; arcuate fasc. and adjacent and deep cortex	Some phonemic paraphasias; word order OK; meaning is appropriate	Same as verbal	Normal to mildly affected	Normal to mildly affected
Isolation of the speech areas	Cortex surrounding F. Sylvius, the peri-Sylvian cortex	Normal if repeating	Severely impaired	Severely impaired but does process speech	Limited to severely impaired; no comprehension
Trans-cortical Motor aphasia	Anterior or mesial frontal	Normal if repeating	Usually impaired	Normal range	Normal to limited
Trans-cortical sensory aphasia	Temporo-parietal surrounding F. Sylvius	Normal to jargon; may be very like Wernicke's pt	Usually impaired	Can distinguish syntactic errors but otherwise severely impaired	Usually impaired
Anomic Amnestic aphasia	Posterior middle temporal; or, diffuse	normal except for nouns which may be omitted, substituted or paraphrased	May be similar to speech output	Usually in normal range	Similar to auditory comprehension
Alexia Agraphia	Supra-marginal & Angular gyri	Usually in normal range	Severely impaired	Usually in normal range	Severely impaired

Note: Alexia may occur without agraphia (lesion of CC and LH's visual cortex)

Clinical syndrome	Locus of lesion	Speech output	Written output	Auditory comprehension	Reading input
Word deafness	Between auditory cortex & superior temporal gyrus	Usually in normal range	Usually in normal range	Hearing is OK but severe impairment of speech comprehension	Usually in normal range

Spontaneity of speaking and writing	Grammatical words (functors)	Fluency	Lexical (content) words	Repetition
Severely impaired, hesitant with frequent pauses	Usually missing with some errors in usage	Mildly to severely impaired	Usually present	Limited as in speech output
Normal range but often repetitious, stereotyped	Present but often inappropriate or erroneous	Normal to hyperfluent	Indefinite, nonspecific nouns; usually paraphasias and often jargon	Impaired to the degree of auditory comprehension
Mildly impaired to near-normal	Occasionally missing to frequently missing	Mildly to moderately impaired	Usually present	Severely impaired with frequent paraphasias
Severely impaired to absent	Present when repeating	Normal when repeating	Present when repeating	Echolalic with completion and correction of minor errors
Severely impaired	Usually present	Normal when repeating	Present	Normal range
Normal range	Usually present	Normal range	Similar to Wernicke's pt.; indefinite nouns with paraphasias and some jargon	Normal range
Normal range	Usually present	Normal range except blocking on nouns	Nouns usually missing, with occasional circumlocutions	Usually normal range
Speaking is normal; writing is often inhibited	Present in speech output	Normal speech range	Present in speech output	Normal range
Normal range	Present	Normal range	Present	Severely impaired

marked impairment (21%) in discriminating correctly pronounced words from those that contained a literal paraphasia, either an inappropriate consonant or vowel.

Alajouanine, Lhermitte, Ledoux, Renaud, and Vignolo (1964) examined a group of fluent jargon aphasics and noted that errors were either phonemic or semantic. Basso, Casati, and Vignolo (1977) tested a group of 50 aphasics on a series of synthesized alveolar stop consonants with different values of (VOT) by requiring them to identify the acoustic boundary between voiced and unvoiced consonants. The data indicate that disordered phonemic output is related to faulty phonemic identification in fluent as well as nonfluent aphasics.

These findings lead one to pose the question of whether subgroups of aphasics may be distinguished on the basis of phonemic discrimination scores alone. This question is particularly interesting in the light of Luria's (1970) hypothesis that the comprehension deficit exhibited by Wernicke's aphasics is due primarily to a disturbance of phonemic perception. Blumstein, Baker, and Goodglass (1977) presented aphasic groups—Broca's, "mixed anteriors" (nonfluent aphasics with comprehension impairments), Wernicke's, and "residual posteriors" (patients with anomic, conduction or transcortical sensory aphasia) with two stimuli that the patients were required to discriminate. The stimuli consisted of two series, one of real words and one of nonsense words. The words were contrasted on the basis of one or more phonological feature. All aphasic groups performed less well with nonsense words than with real words. If Wernicke's aphasics had an impairment based on phonemic discrimination, they should have exhibited the least difference in performance between real and nonsense words since the phonemic aspects of the task were the same. Since this was not the case, Blumstein et al. (1977) concluded that all groups encode the words phonemically and then compare them at a semantic level. Interestingly enough, however, place contrasts were more difficult for the two posterior groups. Since place cues vary as a function of the following vowel, posterior groups may have difficulties in using phonological cues in a linguistically meaningful way.

Other studies have produced less clearcut results in attempting to differentiate between aphasic subgroups on the basis of discrimination of phonemic segments. Daujat, Gainotti, and Tissot (1974) required Broca's and Wernicke's aphasics to match a spoken word with one picture in an array which differed from the target word either phonemically or semantically. Daujat et al. (1974) found no difference in either the quantitative or qualitative performance of the patients on the semantic or phonemic task.

It is clear that the studies described differ not only in their findings but also in the nature of the tasks that each employed and for this reason it is questionable whether or not the experiments all point to one underlying phenomenon. A further complexity is introduced by the fact that within phonological processing, both a peripheral and a more central level seem to exist. Blumstein (1977) presented synthesized consonants to patients with right brain damage and to aphasics. Normal subjects and right brain damaged patients were equally good on the task, but the aphasic patients divided into two groups on the basis of their performance. Some patients gave the same results as normals, others could not identify the stimuli but could discriminate between them normally, and still others were impaired on both discrimination and identification. Blumstein (1977) concluded that phonological processing may involve two levels—a primitive, prelinguistic discrimination level which involves a set of detectors sensitive to acoustic parameters and a level which encodes stimuli along linguistically relevant dimensions. Disruption at different levels will produce different effects on discrimination.

II. Syntax and Semantics

Phonological impairment errors may occur as a result of brain damage relatively independent of any deficit in syntax or semantics. Whether or not damage to the cortex will result in purely articulatory deficits depends upon both the site and extent of the lesion. Lesions restricted to the cortical surface produce qualitatively different deficits than lesions extending into the white matter. In nineteen patients examined by Hécaen and Consoli (1973) with left hemisphere lesions, those with predominantly articulatory disorders had lesions restricted to the cortical surface, whereas those with additional grammatical and comprehension impairments had lesions extending deep into the white matter.

The condition known as Broca's aphasia is now considered to be a complex syndrome involving deficits in grammar and phonological sequencing and propositionizing, though Mohr (1976) considers this syndrome to be a result of a lesion extending well beyond the limits of Broca's area. One of the characteristics that marks the speech of Broca's aphasics is the fact that verbs and unstressed function words at the beginning of sentences are impaired (Jones & Wepmann, 1965; Goodglass & Hyde, 1969), though function words occupying medial positions in sentences are preserved. This telegraphic, agrammatic output has been described as due to an economy of effort caused by a general deficiency in articulation (Isserlin, 1922), which implies a motoric impairment. A Broca's aphasic patient uses a stressed element to alleviate difficulty in bringing the speech output mechanism into action (Goodglass, 1962, 1968), but this is clearly not the whole story. Goodglass (1976) notes that "passive recognition has never been shown to be complete" in agrammatic patients.

Zurif, Caramazza, and Myerson (1972) required normals and agrammatics with intact comprehension to indicate the perceived relationship between function and content words in fifty sentences by noting the words in the sentence that formed the most closely linked pairs. The data were analyzed by means of a hierarchical clustering technique. (Johnson, 1967). Normals produced tight connections between articles and their nouns while Broca's aphasics linked the content words together and ignored the function words to a considerable degree, paralleling the omission of such words in spontaneous speech.

In a further elaboration of this paradigm, Zurif, Green, Caramazza, and Goodenough (1975) varified the semantic qualities of function words somewhat more systematically. The subjects were anterior brain damaged patients with agrammatism but intact comprehension (Broca's aphasics), patients with agrammatism and comprehension deficits (mixed anteriors), and normal subjects. The data indicate that Broca's aphasics although insensitive to function words that mark the beginning of sentence structure (articles and pronouns), are relatively more sensitive to function words that convey semantic relationships (e.g., prepositions); whereas mixed anterior aphasics are insensitive to prepositions in addition to articles and pronouns. These experiments on perceived syntactic relationships partly corroborate the findings by Goodglass (1968) on speech performance of Broca's aphasics, although Zurif et al. (1972) found that Broca's aphasics ignore function words in the beginning of sentences and in the medial positions, whereas Goodglass found medial function words in the speech output of Broca's aphasics to be relatively intact. It is difficult to know the processes involved in the metalinguistic task of perceiving relationships between words, and whether this task reflects an underlying knowledge of syntactic relationships. It is clear, however, that the telegraphic speech of Broca's aphasics cannot be attributed solely to economy of effort. It is also clear that anterior brain damage can interfere with syntactic decoding as well as encoding.

The speech production of individuals with anterior brain damage is strikingly different from that of patients with posterior brain lesions. Wernicke's aphasics, for example, have motorically facile speech with ill-chosen words and phrases which nevertheless adhere to the syntactical rules of English. The Broca's aphasic speaks in clumsy, effortful speech with markedly reduced grammar. A question remains, however, as to whether the speech perception of patients in some way mirrors their speech production (Alajouanine & Lhermitte 1964), and whether it is possible to differentiate among aphasics on this basis rather than on the basis of analysis of spontaneous or elicited speech.

In studies of this problem, we are faced with a wide variety of experimental tasks, and it is unclear exactly which processes these various tasks tap. Goodglass et al. (1970) found that anomics were worse than Broca's and Wernicke's aphasics on the Peabody Picture Vocabulary Test. Broca's aphasics however, were not impaired on tests requiring the encoding of propositions, contrary to expectations. The authors did find however, that a discriminant function analysis identified Broca's and global aphasics correctly, although differentiating poorly between Wernicke's aphasics and the other groups.

Parisi and Pizzamiglio (1970) required aphasic subjects to match one of a pair of pictures to a sentence. The sentence correctly referred to one of the pictures; altering a single syntactical detail would render the sentence applicable to the other picture (e.g., "the boy is pushed by the girl" versus "the girl is pushed by the boy"). Although Wernicke's and global aphasics performed more poorly than Broca's aphasics, a high correlation existed between the scores of Broca's and Wernicke's aphasics when the items were scored in order of difficulty.

This finding was corroborated by Shewan and Canter (1971) in a study in which syntactic structure, level of vocabulary difficulty, and sentence length were varied. Subjects were required to match a spoken sentence to one of four pictures. The effect of increasing the difficulty level of these three factors did not vary between anomics and Wernicke's and Broca's aphasics, leading the authors to conclude that no qualitative difference existed between them.

Although it *is* possible to differentiate between aphasic groups on the basis of their speech output, attempts to discriminate between groups on the basis of tasks that presumably tap some underlying knowledge of meaning or syntax have been less successful. Some success has been obtained by Goodglass et al. (1970) and also by Smith (1974). Furthermore, it has already been noted that Broca's aphasics, but not mixed anterior aphasics (Zurif et al., 1976), formed syntactic associations between nouns and prepositions that signaled a semantic role. However, studies by Parisi and Pizzamiglio (1970) and by Shewan and Canter (1971) have largely been unsuccessful in demonstrating qualitative differences between aphasics in sentence decoding. Until we understand the demands each task makes on the subject, little insight can be obtained into the nature of the information processing disturbances that characterize the various forms of aphasia.

III. The Lexicon

A number of studies have demonstrated the possibility of an internal lexicon based on related and hierarchically organized semantic features (Miller, 1972; Quillian, 1968; Fischler, 1978). Studies investigating the manner in which this hypothetical structure has been disrupted in aphasia lends psychological validity to a theoretical construct and also sheds some light on the nature of the aphasic disorder.

Performance in naming may be disrupted at a number of levels. Caramazza and Berndt (1978) distinguish three stages in the production of names (a) an encoding stage in which features identifying an object are abstracted; (b) a central stage in which features are mapped onto a semantic representation; and (c) a production stage in which the lexical representation is translated into a set of motor commands. Impairment of this process may be caused by disruption of the central organization of lexical items or at a more peripheral level in which retrieval or articulation is impaired.

Studies that address the question of retrieval impairment usually attempt to show that words differ in their accessibility. Gardner (1973) tested anterior and posterior aphasics in a picture naming task in which the items were either "operative" (discrete, manipulable objects) or "figurative." All words were equated for frequency and the extent to which they were picturable. Operative items produced a naming advantage which was explained as being due to a greater number of associations in several sensory modalities that aided retrieval. North (1971) has obtained some evidence that sensory modalities contribute additive information to the retrieval of an objects name.

It seems unlikely, however, that the difficulties experienced by aphasics are simply due to a heightened threshold of excitability. Naming of certain categories, such as color, can be selectively impaired (Geschwind & Fusello, 1966). Theories postulating disruption of retrieval mechanisms as the sole factor in anomia would have to allow for selective disruption to account for this finding. It appears that certain aspects of lexical organization and the mapping of the stimulus object onto this system may be disrupted.

A study by Zurif et al. (1974) examined the relationship between aphasia and lexical organization in a group of patients with anterior or posterior damage relative to a control group. Subjects were given the definition of a number of nouns, half of which were names of humans (husband, knight, wife, etc.) and half of which were animals. The patients were asked to indicate which pair out of three words presented were most similar in meaning. The results indicated that the posterior aphasics did not separate the animal from the human forms, their judgements essentially showing no systematic relationships. Anterior aphasics, however, ordered the words along affective or situational dimensions, and normals ordered the words by using semantic features. Thus, anterior aphasics seem to have lost the linguistically relevant aspects of categorization while retaining those aspects relating to situational factors.

Whitehouse, Caramazza, and Zurif (in press) examined contextual and perceptual variations in the applications of labels to stimuli by aphasics. Variations of the modal "cup" were designed such that either perceptual or contextual dimensions were systematically varied. Perceptually, the picture was altered by either the presence or absence of a handle and the height–width ratio was also varied. Contextually, the pictures were varied to suggest "cup," "bowl," or "glass." Results indicated that anterior aphasics named prototypes correctly and were also sensitive to borderline members between concepts, which were named inconsistently, as one might expect. Posterior aphasics based their naming strategy on one perceptual feature, or made their judgments with no consistency. The results point to an abnormal structuring of semantic elements representing words rather than the failure to activate an intact representation of words.

Howes (1967) found that Broca's aphasics displayed a normal pattern of word associations while anomics and Wernicke's aphasics tended to produce abnormal associations. This finding was corroborated and extended by Lhermitte, Desrouesne, and Lecours (1971) who presented word pairs that were "associated" or "unrelated" to aphasics for their judgments. Aphasics with posterior lesions exhibited a widening of semantic boundaries, erroneously indicating relationships or lack of relationships among words.

Goodglass and Baker (1976), however, examined the associations of a single word by requiring patients to indicate whether words presented to them were related to a picture. They found no evidence for the widening of semantic boundaries. Rather, low comprehension aphasics had difficulty in identifying words functionally or contextually associated with the picture. These patients also had difficulty in producing spontaneous associations elicited by a single word. Goodglass and Baker (1976) maintain that their results are best explained in terms of constriction of semantic boundaries.

Although the notion of widening versus constriction of semantic boundaries in aphasics with posterior lesions is as yet unsettled and may depend on factors such as the nature of the task requirements, evidence for the neuropsychological validity of an internal lexicon is a little more secure. Yamadori and Albert (1973) have reported a case of word category aphasia—a non-modality-specific anomia in conjunction with a comprehension deficit for words in a specific semantic category. Rinnert and Whitaker (1973) compared semantic confusions of patients with a variety of aphasic disorders to corresponding norms for subjects without brain damage. Results indicated that the two classes of data were very similar. Other evidence is obtained from studies of dyslexic patients, indicating semantic substitutions in the reading errors of dyslexic subjects.

IV. Electrical Mapping of the Brain

The application of a weak electric current to the cerebral cortex of awake neurosurgical patients is another method of identifying language zones. Although the neurophysiological effects of introducing an electric current into the brain remain obscure and the variety of experimental manipulations that can be undertaken in the operating room are limited, the results of these studies have had considerable influence on our understanding of the brain's language systems.

Penfield and Roberts (1959) reported results of stimulation mapping in 110 patients. Arrest of speech was evoked from extensive areas in the left hemisphere as well as from peri-Rolandic cortex in the right hemisphere, presumably indicating that much of language cortex or potentially language cortex may directly influence the final common pathway for motor speech. The more aphasic-like responses, repetition (perseveration) and anomia, were only evoked from the left hemisphere classical language zones plus the supplementary motor cortex. Left hemisphere stimulation also evoked distortion and repetition of syllables and words and confusion of numbers while counting. It is interesting to note that Penfield and Roberts did not elicit spontaneous speech from cortical stimulation.

Whitaker and Ojemann (1977) investigated naming errors in three patients using a technique modified from Penfield and Roberts. The earlier studies limited language mapping in each patient to an average of one and a half times, whereas the Whitaker and Ojemann study sampled an average of over 25 different sites in the left hemisphere on an average of two and a half times per site. The significant findings were that a wide area of lateral cortex, including but not limited to the classical language zones, was shown to be involved in language functions, and there was a notable degree of individual variation in how these language sites were represented in the lateral cortex. Subsequent studies (Oje-mann & Whitaker, 1978b) have supported these two generalizations: It is likely that up to half of a cerebral hemisphere may be recruited for language functions and the manner in which it is recruited varies considerably from individual to individual. Ojemann and Whitaker found that the Insula may be part of the language system, that there is probably two functionally distinct parts to the region known as Broca's area, and that in brains of patients suffering from early temporal lobe disease there is more of a commitment to language above the Fissure of Sylvius than in Wernicke's area below it.

Fedio and van Buren (1971) have investigated the left and right tem-poral regions' part in the storing and retrieval of both verbal and non-verbal material, using electrical stimulation techniques. Stimulation of the nondominant side failed to produce any disruption of naming and immediate recall. Naming and retrieval errors occurred with stimulation of the posterior temporoparietal region while stimulation of the anterior region of the temporal lobe resulted in failure to store items.

Ojemann, Fedio, and Van Buren (1968) reported a variety of linguistic phenomena upon stimulation of the thalamus, implicating this structure in language processes (see also Schaltenbrand, Spuler, Wahrens, & Rumler, 1971; Cheek & Taveras, 1966; Smyth & Stern, 1938; Fisher, 1958; Fazio, Sacco, & Bugiani, 1973). Anomic and perseverative errors (repetition of the first syllable of the correct object name during stimula-tion), evoked speech and repetition (continuous use of one word) are obtained upon stimulation of the ventrolateral nucleus of the thalamus. Evidence for lateralization of function at the level of the thalamus was also obtained: Only one patient with a right brain electrode made anomic responses while seven of the patients with left brain electrodes made anomic, perseverative, and repetition errors. Other subcortical areas implicated in the language process are the left pulvinar nucleus and the white matter just lateral to the splenium of the corpus callosum. (Ojemann et al., 1968).

Short-term verbal memory has also been implicated in the functioning of the thalamus (Ojemann, Hoyenga, & Ward, 1971; Ojemann, 1974). Left ventrolateral stimulation significantly shortened the latency of cor-rect recall responses while right ventrolateral stimulation did not. Stimu-lation during presentation also significantly decreased the number of recall errors; stimulation during retrieval increased the number of errors. Ojemann (1976) proposed a model, on the basis of these findings, in which the left ventrolateral nucleus of the thalamus plays a role in a specific alerting response, labeling verbal material in the external environment so that its subsequent retrieval is enhanced, at the same time, inhibiting the retrieval of material already internalized. Interestingly, data were obtained in these studies indicating an inverse relationship between the degree of the "specific alerting response" and postoperative anomia. According to Ojemann (1976), "The greater the effects of the specific alerting response on the short-term memory and latency, the less likely is a postoperative anomia [p. 128]."

Ojemann and Whitaker (1978) have utilized electrical mapping of the brain in bilingual patients with some interesting results. Within the center of the language areas, there are sites that, when stimulated, produce anomic responses in both languages. In areas peripheral to these, stimulation produced interference with only one language. The subject's second language was generally represented in a wider area of cortex than the primary language. While this may simply reflect a higher response threshold to naming in second languages, the authors speculated that during acquisition of a language, a large number of neurons may be needed for execution of naming, but that with proficiency, the number of neurons necessary is reduced. This may have some implications for a theory of automatization processes in the brain.

V. Left-Right Asymmetry

The anatomic model of speech centers in the brain is depicted in the right hemisphere by Wernicke (1874) in the first three sections of his monograph. However, evidence clearly implicating the left hemisphere in language processes is later presented by him, and of course the work of Broca (1865) had already pointed to the inferior part of the third frontal gyrus in the left hemisphere as being involved in speech production. However, Broca (1865) also postulated that in non-right-handers, language is represented in the right hemisphere (Penfield and Roberts, 1959). This hypothesis soon met with problems, after several cases of crossed aphasia appeared in the literature. Today, it is believed, on the basis of studies with aphasics, that 90–99% of all right-handers have language subserved by the left hemisphere (Levy, 1974; Pratt & Warrington, 1972; Penfield & Roberts, 1959); 50–70% of non-right-handers also have language localized in the left hemisphere (Goodglass and Quadfasal, 1954; Hécaen & Sauguet, 1971; Zangwill, 1967).

An additional source of evidence of the asymmetry between left and right hemispheric linguistic processing has been obtained from commissurotomy patients, individuals who have had the connections between the hemispheres surgically destroyed for treatment of epilepsy. Various techniques utilizing the contralateral projection of sensory and motor systems (Sperry, 1975; Levy, 1976; Trevarthen, 1976) initially pointed to a marked asymmetry between the hemispheres for the processing of linguistic material such that the right hemisphere appeared incapable of processing any verbal material whatsoever (Gazzaniga, 1970). However, it later appeared that techniques requiring nonverbal responses on the part of the patient uncovered some verbal ability in the right hemisphere, although processing is restricted to comprehension, in that the right hemisphere appears to be incapable of verbal expression. Zaidel (1973) argues that the right hemisphere of commisurotomy patients had considerable syntactic capabilities, such as "verbs, sentential transformations, and semantically abstract references." Right hemisphere processing of common object nouns (Gazzaniga, 1970; Zaidel, 1976) and adjectives (Gazzaniga, 1976) has also been claimed.

These data should be viewed with caution, however. Commissurotomy patients all have a history of neurological disturbance, in most cases since infancy, and considerable reorganization in the nervous system is likely to have occurred, making any inferences about normal cerebral organization tentative (Whitaker, 1978.) Further, Gazzaniga (1970) has cautioned against overestimating the language capabilities in the right hemisphere in view of cross-cuing strategies evinced by commisurotomy patients. Cross-cuing occurs when one hemisphere correctly processes the stimulus and succeeds in cuing the response of the opposite hemisphere. For example, if a patient is required to report verbally whether a light that was flashed to the left visual field (and the right hemisphere) is green or red, the level of accuracy may increase in time because of a strategy the right hemisphere employs, such as grimacing, to cue the left hemisphere whenever it begins to respond erroneously (Gazzaniga, 1970).

There are some published reports claiming linguistic or communicative disruptions following right hemisphere brain damage. Eisenson (1962) presented evidence that right brain damaged subjects were poorer on a vocabular measure and on a cloze procedure in which the to-be-filled-in word was a conjunction. Several criticisms may be leveled at Eisenson's paper, including the fact that the vocabulary items were unusual, low frequency words, the fact that he did not assess visual field deficits that may or may not have been associated with the brain damage, and, on the cloze test, he scored as an error a number of perfectly correct word choices. Critchley (1962) suggested that right hemisphere damage causes deficiencies in the ability to do creative linguistic processing, as well as hesitation, difficulty in word finding and difficulty in learning novel linguistic material. Perseverative errors have been reported by Marie et al. (1965) after right hemisphere damage; Kinsbourne and Warrington (1962) observed that right brain damaged patients produce paralexic errors.

The problem of the extent to which the right hemisphere is involved in language must be phrased in terms of functional systems. Although it is clear that several peripheral aspects of language may be processed by the right hemisphere in the normal brain (such as visuospatial decoding of letter strings), it is unclear whether the right hemisphere is capable of processing more central aspects of language, such as syntax and semantics. It would indeed appear that an intact dominant hemisphere is a prerequisite for attaining the normal range of syntactic skills, even though the hemisphere is removed at a very early age. Dennis and Kohn (1975; Dennis and Whitaker, 1976) tested three subjects who had undergone surgical removal of the dominant or nondominant hemisphere during infancy. In tasks requiring processing of increasingly complex syntactical forms, subjects with intact right hemispheres had greater difficulty than subjects with intact left hemispheres. The nondominant hemisphere seems to be incapable of fully subserving the function usually mediated by the left hemisphere as far as syntax is concerned, even in the situation where every advantage of functional plasticity is available.

It would seem then that some limitation on the linguistic competence of the nondominant hemisphere is present even at birth, although the full extent of this limitation in the intact adult brain is now known. Studies of hemispherectomized adults add little insight into the matter. Crockett and Estridge (1951) and Smith and Burlund (1966) provide some evidence of speech comprehension and production after dominant hemispherectomy. However, in most of these studies, functional reorganization occurred prior to operation. See Selnes (1976) and Searleman (1977) for discussions. In this regard, French, Johnson, Brown, and Van Buren (1955) have pointed out that hemispherectomy is always of the nondominant hemisphere when loss of function occurred many years previous to the operation since functional transfer takes place in such circumstances. Kinsbourne (1971) obtained evidence for minor hemisphere processing of language after brain damage. The question regarding right hemisphere linguistic capacity in the intact human being cannot be framed in terms of functional reorganization after trauma, since we are concerned with the role of the nondominant hemisphere in language processing in normals, and not only with the plasticity of the nervous system after insult, although the latter does have bearing on right hemisphere potential for language.

VI. The WADA Test

Other clinical data indicating asymmetry for language processing in the CNS are derived from tests of language dominance utilizing intracarotid sodium amytal injection which temporarily deactivates the hemisphere ipsilateral to the side of injection. This procedure is used in patients prior to brain surgery. Milner, Branch, and Rasmussen (1966) have shown that cerebral dominance is more variable in sinistrals than dextrals utilizing data from sodium amytal tests, early left hemisphere damage being a factor in right hemisphere language dominance in sinistrals as well as sinistrality per se. Fedio and Baldwin (1969) have found that injection of sodium amytal into the dominant hemisphere produces a significant slowing in resumption of naming and short term memory for verbal material. The slowing does not occur with minor hemisphere perfusion.

VII. Electroencephalographic Data

Electrophysiological recordings have revealed asymmetries interhemispherically both during reception and production of language. McAdam and Whitaker (1971) observed an increase in the negativity over Broca's area in the left hemisphere prior to spontaneous speech utterances but not preceding nonspeech vocal tract gestures. This finding has been confirmed by Lew, Wada, and Fox (1976) who also obtained a positive correlation between hemispheric laterality for speech, as determined by injection of sodium amytal, and the degree of laterality obtained by measurement of the negative potential prior to speech utterances. Zimmerman and Knott (1974) found that only 22% of stutterers showed asymmetry favoring the left hemisphere as opposed to 80% of normals and concluded that the left and right inferior frontal areas of nonstutterers and stutterers perform differently during speech. The results of McAdam and Whitaker have been replicated and extended by Levy (1977) who obtained reliable hemispheric differences in slow wave activity prior to articulation of sequentially complex utterances. See Morrell and Huntington (1971) for criticisms of slow wave evoked potential analysis prior to speech. Surwillo (1973) recorded word association latency and EEG measures from a number of different age groups (7.5–17 years old) and found that in addition to latency decreasing with age, left hemisphere differences in EEG duration or period partly accounted for the relationship between age and reaction time, whereas right hemisphere differences in EEG period did not.

Asymmetries obtained for language reception have been inconsistent. Buchsbaum and Fedio (1969) presented verbal and nonverbal visual stimuli to subjects and reported that evoked response potentials elicited by words can be distinguished from potentials elicited by nonverbal stimuli. Shelburne (1973) however, found no differences between the visual evoked response potentials to words and nonsense words between left or right parietal or occipital leads. Friedman, Simon, Ritters, and Rapin (1975) also found no asymmetries in the evoked response potentials when subjects were asked to report a key word in a visually presented sentence.

Electroencephalographic asymmetries obtained for auditory stimuli have been more promising. Molfese et al. (1975) obtained left–right differences favoring the left hemisphere in the n_1–p_2 component of the evoked response potential to speech stimuli, whereas nonspeech stimuli produced longer amplitudes in the right hemisphere. Neville (1974) reported evoked response potential amplitude and latency differences elicited by dichotic digits but not by clicks. Other studies have obtained asymmetrical recordings for processing of contextual meaning (Brown, Marsh, & Smith, 1973; Teyler, Harrison, Roemer, & Thompson, 1973) and for linguistic acoustic analysis of a stimulus (Wood et al., 1971).

VIII. Visual Half-Field Studies

Stimuli that are briefly displayed in the right half of the visual field are processed initially by the left hemisphere and vice-versa. The asymmetrical projection of the visual fields have been utilized in the exploration of hemispherical asymmetries for language processing in normals, using reaction time or accuracy scores as dependent measures. (For a review of some of the literature see Dimond and Beaumont, 1976; Moscovitch, 1978; and Madden and Nebes, in Chapter 4.) Models have been proposed that attempt to explain the right visual field (RVF) advantage obtained for verbal material in terms of loss of information due to callosal transfer or in terms of direct access to the linguistically specialized dominant hemisphere (Kimura, 1966, 1973). An alternative explanation has been proposed by Kinsbourne (1970, 1973) in terms of orientation produced by the type of processing required for the task. When left hemisphere processing is required a biasing of attention toward the right visual field is obtained, and right-sided stimulation is thus compatible with such orientation, leading to an advantage in processing.

Data against this model have been obtained by Pirozollo and Rayner (1977) who found that simultaneous presentation of words and faces led to a right visual field advantage for words and a left visual field advantage for faces, indicating that each hemisphere was functioning according to its specialization rather than any consistent asymmetry resulting through an allocation of attention. Similarly, Gardner and Branski (1976) (see Madden and Nebes, in Chapter 4) produced experimental results qualifying Kinsbourne's initial work on orientation produced by concurrent verbal activity.

However, support for the notion of attentional mechanisms influencing visual half-field asymmetries has been obtained by Hellige (1978) and Klein et al. (1976), among others. A recent study by Ledlow (1978) showed that name matches (e.g., A a) for letter pairs produced a RVF advantage only when location was randomized and the magnitude of the advantage depended upon how predictable was the type of match (physical versus name) required. Ledlow et al. (1978) conclude that reaction time in their study measured nonstructural components of laterality, such as attention or orientation. Although it is clear that a simple structural model will not predict these results, it is also not immediately apparent just how allocation of attention shifts with processing certainty and knowledge of location.

While attentional mechanisms would seem to play a part in visual half-field asymmetries, it is also clear that the type of processing required by the task is critical. Furthermore, this may change over time as the subject alters his or her strategy with increasing task familiarity.

Ward and Ross (1977), for example, found that the RVF advantage for letter recognition obtained with backward masking reduced and disappeared with practice. Hardyck et al. (1977) found that a RVF advantage for same–different judgments of word pairs only emerged with a restricted set and with many trials. Hellige (1977) obtained an initial LVF advantage for name matches which then became a RVF advantage with practice and finally disappeared. Hellige (1977) interprets his results in terms of visuospatial processes that are utilized predominantly with initial unfamiliarity, giving way to verbal strategies as the task becomes easier with practice. As yet no satisfactory explanation has been offered as to why visual field asymmetries should actually disappear with practice (e.g., Ward & Ross, 1977; Hellige, 1977). Clearly, such an effect is not limited to the actual stimulus set per se, since Ward and Ross found that even when a new set of letters was substituted after one day of practice, no visual field advantage was obtained, even though a significant RVF advantage was obtained on day one.

It would seem that along with selective orientation, the nature of stimulus encoding in interaction with hemispheric specialization are crucial factors in visual half-field asymmetries.

IX. Dichotic Studies

Dichotic experimentation with digits or nonsense syllables typically yields an advantage for stimuli presented to the right ear (Kimura, 1961) while musical and other nonspeech stimuli, such as environmental sounds, produce a left-ear advantage (Kimura, 1964). These findings have been interpreted in terms of the different specialization of the two hemispheres and subsequent studies have confirmed and extended these results, particularly with regard to the language hemisphere. Experiments have focused on the verification of the psychological validity of phonological distinctive features (Jakobson, 1962; Chomsky & Halle, 1968) and whether the perception and analysis of distinctive features are relegated to the dominant hemisphere.

Studdert-Kennedy and Shankweiler (1970) obtained a right-ear advantage (REA) for the processing of dichotic stop consonants and found that subjects produced a significant number of errors in which all the component features of the stimuli were intact but were recombined incorrectly in the response (e.g., p–d would be reported as b–t). Apparently, the phonetic features of the stimuli were extracted, stored, and recombined, often incorrectly, although the original features of the speech sounds were retained. The data also indicate that when dichotic stimuli share many phonetic features, recombination results in fewer errors than when only one feature is shared.

In a further study, Studdert-Kennedy, Shankweiler, and Pisoni (1972) systematically varied acoustic and phonetic parameters of dichotic speech stimuli. Consonant–vowel syllables having the same vowel endings share both acoustic and phonetic information. When the vowels are different however, only phonetic information is shared, since formant transitions and formant patterns are not the same. The results indicate that the increase in accuracy of report when many features are shared may be due to phonetic information processing, since it occurred regardless of whether or not vowel endings were the same.

Oscar-Berman, Goodglass, and Donnenfeld (1974) examined the effects of shared phonetic features using unilaterally brain-damaged subjects. Whereas normals would be expected to profit from shared phonetic features, left-brain-damaged patients may be unable to do so. The results indicated that left-brain-damaged patients found consonants sharing several features (e.g., p–b) as difficult to process as consonants sharing fewer features (e.g., p–d). Right-hemisphere-damaged subjects did profit from shared phonetic features.

Although evidence exists for left hemisphere specialization for phonetic features, other experiments point to hemispheric processing of acoustic rather than phonetic parameters. Berlin, Lowe-Bell, Cullen, Thompson, and Loomis (1973) found that performance in consonant-vowel recognition tasks declined when isolated formant transitions and to a lesser extent nouns and vowels were introduced in dichotic competition with consonant–vowel stimuli. The experiment by Studdert-Kennedy et al. (1972) showed that, in addition to enhanced performance when phonetic features were shared, a greater right-ear advantage occurred when consonant–vowel stimuli shared auditory features. Cullen, Thompson, Hughes, Berlin, and Samson (1974) interpret these results in terms of a central additive acoustic processor. When a large number of acoustic features overlap, confusion occurs and performance favors the right ear. A similar notion is invoked in the experiments of Crowder and Morton (1969) and Morton, Crowder and Prausin (1971) pointing to a precategorical acoustic storage sensitive to nonlinguistic aspects of speech.

It is possible that along with a generalized speech processor in the left hemisphere, an analyzer also exists that processes auditory features (Cutting, 1974) and that different tasks tap these processes differentially. Cutting (1974) compared performance on discrimination of CV (consonant–vowel) stimuli and C'V syllables (identical to the CV stimuli but with inappropriate F1 transitions) with dichotic recognition. The results indicated that although both CV and C'V segments yield identical right-ear advantages, only the CV stimuli produce a discrimination curve characteristic of categorical perception. Cutting (1974) interpreted his results as indicating the operation of phonetic short-term memory in the discrimination of CV segments. The absence of categorical perception with C'V stimuli seems to point to a purely auditory component in the processing of these stimuli. The right-ear advantage was obtained for dichotic presentation of both classes of stimuli and might indicate, that in both cases, purely auditory processes are utilized.

It would seem that dichotic listening experiments either tap phonetic or acoustic aspects of hemispheric specialization. It is often difficult to determine the conditions necessary for ensuring phonetic or acoustic processing, as is evident in the original failure to obtain a right-ear advantage for vowels (Studdert-Kennedy & Shankweiler, 1970). Liberman, Cooper, Shankweiler, and Studdert-Kennedy (1967) suggested that the relatively more encoded nature of consonant sounds may engage perceptual process localized in the left hemisphere, whereas vowels will involve either right hemisphere mechanisms or both left and right hemisphere processes. However, Weiss and House (1973) obtained a right-ear advantage for vowels masked by white noise and suggested that perceptual difficulty rather than encodedness per se is a key factor limiting the right-ear advantage for vowels. Their hypothesis was sub-sequently examined by Godfrey (1974), who manipulated vowel dura-tion, acoustic–phonetic distinctness, and signal–noise ratio. Results seem to point to dichotic competition at an auditory rather than a phone-tic level. The right-ear advantage obtained for vowels under increasing perceptual difficulty is explained by Godfrey (1974) in terms of a pre-categorical acoustic storage to which the left hemisphere has privileged access.

Finally, dichotic (and, less successfully, monotic) presentation has been used to investigate left hemisphere specialization for other aspects of language. Zurif and Sait (1970) presented nonsense sequences dichoti-cally that either retained the grammatical structure of English ("the wak jud shendily") or were unstructured, though retaining the same func-tion words, nonsense syllable stems, and bound morphemes. The struc-tured sentences were recorded with proper sentential intonation while the unstructured sequences were not. A significant right-ear advantage was obtained only in the structured condition. Also, when syntax was kept constant and intonation varied, only the intonation condition yielded a right-ear advantage (Zurif & Mendelsohn, 1972). When acoustic parameters, such as intonation, are utilized for linguistic deci-sions, they are associated with left hemisphere mechanisms, whereas other sounds, processed independently of linguistic stimuli, yield a right hemisphere advantage (King & Kimura, 1972).

Bever (1971) has found evidence for left hemisphere processing of syntax in normals using monotic presentation. Some of the sentences presented maintained a noun–verb–noun sequence whereas others in-terrupted this sequence. Bever found that errors were often produced by converting a sequence that did not isolate the noun–verb–noun cluster into one that did and this is more likely to occur when sentences were presented to the right ear. Since this result only emerged with a two second delay between presentation and recall, the laterality effect ap-pears to be connected to memory rather than perceptual processes.

X. Development of Speech and Language and CNS Maturation

As the brain matures, language develops into an exceedingly com-plex system presumed to be predominantly subserved by the left hemi-sphere in normal right-handed individuals. Lenneberg (1967) has sug-gested that a critical period for language exists such that there is a limited time span during cortical development in which maturational processes interact with the environment to produce language functioning. On reviewing biochemical, anatomical, and electrophysiological studies of maturation, Lenneberg inferred that the critical period for language spans the ages of 2–13 years; prior to age 2, language does not appear, due to insufficient cerebral maturation. Between the ages of 2 and puberty, cerebral dominance is established, language develops in its entirety, and the brain loses its ability to reorganize and adapt to injury.

The notion of gradual development of cerebral dominance implies the possibility of equipotentiality for language at birth. Many studies have documented the lack of correlation between side of lesion and later general language performance in children (Basser, 1962; Carlson, Netley, Hendricks, & Pritchard, 1968). As early as 1868, Cotard observed that individuals who were hemiplegic from infancy might not show aphasia, even though the entire left hemisphere was atrophied. However, the plasticity of the brain during early years and its ability at this stage to reorganize and recover from injury, does not rule out the possibility of very early functional specialization. Annett (1973) investigated language in right and left hemiplegics who incurred damage before 13 months of age and found that left-sided insult resulted in greater frequency of language impairment than right-sided lesions. Studies with children in whom the entire left or right hemisphere has been removed at infancy have indicated that the isolated right hemisphere is less able to respond to the syntactic aspects of speech than the left hemisphere (Dennis & Kohn, 1975; Dennis & Whitaker, 1976). It would seem that the earlier studies which argued for hemispheric equipotentiality simply used superficial language measures. Although the phonological and cognitive-semantic aspects of language seem to be quite well mediated by the right hemisphere, a number of aspects of syntax may not be; the best evidence now suggests that the two hemispheres are not equipotential at birth but that their functional asymmetry is hard-wired, probably genetic in origin.

Anatomically, asymmetries exist in the gross configuration of the human cerebral cortex on the upper surface of the temporal lobe, such that the left planum temporal is larger than the right in 65% of adult brains (Geshwind & Levitsky, 1968). This finding has been confirmed in fetuses and newborns (Wada, 1976). Although this structural asymmetry may have some connection with the functional specialization for language, it is unlikely that there is a perfect relationship between the two. Levy (1974) has estimated that 99.67% of dextrals have left hemisphere dominance for language while 11% of the cases reported by Geshwind and Levitsky (1968) have a larger right planum temporale. Of course, the possibility always exists that a higher percentage of persons

may have right-sided or bilateral speech dominance than has been previously assumed (Wada, Clarke, & Hamm, 1975) but this is in direct
contrast with clinical evidence.

Studies with normal neonates and young children have obtained evidence for very early lateralization of linguistic processes. Entus (1977)
measured recovery of high amplitude sucking responses to changes in
verbal (CV syllables) or nonverbal stimuli (music). Stimuli were presented dichotically and varied in either the right or left ear. The results
indicate that recovery of sucking was greater for changes in the right ear
with speech and greater in the left ear with music. Molfese (1977) obtained asymmetrical recordings of evoked potentials in neonates to verbal and nonverbal auditory material. Dichotic studies have obtained a
right-ear superiority for verbal material in children as young as 2–3 years
of age (Nagafuchi, 1970; Yeni-Komshian, 1973; Hiscock & Kinsbourne,
1976) although other studies have failed to obtain a right-ear advantage in
very young children (Darby & Satz, 1973; Bryden, 1973) or have shown
an increasing right-ear advantage with age (Satz, Bakker, Goebel, &
Vander Vlugt, 1975; Bryden et al., 1973).

Tachistoscopic studies have also yielded ambiguous results. Carmon,
Nachson and Storinsky (1976) employed a recognition task of single
Hebrew letters, four letter Hebrew words, two-digit numbers, and four-
digit numbers. Right visual field superiority was found in the case of 10-
and 12-year-old children but not for 6- and 8-year-old children. No visual
field superiority was found in any group for single letter identification.
Barroso (1970) has also obtained evidence for differences between age
groups on verbal and nonverbal tachistoscopic tasks. Children 6, 8, and
9 years old gave no visual-field advantage for verbal and nonverbal
stimuli while appropriate visual-field effects were obtained for older
children. However, Witelson (1977); Marcel, Katz, and Smith (1974); and
Reitsma (1975) all obtained significant right visual field superiorities for
verbal material in children younger than 9 years old.

It would seem that the contradictory evidence may be resolved in part
by an understanding of exactly what cognitive processes are utilized in
various tachistoscopic and dichotic tests of language lateralization.
Brown and Jaffe (1974) have hypothesized that cerebral dominance is a
continuous process that evolves throughout life. It is conceivable that
certain peripheral aspects of speech processing are lateralized both corti-
cally and subcortically at a very early age and perhaps even before birth.
Other aspects of speech and language may become lateralized over time.
This does not necessarily mean that equipotentiality exists for certain
linguistic processes, since there may be an innate gradient favoring one

or the other hemisphere depending on the nature of the cognitive process involved.

The impressive ability of the neonate to discriminate between phonetic features (Eimas, Siqueland, Juszyck, & Vigonito, 1971; Morse, 1974, Moffit, 1971) has led to the inference that categorical phonetic processing may be innately determined (Morse, 1976; Eimas, 1974). Selnes and Whitaker (1977) have suggested that categorical speech perception is a property of the auditory system of higher mammals since chinchillas (Kuhl & Miller, 1975) and rhesus monkeys (Morse, 1976) have also demonstrated evidence of between-category discrimination of speech sounds. A study by Walker and Halas (1972) suggests that the neural mechanisms involved may be subcortical.

It is possible that the processing of speech segments by neonates may bear only a superficial resemblance to that of adults, since at birth the postthalamic component of the auditory system is immature (Yakovlev & Lecours, 1967) and only reaches completion at 4–5 years of age. Presumably, the nature of speech perception will change as the auditory system becomes more mature.

As the brain develops, language and speech processing becomes more refined and complex. Milner (1976) has correlated the development of the brain with language acquisition. Whitaker and Bub (in preparation) have done the same for speech production. As the cortex innervating the speech organs develops, the sounds the young child is capable of uttering change. Initially, speech sounds or babbling are probably mediated by subcortical structures due to the immature state of the cortex (Lecours, 1975). The sounds produced during early infancy may, therefore, bear little resemblance to later speech output. Jakobson (1968) has shown that children, at later stages of development, are no longer able to produce the sounds they emitted as infants, perhaps due to the change in control of speech sound from subcortical to cortical.

Cortical innervation of the speech organs develops relatively late (Humphrey, 1969, Conel, 1939–1964). As the corticobulbar tract matures, control is first obtained over lip rounding and closure. Studies of speech output of children at 3½ years of age indicate that the first sounds produced are bilabials (Berry & Eisenson, 1956; Wellman, Call, Mengiot, & Bradbury, 1931; Templin, 1953). Control is subsequently obtained over the back of the tongue, glottals and velar consonants emerge almost a year after bilabial sounds. Fricatives are generally the last sounds to emerge. These consonants require an extremely delicate balance of protagonist and antagonist muscles of the tongue to create the narrow groove that maintains turbulent air flow (Hardcastle, 1976). One

may infer that a certain level of coordination of the vocal tract musculature is necessary before fricatives can be uttered. Kent (1977) has shown
that intersubject standard deviations for the fundamental frequency
measurements of vowel sounds diminish with maturity, indicating that
neuromuscular coordination of speech organs indeed increases for a
relatively protracted period after birth.

Finally, it should be mentioned that the receptive aspects of speech
and language generally develop more rapidly than the productive aspects (Smith, 1973; Morton & Smith, 1974). In accordance with this,
the corticobulbar tract and Broca's area are still relatively poorly developed at 4 years of age (Conel, 1939–1964). Wernicke's area, thought
to mediate receptive aspects of language, is equal in development
on a number of criteria, at 4 years of age, to the visual association
cortex.

Bibliography

Alajouanine, T., & Lhermitte, F. Aphasia and physiology of speech. In D. M. Rioch &
    E. A. Weinstein (Eds.), *Disorders of communication*. Baltimore: Williams and Wilkins, 1964.
Alajouanine, T., Lhermitte, F., Ledoux, P., Renaud, D., & Vignola, L. A. Les composantes
    phonemiques et semantiques de la jargonaphasie. *Revue Neurologique*, 1964, *110*, 5–20.
Annett, M. Laterality of childhood hemiplegia and the growth of speech and intelligence.
    Cortex, 1973, *9*, 4–33.
Barroso, F. Hemispheric asymmetry of function in children. In R. W. Rieber (Ed.), *The
    neuropsychology of language*. New York: Plenum Press, 1976.
Basser, L. S. Hemiplegia of early onset and the faculty of speech with special reference to
    the effects of hemispherectomy. *Brain*, 1962, *85*, 427–460.
Basso, A., Casati, G., & Vignola, L. A. Phonetic identification defect in aphasia. *Cortex*,
    1972, *13*, 84–96.
Bastian, H. C. Some problems in cornexion with aphasia and other speech defects. *Lancet*,
    1897, *I*, 1005–1017, 1132–1137, 1187–1194.
Bay, E. Aphasia and nonverbal disorders of language. *Brain*, 1962, *85*, 412–426.
Berlin, C. I., Lowe-Bell, S. S., Cullen, J. K., Jr., Thompson, C. L., & Loovis, C. F.
    Dichotic speech perception: An interpretation of right-ear advantage and temporal
    offset effects. *Journal of the Acoustical Society of America*, 1973, *53*, 699–703.
Berry, M. F., & Eisenson, J. *Speech disorders*. New York: Appleton-Century-Crofts, 1956.
Bever, T. The nature of cerebral dominance in speech behavior of the child and adult. In R.
    Huxley & E. Ingram (Eds.), *Language acquisition: Models and methods*. New York:
    Academic Press, 1971.
Blumstein, S. E. The perception of speech in pathology and ontogeny. In A. Caramazza &
    E. Zurif (Eds). *The acquisition and breakdown of language*. Baltimore: Johns Hopkins Uni-
    versity Press, 1977.
Blumstein, S. E., Baker, E., & Goodglass, H. Phonological factors in auditory comprehen-
    sion in aphasia. *Neuropsychologia*, 1977, *15*, 19–30.
Broca, P. Remarques sur la siege de la faculte du langage articule, suivies d'une observa-
    tion d'aphemie (perte de la parole). *Bulletin de la Societe d'Anatomie*, 1861, *6*, 330–357.

Broca, P. Sur la siege de la faculte du langage articule. *Bulletin de la Societe d'Anthropologie,* 1865, *6,* 377–395.

Brown, J. W. Lateralization: A brain model. *Brain and Language,* 1973, *5,* 258–262.

Brown, J. W., & Jaffe, G. Hypothesis on cerebral dominance. *Neuropsychologia,* 1975, *13,* 107–111.

Brown, W. S., Marsh, J. T., & Smith, J. C. Contextual meaning effects on speech evoked potentials. *Behavioral Biology,* 1973, *9,* 755–761.

Bryden, M. P. Perceptual asymmetry in vision: relation to handedness, eyedness and speech lateralization. *Cortex,* 1973, *9,* 418–435.

Bryden, M. P., & Allard, F. Dichotic listening and the development of linguistic processes. In M. Kinsbourne (Ed.), *Hemispheric asymmetries of function.* New York: Cambridge University Press, 1975.

Buchsbaum, M., & Fedio, P. Visual information and evoked response from left and right hemispheres. *Electroencephalography and Clinical Neurophysiology,* 1969, *26,* 266–272.

Caramazza, A., & Berndt, R. S. Semantic and syntactic processes in aphasia: A review of the literature. *Psychological Bulletin,* 1978, *85,* 898–918.

Carlson, J., Netley, S., Hendrick, E. B., & Pritchard, J. A re-examination of intellectual disabilities in hemispherectomized patients. *Transactions of the American Neurological Association,* 1968, *93,* 198–201.

Carmon, A., Nachson, I., & Storinsky, R. Developmental aspects of visual hemiyield differences in perception of verbal material. *Brain and Language,* 1976, *3,* 463–469.

Cheek, W. R., & Taveras, J. Thalamic tumors. *Journal of Neurosurgery,* 1966, *24,* 505–513.

Chomsky, N., & Halle, H. *The sound pattern of English.* New York: Harper and Row, 1968.

Conel, J. L. *The postnatal development of the human cerebral cortex.* Cambridge, Mass.: Harvard University Press, 1939–1964.

Critchley, M. D., Jacksonian ideal and the future with special reference to aphasia. *British Medical Journal,* 1960, *2,* 6–12.

Critchley, M. Speech and Speech-loss in relation to the duality of the brain. In V. B. Mountcastle (Ed.), *Interhemispheric relations and cerebral dominance.* Baltimore: Johns Hopkins University Press, 1962.

Crockett, H. C., & Estridge, N. M. Cerebral hemispherectomy. *Bulletin of the Los Angeles Neurological Society,* 1951, *16,* 71–87.

Crowder, R. G., & Morton, J. Precategorical acoustic storage (PAS). *Perception & Psychophysics,* 1969, *5,* 365–373.

Cullen, J. K., Thompson, C. L., Hughes, L., Berlin, C. I., & Samson, D. S. The effects of varied acoustic parameters on performance in dichotic speech perception tasks. *Brain and Language,* 1974 *1,* 307–323.

Culting, J. E. Different speech-processing mechanisms can be reflected in the results of discrimination and dichotic listening tasks. *Brain and Language,* 1974, *1,* 363–375.

Darby, R., & Satz, P. Developmental dyslexia: A possible lag mechanism. Unpublished Master's thesis, University of Florida, 1973 (see Satz et al., 1975).

Darley, F. L. *Diagnosis and appraisal of communication disorders.* Englewood Cliffs, N.J.: Prentice-Hall, 1964.

Daujat, C., Gainotti, G., & Tissot, R. Sur Quelques aspects des troubles de la compréhension dans l'aphasie. *Cortex,* 1974, *10,* 347–359.

Dennis, M., & Kohn, B. Comprehension of syntax in infantile hemiplegics after cerebral hemidecortication: Left hemisphere superiority. *Brain and Language,* 1975, *2,* 475–486.

Dennis, M., & Whitaker, H. A. Language acquisition following hemidecortication: Linguistic superiority of the left over the right hemisphere. *Brain and Language,* 1976, *3,* 404–433.

Eimas, P. D. Auditory and linguistic processing of cues for place of articulation by infants. *Perception & Psychophysics*, 1974, *16*, 513–521.

Eimas, P. D., Siqueland, E. R., Juszyck, P., & Vigonito, J. Speech perception in infants. *Science*, 1971, *171*, 303–306.

Eisenson, J. Language and intellectual modifications associated with right cerebral damage. *Language and Speech*, 1962, *5*, 49–53.

Entus, A. K. Hemispheric asymmetry in processing of dichotically presented speech and nonspeech stimuli by infants. In S. Segalowitz & F. Gruber (Eds.), *Language development and neurological theory*. New York: Academic Press, 1977.

Fazio, C., Sacco, G., & Bugiani, O. The thalamic hemorrhage. *European Neurology*, 1973, *9*, 30–43.

Fedio, P., & Baldwin, M. Dysnomia and short-term memory impairment from intracarotid sodium anytal. *Excerpta Med. Found. Int. Congr. Ser.* 1909, *193*.

Fedio, P., & Van Buren, J. M. Cerebral mechanisms for perception and immediate memory under electrical stimulation in conscious man. Bethesda: *Lang. Neurol. Branch*, Nat. Inst. Neurol. Dis. Stroke. Unpublished Manuscript, 1971.

Fischler, I., Associative facilitation without expectancy in a lexical decision task. *Journal of Experimental Psychology, Human Perception and Performance.* 1977, *3.* 18–27.

Fisher, C. M., Clinical syndrome in cerebral hemorrhage. In W. S. Fields (Ed.), *Pathogenesis and treatment of cerebrovascular disease*. Springfield, Ill.: Charles C Thomas, 1958, pp. 318–342.

French, L. A., Johnson, D. R., Brown, I. A., & Van Bergen, F. B. Hemispherectomy for control of intractable convulsive seizures. *Journal of Neurosurgery*, 1955, *12*, 154–164.

Friedman, D., Simson, R., Ritter, W., & Rapin, I. Cortical evoked potentials elicited by real speech words and human sounds. *Electroencephalography and Clinical Neurophysiology*, 1975, *38*, 13–19.

Gainotti, G., Ibba, A., & Caltagirone, C. Perturbations acoustiques et semantiques de la comprehension dans l'aphasie. *Revue Neurologique*, 1975, *131*, 645–649.

Gardner, E., & Branski, D. Unilateral cerebral actuation and perception of gaps: A signal detection analysis. *Neuropsychologia*, 1976, *14*, 43–53.

Gardner, H. The contribution of operativity to naming capacity in aphasic patients. *Neuropsychologia*, 1973, *11*, 213–220.

Gazzaniga, M. S. *The bisected brain*. New York: Appleton-Century-Crofts, 1970.

Geffen, G., Bradshaw, J. L., & Wallace, G. Interhemispheric effects on RT to verbal and nonverbal visual stimuli. *Journal of Experimental Psychology*, 1971, *87*, 415–422.

Geschwind, N., & Fusillo, M. Color naming defects in association with alexia. *Archives of Neurology*, 1966, *15*, 137–146.

Geschwind, N., & Levitsky, W. Left/right asymmetries in temporal speech region. *Science*, 1968, *161*, 186–187.

Godfrey, J. J. Perceptual difficulty and the right ear advantage for vowels. *Brain and Language*, 1974, *1*, 323–337.

Goodglass, H. Redefining the concept of agrammatism in aphasia. *Proceedings of the International Speech and Voice Therapy Conference*, 12th, Purdue, 1962, pp. 108–116.

Goodglass, H. Studies on the grammar of aphasics. In S. Rosenberg & G. Koplin (Eds.), *Developments in applied psycholinguistics research*. New York: Macmillan, 1968.

Goodglass, H. Agrammatism. In: H. A. Whitaker & H. A. Whitaker (Eds.), *Studies in neurolinguistics* (Vol. 2.). New York: Academic Press, 1976.

Goodglass, H., and Baker, E. Semantic field, naming and auditory comprehension in aphasia. *Brain and Language*, 1975, *3*, 359–374.

Goodglass, H., Gleason, J. B., & Hyde, M. Some dimensions of auditory language comprehension in aphasics. *Journal of Speech and Hearing Research*, 1970, *13*, 595–606.

Goodglass, H., & Hyde, M. R. How aphasics begin their utterances. In H. Goodglass. *New measures of aphasic symptom variables.* Unpublished Progress Report, MSPHS Grant M-1802. 1969, Boston.

Goodglass, H., & Quadfasal, F. A. Language laterality in left handed aphasics. *Brain,* 1954, 77, 521–548.

Hardcastle, V. *The physiology of speech production* New York: Academic Press, 1976.

Hardyck, C., Tzeng, O. J. L., & Wang, W. S. Y. Cerebral lateralization of function and bilingual decision processes: is thinking lateralized? *Brain & Language,* 1978, 5, 56–72.

Hécaen, H. Clinico-anatomical and neurolinguistic aspects of aphasia. In G. Talland & M. Wough (Eds.), *Memory disorders.* Boston: Atlantic Press, 1969.

Hécaen, H., & Consoli, S. Analyse de troubles du langage au cours du lesions de l'aire de Broca. *Neuropsychologia,* 1973, 11, 377–388.

Hécaen, H., & Sauget, J. Cerebral dominance in left-handed subjects. *Cortex,* 1971, 7, 19–48.

Hellige, J. B. Changes in same-different laterality patterns as a function of practice and stimulus quality. *Perception & Psychophysics,* 1976, 20, 267–273.

Hellige, J. Visual laterality patterns for pure-versus mixed-list presentation. *Journal of Experimental Psychology: Human Perception and Performance,* 1978, 4, 121 131.

Hiscock, M., & Kinsbourne, M. Perceptual and motor measurements of cerebral lateralization in children. *Paper presented at the 37th annual meeting of the Canadian Psychological Association.* 1976, Toronto, Ontario.

Howes, D. Some experimental investigation of language in aphasia. In K. Salzinger and S. Salzinger (Eds.), *Research in verbal behavior and some neurophysiological implications.* New York: Academic Press, 1967.

Humphrey, T. Postnatal repetition of human prenatal activity sequences. In R. J. Robinson (Ed.), *Brain and early behavior.* New York: Academic Press, 1969.

Isserlin, M. Uber Agrammatismus. *Zeitschrift fur die Gesamte Neurologie und Psychiatrie,* 1922, 75, 332–416.

Jakobson, R. *Child language, aphasia and phonological universals.* The Hague: Mouton Publishers, 1968.

Johns, D. F., & Lapointe, L. L. Neurogenic disorders of output processing: Apraxia of speech. In H. A. Whitaker & H. A. Whitaker (Eds.), *Studies in neurolinguistics* (Vol. 2). New York: Academic Press, 1976.

Jones, L. F., & Wepman, J. M. *Grammatical indicants of speaking styles in normal and aphasic speakers.* Publication No. 46. Chapel Hill: University of North Carolina Psychometric laboratory, 1965.

Kent, R. Anatomical and neuromuscular maturation of the speech mechanism. Evidence from acoustic studies. *Journal of Speech and Hearing Research,* 1976, 19, 421–447.

Kimura, D. Cerebral dominance and the perception of verbal stimuli. *Canadian Journal of Psychology,* 1961, 15, 166–171.

Kimura, D. Left-right differences in the perception of melodies. *Quarterly Journal of Experimental Psychology,* 1964, 16, 355–358.

Kimura, D. Dual functional asymmetry of the brain in visual perception. *Neuropsychologia,* 1966, 4, 275–285.

Kimura, D. The asymmetry of the human brain. *Scientific American,* 1973, 228, 70–78.

King, F. L., & Kimura, D. Left-ear superiority in dichotic perception of vocal nonverbal sounds. *Canadian Journal of Psychology,* 1972, 26, 111–116.

Kinsbourne, M. The cerebral basis of lateral asymmetries in attention. *Acta Psychologica,* 1970, 33, 193–201.

Kinsbourne, M. The minor hemisphere as a source of aphasic speech. *Transactions of the American Neurological Association,* 1971, 96, 141–145.

Kinsbourne, M. The control of attention by interaction between the cerebral hemispheres. In S. Kornblum (Ed.), *Attention and performance IV*. New York: Academic Press, 1973.

Kinsbourne, M., & Warrington, E. K. A variety of reading disabilities associated with right hemisphere lesions. *Journal of Neurology, Neurosurgery and Psychiatry*, 1962, *25*, 339–344.

Klein, D., Moscovitch, M., & Vigna, C. Attentional mechanisms and perceptual asymmetries in tachistoscopic recognition of words and faces. *Neuropsychologia*, 1976, *14*, 55–66.

Kuhl, P. K., & Miller, J. D. Speech perception by the chinchilla: phonetic boundaries for synthetic VOT stimuli. *Journal of the Acoustical Society of America (suppl.)*, 1975, *57*, 549, Abstr. X13.

Lebrun, Y. Neurolinguistic models of language and speech. In Whitaker, H. A. & Whitaker, H. A. (Eds.), *Studies in Neurolinguistics* (Vol. 2). New York: Academic Press, 1976, pp. 1–30.

Lecours, A. R. Myelogenetic correlates of the development of speech and language. In E. H. Lenneberg & E. Lenneberg (Eds.), *Foundations of language development*. New York: Academic Press, 1975.

Ledlow, A., Swanson, J. M., & Kinsbourne, M. Reaction times and evoked potentials as indicators of hemispheric differences for laterally presented name and physical matches. *Journal of Experimental Psychology*, 1978, *4*, 440–454.

Lenneberg, E. *Biological foundation of language*. New York: Wiley, 1967.

Levy, J. Psychobiological implications of bilateral asymmetry. In S. J. Dimond & J. C. Beaumont (Eds.), *Hemisphere function in the human brain*. London: Paul Elek, 1974.

Levy, R. S. The question of electrophysiological asymmetries preceeding speech. In H. A. Whitaker & H. A. Whitaker (Eds.), *Studies in neurolinguistics*, (Vol. 3). New York: Academic Press, 1977.

Lhermitte, F., Desrouesne, J., & Lecours, A. R. Contribution a l'etude der troubles semantiques dans l'aphasie. *Revue Neurologique*, 1971, *125*, 81–101.

Liberman, A., Cooper, A., Shankweiler, D. P., & Studdert-Kennedy, M. Perception of the speech code. *Psychological Review*, 1967, *74*, 431–461.

Low, M. D., Wada, J. A., & Fox, M. EEG localization of conative aspects of language production in the human brain. *Electroencephalography and Clinical Neurophysiology*, 1976, *37*, 418–419.

Luria, A. Neuropsychology in the local diagnosis of brain damage. *Cortex*, 1964, *1*, 3–18.

Luria, A. R. *Higher cortical functions in man*. New York: Basic Books, 1966.

Luria, A. *Traumatic aphasia*. The Hague: Mouton, 1970.

Marcel, T., Katz, L., & Smith, M. Laterality and reading proficiency. *Neuropsychologia*, 1974, *12*, 131–139.

Marcie, P., Hécaen, H., Dubois, J., & Angelergues, R. Les troubles de la realisation de la parole au cours de lesions de l'hemisphere droit. *Neuropsychologia*, 1965, *3*, 217–247.

Marshall, J. C., & Newcombe, F. Variability and constraint in acquired dyslexia. In H. A. Whitaker & H. A. Whitaker (Eds.), *Studies in neurolinguistics*, (Vol. 3). New York: Academic Press, 1977.

McAdam, D. W., & Whitaker, H. A. Language production: Electroencephalographic localization in the normal human brain. *Science*, 1971, *172*, 499–502.

McKeever, W. F., Gill, K. M., & Vandeventer, A. D. Letter versus dot stimuli as tools for splitting the normal brain with reaction time. *Quarterly Journal of Experimental Psychology*, 1975, *27* 363–373.

McKeever, W. F., Vandeventer, A. D., & Suberi, M. Avowed, assessed and familial handedness and differential processing of brief sequential and nonsequential visual stimuli. *Neuropsychologia*, 1973, *11*, 235–238.

McKeever, W. F., & Vandeventer, A. D. Dyslexic adolescents: evidence of impaired visual and auditory language processing associated with normal lateralization and visual responsivity. *Cortex*, 1975, *11*, 361–378.

Miller, G. A. English verbs of motion: A case study in semantics and lexical memory. In A. W. Melton & E. Martin (Eds.), *Coding processes in human memory.* Washington: Winston, 1972.

Milner, B., Branch, C., & Rasmussen, T. Evidence for bilateral speech representation in non-right-handers, *Transactions of the American Neurological Association*, 1966, *91*, 306–308.

Milner, E. CNS Maturation and Language Acquisition. In H. A. Whitaker & H. A. Whitaker (Eds.), *Studies in neurolinguistics*, (Vol. 1). New York: Academic Press, 1976.

Moffitt, A. R. Consonant cue perception by twenty-to-twenty-four-week-old infants. *Child Development*, 1971, *42*, 717–731.

Mohr, J. P. Broca's area and Broca's aphasia. In H. A. Whitaker, & H. A. Whitaker, (Eds.), *Studies in neurolinguistics*, (Vol. 2), New York: Academic Press, 1976.

Morton, J. Crowder, R. G., & Proussin, H. A. Experiments with the stimulus suffix effect. *Journal of Experimental Psychology Monograph*, 1971, *91*, 169–190.

Morton, J., & Smith, N. V. Some ideas concerning the acquisition of phonology in current problems in psycholinguistics. Paris: *Editions du C.N.R.S.*, 1974, 161–176.

Molfese, D. L. Infant cerebral asymmetry. In S. Segalowitz & F. Gruber (Eds.), *Language development and neurological theory.* New York: Academic Press, 1977.

Molfese, D. L., Freeman, R. B., Jr., & Palermo, D. S. The ontogeny of brain lateralization for speech and nonspeech stimuli. *Brain and Language*, 1975, *2*, 356–368.

Morrell, L. K., & Huntington, D. A. Electrocortical localization of language production. *Science*, 1971, *174*, 1360–1361.

Morse, P. A. Infant speech perception: A preliminary model and review of the literature. In R. Schiejetbusch & L. Lloyd (Eds.), *Language perspectives: acquisition, retardation and intervention.* Baltimore: University Park Press, 1974.

Morse, P. A. Speech perception in the human infant and rhesus monkey. In S. R. Harnad, H. D. Steklis, & J. Lancaster, (Eds.), *Origins and evolution of language and speech. Annals of the New York Academy of Sciences* 1976, *V280.*

Moscovitch, M., Saillion, D., & Christie, D. Early versus late stages of processing and their relation to functional hemispheric asymmetries in fact recognition. *Journal of Experimental Psychology: Human Perception Performance*, 1976, *2*, 401–416.

Nagafuchi, M. Development of dichotic and nonaural hearing abilities in young children. *Acta Otolaryngolica*, 1970, *69*, 409–414.

Neville, H. Electrographic correlates of lateral asymmetry in the processing of verbal and nonverbal auditory stimuli. *Journal of Psycholinguistic Research*, 1974, *3*, 151–163.

Nielson, J. M. *Agnosia, Apraxia, aphasia: Their value in cerebral localization.* New York: Hoeber, 1946.

Ojemann, G. A., Speech and short term verbal memory alterations evoked from stimulation in pulvinar. In I. S. Cooper, H. Riklan, & P. T. Rakic (Eds.), *The pulvinar co. complex.* Springfield, Ill.: Charles C. Thomas, 1974, pp. 173–184.

Ojemann, G. A. Subcortical Language Mechanisms. In H. A. Whitaker & H. A. Whitaker (Eds.), *Studies in neurolinguistics*, (Vol. 2). New York: Academic Press, 1976.

Ojemann, G. A., & Fedio, P. Effect of stimulation of the human thalamus and parietal and temporal white matter on short term memory. *Journal of Neurosurgery*, 168, *29*, 51–59.

Ojemann, G. A., Fedio, P., & Van Buren, J. Anomia from pulvinar and subcortical parietal stimulation. *Brain*, 1968, *91*, 99–116.

Ojemann, G. A., Hoyenga, D., & Ward, A. A., Jr. Prediction of short term verbal memory disturbance after ventrolateral thalamotomy. *Journal of Neurosurgery*, 1971, *35*, 203–210.

Ojemann, G. A., & Whitaker, H. A. The Bilingual brain. *Archives of Neurology*, 1978(a), *35*, 409–412.

Ojemann, G. A. & Whitaker, H. A. Language localization and variability. *Brain and Language*, 1978(b), *6*, 239–260.

Oscar-Berman, M. Goodglass, H. & Donnenfeld, H. Dichotic ear-order effects with non-verbal stimuli. *Cortex*, 1974, *10*, 270–277.

Oscar-Berman, M., Zurif, E., & Blumstein, S. *Effects of unilateral brain damage on the processing speech sounds.*

Parisi, D., & Pizzamiglio, L. Syntactic comprehension in aphasia. *Cortex*, 1970, *6*, 204–215.

Penfield, W., & Roberts, L. *Speech and Brain mechanisms*. Princeton, N.J.: Princeton University Press, 1959.

Pirozzolo, F., & Rayner, K. Hemispheric specialization in reading and word recognition. *Brain and Language*, 1977, *4*, 248–261.

Pratt, R. T. C., & Warrington, E. E. The assessment of cerebral dominance with unilateral ECT. *British Journal of Psychiatry*, 1972, *121*, 327–328.

Quillian, M. R. Semantic memory. In Minsky, M. (Ed.), *Semantic information processing*. Cambridge, Mass.: MIT Press, 1968.

Reitsma, P. Visual asymmetry in children. In *Lateralization of brain function*. Boerhaawe Committee for Postgraduate Education: University of Leiden Press, 1975.

Rinnert, C., & Whitaker, H. A. Semantic confusions by aphasic patients. *Cortex*, 1975, *9*, 56–81.

Rosenbek, J., Wertz, R. T., & Darley, F. L. Oral sensation and perception in apraxia of speech and aphasia. *Journal of Speech and Hearing Research*, 1973, *16*, 22–36.

Sasanuma, S., & Fujimura, O. Selective impairment of phonetic and non-phonetic transcription of words in Japanese aphasic patients: Kana vs. kanji in visual recognition and writing. *Cortex*, 1971, *7*, 1–18.

Satz, P., Bakker, D. J., Goebel, R., & Vander Vlugt, H. Developmental parameters of the ear asymmetry: A multivariant approach. *Brain and Language*, 1975, *2*, 171–185.

Schaltenbrand, G., Spuler, H., Wahrens, W., & Rumler, B. Electroanatomy of the thalamic ventro-oral nucleus based on stereotaxic stimulation in man. *Zeitschift fur Neurologie*, 1971, *199*, 259–276.

Searleman, A. A review of right hemisphere linguistic capabilities. *Psychological Bulletin*, 1977, *84*, 503–528.

Selnes, O. A. A note on the representation of language in the right hemisphere of of right-handed people. *Brain and Language*, 1975, *3*, 583–590.

Selnes, O. A., & Whitaker, H. A. Neurological substrates of language and speech production. In S. Rosenberg. *Sentence production: Developments in research and theory*. New Jersey: Erlbaum, 1977.

Shankweiler, D., & Harris, K. S. An experimental approach to the problem of articulation in aphasia. *Cortex*, 1966, *2*, 277–292.

Shankweiler, D., & Studdert-Kennedy, M. A continuum of lateralization for speech perception? *Brain and Language*, 1975, *2*, 212–225.

Shelburne, S. A., Jr. Visual evoked responses to word and nonsense syllable stimuli. *Electroencephalography and Clinical Neurophysiology*, 1972, *32*, 17–25.

Shewan, C. M., & Canter, G. J. Effects of vocabulary, syntax and sentence length on auditory comprehension in aphasic patients. *Cortex*, 1971, *7*, 209–226.

Smith, A., & Burkland, C. W. Dominant hemispherectomy. *Science*, 1966, *153*, 1280–1282.

Smith, N. V. *The acquisition of phonology: A case study*. Cambridge, Mass.: Cambridge University Press, 1973.

Smyth, G. E., & Stern, K. Tumors of the thalamus—a clinico-pathological study. *Brain*, 1938, *61*, 359–374.

Sperry, R. W. Lateral specialization in the surgically separated hemisphere. In F. O. Schmitt & F. G. Worden (Eds.), *The neurosciences* (Vol. 3). Cambridge, Mass.: MIT Press, 1974.

Studdert-Kennedy, M., & Shankweiler, D. Hemispheric specialization for speech perception. *Journal of the Acoustical Society of America*, 1970, *48*, 579–594.

Studdert-Kennedy, M., Shankweiler, D., & Pisoni, D. Auditory and phonetic processes in speech perception: Evidence from a dichotic study. *Cognitive Psychology*, 1972, *5*, 455–466.

Surwillo, W. W. Word association latency in normal children during development and the relation of brain electrical activity. *Psychophysiology*, 1973, *10*, 154–165.

Templin, M. D. Norms on a screening test of articulation for ages three through eight. *Journal of Speech and Hearing Disorders*, 1953, *18*, 323–331.

Teyler, T., Harrison, T., Roemer, R., & Thompson, R. Human scalp recorded evoked potential correlates of linguistic stimuli. *Journal of the Psychonomic Society Bulletin*, 1973, *1*, 333–334.

Trevarthen, C. Analysis of cerebral activities that generate and regulate consciousness in commissurotomy patients. In S. Dimond & J. G. Beaumont (Eds.), *Hemisphere function in the human brain*. London: Paul Elek Ltd., 1974.

Wada, J. A. Cerebral anatomical asymmetry in infant brains. In Kimmura, D. (chm.), Sex differences in brain asymmetry. *Fourth annual meeting of the society of neuroscience*. St. Louis, Mo. 1976, *No. 695*, p. 456.

Wada, J. A., Clarke, R., & Hamm, A. Cerebral hemispheric asymmetry in humans. *Archives of Neurology*, 1975, *32*, 239–246.

Walker, J. L., & Halas, E. S. Neural coding at subcortical nuclei. *Physiology and Behavior*, 1972, *8*, 1099–1106.

Ward, T., & Ross, L. Laterality differences and practice effects under central backward masking conditions *Memory and Cognition*, 1977, *5*, 221–226.

Weiss, M. S., & House, A. S. Perception of dichotically presented vowels. *Journal of the Acoustical Society of America*, 1973, *53*, 51–58.

Wellman, B. L., Case, I. M., Menglot, I. G. & Bradbury, D. E. Speech sounds of young children, *University of Iowa studies in child welfare*, 1931, *5*.

Wernicke, C. *Der aphasische symptomenkomplex*. Breslau: Cohn and Weigert, 1874.

Whitaker, H. A. *On the representation of language in the human brain*. Edmonton: Linguistic Research, Inc., 1971.

Whitaker, H. A. The fallacy of the split brain research. *SISTM Quarterly and Brain Theory Newsletter*, 1978, *2*, 8–10.

Whitaker, H. A. Levels of impairment in disorders of speech. In *VIIIth International Congress of Phonetic Sciences*. In Press.

Whitaker, H. A., & Ojemann, G. A. Graded localization of naming from electrical stimulation mapping of left cerebral cortex. *Nature*, 1977, *270*, 50–51.

Whitaker, H. A., & Ojemann, G. A. Laterlization of higher cortical functions: A critique. In S. J. Dimond & D. A. Blizard. *Evolution and lateralization of the brain*. Annals of the New Academy of Sciences: The New York Academy of Sciences, 1977.

Whitaker, H. A., & Selnes, O. A. Anatomic variation in the cortex: Individual differences and the problem of the localization of language functions. *Conference on origins and evolution of language and speech*. New York: New York Academy of Sciences, 1975.

Whitaker, H. A., & Selnes, O. A. Anatomic variations in the cortex: Individual differences and the problem of the localization of language functions. In S. R. Harnad, H. D.

Steklis, & J. Lancaster, (Eds.), *Annals of the New York Academy of Sciences.* (Vol. 280). Origins and evolution of language and speech, 1976.

Whitehouse, Caramazza and Zurif. Naming in aphasia: Interacting effects of form and function. *Brain and Language,* 1973, *6,* 63–75.

Witelson, S. Early hemisphere specialization and interhemisphere plasticity: An empirical and theoretical review. In S. Segalowitz & F. Gruber (Eds.), *Language Development and neurological theory.* New York: Academic Press, 1977.

Wood, C. C., Goff, W. R., & Day, R. S. Auditory evoked potentials during speech perception. *Science,* 1971, *173,* 1248–1251.

Wyllie, J. *The disorders of speech.* Edinburgh: Oliver, 1894.

Yakovlev, P. E., & Lecours, A. R. The myelogectic cycles of regional maturation of the brain. In A. Minkowski (Ed.), *Regional development of the brain in early life.* Philadelphia: Dowis, 1967.

Yamadori, A., & Albert, M. L. Word category aphasia, *Cortex,* 1973, *9,* 112–125.

Yeni-Komshian, G. Cited in Witelson, P. In S. Segalowitz & F. Gruber (Eds.), *Language development and neurologica theory.* New York: Academic Press, 1977.

Zaidel, E. Linguistic competence and related functions in the right hemisphere of man following cerebral commissurotomy and hemis pherectomy. Unpublished doctoral dissertation, California Institute of Technology, 1973.

Zangwill, O. L. Speech and the minor hemisphere. *Acta Neurologica Belgica,* 1969, *67,* 1013–1020.

Zimmerman, G. N., & Knott, J. R. Slow potentials preceding speech in stutterers and normal speakers. *Electroencephalography and Clinical Neurophysiology,* 1973, *36,* 216.

Zurif, E., & Caramazza, A. and Myerson, R. Grammatical judgments of agrammatic patients. *Neuro-psychologia,* 1972, *10,* 405–417.

Zurif, E., Caramazza, A., Myerson, R., & Galvin, J. Semantic feature representations for normal and aphasic language. *Brain and Language,* 1974, *1,* 167–187.

Zurif, E. B., Green, E., Caramazza, A., & Goodenough, W. C. Metalinguistic judgments of aphasic patients: Sensitivity to junctors. *Cortex,* 1975

Zurif, E. B., & Mendelsohn, M. Hemispheric specialization for the perception of speech sounds: The influence of intonation and structure. *Perception & Psychophysics,* 1972, *11,* 329–332.

Zurif, E. B., & Sait, P. E. The role of syntax in dichotic listening. *Neuropsychologia,* 1970, *8,* 239–244.

Chapter VI

Cerebral Asymmetry and the Psychology of Man

JERRE LEVY

I. Introduction

Until recently, the anatomy, physiology, and organization of the central nervous system seemed irrelevant to the understanding of human behavior for most psychologists. Even physiological psychologists appeared to believe that, though something might be learned about rat behavior by studying rat brains, human psychology was much too complex to yield to a neurological analysis. Nevertheless, for well over a hundred years, neurologists and a few iconoclastic psychologists had been studying the behavior patterns of patients suffering from brain damage in, an attempt to understand how higher cognitive functions were integrated by neural tissue. Great progress was made in delineating the so-called primary projection areas for vision, hearing, touch, and motor control, but until the middle of the twentieth century the only firm generalization regarding higher processes was that speech was localized in the left cerebral hemisphere in most right-handers. Indeed, the majority of researchers believed that the left side of the brain was dominant not only for speech, but also for the processing of all sensory input and the control of motor output. The right hemisphere was believed to be little more than a defective automaton whose sole function was to relay information to the other half of the brain. In effect, to study human psychology was to study the functions of the left hemisphere,

245

THE BRAIN AND PSYCHOLOGY

and it could hardly be of great import to students of human behavior that a half brain, rather than a whole brain, generated the content of their research.

The notion that man is a half-brained species was not only peculiar from a theoretical standpoint, but had been contradicted by observation almost from its inception. Hughlings Jackson, in 1864 (Taylor, 1958) suggested that the right cerebral hemisphere played a special role in perception. In describing a patient with a right hemisphere tumor, he said "She did not know objects, persons and places . . . there was what I would call 'imperception', a defect as special as aphasia." In fact, seventeen years before Broca (1861) published his classical paper on speech localization, Wigan (1844) had concluded, on the basis of the fact that the cerebral organ is double, that "a separate and distinct process of thinking or ratiocination may be carried on in each cerebrum simultaneously." Nevertheless, such ideas had little impact on the thinking of most neurologists, and even Weisenberg and McBride's (1935) report that patients with injury to the right side of the brain displayed a specific defect in the manipulation of forms and in the appreciation of spatial relationships did not significantly affect the generally held belief that thought and behavioral control were centered in the left hemisphere.

Many studies of patients suffering from unilateral brain damage emerged during subsequent years, all suggesting that the right hemisphere was as superior to the left in certain capacities as was the left to the right in language (Paterson and Zangwill, 1944; McFie, Piercy, and Zangwill, 1950; Hécaen, Penfield, Bertrand, and Malmo, 1956; Ettlinger, Warrington, and Zangwill, 1957; Reitan and Tarshes, 1959; Hécaen and Angelergues, 1962), and though many researchers were coming to doubt the validity of the concept of a dominant left hemisphere, Alajouanine and Lhermitte (1963) maintained that the various findings confirmed the classical view. In particular, they attributed the symptoms of right hemisphere injury to a pathological release of activity in the left side of the brain. Thus, in spite of the considerable body of evidence that had accumulated by the early 1960s showing that certain disorders were specifically associated with damage to the right hemisphere, it was still theoretically possible to deny it a specialized role in higher cognitive functions. Indeed, since any behavioral consequences of a neurological lesion can always be explained as reflecting disinhibition of intact neural tissue, no amount of data from patients with unilateral cerebral injury can establish superiority or dominance of one hemisphere over the other. It was, perhaps, partly because of these theoretical difficulties that so little attention was directed to hemispheric laterality in American psychology. In fact, in the third edition of Hilgard's *Introduction to Psychology* (1962), there is only a single passage referring to lateral differences in the two sides of the human brain (p. 45) and, here, the author even disputes the view that language itself is unilaterally organized, saying, "Speech is far too complex to be localized in this simple manner...."

However, resistance to the idea that each side of the human brain was predominant in and specialized for a set of functions for which the other side was deficient cannot be due entirely to the interpretative ambiguity of symptoms from neurological lesions. Mishkin and Forgays (1952), Orbach (1953), Heron (1957), and Terrace (1959) had found a right visual field superiority in the recognition of tachistoscopically presented verbal stimuli, and Terrace (1959) had also found that 17 of 24 normal people with perceptual asymmetries on a form recognition task were superior in the **left** visual field, whereas only 7 were superior in the right visual field, exact $p = .032$. These findings were not, however, taken to indicate asymmetries of the cerebral hemispheres. The first study of perceptual asymmetries in normal people that was interpreted to indicate lateral differences in the brain was published by Kimura (1961). She suggested that the right visual field superiority for verbal stimuli implied left hemisphere specialization for language. This interpretation was, however, challenged on the ground that left-to-right reading habits could generate such an asymmetry. The fact that Barton, Goodglass, and Shai (1965) subsequently found that Israelis who read from right to left also manifest a right field superiority for verbal material, and that Kimura (1966) demonstrated a left field superiority for a dot enumeration task in Canadians, seemed to have little impact in challenging the classical view. The notion that the human right hemisphere surpasses the left in a variety of nonlinguistic functions and has a different mode of thinking was apparently so discordant with generally held opinions that only a dramatic proof of its validity could gain its widespread acceptance.

It is difficult to avoid the conclusion that a fundamental philosophical dilemma precluded the acceptance of either Hughlings Jackson's ideas or of the implications of observations from neurological or normal populations gathered since. Sherrington (1947) stated that the

> self is a unity . . . it regards itself as one, others treat it as one. It is addressed as one, by a name to which it answers. The Law and State schedule it as one. It and they identify it with a body which is considered by it and them to belong to it integrally. In short, unchallenged and unargued conviction assumes it to be one. The logic of grammar endorses this by a pronoun in the singular. All its diversity is merged in oneness [p. xvii].

Yet, if the two hemispheres differ, if each has its own capacities, ways of thinking, intentions to act, and perhaps value systems, then by certain definitions of "person," there would be, as Puccetti (1973) says, "two persons" housed in the same body, a proposition which, on introspective grounds, is exceedingly difficult to accept. As long as it was possible to attribute the various symptoms of neurological lesions to pathological release of activity in the left hemisphere or the various perceptual asymmetries of normal people to any of several mundane factors, the conclusion that each hemisphere has its special mind could be and was denied. It should be recognized that though psychology only has recently come to appreciate the fact and significance of cerebral asymmetry in the human brain, the evidence has been available for over a hundred years. As Kuhn (1962) emphasized, mere facts are forced into conventional paradigms of thought until such time as assimilation is not possible. When the old paradigms utterly fail in the face of accumulating evidence, then a paradigmatic revolution occurs in which the theoretical framework itself accommodates to the observations.

Just such a revolution has occurred and is evident in the fact that no introductory psychology texts published prior to the beginning of the 1970s even discussed the differential specialties of the two sides of the brain (except to mention speech localization), while almost all those published since 1974 describe hemispheric differences as a major defining aspect of human brain organization (e.g., Davidoff, 1976; Geiwitz, 1976; Lazerson, 1975; Kagan and Havemann, 1976; Liebert and Neale, 1977; Lindzey, Hall, and Thompson, 1975; McGaugh, Thompson, and Nelson, 1977; Morgan and King, 1975; Morris, 1976). Unlike the earlier edition of Hilgard's introductory text in which even speech localization was doubted, the 1975 edition (Hilgard, Atkinson, and Atkinson, 1975), states that "The ... left hemisphere governs our ability to express itself in language. It can perform many complicated sequential and analytic activities and is skilled in mathematical computations. ... The right hemisphere appears to have a highly developed spatial and pattern sense. It is superior to the left hemisphere in constructing geometric and perspective drawings [pp. 52, 53]." Judging from the citations in the various texts, the revolution in American psychology regarding cerebral asymmetry was stimulated in large part by the observations of Roger Sperry and his colleagues of human neurological patients in whom all the cerebral commissures connecting cortical regions of the two hemispheres had surgically separated (Sperry, 1974).

II. The Split-Brain Patient

A. The Split-Brain Syndrome

It had been discovered during the 1940s that surgical division of the corpus callosum was an extremely effective procedure for reducing the frequency and severity of epileptic seizures in patients for whom other therapies had failed (Van Wagenen and Herren, 1940). Eventually, 26 people underwent this therapeutic surgery. Akelaitis (Smith and Akelaitis, 1942; Akelaitis, 1941a,b,c; 1942a,b; 1943; 1944; Akelaitis, Risteen, Herren, and Van Wagenen, 1942; Akelaitis, Risteen, and Van Wagenen, 1943) immediately recognized the potential value of the procedure in gaining an understanding of hemispheric function. In contrast to patients with unilateral brain damage, commissurotomy patients possess two relatively normal hemispheres whose functions, presumably, can be separately tested. The Akelaitis investigations were, however, disappointing. The various tests administered revealed no differences between commissurotomy patients and normal subjects that could be attributed to callosal disconnection. The patients behaved as if both hemispheres had access to information from both sides of the body. The absence of any obvious deconnection syndrome led Lashley to suggest jokingly that the sole function of the corpus callosum was to support the brain. As was subsequently discovered in Sperry's laboratory, split-brain patients have a variety of mechanisms by which they can generate integrated and essentially normal behavior patterns, and highly refined tests are necessary to reveal the functional consequences of commissurotomy. The failure of Akelaitis to discover these consequences may be attributed predominantly to inadequacies in test procedures.

In 1962, a second series of split-brain patients became available for psychological investigation. Bogen and Vogel (1962) published a case report of a patient in whom all the neocortical commissures had been severed, and in the same year Gazzaniga, Bogen, and Sperry (1962) described various aspects of this patient's behavior. They reported that in naming tasks, the patient performed normally when objects were placed in the right hand or were shown in the right visual half-field but was totally unable to describe stimuli felt by the left hand or presented in the left visual half-field. It appeared that each hemisphere was completely out of conscious contact with the other, and that only the left hemisphere could speak. Though the left hand typically was unable to carry out skilled motor tasks upon verbal command, it was **superior** to the right in visual constructional tasks such as drawing. Thus, division of the anatomical connections between the halves of the brain produced a splitting of consciousness as well. The same split-brain syndrome was seen in later patients, and it was clear that each separated hemisphere had its own perceptions, motivations, memories, and stream of consciousness, completely isolated from and inaccessible to those of the other side of the brain (Sperry, Gazzaniga, and Bogen, 1969).

The existence of two separate behaving systems in the commissurotomy patient can be accommodated into the "single-minded" view of Sherrington if only one half-brain were conscious, and this is precisely the position of Eccles (1970, 1973). He believes that only the left hemisphere is conscious, the right being merely an automaton; but if so, is the aphasic patient with left hemispherectomy no longer a person? Is it merely an unconscious right hemisphere that constructs puzzles, plays music, paints pictures, and emotionally reacts in a thoroughly human way? More recently, Le Doux, Wilson, and Gazzaniga (1977) have also avoided the double-mind problem, suggesting, like Eccles, that there is consciousness only where language is present, and that it is only in the praxic skills of the left hand that the right hemisphere manifests superiority. They maintain that there is no evidence whatsoever of any cognitive superiorities of the right hemisphere of split-brain patients. Indeed, Gazzaniga, Bogen, and Sperry (1965) had suggested that "lateral specialization lies more in the motor-executive or expressive sphere than in sensory-perceptual components of performance." If it is only the output unit for praxis of the right hemisphere that surpasses that of the left, there is little need for positing two different specialized "core processors."

Though Eccles does not deny the possibility that the right hemisphere, though unconscious, may surpass the left in a variety of functions, Gazzaniga and colleagues not only deprive the right side of the brain of consciousness, but also of any special processing programs. In the initial split-brain studies, it was found that though the right hemisphere was speechless, it could **understand** some aspects of language, and that though the left hemisphere was incompetent at constructional praxis, it could correctly **match** visual patterns (Gazzaniga et al., 1965; Bogen and Gazzaniga, 1965; Bogen, 1969a). Thus, the conclusion that hemispheric specialization may reside in the expressive aspects of behavior was not unreasonable when the suggestion was first made. In fact, the tests administered in these early studies were ill-designed to reveal hemispheric differences in information processing and cognition. The recognition of simple words or sentences or the ability to match simple designs can be accomplished by other mammals, and it would be rather remarkable if either human hemisphere were cognitively less competent than a monkey brain. If cognitive differences exist between the half-brains, they would be expected to be revealed only by tasks sufficiently difficult to challenge the specialized and superior hemisphere. How competent is the right hemisphere at phonetic analysis; at the decoding of complex syntactical structure? How competent is the left hemisphere at three-dimensional visualization; at encoding and remembering random shapes that are resistant to verbal description? Only if it were demonstrated that the hemispheres are equally skilled at these relatively difficult tasks could it be legitimatly concluded that they are cognitively symmetrical.

B. Hemispheric Specialization for Cognition
   in Split-Brain Patients

A consideration of observations from unilaterally brain damage patients suggests that the disorders of the left hemisphere in skilled constructional tasks are a secondary consequence of a poorly developed understanding of spatial relationships. In fact, the so-called constructional apraxia of this hemisphere is actually a manifestation of a visuospatial agnosia. To test this possibility, Levy-Agresti and Sperry (1968; Levy, 1974) designed a test that required no constructional skills, but that depended on three-dimensional visualization. The test was a cross-model modification of the Spatial Relations subtest of the Differential Aptitude Test Battery, appropriate for testing separately the left and right hemispheres of split-brain patients. A series of 13 items was constructed, each item consisting of three small wooden blocks that were similar, but not identical in shape or in the relation of smooth and rough surfaces, and a choice card that depicted each of the three blocks in opened-up, two-dimensional form. On any given test run, one block from each of the 13 items was presented to one of the hands to palpate, the hand hidden from the subject's view, and choice cards were displayed in free vision from which the matching choice was to be selected.

It had been repeatedly demonstrated in split-brain patients that tactile information regarding shape was strictly confined to the hemisphere contralateral to the stimulated hand. Although both hemispheres had access to the choice card in the cross-model test, only one hemisphere was aware of the stimulus on any given trial. Test performance for the left and right hands was dependent on how well the right and left hemispheres, respectively, could mentally fold the choice drawings and match them with the wooden block.

Six split-brain patients were first given a much simpler version of the final test to instruct them in the task to be performed and to determine whether they were capable of doing the task at all. Two patients (M. K. and R. Y.), both with evidence of right hemisphere damage, completely failed to even grasp the concept of matching a two-dimensional drawing to a three-dimensional shape and were not given the final test. It should be noted that a normal 7-year-old child passed the final test easily and understood the instructions immediately.

Of the four patients (L. B., N. G., A. A., and N. W.) given the final test, three displayed above-chance performance with one or both hands.

N. G. performed at chance with both hands. N. G.'s performance IQ on the Wechsler Adult Intelligence Scale (WAIS) was only 71. Her verbal IQ (VIQ) was in the low-normal range, suggesting more damage to the right hemisphere than to the left. A. A. and N. W. performed at chance with their right hands, but above chance with their left. A. A., however, may have a sensory defect on the right side of his body, so that his left hand superiority may be a reflection of this. However, N. W. is likely to have right hemisphere damage. Her verbal and performance WAIS scores were 97 and 89, respectively. The superiority of her left hand on the cross-modal test occurred in spite of probably asymmetric damage to the right hemisphere. L. B. scored above chance with both hands, but was vastly superior with his left. His VIQ is 110 and his performance IQ (PIQ) 100.

Not only was the right hemisphere found to be superior to the left in this spatial relations task, but the strategies employed by the hemispheres in solving the problems differed. The right hemisphere performed best on those items in which the choices were easy to differentiate visually, and worst on those in which visual differentiation of the choices was difficult. The left hemisphere performed best on items in which the choice drawings were easy to describe verbally, and worst on those that were resistant to verbal description. Indeed, only 36% of the variance in the rank order of item difficulty for one hand could be accounted for by the rank order of difficulty for the other hand in L. B., the only subject scoring above chance with both hands. However, 56% of the variance in the rank order of item difficulty for N. W.'s left hand was accounted for by the rank order of difficulty for L. B.'s left hand, and 69% of the variance in rank order of difficulty for L. B.'s right hand was accounted for by the rank order scores of an unoperated epileptic control subject. In other words, the orders of difficulty for L. B.'s two hands were less similar than L. B.'s and N. W.'s left hands or than L. B.'s right hand and the scores of an unoperated subject. On the basis of these findings, Levy-Agresti and Sperry (1968) suggested that "the mute . . . hemisphere is specialized for gestalt perception, being primarily a synthesis in dealing with information input. The speaking . . . hemisphere, in contrast, seems to operate in a more logical, analytic, computer-like fashion [p. 1151]."

The data collected in this study were the first in split-brain patients to suggest that the hemispheres differed in their modes of thinking and information processing strategies, not merely in executive capacities. In 1969, after an extensive review of this literature and completely independently of our recently published findings in split-brain patients, Bogen (1969b) reached the same conclusion. He said, "In the human, where *propositional* though is typically lateralized to one hemisphere, the other hemisphere evidently specializes in a different mode of thought, which may be called *appositional* [pp. 157–158]." Since 1968, split-brain research has concentrated on delineating the nature of those thought processes that characterize the differential specializations of the two sides of the brain. The possibility that deficiency syndromes resulting from right hemisphere lesions were the consequence of a pathological release of activity in the left hemisphere and that the right hemisphere had no specialties of its own was no longer tenable, as Alajouanine and Lhermitte had suggested (1963). The conclusions reached by Levy-Agresti and Sperry (1968) and Bogen (1969b) began to gain widespread acceptance in the psychological community.

A large number of researchers today believes that human cognition, normal or pathological, can only be understood by considering the laterally differentiated functions of the two sides of the brain. Evidence has accumulated that schizophrenia, affective psychosis, and infantile autism result from a unilateral cerebral dysfunction, and that differences in cognitive structure in the sexes and among people of the same sex are associated with variations in the lateral organization of the cerebral hemispheres. Patterns of cognitive ability on standardized psychometric tests and changes in those patterns with development have been related to cerebral asymmetry. Since human cognition is a reflection of cortical activity, and if the left and right cortices differ in the nature of their integrative processes, it is inevitable that all aspects of human thinking will reflect their asymmetrical neurological substrates.

A converging body of evidence from unilaterally brain-damaged patients, from investigatings of normal people, and from split-brain research points to the conclusion that the left hemisphere is vastly superior and dominant to the right in linguistic processing, that it thinks logically, deductively, analytically, and sequentially, that its linguistic superiority derives from fundamental differences in the way it processes, decodes, encodes, and arranges information. The right hemisphere is superior and dominant to the left in visuospatial construction, in recording the literal properties of the physical world, in visualizing the relationships of objects in space, and probably, in reaching accurate conclusions in the absence of logical justification. Further, the hemispheres differ in their propensity to control behavior as a function of task demands.

A brief survey of recent findings with split-brain patients will illustrate the kinds of hemispheric differences that have been seen. The right hemisphere has been shown to understand simple spoken or written language (Gazzaniga and Sperry, 1967), but it apparently has grave difficulties in syntactic understanding. Gazzaniga and Hillyard (1971) found that when shown a picture of some activity, the right hemisphere could not distinguish a correct from an incorrect oral description of the stimulus with respect to subject versus object in semantically unconstrained situations, to singular versus plural, or to present versus future tense. The only grammatical dimension that was correctly discriminated was affirmative versus negative. These results suggest that the right hemisphere's capacity to follow oral instructions depends on an extraction of major content words that are, in the simple instructions it receives, sufficient to communicate the essential information. Further, though the word comprehension vocabulary of the right hemisphere on the Peabody Picture Vocabulary Test is at the approximate level of a 12-year-old child (Zaidel, 1976a), on the Token Test, which measures comprehension of complex instructions such as, "Put the red circle between the yellow rectangle and the green rectangle," the right hemisphere scores at the level of a 4-year-old child (Zaidel, 1977). The lack of semantic constraint and the load that is placed on short-term memory in the Token Test apparently taxes the right hemisphere beyond its linguistic limit. The above studies illustrate the radical differences in the structure of language comprehension in the hemispheres. It may not be valid to describe the right hemisphere's comprehension capacities as language at all. Patterson (personal communication) has shown that a 4-year-old gorilla, Koko, scores at an age level comparable to human children on the Peabody Picture Vocabulary Test given with oral instructions, and as any dog owner can testify, most pet dogs raised in human families comprehend at least a limited vocabulary of words (sit, stay, come, no, etc.).

Assuming that the human right hemisphere is considerably more intelligent than both hemispheres of an ape or a dog, it would be expected that it could acquire a more extensive comprehension vocabulary. But the profound syntactical failures displayed provide little evidence that it possesses language in the sense of the left hemisphere. It might be argued that the dog comes to understand various words by a simple sound-meaning associative process, whereas language comprehension in people depends on a sequential phonetic analysis of a word's phonemic components. While this may be true for the left hemisphere, there is no evidence that the right hemisphere possesses any capacity for phonetic analysis at all. Levy and Trevarthen (1977; Levy, 1974) found that though the right hemisphere could correctly indicate assent or disagreement that it had seen an object named by the experimenter, behavior was random if it was required to indicate whether the object it had seen had a name that *rhymed* with a named object. If the right hemisphere had seen, for example, a picture of a bee, it had no idea whether or not the name of this object rhymed with "key." Further, Zaidel (1976b) showed that the right hemisphere was totally incapable of pointing to a printed letter designating the stop consonant of consonant-vowel (CV) syllables that it heard. This incapacity contrasts strongly with the right hemisphere's ability to point to a real word spoken by an experimenter. It appears that words are perceived by the right hemisphere as unanalyzed wholes and that meaning is elicited directly by the acoustic gestalt. In summary, whereas the right side of the brain can extract a great deal of meaning from spoken and written language, its extremely deficient capacities at syntactic and phonetic analysis give no evidence that it possesses a linguistic system even remotely similar to that of the left hemisphere. The strategies it utilizes to derive meaning from words or phrases appear to be similar in all respects to those of other mammals, and its superiority to animals in language comprehension may be attributed to its higher intelligence. Though the quantitative differences between the hemispheres of split-brain patients in their capacity to understand language are less than studies of unilaterally brain damaged patients would have led us to expect, the qualitative differences in the methods used to achieve comprehension are profound, and even greater than could have been predicted. As had been suggested by Levy-Agresti and Sperry (1968) and Bogen (1969b), the hemispheres differ not so much in how they **perform,** but rather in the ways they **think.**

This conclusion holds equally for certain nonlinguistic capacities in which the left hemisphere is deficient. Levy, Trevarthen, and Sperry (1972) tested the hemispheres of split-brain patients on two aspects of performance: (a) the tendency to take control of behavior under competitive conditions; and (b) the relative ability of each hemisphere when it took control. In this series of tests, two stimuli were presented simultaneously, one to each hemisphere, under tachistoscopic conditions. Subjects were required to either select a matching stimulus from a set in free vision, or to name or describe the stimulus seen. The stimuli consisted of faces or nonsense shapes, for which names were taught, common objects for which names were known, or three-component vertical arrays of X's and squares. On the vast majority of matching trials, the right hemisphere took control of behavior, selecting a choice matching the stimulus it had seen; erroneous choices were made as often as left hemisphere matches. Excluding trials on which left hemisphere matches were made, errors and chance guessing constituted 7%, 25%, 2%, and 40% of total responses on the faces, nonsense shapes, common objects, and chain pattern tests, respectively.

On naming trials, the left hemisphere stimulus was named on the majority of occasions and, excluding trials on which right hemisphere stimuli were named, errors and chance guessing constituted 47% of responses to the faces test, 68% of responses on the nonsense shapes test, 3% of responses on the common objects test, and 26% of responses on the chain pattern test.

These results show several very interesting aspects of hemispheric differentiation. First, when a simple match is required, the right hemisphere dominates behavior, even though the left hemisphere could have controlled responding. Left hemisphere dominance for naming was, of course, expected. Second, the dominance of the right hemisphere for matching occurred independently of its ability as indexed by error rates. Though its matching performance for faces and nonsense shapes was considerably better than was the naming performance of the left hemisphere, the hemispheres performed equally well on the common objects test, and the left hemisphere's naming performance on the chain pattern test was superior to the right hemisphere's matching performance. The instruction to match physically two objects apparently activated the right hemisphere which then assumed almost total control over behavior, even when it was relatively poor at performing a given task. Hemispheric dominance seems to be more determined by a hemisphere's imagined than real capacity.

The ability differences are interesting also. Even though the patients could readily repeat names they had been taught for faces and nonsense shapes, the left hemisphere seemed to have difficulty encoding the images well enough to permit accurate identification. For objects that had been well-known since early childhood, there was no difficulty at all, and on patterns whose components were sequentially arranged and easily decomposable, performance exceeded that of the right hemisphere.

The difficulty manifested by the left hemisphere in identifying faces and nonsense shapes is completely consistent with inferences drawn from patients with right hemisphere damage. The left hemisphere is not only inferior to the right in spatial transformational tasks tested by the cross-modal test described previously, but also in the apprehending and remembering of visual configurations for which no verbal labels had been available in long-term memory. The equally good performances of the two hemispheres on pictures of objects whose names had been known since early childhood is congruent with Milner's observations (1967) that recognition of common objects is unimpaired whether patients suffer from right or left hemisphere lesions. The superiority of the left hemisphere on the chain pattern test apparently results from its superior means for encoding the stimulus information. An analysis of error patterns revealed that the right hemisphere, but not the left, displayed a very large number of transformation errors. A pattern such as X-X-square, for example, was frequently matched with square-square-X. It seems that the left hemisphere sequentially labeled each of the three components of the stimulus, transforming the spatial ordering into a well-encoded temporal order that was retained and guided the response. In contrast, the right hemisphere appeared to attempt an encoding of the stimulus as a spatial gestalt. While such a strategy works well with stimuli in which the arrangement of components defines the meaning of the stimulus or that form a "good gestalt," it breaks down with stimuli lacking such "visual syntax."

Levy et al. (1972) also noted that the hemispheres manifested strategic differences with faces and nonsense shapes, the left hemisphere searching for distinctive subordinate features that could be verbally labeled, the right hemisphere extracting the critical form invariants that served to identify the whole stimulus. Thus, the left hemisphere's disability in identifying faces or nonsense shapes, like the right hemisphere's disability in comprehending language, derives from its specialized mode of thinking that is poorly designed for the task. The relatively good performance of the left hemisphere compared to the right on identification of the chain patterns seems to be a reflection of those same cognitive differences responsible for the left hemisphere's linguistic superiority.

The tendency of the right hemisphere to control behavior when the patients are instructed to point to a choice physically identical with a stimulus they had seen is due to the cognitive requirements of the task, and **not** to a dominance of the right hemisphere for pointing. When two words are presented simultaneously, one to each hemisphere, and patients must point to a picture named by the word, or when pictures are presented and patients must point to other pictures whose names rhyme, the left hemisphere assumes control over behavior (Levy and Travarthen, 1977). Though the right hemisphere is totally incompetent at rhyming, it is perfectly capable of reading the simple words in the word-picture task. Consequently, the dominance of the left hemisphere for a simple reading task cannot be attributed to right hemisphere incapacity but to differences in how the hemispheres **perceive** their competence. Other studies have shown that when the same input and choice stimuli are used under different instructional conditions, hemispheric dominance is controlled by instruction. Thus, if told to select choices that **look** similar to what they have seen (e.g., a hat with a brim when the stimulus is a cake on a cake plate), the right hemisphere dominates, but if told to select choices that **go with** or that would be **used with** the stimulus seen (e.g., a knife and fork to go with the cake), the left hemisphere dominates (Levy and Trevarthen, 1976).

Neither the nature of stimuli, choices, nor responses, or even actual hemispheric capacity, determines hemispheric dominance. Rather, a hemisphere's propensity to control behavior seems to be a function of how it perceives the cognitive requirements for a given task. If those requirements call for literal encoding of sensory information or visualization of spatial relations, the right hemisphere assumes and maintains control, even if it turns out that the particular task is poorly processed by the controlling hemisphere. If there appears to be a requirement for speaking, phonetic analysis, semantic decoding of words, or for the derivation of conceptual categories, the left hemisphere assumes and maintains control, even if on the particular task, the right hemisphere is as competent as the left.

The various studies described, as well as others, leave little doubt that both sides of the brain are highly specialized neurological computers, each predominant in and superior for differing sets of functions, functions that complement those of the other hemisphere. The differences in manifest performance between the hemispheres on various types of problems are considerably less dramatic than the differences in strategy used to solve those problems. Both sides of the brain possess a human level of intelligence and both are highly adaptive at utilizing their specialized processes for dealing with a variety of cognitive tasks. Only when those tasks are totally incapable of solution by a hemisphere's special neural program, or when the level of intelligence of a hemisphere is insufficient for discovering how to apply its skills to a highly unusual task, will radical differences in actual performance be observed. The right hemisphere manifests almost no competence at speech and rhyming, and the left hemisphere manifests little competence at visualizing the three-dimensional form of a two-dimensional representation or at remembering and identifying meaningless visual or tactile (Milner and Taylor, 1972) configurations. In contrast, the right hemisphere extracts a good deal of meaning from language, though using quite probably, the same mechanisms used by other mammals, and the left hemisphere extracts significant meaning from nonlinguistic stimuli, though probably using sequential, analytic processes. In summary, the fundamental differences in the two sides of the brain reside in their profoundly different approaches to the world of experience and in their differing propensities to control behavior as a function of the perceived cognitive strategies demanded. There can no longer be any doubt that rather than being a half-brained species, we are a two-brained species, each brain having its special mind.

Given the foregoing picture of hemispheric specialization, it is of interest to determine how these specializations are integrated and manifested in the intact individual and to assess the relationship between patterns of lateral organization and psychological function. In the sections to follow, studies on variations in hemispheric lateralization and cognition are discussed.

III. Individual Differences in Human Brain Organization

Though the pattern of asymmetric hemispheric function discussed in preceding sections appears to be valid for most individuals, there are a number of variations that differentiate people by age, sex, handedness, hand posture during writing, eye dominance, and psychological structure. Though the cerebral hemispheres are anatomically, electrophysiologically, and behaviorally lateralized at birth, both infant hemispheres possess an enormous plasticity in their capacity for assuming the other hemisphere's functions. There are sex differences in relative rate of left and right hemisphere maturation, degree of lateral differentiation in adulthood, and intrahemispheric organization. A number of behavioral traits and asymmetries, such as handedness, hand posture during writing, and eyedness, are correlated with variations in cerebral asymmetry: The direction and degree of cerebral laterality vary with hand posture and the direction of behavioral asymmetries. Even among individuals having well-lateralized brains in the typical direction, the tendency of one or the other hemisphere to dominate affective responses, cognitive processing, and behavioral control is correlated with variations in personality structure. Certain classes of psychiatric patients manifest profound abnormalities in either the balance of hemispheric dominance, in the capacity of one hemisphere to utilize its specialized programs, or both. Extreme sociocultural environments during development can affect, radically and asymmetrically, hemispheric maturation, competence, or usage. Perinatal stress on the infant brain can shift patterns of lateral development.

Probably the only people who have the "classical" cerebral laterality pattern—the hemispheres being strongly lateralized with language and related functions almost entirely confined to the left hemisphere with a normal balance of hemispheric dominance—are adult, right handed, right eyed males with a normal, noninverted hand posture during writing; who have no left handed relatives, were free from birth stress, whose sensory functions are intact, who suffer no psychotic illness, and who were reared in a relatively normal environment. Such individuals probably constitute no more than 15% of the population. The remaining 85% of us manifest various deviations from this standard pattern either in direction or degree of hemispheric lateralization, intrahemispheric organization, plasticity of one hemisphere to assume the other hemisphere's functions, or in dominance relations of the hemispheres with respect to behavioral control. Far from being a species-specific trait, the standard laterality pattern is but one among many in the human population.

In the following sections, the nature of the observed variations will be highlighted, and the possible causes of individual differences in lateral organization will be discussed.

A. Developmental Variations

Traditionally, the neonatal human brain was thought to be symmetric in function: Each hemisphere had the capacity for developing the full range of cognitive abilities of both sides of the brain. Lateralization of function was presumed to develop with age, each hemisphere becoming progressively more specialized and less capable of assuming the other hemisphere's functions, so that by puberty lateralization was complete (Lenneberg, 1966). This conclusion was based on the fact that, though left hemisphere lesions in children typically produce aphasia, the deficit is almost always transient; within two years following the trauma no residual defects remain. In adult cases with left-sided damage, the majority not only develop aphasia, but aphasic symptoms are permanent. When recovery occurs, it is rapid; symptoms disappearing within three months, suggesting that lesions spared the main language areas and that the aphasic symptoms resulted from a temporary disruption of the language centers, possibly due to trauma-induced swelling of brain tissues. In prepubertal children, recovery of function is a protracted process, the majority having residual symptoms after three months, and about one-third having residual symptoms even after a year, and almost all recovering by the end of two years.

In addition to differences between children and adults in recovery patterns, the aphasic symptoms differ. In young children, a lesion to Wernicke's area produces mutism and agrammatism. A lesion to the same area in a 10-year-old is likely to produce anomia, as well as a phonemic aphasia in which patients are asked to name some object such as an ashtray, and fail to do so even when given a cue such as "ashtr—."

Phonemic aphasia is a deterioration of anomia. Phonemic aphasias are common in adults with Wernicke's lesions, and in later adult life, jargon aphasia, which is a further deterioration of phonemic aphasia (Brown and Hécaen, 1976), is likely to occur. According to Brown and Hécaen, localization of function within a hemisphere progresses throughout life, so that functions having a widespread cortical representation become increasingly more localized with age. Observations of clinical cases suggest progressive lateralization of function as well as progressive localization of function within a hemisphere.

However, recent data show that the neonatal hemispheres are not functionally equipotential and that they are asymmetric, even in manifest function. The majority of infants displays a rightward tonic neck reflex, and the direction of the reflex is correlated with handedness at age 10 (Gesell and Ames, 1947). Turkewitz, Gordon, and Birch (1965) and Turkewitz, Birch, Moreau, Levy, and Cornwell (1966) found that most infants lie with the head turned to the right. Siqueland (1964) and Siqueland and Lipsett (1966) found right head turning to be more easily conditioned than left head turning in infants. Wickelgren (1967) found that infants 2–5 days of age showed a pronounced tendency to deviate their eyes to the right. All these findings suggest greater left than right hemisphere activation in infants. The question is whether this more activated hemisphere is, in any way, specialized for language functions.

In adults, there is an asymmetric blocking of the alpha rhythm over the hemisphere engaged in specialized cognitive processing (Morgan, McDonald, and MacDonald, 1971). The infant's homologue of the alpha rhythm is a 4-Hz wave, and Gardiner and Walter (1977) found selective blocking of this rhythm over the left hemisphere of infants to verbal stimuli and over the right to musical stimuli. Molfese (1977) found larger evoked potentials to musical chords over the infant right hemisphere and to CV syllables over the left hemisphere. Using dishabituation of nonnutritive sucking as a measure of discrimination, Entus (1977) observed greater discrimination of music with the left ear and of speech with the right ear in infants. These results were confirmed by Best and Glanville (1978) with dishabituation of heart rate as the discriminative measure in infants from 3 to 5 months of age. One sees, then, that with both electrophysiological and behavioral measures, the infant brain is functionally lateralized in the same direction as is seen in the majority of adults.

Witelson (1977) has provided a massive review of the literature on lateralization in children as measured by dichotic listening, tachisto-scopic, and dichhaptic tests of functional asymmetry. In brief, her review led her to the conclusion that **degree** of lateral differentiation remains invariant throughout the developmental period, that there is no evidence that lateralization of function is a progressive, developmental phenomenon. The magnitude of perceptual asymmetries in children from the earliest ages at which this has been measured (about age 2) is as great as that seen in adults. Obviously, children manifest increasing cognitive development of both hemispheres so that the cognitive domain that can be integrated becomes progressively larger with maturation. This means that no hemispheric differences can be expected to be found for cognitive operations beyond the intellectual capacities of the child, since neither hemisphere would have acquired the specialized capacities required. For example, a 3-year-old would be unlikely to show superior left hemisphere abilities for interpreting a passage from Shakespeare. Also, a 3-year-old might show only a very slight left hemisphere advantage for matching of rhyming words simply because the left hemisphere has not yet developed its capacities in this domain, but this would not imply that lateralization was still in the process of development, but merely that cognition was still immature. It is when overall performance level is controlled that the magnitude of asymmetries appears to remain invariant.

Taken in conjunction with clinical findings, the studies on normal infants and children suggest that there is a major distinction between plasticity of hemispheric function and manifest lateralization of function. While lateralization of function is present at birth, and its magnitude remains unchanged throughout life, there can be little doubt that the plastic capacity of each side of the brain to assume the other hemisphere's functions becomes increasingly reduced with maturation, and that for the majority, is lost entirely by puberty.

It should be mentioned that even in the young infant, this plasticity is incomplete. Dennis and Kohn (1975) found that adult infantile hemiplegics with left hemispherectomy were inferior to those with right hemispherectomy in the comprehension of passive voice sentences; the latter group showing no deficits, the former group displaying little evidence of any comprehension for semantically unconstrained sentences. Kohn and Dennis (1974) also found that adult infantile hemiplegics with right hemispherectomy were deficient on visuospatial problems as compared to patients with left hemispherectomy. Thus, while each hemisphere of the infant has a remarkable ability to subsume the functions of the removed half-brain, the ability is limited to certain types of cognitive operations. In the split-brain patient, the right hemisphere's "language" is specifically limited in syntactic understanding; it may be that in cases of left hemispherectomy in infantile hemiplegics, the language of the remaining right hemisphere utilizes alternative strategies for the accomplishment of language performance. In the Kohn and Dennis (1974) study, patients with right hemispherectomy performed adequately on visuospatial tasks that could be performed by normal 10-year-olds and showed deficiencies only on those tasks dependent on later stages of cognitive maturation.

It is as if the infant left hemisphere, in the absence of the right, has the competence to develop a restricted level of visuospatial function, and perhaps even this is mediated through unusual processing strategies. In normal people, certain tests of presumed visuospatial function can be performed using verbal–analytic strategies. By memorizing a set of street names and a sequence of right and left turns, it is possible to negotiate through a strange city, totally bypassing the need to form mental images. In infantile hemiplegics with hemispherectomy or in children with unilateral brain damage, it is conceivable that recovery of function represents the development of processing strategies quite different from those normally utilized for the performance of various functions. Plasticity may be more a matter of learning to apply processing strategies specialized in one hemisphere to behaviors normally dependent on the specialties of the other hemisphere, than of the development of new neurological pathways and processing strategies normally associated with the damaged or removed half-brain. Adults may be unable to learn to apply the strategies of one hemisphere to tasks formerly performed by the other, just as they are unable to learn a second language with anything like the fluency and ease of children. The progressive within-hemisphere localization of function that Brown and Hécaen (1976) have discussed may be a critical aspect of the loss of hemispheric plasticity. Further studies will be required to discover whether children with recovered language following left hemisphere lesions depend on unusual processes for language performance.

In addition to the bifunctional competence that a hemisphere develops when the other is damaged or removed in early childhood, the same type of bifunctional development occurs in cases of agenesis of the corpus callosum (Jeeves, 1972; Netley, 1977; Saul and Sperry, 1968). At birth, each hemisphere apparently possesses a primary program of specialization that becomes progressively refined and more competent with maturation and a capacity for integrating behaviors normally programmed by the other half-brain. This capacity in the normal child seems to become increasingly restricted with development, under the influence of inhibition mediated via the corpus callosum from the other half-brain. With early hemispheric damage or callosal agenesis no such inhibition occurs, and the secondary capacity matures to the level of competence seen in adult infantile hemiplegics. In normal children, it cannot be said that the degree of lateral differentiation increases, but lateralization apparently would **decrease** were it not for the mutual inhibition of secondary capacities exerted by each hemisphere on the other.

It seems clear that lateralization of cerebral function is a prenatally determined biological trait of the human species that can be strongly affected by early cerebral abnormalities. To what extent do sociocultural factors affect lateral development?

The effect of culture on handedness is obvious. During earlier times in American culture, left-handedness was severely punished, and in many other cultures today even more severe inhibition of sinistrality is practiced. As evidence for these assertions, the frequency of left-handedness as measured by writing hand varies widely from culture to culture and within the same culture over time, and these variations can be directly related to the degree of cultural pressure to be right-handed. The frequency of left-handed writers has increased in the U.S. from 2.2% in 1932 to over 11% by 1972 (Levy, 1976). Further, in the Detroit school system, where no pressure was exerted on children by teachers to be right handed, the frequency of sinistral writers in 1932 was 7.5% (Pyle and Drouin, 1932), clearly reflecting the unusually low level of dextral conformity demanded for this time period.

Though cultural induction of dextrality for a specifically trained unimanual skill can and does occur, individuals adopting the right hand for a given activity in consequence of such social pressure do not, thereby, become right-handers. Teng, Lee, Yang, and Chang (1976) found that though only 1% of Taiwanese use the left hand for writing, so strongly is sinistral writing punished in this culture, the distribution of continuously scored manual dominance on a variety of activities is highly similar to that seen in western societies. In other words, for unimanual activities not specifically conditioned to be performed by the right hand, sinistrality was manifested and there was little evidence of any generalization from dextrally trained skills to others that were ignored by the culture. We may conclude that sociocultural effects on handedness are confined to those manual activities that are directly trained and that sufficiently refined tests can reveal the basic pattern of manual dominance that would have emerged in the absence of social pressure. In summary, sociocultural factors appear to have only the most superficial effects on handedness, and it is unlikely that normal variations in these factors produce any fundamental reorganization of the brain.

However, extreme environments may well produce radical changes in brain organization. Neville (1977), in an examination of congenitally deaf children, found the patterns of cerebral lateralization to differ from those of normal children and to vary as a function of whether or not the child was conversant in American Sign Language. In normal children the visual evoked response (VEP) is larger over the right than left hemisphere, but in nonsigning deaf children, evoked response magnitude was found to be small and little hemispheric asymmetry was seen. In signing deaf children, the VEP was larger over the left hemisphere than right. These results suggest that in the absence of either oral or sign language, the brain becomes underreactive and little lateral differentiation of response develops. In normal hearing children the visuospatial right hemisphere develops a greater response to visual signals than the left, but in deaf signing children, for whom language is purely visual, it appears that the left linguistic hemisphere becomes asymmetrically responsive to visual signals.

In unpublished data, Neville also found that on tachistoscopic tests, deaf signers not only show a left hemisphere (right visual field) superiority for discriminating hand signs, but also for a dot location task that, in normals, is better performed by the right hemisphere. It is possible that the effects seen by Neville result from differential attentional effects in the different groups of children, with arousal having a high threshold in nonsigning deaf children, being asymmetrically allocated to the right hemisphere in hearing children, and to the left hemisphere in signing deaf children in response to visual signals. Living in a silent world with no access to a formal communication system could reasonably be expected to make a child underresponsive to external stimulation; whereas for a signing deaf child, any visual signal could serve to alert the linguistic left hemisphere in preparation for processing. It is conceivable, of course, that the Neville results reflect an actual change in the organizational properties of each hemisphere, so that were it possible to trace the neurological pathways responsible for differential hemispheric function, it would be found that the left hemisphere of the signing deaf was more similar to the right hemisphere than was the case in hearing people, and that the right hemisphere was incompletely matured. If this were the case, one would expect that the signing deaf would manifest specific deficiencies on pure spatial function not involving communication or the understanding of social interaction. There is no evidence for such a deficiency, and it seems more likely that it is the dynamical properties of attention and arousal that have changed.

In addition to the change in lateral functioning that results from deafness, a rather profound change can also be produced by extreme environmental deprivation. Genie, the child of a blind mother and psychotic father, was found at the age of 13 years 7 months after having been isolated from all human contact in a small locked room from the age of 20 months (Curtiss, 1977). At the age of 20 years, dichotic listening and tachistoscopic tests, as well as studies of Genie's auditory and visual evoked responses, indicate that her response to language, as well as to other stimuli, is mediated almost entirely by the right hemisphere. It would appear that the failure of Genie to utilize her left hemisphere for cognitive processing and behavioral control is due to the extreme deprivation of adequate stimuli for left hemisphere development that she suffered throughout childhood. Just as deprivation studies with animals have shown specific functional degeneration of neural tissue when adequate stimulation is absent during development, so it appears that the human left hemisphere is dependent on social-linguistic interaction during the critical childhood period for normal maturation.

While the nonsigning deaf show little evidence of cerebral asymmetry, and the signing deaf, an abnormally reactive left hemisphere to visual stimulation, Genie manifests an almost total absence of left hemisphere processing. Congenitally deaf children, if they lack sign language, still have the opportunity for communicative interaction with others, and if proficient in sign language, have a well-developed linguistic system highly dependent on visual processing. Genie, in contrast, had no communicative interaction of any type except as the victim of abuse from the age of 20 months until adolescence. She had no social world, heard no language, had no opportunity to even learn gestual communication, and was severely punished if she vocalized at all. On all cognitive tests depending on left hemisphere function, Genie is profoundly defective, but on tests depending solely on right hemisphere function, she scores well **above** the normal adult level. Indeed, on some tests she was above the 98th percentile. It would appear that even the sensory-deprived environment of Genie's childhood is sufficient for right hemisphere development, but lack of a social environment during the critical childhood period evidently irrevocably blocks normal left hemisphere function.

The social environments imposed by deafness, and in the case of Genie, must be considered extreme conditions, and we may ask what evidence there is that social variation within normal limits produces effects on the development of cerebral lateralization. Geffner and Hochberg (1971) reported that children from a low socioeconomic background only demonstrated a right ear advantage on verbal dichotic listening tests at age 7, whereas middle class children manifested a right ear advantage by age 4. One cannot know from this observation whether the differing environments actually produced a change in brain organization, whether the apparent laterality difference was simply an artifact of differing performance levels (Levy, 1977), or whether there may have been genetic differences in the two groups that were responsible for the differing performances. However, Bever (1971) examined ear dominance in two groups of low-SES children, one of which had been exposed to an enrichment program. Though IQs and performance levels were the same for the two groups, only the enriched group showed a right ear superiority. This group also manifested greater handedness development.

Though the Bever results seen to suggest that environmental enrichment promotes lateralization, there is, as discussed, no evidence that lateralization develops. Conceivably, Bever's enriched and control groups were differentiated in some way prior to the enrichment manipulation. If cerebral laterality, as measured on appropriate tests whose cognitive requirements are not beyond the age group measured, remains unchanged from the age of 2 or 3 years to adulthood, it makes little sense to posit different rates of lateralization in children as a function of environmental enrichment. What clearly does change with age is the level of cognitive maturation; if some test of laterality requires abilities beyond the cognitive level of the child, no perceptual asymmetries could be observed since neither hemisphere would be competent for the task at hand. In Bever's study, however, the overall **performance** levels of the two groups were the same. Possibly, environmental enrichment changes attentional strategies that might underlie the observed asymmetries.

There are other complexities in interpreting the Bever data. Starck, Genesee, Lambert, and Seitz (1977) compared ear scores of monolingual speakers of English versus trilinguals in English, French, and Hebrew. The subjects in this study were Jewish children in kindergarten, first, and second grades. In a first study, a right ear superiority was seen in trilinguals, though not monolinguals, but a second study failed to confirm this. In the second study, though nonsignificant, monolinguals had a larger asymmetry than trilinguals (in monolinguals, right ear = 115% of the left ear; in trilinguals, right ear = 110% of left ear). It must be concluded, therefore, that the initial conclusion represents a Type I error and that there was no effect of multilingualism on lateralization. If the presumed linguistic enrichment in Bever's study increased lateralization, it would be expected that the language enrichment of the trilingual children would have the same effect.

Thus there is little evidence to support the view that normal sociocultural variations affect lateral development of the brain. Whether groups classified by socioeconomic status may differ, for other reasons, in performance profiles on laterality tests is still open. Knox and Kimura (1970) found clear right ear superiorities in low-SES children even in their youngest age group (age 5), though Geffner and Hochberg (1971) did not. Also, Dorman and Geffner (1974) found right ear superiorities in 6-year-olds from a low SES background as strong as those seen in children from a middle-SES background. Geffner and Dorman (1976) saw no SES difference for ear asymmetries in 4-year-olds. The weight of evidence suggests that SES has little effect on laterality patterns, either directly or via its correlations with other variables. In the normal child, the brain is lateralized at birth; and in the absence of early brain damage, given a normal social environment, cerebral maturation seems to follow a standard developmental program. Each hemisphere gains in cognitive competence for its specialized functions and progressively loses the capacity for integrating behaviors under control of the other side of the brain. Only in the presence of neurological damage or extreme environmental deprivation is this developmental program disrupted.

B. Manual, Ocular, and Pedal Correlations with Cerebral Laterality

That handedness and cerebral laterality are related phenomena has been recognized for many years. Though the large majority of dextrals have language localized in the left hemisphere; sinistrals are heterogenous with respect to cerebral lateralization, some having language integrated by the left hemisphere, some by the right, and some having partial bilateralization of function (see Levy, 1974, for review). The probability of aphasia in left- and ambihanded individuals is considerably higher than would be expected were linguistic functions completely unilaterally organized. In such a case, if lesions are randomly distributed to the left and right hemispheres, only half the patients would develop aphasia. In fact, of the 52 patients studied by Conrad (1949), Humphrey and Zangwill (1952 a,b), and by Goodglass and Quadfasal (1954), half with left and half with right sided damage, almost 75% displayed language disorders, indicating that in almost 25% of the group, injury to the subordinate language hemisphere could produce at least a temporary aphasia. Further support for the view that in a substantial proportion of sinistrals, linguistic functions are partially bilateralized, derives from the frequency of aphasia recovery. In the Conrad, Humphrey, and Zangwill, and Goodglass and Quadfasal patients, half of those who initially became aphasic, recovered. In contrast, Luria (1970) found that after left hemisphere damage, 100% of fully dextral patients from dextral families suffered language disorders, and in 97% the disorder was permanent. Incomplete dextrality or familial sinistrality was associated with a lower initial aphasia rate following injury to the left side of the brain and a higher frequency of recovery.

Although conclusions regarding the direction and degree of cerebral lateralization in completely right-handed individuals from dextral families can be inferred with confidence from aphasia data, the same is not true of other groups. A disruption of language in the latter may occur even when it is the subordinate verbal hemisphere that is damaged, and recovery of linguistic functions may occur when the more specialized verbal hemisphere is damaged. In cases of transient aphasia, it is impossible to say whether the injured or the noninjured hemisphere was the primary site of speech, and to deduce the relation between degree and direction of lateralization. One firm generalization can be made from such studies: Sinistrality or ambilaterality in an individual or in members of his family increases the probability of right hemisphere language and of partial bilateralization of linguistic functions. Whether right or left hemisphere speech in these groups is more related to bilateral representation cannot be deduced.

Another problem concerning the determination of cerebral lateralization in left-handers is that some left-handers appear to represent a normal human variation, while others appear to be a pathological population whose left-handedness results from subtle or overt damage to the left hemisphere during early development (Bakan, Dibb, and Reed, 1973), and there is no reason to suppose that cerebral laterality patterns should be the same in both groups. If early left hemisphere damage is minor and produces no obvious neurological signs, handedness may shift to the left while leaving language centered in the left hemisphere, but if there is clear clinical evidence of early injury to the language regions of the left hemisphere, handedness is likely to shift to the left and language to the right.

In groups of left-handers with no known history of early damage to the left hemisphere, one approach to the problem of distinguishing normal from pathological left-handers has been to separate subjects according to family history of handedness. Statistically, left-handers with left-handed relatives consist predominantly of normal left-handers, whereas those having only dextral relatives would more likely represent pathological cases. Hécaen and Sauguet (1971) found that in nonfamilial sinistrals, aphasic symptoms were associated solely with left hemisphere lesions and 76% of patients in this group were above the median in strength of left-handedness. In contrast, among familial sinistrals, aphasia was equally likely from either right or left hemisphere lesions, and 40% were above the median in strength of left-handedness. These observations strongly suggest that the nonfamilial group, though having no clinical signs of early brain damage, were shifted dextrals in consequence of early cerebral stress to the hand control region of the left hemisphere, and though handedness was shifted, language remained in the left side of the brain. In the familial, presumably nonpathological group of left-handers, cerebral lateralization was variable with respect to direction and degree.

These conclusions have been confirmed in nonclinical populations also, using dichotic and/or tachistoscopic tests of perceptual asymmetry as indices of cerebral laterality. Zurif and Bryden (1969) found right hemisphere language to be more probable in familial than in nonfamilial sinistrals, as did Varney and Benton (1975). Carter-Saltzman (1978) found, on a verbal dichotic test, that nonfamilial sinistrals manifested a mean right ear–left hemisphere superiority, and variance in ear difference scores was smaller than that of right handers from dextral families $F(185,6) = 4.12$, $p < .05$, one-tailed, confirming the almost invariable left hemisphere language localization in sinistrals with no left-handed relatives. The familial sinistrals in Carter-Saltzman's sample had a mean left ear–right hemisphere superiority, and the variance in ear difference scores was larger than for right-handers from dextral families $F(15,185) = 2.29$, $p < .05$, one-tailed, demonstrating the heterogeneity of cerebral laterality patterns in this group of left-handers. In support of the view that familial sinistrals typically represent a neurologically normal group, and nonfamilial sinistrality is often a reflection of shifted handedness and perinatal stress, Carter-Saltzman found that, compared to dextrals, reading performance of the familial group was nonsignificantly superior, but that the nonfamilial group was significantly inferior, $t(117) = 2.29$, $p = .011$, one-tailed.

Thus, in apparently normal left-handers, those with sinistral relatives display great variation in the pattern of lateral organization, whereas those without sinistral relatives may consist of a high proportion of individuals in whom handedness, but not language, has shifted in consequence of early, undiagnosed cerebral stress. It may be expected in pathological populations in which the frequency of sinistrality is increased, that a substantial proportion would represent shifted dextrals. Those with no known history of early left hemisphere damage would, like the nonfamilial sinistrals observed by Hécaen and Sauguet (1971), Zurif and Bryden (1969), and Carter-Saltzman (1978), be likely to have language still centered in the left hemisphere. In contrast, those with known early damage to the language regions of the left side of the brain would be likely to have language shifted to the right hemisphere.

Rasmussen and Milner (1977) confirmed this prediction in a group of epileptic patients. Bolin (1953) has shown that sinistrality is increased in this group. Of left-handed epileptics without clinical evidence of early cerebral injury, 70%, 15%, and 15%, respectively, manifested left, bilateral, and right hemisphere language. The results were obtained using the Wada technique to assess language localization, in which one hemisphere is briefly inactivated by injection of sodium amobarbitol into the internal carotid artery. The small proportion showing right hemisphere language is consistent with the supposition that this group of patients contained a larger fraction of shifted dextrals compared to normal, familial sinistrals. In epileptics with known early damage to the left hemisphere, a rare condition in normal groups of sinistrals, 28%, 19%, and 53%, respectively, had left, bilateral, and right hemisphere language. The increase in bilateral language representation compared to the group without known early injury was not significant [$\chi^2(1) = .53, p = .47$], but the distribution in the direction of lateralization in those with unilateral language was significantly different [$\chi^2(1) = 42.93, p < .0001$].

The Rasmussen and Milner results, taken in conjunction with observations of normal populations and of neurological patients who were normal, prior to lesions incurred in adulthood, offer support for the view that minor perinatal cerebral stress, insufficient to produce overt clinical signs, often does induce left-handedness while leaving language specialized to the left. Major left cerebral damage is likely to shift both handedness and language. Thus, in normal samples of left-handers, right hemisphere language would almost never be pathological in origin; left hemisphere language could either represent a normal variant or minor stress during early development. When right cerebral language is pathological in left-handers, it is found almost exclusively in patient populations who suffered major left hemisphere damage during infancy. Rasmussen and Milner found that even gross early damage to the left hemisphere did not induce a shift of language to the right hemisphere if the injury spared the primary speech zones.

In considering cerebral lateralization in left-handers, it is of major importance to distinguish between those who are native sinistrals and those whose handedness has been shifted due to early cerebral stress. In the latter, a further distinction must be made between those in whom handedness alone has shifted and early stress was minor, and those in whom both handedness and language have shifted and damage to the language areas of the left hemisphere was severe. To reiterate, in apparently normal subjects, only the first two groups of left-handers are likely to be represented, the former being heterogeneous with respect to degree and direction of laterality, the latter typically having left cerebral language.

The fact that Rasmussen and Milner found no increase in bilateral language representation in their patients with known early left hemisphere injury suggests that bilateralization of function is likely to represent a normal variation, but their data do not allow a determination of the relation of bilateralization of linguistic function to the location of the major language hemisphere. There is no reason to supose that because aphasia may follow inactivation of either or neither hemisphere (the index of speech bilateralization used by Milner and Rasmussen), that language is symmetrically organized. Though lateralization may be extremely weak, it is still likely that one hemisphere leads the other in the control of language function. A basic question is whether in normal, native left-handers, weak cerebral lateralization is assoicated more with a left or with a right hemisphere localization of the major language centers, or whether degree and direction of lateralization are uncorrelated.

Relevant to this issue is the finding of Satz, Achenbach, Pattishall, and Fennell (1965) that left-handers with left hemisphere language had smaller perceptual asymmetries than did right-handers; those with right hemisphere language had larger asymmetries, suggesting that weak lateralization in normal left-handers is specifically associated with left hemisphere language. If so, the majority of transient aphasics probably have their primary language areas on the left, regardless of the side of the inducing lesion. Levy and Reid (1976, 1978) in adults, and Reid (1980) in children, found a strong directional association between degree of lateralization and location of the language hemisphere in left-handers. In sinistrals with left hemisphere language, cerebral lateralization was weak, and in those with right hemisphere language it was at least as strong, if not stronger, than in right-handers. Levy and Reid's analysis (1978) of error patterns on their verbal tachistoscopic test indicated that the nonverbal hemisphere tended to permute the letters of nonsense syllables in right-handers, and in left-handers with right hemisphere language. This was not so in left-handers with left hemisphere language. In these subjects, the hemispheres were equally proficient at maintaining the correct order of stimulus elements, further evidence for bilateralization of language in this group.

Levy and Reid (1976, 1978) had run pretests on all potential subjects to exclude those having asymmetric visual thresholds, so that the frequency of pathological sinistrality was probably reduced in their sample. A reanalysis of the Levy and Reid data showed that familial sinistrality was unrelated to either degree of lateralization or to performance levels on the verbal and spatial tachistoscopic tests in left-handers having right hemisphere language, and performance levels at least equaled those of right-handers. Of the 24 subjects in this group, 15 had first-degree sinistral relatives and one had a left-handed grandparent. This gives additional weight to the conclusion that in sinistrals from normal populations, those with right hemisphere language represent a completely normal, nonpathological variation.

Among the 24 sinistrals with left hemisphere language, 15 also had first-degree left-handed relatives. On a composite performance measure derived from the two tachistoscopic tests (verbal and spatial), these 15 familial sinistrals did not differ from right-handers, but nonfamilial sinistrals were significantly inferior to right-handers [$t(31) = 4.12$, $p <$ .001], suggesting that in the subgroup of left-handers having left hemisphere language and no sinistral relatives, the probability of a pathological origin of sinistrality is increased. Inspection of individual performance scores of the 9 subjects in this category revealed that only 5 appeared to have a significant processing deficit. Since native left-handers cannot always be expected to have left-handed relatives, this observation is not surprising.

To summarize, both clinical data as well as laterality studies in normal groups are consistent in showing that only a minority of cases of sinistrality can be attributed to early cerebral damage, and that among the majority of left-handers who are free of such injury, some have strongly lateralized right hemisphere language and the remainder have weakly lateralized left hemisphere language. In cases of early cerebral stress to the left hemisphere, language typically remains localized to the left if stress is mild, but shifts to the right if damage is severe and impinges on the primary language areas. Though some of the variance in direction, and possibly degree, of lateralization is due to pathological causes, it must be concluded that the major portion has its origin in normal factors acting during the prenatal period.

This conclusion is strengthened by the facts that (a) the brain is functionally lateralized at birth; (b) anatomical asymmetries homologous with those in adults (Geschwind and Levitsky, 1968) are seen in infants (Witelson and Pallie, 1973; Wada, Clarke, and Hamm, 1975); and (c) by recent observations showing that variations in cerebral anatomy are correlated with handedness. LeMay and Culebras (1972) found that 86% of dextrals showed an expansion of the left parietal operculum, a region in the midst of the posterior language area, as measured by carotid angiograms. Only 5% displayed symmetry and 9% showed a right side expansion. In contrast, 67% of sinistrals had symmetric parietal opercula, 17% had a left side expansion, and 11% had a right side expansion. Also, 6 of the 18 left-handers were given the Wada test and were diagnosed as having left hemisphere language. All 6 had equally enlarged parietal opercula on the left and right, adding additional evidence to the view that when the major language areas are localized to the left hemisphere in left-handers, lateral differentiation is weak. Interestingly, LeMay and Culebras described a right-handed patient who developed aphasia after a right cerebral lesion; in this patient there was little asymmetry of the left and right parietal opercula. In all individuals with the major language hemisphere ipsilateral to the dominant writing hand, cerebral functions may tend to be partially bilateralized.

In Levy and Reid's (1976, 1978) and Reid's (1980) studies, left-handers with left hemisphere language and the one right-hander who had right hemisphere language, used an inverted writing posture, the hand held above the line of writing and the tip of the pencil pointing toward the bottom of the page. Left-handers with right hemisphere language and right-handers with left hemisphere language adopted the typical, noninverted posture, the hand held below the line of writing and the tip of the pencil pointing toward the top of the page. With direction of cerebral lateralization jointly indexed by two tachistoscopic tests (one verbal, one spatial), 70 of the 73 Levy and Reid subjects displayed this association between hand posture during writing and the crossed or uncrossed relation between the language hemisphere and the dominant writing hand, including all 24 dextrals with the normal posture (Group RN), all 24 sinistrals with the normal posture (Group LN), the one right-hander with the inverted posture (Subject RI), and 21 of 24 sinistrals with the inverted posture (Group LI). In the last group, perceptual asymmetries (and presumed degree of cerebral lateralization) were so small that any unreliability or imperfect validity of the indexing measure could easily result in misclassification of subjects. Only one of the three LI subjects displayed a group-atypical laterality pattern on both tachistoscopic tests, and even in this case, neither the asymmetry score on the verbal test nor the spatial test was of sufficient magnitude to reject the hypothesis of no field difference.

That hand posture is a reflection of central neurological organization, rather than an adaptation to the left-to-right direction of writing, is not only demonstrated by the Levy and Reid (1976, 1978) and Reid (1980) results, but also by the fact that a small proportion of dextrals also adopt the inverted posture, and that in Israel, where writing proceeds from right to left, the inverted posture is more prevalent among left- than right-handers (Gur and Gur, personal communication; Shanon, in press).

Smith and Moscovitch (1978) confirmed the hand posture effect on cerebral lateralization using the same tachistoscopic tests as Levy and Reid, but saw no effect of hand posture with a verbal dichotic test. It is possible that, as the authors suggest, auditory aspects of language are differently lateralized in LI subjects than are visual aspects, or that dichotic tests have too low a validity to index cerebral laterality correctly. Berlin and Cullen (1977) have discussed the variety of factors that can affect ear asymmetry scores that are unrelated to hemispheric laterality, and even among right-handers it is rare to find more than 80% displaying a right ear–left hemisphere advantage for verbal material. Also, in Reid's study (1980), tactile tests of lateralization were used and the same results were found as with Levy and Reid's tachistoscopic tests, and it seems a priori unlikely that only acoustic aspects of language have a unique organization. This possibility, however, cannot be ruled out and further studies are required to resolve the issue.

An obvious question is why people having at least some aspects of language lateralized to the hemisphere ipsilateral to the dominant hand should use an inverted hand posture, and the answer must depend on the mechanisms by which the writing hand is controlled in such individuals. Clearly, writing requires access to the linguistic integration areas of the brain, but language functions are, to some extent bilateralized in ipsilateral people and it could be postulated that the lingusitically subdominant hemisphere controls writing via the normally crossed motor pathways. At least one study seems to render such an hypothesis unlikely. Hécaen, Angelergues, and Douzens (1963) found that left hemisphere lesions in left-handers that result in aphasic disorders also produce agraphia. If writing were programmed by the right hemisphere in such people, no agraphia would have been seen. However, Heilman, Coyle, Gonyea, and Geschwind (1973) described the case of a left-handed man who wrote with the right hand. Following a right hemisphere lesion and left hemiplegia, this patient was totally free of aphasic symptoms but had a profound agraphia of the right hand.

That the motor pathways were predominantly crossed in this patient is affirmed by his left hemiplegia. Probably, this patient had written with the right hand as a result of cultural pressure, and in the absence of such pressure would have used the left hand. The absence of aphasia indicates that speech was localized to the left, and Heilman et al. (1973) suggest that the right hemisphere was specialized for manual praxis and that praxic signals from the right were transcommissurally conveyed to the left to be integrated with linguistic information. Under their interpretation, the final common path to the right hand was in the left hemisphere.

If the Heilman et al. patient typifies left-handers with left hemisphere language, then, in these people, lesions to either side of the brain would be expected to produce agraphia and the Hécaen et al. (1963) and Heilman et al. (1973) observations would not be incompatible. Both would be consistent with the possibility that the language subdominant hemisphere in such people participates directly in the control of writing, and not merely as a transfer station for control signals originating in the language dominant left hemisphere. However, neither study is consistent with the hypothesis that in individuals with an ipsilateral relation between speech and the writing hand, writing is solely dependent on the contralateral hemisphere. The bihemispheric control hypothesis leads to the prediction that in all left-handers, injury to the right hemisphere should produce agraphia, and that the agraphia rate should be as high as for right-handers with left hemisphere injury. Disconfirming this prediction is the observation of Hécaen and Sauguet (1971) that the frequency of agraphia in sinistrals after right side damage is extremely small; significantly smaller than in dextrals or sinistrals with left side damage. The agraphia rate in the latter group did not differ.

Geschwind (personal communication) reports that the Hécaen and Sauguet patients were studied some months after incurring damage when reorganization of function to the intact hemisphere of bilateralized sinistrals would have been complete. He explains the low agraphia rate after right side lesions as being due to recovery of writing, using the right hand, after linguistic processes have become reintegrated on the left. However, if reorganization had occurred, it would be expected that sinistrals with left side damage would have shown a similar recovery. Not only did Luria (1970) find that recovery from an initial aphasia after left hemisphere lesions in sinistrals is quite prevalent, but Levy and Reid (1976, 1978) and Reid (1980) observed that left-handers with left hemisphere language were very weakly lateralized, precisely the group expected to manifest a high frequency of lateral reorganization after lesions. The finding of Hécaen and Sauguet that agraphia was as probable in sinistrals with left hemisphere damage as in dextrals is not consistent with the reorganization interpretation; such an interpretation is not, therefore, adequate to explain the low agraphia rate after right side damage in sinistrals.

Possibly, in people with the ipsilateral relation between the primary verbal hemisphere and the dominant hand (hereafter referred to as "ipsilateral" people), the hand is directly controlled by the uncrossed motor pathways (Levy, 1974). To examine this conjecture, Moscovitch and Smith (1979) compared RT's by the two hands to signals displayed in the left or right sensory field using a Donders' type c-reaction (Donders, 1868). In their paradigm, a given hand always responded on any fixed block of trials whenever a signal appeared to the left or right, and no response was given when no signal appeared. In simple reaction time tasks (Donders' a-reaction), in which a fixed response is always given to an invariable stimulus, normal right-handers respond faster to signals ipsilateral to the responding hand. The advantage of the uncrossed signal–hand combination derives from the directness of neural pathways (Poffenberger, 1912). With the crossed signal–hand combination, assuming that motor control is crossed, a response can be initiated only after relay of sensory information across the cerebral commissures to the hemisphere controlling the response. In the c-reaction paradigm, the neural pathway effect is also observed, but only for visual signals (Berlucchi, Crea, Di Stefano, and Tassinari, 1977). With tactile (Broadbent and Gregory, 1962) or auditory (Callan, Kliesz, and Parsons, 1974) signals, the effect of the spatial compatibility of the response key and the signal overwhelms any effect of the neural pathways. Even if a response hand is crossed so that it must depress a key on the opposite side of space, the uncrossed key–signal (and crossed hand–signal) combination yields faster reactions. Even more powerful spatial compatibility effects appear with the Donders' b-reaction, in which variable responses are given as a function of the particular signal presented, and no stimulus modality can reveal the organization of neural pathways.

Moscovitch and Smith always had subjects respond to a key ipsilateral to the hand, so that spatial compatibility and neurological effects were completely confounded, working jointly to produce a superiority for the uncrossed signal–hand combination in subjects with normal crossed motor control, and in opposing directions for any subjects having uncrossed motor control. In subjects having the normal hand posture, both left- and right-handers, and a presumed contralateral language organization, they found, as expected, the usual advantage for signals ipsilateral to the responding hand, regardless of signal modality. In subjects with the inverted hand posture, including one right-hander, and presumed ipsilateral language organization, the same uncrossed superiority was seen for the auditory and tactile tests, an effect that may be attributed to stimulus–response compatibility, but on the visual test, faster reactions were given to signals contralateral to the responding hand, in spite of the fact that any spatial compatibility effects would operate in the opposite direction. These results provide strong support for the hypothesis that individuals having an inverted hand posture, and having ipsilateral language, actually control the hand via the uncrossed pyramidal pathway. However, given the modality-specific effect, Moscovitch and Smith favor the view that such people have a peculiar organization only with respect to the visual system. As noted, the modality-specific results could have been expected on the basis of earlier research, and the postulate that motor control is only unusual in response to visual, but not to auditory and tactile, signals, is premature. The data do not demand such an interpretation; if they are replicated with the Donders' a-reaction paradigm, more serious attention will have to be devoted to this hypothesis.

Assuming that the Moscovitch and Smith observations actually indicate a general reliance on the uncrossed motor tracts for manual control in ipsilateral people, we need to understand the underlying neurological basis for this organization. In most people, about 80% of the pyramidal fibers decussate in the lower medulla to effect contralateral control, and the crossed tracts are about four times larger than the uncrossed tracts. If such crossed predominance also prevails in ipsilateral people, it is difficult to imagine why motor control should be ipsilateral. Fidelity of movement would be expected to be correlated with the size of the mediating pathway, and the hand contralateral to the controlling hemisphere should be superior. Although it is possible that some people depend on the smaller, ipsilateral tracts, available knowledge does not permit any interpretation of why this might be so. Alternatively; it might be that in ipsilateral people, there is a predominance of uncrossed fibers. There is anatomical variation among people in the percentage of decussating pyramidal fibers in the lower medulla, ranging from complete crossing to the total absence of the medullary motor decussating (Flechsig, 1876; Nyberg-Hansen and Rinvik, 1963; Verhaart and Kramer, 1952), and it could be that individuals in whom only a minority of pyramidal fibers decussate have uncrossed motor control. Most neurologists, however, assume that fibers in the uncrossed tracts decussate at the level of synapse with motor neurons in the spinal cord, though evidence in people pertinent to this issue is not available. On a priori grounds, it seems unlikely that major anatomical variations in the pyramidal decussation would be functionally compensated by spinal cord decussation, since such a compensatory reaction would require that ipsilateral embryonic axons "know" that they have failed to cross in the lower medulla. When optic fibers of the amphibian are prevented from crossing in the optic chiasm, they make no attempt to cross at deeper levels of the nervous system and make perfectly normal, though highly maladaptive, synaptic contacts with the ipsilateral optic tectum (Sperry, 1945).

Additional considerations suggest that ipsilateral people might have a predominance of uncrossed motor fibers. Levy and Reid (1976, 1978) found that these individuals differed from others in adopting the inverted hand posture (itself an indication that motor control pathways are unusual) and had weakly lateralized brains with partial bilateralization of function, a pattern of hemispheric organization also occurring in patients with callosal agenesis (Jeeves, 1972; Saul and Sperry, 1968; Netley, 1977). Callosal agenesis is associated with other failures of midline development (François, Eggermont, Evens, Logghe, and De Bock, 1973), and it might be that callosal agenesis and failure of pyramidal decussation are associated and are reflections of a generalized midline blockage occurring during the embryonic period when fibers from these systems would normally cross the midline. It may be that ipsilateral people have the organization they do precisely because of such midline blockage, and that their weak lateral differentiation is a consequence of partial callosal dysgenesis. The symptoms of even total agenesis are usually so minor that it is typically discovered only at autopsy; of those cases discovered during life, refined tests are necessary to differentiate between them and normal individuals (Ferriss and Dorsen, 1975). Under this hypothesis, the frequency of sinistrality should be increased in patients with callosal agenesis since this would be correlated with an uncrossed predominance of pyramidal fibers. This expectation is confirmed: Left- or ambihandedness is observed in almost half the cases described (Saul and Gott, 1976; Ferriss and Dorsen, 1975; Ettlinger, Blakemore, Milner, and Wilson, 1972; Lehmann and Lampe, 1970).

The major problem with the foregoing ideas is that though homolateral hemiplegia has been observed after unlateral lesions (Billet, 1961; Czochra, 1962; Ectors and Achslogh, 1959; Mastrobuono and Munarini, 1963; Zenner, 1898), clinical neurologists report that its frequency is quite low, considerably lower than the frequency of ipsilateral language. Even when the syndrome is observed, it is usually attributed to compression of the contralateral brainstem by a mass lesion. Milner (personal communication) has never observed a case of ipsilateral hemiplegia following injection of sodium amobarbitol in the left or right internal carotid artery. If some 6% of people have predominance of uncrossed motor fibers, the same proportion should be seen with ipsilateral hemiplegia.

The only obvious explanation of the mechanism of hand control in ipsilateral individuals that is consistent with all available data is that the hand is controlled by the uncrossed pathway which, as in other people, is considerably smaller than the crossed pathway. As discussed, though such a possibility is conceivable, the reasons for the existence of such an organization and the means by which movement fidelity would be generated present serious conceptual difficulties. We are, consequently, left in the very unsatisfactory position that each of the possible explanations of ipsilateral hand control is congruent with some findings and either incongruent with others or conceptually objectionable. The resolution of this problem is likely to provide major advances in our understanding of brain–behavior relationship, but it will have to await additional research.

The complexities of the issues involved in understanding the relation between cerebral and behavioral asymmetries highlights the need for keeping a firm focus on neuroanatomy. The assumption of the nineteenth century that manual and cerebral laterality were perfectly correlated arose from a failure to appreciate the possibility that motor control mechanisms, from cortical levels downward, may not be identical in all people. Though the majority may have language and praxic skills specialized to the same hemisphere, this may not be true of all, and while the typical individual may have a predominantly crossed motor control system, some may possess a predominantly uncrossed system. Manual dominance must necessarily result from an interaction between the direction of cerebral lateralization and the functional anatomy of the controlling pathways, and variations in the latter mean that handedness and laterality of the brain must be imperfectly correlated. The factors underlying cerebral asymmetry and asymmetries of behavioral function must be considered to be only partially overlapping, and there is no a priori reason to expect perfect associations.

This restriction holds not only for handedness, but also for any other behaviorally lateralized trait. Left-foot dominance, for example, has been found in 22% of students, only 11% of whom were observed to be left-handed (Peters and Durding, 1979). These data can be understood on the basis of differential control mechanisms for handedness and footedness. There appears to be a substantially greater competence of the ipsilateral hemisphere in most people to control the legs than the hands, possibly because of proportionately more pyramidal fibers for leg control in the uncrossed tract, and possibly because of recrossing of axons at the synaptic level for leg control in the crossed tract (Nathan and Smith, 1973). There is no need to posit varying cortical effects on handedness and footedness, though these may be present, since known variations in the distribution of motor fibers to the upper and lower limbs can account for the observations.

Ocular dominance has been the subject of much controversy, some asserting that it has no relation with handedness (Coren and Kaplan, 1973) and, by implication, none with cerebral laterality. Part of the problem has arisen from the fact that different measures of eye dominance measure different things, but a major difficulty is that there is little understanding of either the neurological basis of ocular dominance or of its function. One possibility is that eye dominance serves to inhibit double images for objects nearer or farther away than a point of fixation. Were both eyes equally dominant in sighting, objects closer than the point of fixation would be seen contralaterally displaced by each eye. If a single eye dominates sighting, only single images will be seen, reducing the complexity of the visual scene to be analyzed.

However, nothing is known regarding the neurology of the attentional mechanisms responsible for eye dominance. Each eye projects its sensory input bilaterally, from the nasal retina to the contralateral hemisphere and from the temporal retina to the ipsilateral hemisphere. It may be that a hemisphere tends to facilitate its crossed input more than its uncrossed input so that images projected on the nasal retinae have an attentional advantage over those on the temporal retinae. The far periphery is only projected on the nasal retinae, the temporal retinae being blind for these regions of space. Thus, it would make adaptive sense for an organism with the visual anatomy of man to be relatively more sensitized to input projected to the nasal retinae so that alterting and orientation responses could be rapidly mediated to stimuli still outside the visual fields of the temporal retinae.

Hayashi and Bryden (1967), on a verbal tachistoscopic task, found a right visual field superiority only in subjects with superior right eye acuity, and no difference between fields for subjects with superior left eye acuity. These results suggest that the nasal retina was a superior pathway compared to the temporal retina, the retinal effects summating with hemispheric effects in subjects with better right eye acuity and opposing hemispheric effects in subjects with superior left eye acuity. These observations are consistent with the suggestion that a hemispheric effect selectively facilitates visual input from the opposite eye, and that ocular dominance may reflect a facilitating asymmetry between the two hemispheres.

Handedness and ocular dominance, in fact, appear to be strongly associated. Merrel (1957) found that of 464 dextral writers, 327 (70.5%) were right-eyed and 137 (29.5%) were left-eyed. Among 33 sinistral writers, 20 (60.6%) were left-eyed and only 13 (39.4%) were right-eyed $\chi^2(1) = 13.79$, $p < .0002$. Gur, Levy and Van Auken (1978) found 205 (77.1%) of 266 right-handers to be right-eyed and 61 (22.9%) to be left-eyed. Of 159 left-handed writers, only 77 (48.4%) were right-eyed and 82 (51.6%) were left-eyed. The difference in distributions was highly significant $\chi^2(1) = 36.56$. $p < .0001$.

These results in general suggest that the verbal hemisphere asymmetrically facilitates visual input from the contralateral eye. The predominance of right-turning tendencies in infants, discussed earlier, is indicative of greater left than right hemisphere arousal, and in adults, alpha activity is more prevalent over the right than the left hemisphere (Morgan, McDonald, and MacDonald, 1971; Morgan, MacDonald, and Hilgard, 1974), again indicating an arousal advantage of the left hemisphere. Also, when hemispheric activation is assessed by the direction of lateral eye movements as a first behavioral response to questions, alpha activity is found to be lower in left than in right hemisphere activators (Bakan and Svorad, 1969). It may be that this generalized arousal asymmetry in favor of the verbal hemisphere generates greater attention for visual input to the nasal retina of the contralateral eye. Also, eye dominance may reflect an initial left hemisphere bias at birth that is reinforced by environmental experience: the more "alert" eye at birth provides more information to the infant and, thus, that eye may further increase its attentional advantage.

The question may be raised as to why the association between eyedness and handedness is imperfect. The variation in cerebral lateralization in left-handers is sufficient to account for the eyedness variations, but in right-handers, some 25–30% are left-eyed, though the vast majority have left hemisphere language. If eyedness merely reflects a relative arousal bias in favor of the left hemisphere, left-eyed dextrals may have a reversed arousal relation with an arousal advantage of the spatial right hemisphere. Gur and Gur (1978) found that left-eyed dextrals fail to manifest the typical right visual field of advantage for verbal material seen in right-eyed dextrals. This observation could be due to a conflict between the processing specialties of the left hemisphere and an arousal bias of the right hemisphere.

Gur, Levy, and Van Auken (1978), though finding that left-eyedness was less prevalent in strong dextrals (21% left-eyed) than in weaker dextrals (25% left-eyed), did not find the difference to be significant $\chi^2(1) = .78, p = .38$, and if arousal relations alone are responsible for left-eyedness in right handers, one would expect dextrality to be weaker in left-eyed individuals. Nevertheless, the causes of left eyedness may have been different in the two groups. Birth histories collected from mothers of subjects, showed that in strong dextrals, left-eyedness was associated with birth stress, as rated on a four-point scale, while in weaker dextrals it was not. Among the former group of 144 subjects, left-eyedness was found in 12.3%, 19.5%, 38.5%, and 75%, respectively, in the no, mild, strong, and severe stress categories.

It appears that eyedness, like handedness, is determined by multiple factors, some innate and closely related to cerebral laterality and some related to birth trauma. It may be that when the infant brain is subjected to trauma, eyedness is the first dimension of laterality to shift, followed by handedness when the hand control region of the left hemisphere is damaged, and lastly, by language itself when trauma is severe and invades the language centers. Eyedness is likely to reflect a generalized attentional phenomenon so that minor stress almost anywhere in the left hemisphere could be sufficient to shift eye dominance.

That eyedness, though susceptible to the effect of perinatal stress, is largely innate is suggested by several considerations. First, it has been established that eyedness and handedness are strongly correlated, and this correlation holds in spite of the relatively high frequency of pathological left-eyedness in right-handers. Second, handedness in conjunction with hand posture, is almost a perfect predictor of cerebral lateralization which is present at birth, and handedness seems to be programmed during the prenatal period. Gesell and Ames (1947) found the direction of the tonic neck reflex in infants as young as 28 weeks postconceptional age to be predictive of handedness at age 10. Also, fingerprint patterns, which are highly heritable and formed by the 18th gestational week, are correlated with handedness (Rife, 1943). Third, and most importantly, Merrell (1957) found a strong familial effect for eyedness: over 75% of the children of parents concordant for right-eyedness were right-eyed, about 56% of the children of parents discordant for eyedness were right-eyed, and only 46% of the children of parents concordant for left-eyedness were right-eyed, $\chi^2(2) = 28.75$, $p < .001$.

That a major portion of the variance in lateralized traits is due to factors acting prior to birth can hardly be doubted given the available evidence. Morgan (1977) has suggested that these factors reside entirely in the mother and are probably mediated though cytoplasmic constituents present in the unfertilized ovum. Churchill, Igna, and Senf (1962) found that position of the fetus during delivery (left occiput anterior—LOA—and head turned toward right, or right occiput anterior—ROA—and head turned toward left) was predictive of handedness at age 2, and postulated that asymmetrical damage to the right hemisphere in the case of LOA deliveries and to the left hemisphere in the case of ROA deliveries determined subsequent handedness. Both the Morgan and Churchill et al. hypotheses would predict that the familial effect is mediated entirely through the mother, and the Churchill et al. suggestion cannot account for the variability in the direction of cerebral laterality in left-handers. Further, the fact that the nonverbal hemisphere is as highly specialized as the verbal hemisphere and appears to be as free from pathology is not compatible with the idea that handedness is generated through injury to the nonverbal hemisphere. Also, both functional and anatomical asymmetries of the hemispheres are manifest at birth, and asymmetrical perinatal injury could not produce such instantaneous lateral differentiation. The Morgan hypothesis is disconfirmed by Merrell's finding (1957) that when parents are discordant for eyedness, the proportions of left-eyed children do not differ as a function of whether it is the father or mother who is left-eyed. When the father is left-eyed, 43.4% of the children are left-eyed and when the mother is left-eyed, 44.8% of the children are left-eyed, $\chi^2(1) = .016$, $p = .90$.

Eyedness, since it is much freer from possible socio-cultural determinants than is handedness, is a better trait to investigate for possible prenatal materanal effects. Any maternal effect that may be found for handedness could easily be attributable to postnatal socio-cultural factors, though even for handedness there is very little evidence of a greater correlation between mothers and children than between fathers and children. In matings discordant for handedness, Merrell (1957) found a **higher** percentage of sinistral progeny when the father was left-handed, Falek (1959) and Annett (1973) found a **lower** percentage, and Rife (1940) found no difference in porportions. The Merrell and Falek samples for parent–child handedness are too small to allow any conclusions to be drawn, and Annett did not replicate her findings when considering handedness relations between the parental and grand parental generations. In summary, the available evidence strongly supports the view that much of the variation in lateralized traits is of genetic origin, and that the imperfect correlations among these various traits result from only a partial overlap in the causative factors underlying them.

Neither dextrality, right-eyedness, nor left hemisphere language can be considered to be a species-specific trait. We are polymorphic with respect to lateral organiation and our variations derive, in large part, from our evolutionary heritage.

C. Sex Differences

The psychological literature is replete with studies showing sex differences in a variety of functions (Maccoby and Jacklin, 1974; Hutt, 1972), and sex differences have also been found in the lateral organization of the cerebral hemispheres. Rudel, Denckla, and Spalten (1974), Witelson (1976), and Reid (1980) found that in right-handed children, the right hemisphere of boys matures earlier than that of girls as manifested in greater left-sided perceptual asymmetries for spatial material at younger ages. Kimura (1967), Bryden (1970), Pizzamiglio and Cecchini (1971), Van Duyne and D'Alonzo (1976), and Reid (1980) all found earlier and more pronounced left hemisphere maturation in girls, as seen in greater right-sided perceptual superiorities for verbal material. Consistent with these functional differences in the relative rates of hemispheric maturation, Lansdell (1964), in a reanalysis of Conel's (1963) study of eight brains of 4-year-old children found that in four out of the five female brains, myelinization of the precentral gyrus was greater in the left hemisphere than in the right, whereas in all three male brains, myelinization was greater in the right hemisphere than in the left. The exact probability of finding this extreme a sex difference in the observed direction is .071. Although not reaching a conventional level of significance due to the small sample size, it is more probable that a real difference exists than that it does not. Witelson and Pallie (1973), in an examination of 14 infant brains, found females to exhibit a greater left hemisphere development of the planum temporale than males.

While some have concluded, on the basis of such observations, that lateralization per se increases with development, functions of the right hemisphere of females and of the left hemisphere of males being relatively retarded in lateral differentiation, it was noted earlier that there is no reason to suppose this to be the case. When, at a young age, no hemispheric asymmetries are seen for a particular cognitive task, it is almost certainly due to simple cognitive immaturity of the specialized hemisphere and the forced reliance on nonlaterally differentiated processes that are replaced, with subsequent development, by laterally specialized and more competent cognitive strategies. Thus, the developmental sex differences observed relate not to differences in the rates at which left and right hemisphere functions become laterally differentiated, but to the rates at which the cognitive strategies of a hemisphere, via its specialized program, become functionally competent to integrate task demands.

The apparently differing maturational rates of the two sides of the brain in boys and girls are concordant with the sex differences in the maturation of verbal and spatial function. Boys surpass girls on tests of spatial function by 4 years of age. Wilson (1975) found male twins to be superior to their female co-twins on a maze test at all ages studied (ages 4 through 6). Porteus (1965) observed male superiority on his maze test in children of nearly a hundred different cultures. Girls verbalize more in response to the mother (Lewis and Freedle, 1972; Lewis, 1969) and language develops earlier in girls than in boys (Moore, 1967; Clarke-Stewart, 1973). The male superiority in visuospatial function is maintained at least through late middle age (Porteus, 1965; Davies, 1965), as is the female superiority on tests of verbal fluency (Eisenberg, Berlin, Dill, and Frank, 1968; Stevenson, Klein, Hale, and Miller, 1968; Backman, 1972; Rosenberg and Sutton-Smith, 1964, 1969).

It has been argued that sex differences in cognition result from differential reinforcement in boys and girls for different abilities. Under this hypothesis, it would have to be supposed that the sex variation in hemispheric development is induced by socially conditioned behavior, (i.e., that the left hemisphere of girls matures rapidly in response to the reward for verbal behavior, and that the right hemisphere of boys matures rapidly in response to the reward for skilled spatial–mechanical performance). Under this hypothesis, it should be the right hemisphere of girls and the left hemisphere of boys that matures more rapidly in children with the right hemisphere language–left hemisphere spatial laterality pattern.

Reid (1980) examined this issue in left-handed children having inverted and noninverted writing postures. In 8-year-olds, the LI subjects were weakly lateralized, but, like dextrals, both boys and girls had a right-hand superiority on Reid's tactile temporal pattern test and a left-hand superiority on a tactile nonsense shapes test, confirming results of Levy and Reid (1976, 1978). The LN subjects were strongly lateralized in the opposite direction, again confirming Levy and Reid, and both boys and girls had a right-hand superiority on the nonsense shapes test and a left hand superiority on the temporal pattern test. In 5-year-olds, a manual asymmetry was displayed on only one of the two tests. Girls in the LI group, like right-handed girls, had a right hand (left hemisphere) superiority on the temporal pattern test and no hand difference on the nonsense shapes test, while boys in the LI group, like right-handed boys, had a left-hand superiority (right hemisphere) on the nonsense shapes test and no hand difference on the temporal pattern test. In the 5-year-olds of group LN, girls had no asymmetry on the temporal pattern test, and a right-hand (left hemipshere) superiority on the nonsense shapes test, and boys had no asymmetry on the nonsense shapes test, and a left-hand (right hemisphere) superiority on the temporal pattern test. In other words, Reid found that irrespective of the nature of cognitive specialization, the left hemisphere of girls and the right hemisphere of boys mature earlier.

On standardized cognitive tests, Reid found the typical verbal–spatial sex difference in her dextral and LI children. In LN children, girls were superior in spatial abilities and boys in verbal abilities, evidently reflecting the greater maturation of the spatial left hemisphere of girls and of the verbal right hemisphere of boys. There are no reasonably conceivable means by which social factors could selectively reinforce verbal function in girls with left hemisphere language and spatial function in girls with right hemisphere language, or spatial function in boys with left hemisphere language and verbal function in boys with right hemisphere language. The only rational interpretation that can be given to the Reid data is that biological differences in males and females are responsible for the differing maturational rates of the two hemispheres, and that the usual cognitive sex differences observed result from the fact that 95% of the human population has linguistic functions localized to the left and nonverbal functions localized to the right. In the 5% who have a reversed laterality pattern, cognitive sex differences are also reversed.

Unfortunately, the simple conclusion that females are relatively superior in left hemisphere functions and males in right hemisphere functions cannot be correct. While it is true that consistent differences are found in favor of males in certain abilities asymmetrically integrated by the right hemisphere and in favor of females in other abilities integrated by the left hemisphere, there are a variety of capacities that reveal a reversed hemisphere-by-sex interaction. Females surpass males in the perception of fine visual detail (Andrew and Paterson, 1946; Schneidler and Paterson, 1942; Bennett, Seashore, and Wesman, 1959), in understanding the meaning of facial expression (Buck, Savin, Miller, and Caul, 1972), in face recognition (Bahrick, Bahrick, and Wittlinger, 1975), and in identifying the affective implications of tone of voice (Soloman and Ali, 1972), all of which are unequally dependent on right hemisphere processing. Most studies find that the sexes do not differ on tests of vocabulary (Maccoby and Jacklin, 1974), though a few find a female superiority (achenbach, 1969; Very, 1967) and others find a male superiority (Brimer, 1969; Dykstra and Tinney, 1969; France, 1973; Corah, 1965). On the assumption of a female left hemisphere superiority, females should consistently score higher on vocabulary tests than males. On the Differential Aptitude Test of verbal reasoning (as opposed to verbal fluency), Bennett, Seashore, and Wesman (1959) found males to score higher than females. Males also surpass females in amount and range of general information (Miele, 1958). None of these findings can be reconciled with a general male inferiority in left hemisphere functions. Particularly striking is the great male superiority over females in the formal use of language as a tool for logic: In almost all studies, in spite of a sex equality in simple arithmetic computation, males surpass females in mathematical reasoning (Hilton and Berglund, 1971; Svensson, 1971; Droege, 1967; Very, 1967).

In general, it appears that females surpass males in all those functions that depend on a rapid encoding of unstructured information and on the retention of that information for use in adaptive output even when a logical justification of conceptual relationships cannot be specified, particularly in social-communicative interactions. As Douglas, Ross, and Simpson (1968) found, girls learn and remember information by memorization whether the memorized material is understood or not, and the general female superiority in incidental learning from watching films (Hale, Miller, and Stevenson, 1968; Stevenson, Hale, Klein, and Miller, 1968) and in verbal memory (Amster and Wiegand, 1972; Felzen and Anisfeld, 1970; Finley and Frenkel, 1972; Milburn, Bell, and Koeske, 1970) may well depend on the female ability to store in and recall from memory information that, at the time of input, bears no particular relation with well-formed concepts. Whether that information is in the form of perceptual details, faces, facial expressions, tone of voice, words, algorithms for arithmetic operations, or spelling patterns, and whether predominantly encoded by the right or left hemisphere, females have a general memorial advantage over males when that information cannot be placed in a well-formed logical structure. It can subsequently be integrated and utilized in reaching valid conclusions and in controlling adaptive behavior even when a rigorous specification of controlling relations cannot be given. Thus, females may be remarkably accurate in reading the affective and motivational states of others, in describing various details of facial features and voice tone, and in giving direct quotations of conversations heard as justifications for the conclusions they reach, while, at the same time, being quite unable to explain why the various remembered details imply the conclusions they do. Were functional and neurological structures isomorphic, one might suppose that functions are diffuse and boundaries between functional systems relatively open in the female brain.

Male superiorities consistently emerge on those functions that depend on the extraction of spatial or logical relationships, independently of the contextual components of the systems forming those relationships, and whether right or left hemisphere processes are used. Douglas, Ross, and Simpson (1968) found that boys typically try to master the underlying principles of material they learn, as if information can only be retained and utilized when placed in a tightly organized conceptual system. The fact that males are more field-independent than females (Keogh and Ryan, 1971; Corah, 1965; Saarni, 1973; Okonji, 1969; Fiebert, 1967) is consistent with the idea that males may ignore the contextual aspects of relational systems, predominantly extracting the formal associations among physical or linguistic components and ignoring the incidental properties those components may have. For a female, the vast difference between a geographical region and its symbolic representation on a map may produce profound interference in perceiving the isomorphism between the two, but for a male, those differences may be minor because the geography itself may have been encoded in terms of precisely those relations depicted on the map. Language for a female may consist in the total meaning derived, not only from denotative content, but from the connotative content as specified by social context, tone, expression, and bodily movement, but for a male, denotative meaning may override all other considerations. Thus, in a purely formal language like mathematics, whose meaning is entirely denotative, males exhibit a superiority, while in natural language communication, both receptive and expressive, females exhibit a superiority.

Bhavani and Hutt's finding (Hutt, 1972) that on a test of divergent thinking, females generate more overall responses, but the proportion that are original is less than in males, may be due to a female dependence on remembered associations and a male dependence on associations derived from structured cognitive principles. Frederiksen and Evans (1974) also found that on Guilford's Consequences test, females surpassed males in the number of obvious consequences, and males surpassed females in the number of remote consequences; again suggesting a memorial dependence in women and a derivational dependence in men. It is of relevance also that when sex differences are found in the Remote Associations Test, women generally exceed men (Maccoby and Jacklin, 1974). This test depends on forming an association between conceptually unrelated ideas solely on the basis of the identity of a single word that is related with all concepts (Example: "Cottage, Blue, Rat"; Answer: "Cheese") and would seem to depend not only on verbal fluency, but also on easy access among unrelated concepts. It appears that for males, if function mapped directly onto neurology, we would expect to find highly localized, well-bounded functional systems with restricted pathways mediating logical associations among structured memories.

From the foregoing considerations, it may be seen that sex differences in cognitive structure cannot be solely due to better developed right hemisphere functions in males and better developed left hemisphere functions in females. The cognitive differences observed strongly suggest that within-hemisphere organization is profoundly different in the two sexes. In left hemisphere processes, females exceed males in those dependent on rote verbal memory, fluency, and relatively free associative connections among conceptually distant ideas; males exceed females in those dependent on analytic reasoning and abstraction of formal denotative content. In right hemisphere processes, females exceed males in perceptual speed and memory for unstructured incidental sensory input and for the integration of contextual situations; males exceed females in the extraction of formal spatial relationships and in their independence from the sensorial constraints of the perceptual field. It may be that females surpass males in interhemispheric integration of remotely related information, as in their superior ability to relate language to nonverbal aspects of communication, and that males surpass females in interhemispheric integration of the formal properties of spatial and logical concepts, as in their partial reliance on spatial constructs for mathematical performance (Werdelin, 1961; Mellone, 1944). There is no spatial factor in the mathematical skills of girls.

Anatomical and functional evidence suggest that within and between hemispheres, functions are more diffusely organized in females and more strongly localized in males. Wada, Clarke, and Hamm (1975) in an examination of 100 adult brains found that the difference in size of the left and right temporal planes was larger in males than in females, suggesting less lateralization of verbal functions in the latter. Lansdell and Davie (1972) compared verbal and nonverbal factor scores from the Wechsler-Bellevue Intelligence Test of 74 neurological patients with and without a massa intermedia, a midline thalamic structure consisting of the rhomboid and central median nuclei. In all groups of patients in the Lansdell and Davie sample, verbal scores exceeded nonverbal scores **except** in males lacking a massa intermedia.

There is good reason to suppose that the massa intermedia plays an important role in maintaining equal arousal of the two hemispheres. First, the nuclei of the massa intermedia are part of the diffuse thalamocortical system and stimulation of them leads to a widespread disturbance of large cortical areas. Bilateral responses in both sides of the cortex are induced; the bilateral spread is not mediated via the corpus callosum or anterior commissure, and a lesion of the central medial nucleus interferes with contralateral responses (Kerr and O'Leary, 1957). Second, if the massa intermedia plays the role suggested, it would be of high adaptive value in animals with symmetric brains, but might be expected to interfere with the selective hemispheric activation necessary for good cognitive performance in people with well lateralized brains. In primates other than man, the massa intermedia is almost always present and is quite large, but in man it is small and is absent in a substantial minority of the population (Sarnat and Netsky, 1974), strongly suggesting that agenesis of the massa intermedia is a recent evolutionary adaptation to the asymmetric brain of man. Third, agenesis of this structure is more frequent in males than females: Morel (1947) found only 14% of females with agenesis, but 28% of males. In the Lansdell and Davie sample, 33% of females and 40% of males were lacking the massa intermedia, unusually high proportions for both sexes. If the male brain is more asymmetric than the female brain, interference with selective hemispheric activiation would be expected to degrade male performance to a greater extent, and it may be that selective factors favoring agenesis of the massa intermedia have acted more strongly in males than in females. Given that in primates other than man, the massa intermedia is almost always present, it is unlikely that its development is controlled by genes on the sex chromosomes. It is more probable that expression of autosomal genes is affected by gene products of loci on the sex chromosomes (i.e., that in our species, massa intermedia development is a sex-limited, but not a sex-linked, trait).

Considering the likely role of the massa intermedia, the Lansdell and Davie results suggest that spatial function in males is almost entirely dependent on the right hemisphere, and that absence of the massa intermedia permits full right hemisphere activation with no competition from the left hemisphere for processing control. In females, it appears that nonverbal functions may be integrated by either hemisphere. If so, activation relations between the hemispheres of the female brain should be relatively unimportant in female performance.

The failure of the presence or absence of the massa intermedia to affect verbal performance in males may have been due to a general left hemisphere processing dominance in the Lansdell and Davie patients. In all groups, verbal performance exceeded spatial performance, though the difference was not significant in males lacking a massa intermedia. Lansdell and Smith's finding (1975) that following left hemisphere damage, verbal functions partially recover with time, whereas after right hemisphere damage, nonverbal functions show no improvement, is consistent with the conclusion that neurological patients with generalized cerebral dysfunction develop an inbalance in activation in favor of the left hemisphere. The relatively intact verbal performance seen in all groups may reflect an overall dominance of processing control by the left side of the brain in neurological samples. Right hemisphere activation in such groups may require an unusual capacity to override the left hemisphere bias, a capacity that may depend on the absence of the massa intermedia.

Other evidence that males, more than females, depend on the functions of a single hemisphere for the performance of cognitive tasks was obtained by McGlone and Kertesz (1973). In female patients with left hemisphere lesions, spatial and verbal performance was correlated, both functions being depressed by left side lesions, but in males no such relation was seen. Further, right hemisphere lesions depressed spatial performance more in males than in females. Sherman (1974), in a reanalysis of Meyer and Jones's (1957) data, found that left temporal lobectomy depressed spatial performance to a much greater extent in females than in males, again suggesting that nonverbal functions are strongly lateralized in the male brain, but not in the female brain.

Studies with normal subjects support and extend this conclusion. Females exhibit smaller and less consistent hemispheric asymmetries on both nonverbal and verbal tests (Bryden, 1966; Kimura, 1969, 1973; McGlone and Davidson, 1973; Levy and Reid, 1976, 1978; Ehrlichman,

1972; Remington, Krashen, and Harshman, 1973). It therefore appears that although the left hemisphere matures earlier in females and the right hemisphere matures earlier in males, the nature of within-hemisphere organization differs for the two sexes. While the two hemispheres of females are clearly laterally differentiated, both hemispheres, to some extent, appear to participate in integrating those functions predominantly specialized to the other side of the brain. The "language" or processing strategies of the female hemispheres are more similar than those of males, and for this reason, there may be a more automatic and less consciously structured communication between the hemispheres of females. In males, in whom the hemispheres differ greatly in their thought strategies, interhemispheric communication and integration may depend on a highly structured information code that can be decoded and utilized by the other side of the brain.

The cognitive sex differences that have been observed, and the greater bilateralization of functions in females than males, suggest that in both hemispheres of the male, the neurological substrates of cognitive systems are well localized and bounded, with interrelations among them controlled by highly structured concepts. The physical–spatial constructs of the right hemisphere and the linguistic–symbolic contructs of the left hemisphere can be integrated and mapped onto one another only via restricted formal invariants that they share. The male, in some sense, can be considered to be an analytic geometer. In contrast, in both hemispheres of the female, the neurological substrates of cognitive processes seem to be more diffusely organized and relatively unbounded; associative interconnections between them are widespread and unrestricted. Similarly, the integration of left and right hemisphere processes appears to reflect a greater freedom of association that does not depend on formal conceptual relationships. Each type of brain organization has its own virtues and deficits. A highly structured system automatically excludes arousal of concepts and memories peripheral to a given organization of the world of experience or thought and enhances the probability that formal principles governing that organization can be derived and subsequently applied in other situations. On the other hand, the power of such a system in this domain would be reflected as a deficiency in perceptual speed, verbal fluency, unstructured memory, and in the ability to grasp intuitively the implications of a set of events whose interrelations cannot be formally specified. A diffuse cerebral system would be expected to generate precisely the opposite pattern of abilities and impairments.

The earlier maturation of the female left hemisphere may reflect the nature of female verbal functions. Even a quite young child could be expected to have sufficient cognitive maturation to permit the acquisition of associative verbal memories that could be utilized for productive output, but the acquisition of formal symbolic representations would be considerably delayed. If the female left hemisphere is designed to acquire and utilize language as a tool for fluent communication, and the male left hemisphere is designed to acquire and utilize the rules of language as a tool for thought, left hemisphere functions would mature earlier in females simply due to the differing levels of cognitive maturation required for these two different aspects of language. Biologically, more rapid left hemisphere maturation in females may be due to a major adaptive dependence of females on social competence. The earlier maturation of the male right hemisphere can be explained on the grounds that if both hemispheres of the male are designed to derive well-structured organizational schemata, those that must develop first would depend on sensorimotor and perceptual integrations, symbolic conceptual integrations being delayed to a later stage of maturity due to the greater cognitive complexity required. Concrete principles governing relationships in the physical world can be expected to be acquired well before those relationships can be formalized in symbolic representations, and according to Piaget (1954), such formalization is dependent on a prior acquisition of experiential principles. Thus, right hemisphere maturation in the male may be a prerequisite to the subsequent development of male left hemisphere functions.

It may be that the functions of the earlier developing hemisphere in both sexes condition the maturation of functions in the other side of the brain, so that these develop predominantly in service of the earlier developing functions. The perceptual systems of the female right hemisphere may be activated and directed by left hemisphere commands; the analytical systems of the male left hemisphere may be activated and directed by right hemisphere commands. In that small group of the population with right hemisphere language, it may be the analytical right hemisphere of males and the perceptual left hemisphere of females that direct and coordinate hemispheric functions. If it is true that the leading hemisphere is the left for females and the right for males, the conditions under which each hemisphere's activities come into play and the ways in which they are used for adaptive behavior would be expected to be different for the sexes. Male analytical functions may be activated in response to an attempt to formalize physical relationships and principles in typical right-handers. In males with right hemisphere language, spatial–geometric representations may be activated in response to attempts to visualize the implications of logical associations. In female right-handers, perceptual processes may be aroused in response to attempts to derive meaning from communicative interactions or to reify symbolic representations. In females with right hemisphere language, verbal functions may be aroused in response to attempts to apply symbolic meaning to perceptual experience. The various observations regarding differences in males and females in attitudes, orientation, values, and cognitive capacities, as well as the known differences in hemispheric development and organization, are congruent with the foregoing suggestions.

Though the Reid data (1980) rule out the possibility that sociocultural factors could be responsible for the differing developmental rates of the two hemispheres of boys and girls, it is reasonable to ask whether such factors might be responsible for the ultimate degree of lateral differentiation in adults. The little evidence available on this question strongly suggests that biological factors underlie the differing degrees of lateralization, as well as the asymmetry in maturational rate of the hemispheres. First, Weiss and Gordon (personal communication, 1977) and Netley (1977) found that in women with Turner's syndrome, the hemispheres are very weakly lateralized, verbal functions being bilateralized, with verbal performance intact and spatial performance greatly depressed (Alexander, Ehrhardt, and Money, 1966). In Turner's syndrome, one of the two sex chromosomes is missing, and females with this condition have only a single X chromosome. Though the ovaries begin to differentiate in the embryo, they rapidly undergo dysgenesis and, by birth, are represented by nonfunctional streaks. Thus, any biochemical products of the normal fetal ovaries are absent in Turner's patients and these products may be critical in promoting lateral differentiation and maturation by right hemisphere functions. It may be that normal differences in male and female fetuses in the absolute amount of gonadal products—the male fetal gonads being considerably more active—produce the observed cerebral differences. If so, it could be predicted that in chromosomal and anatomic females with an overabundance of fetal sex steroids, either from maternal progesterone injections or from abnormal testosterone output from pathological fetal adrenals, the brain should be more lateralized with the right hemisphere maturing more rapidly than in normal females. No studies are yet available pertinent to this issue, except the finding that such fetally androgenized girls are more masculine in their outlooks and attitudes (Money and Ehrhardt, 1972) than a control sample of normal girls.

Waber (1976) found, in a group of 13-year-old girls and 16-year-old boys, that late maturers of both sexes manifested greater ear asymmetries on a verbal dichotic test and higher spatial ability than did early maturers. Verbal ability was unrelated to stage of pubertal development.

In younger children (10-year-old girls and 13-year-old boys), spatial ability was also superior in late maturers, but pubertal development had no relation with ear asymmetries. The actual levels of performance on the dichotic test and on cognitive tests could not be determined from the data presented by Waber since only ear difference scores were given for the former and scores had been converted to z-scores within age groups for the latter. Sexes could not be compared on either verbal or spatial ability since chronological ages were matched only for 13-year-olds, and only difference scores between verbal and spatial performance were presented. Thus, it is not possible to determine the possible interrelations among ear performance scores, cognitive performance scores, difference scores, sex, and chronological age.

Waber interprets her results as meaning that sex differences in brain organization and cognitive structure are an artifact of sex differences in maturational rate. Whether such an interpretation is even permissible depends on the nature of unreported data concerning relative spatial ability for the two sexes at varying ages and stages of pubertal development. More important is the fact that age of pubertal onset is biologically determined, partly genetic, and strongly related to sex. The same factors that control onset time of puberty could control both brain organization and cognitive structure. Puberty in girls with Turner's syndrome is typically induced rather late in development and this is not associated with strong lateralization; rather, lateralization is weak and spatial ability poor. Clearly, if a delay in pubertal hormones is the causal factor in permitting strong lateralization, Turner's girls, who may not receive hormone therapy until age 15 or later, should have a masculine brain organization and cognitive structure.

Age of pubertal onset in gonadally normal people may well be partially programmed by the nature and quantity of fetal sex steroids—low levels of androgens or estrogens inducing early puberty and a feminine cerebral pattern, high levels inducing a late puberty and a masculine cerebral pattern. As Waber maintains, age of puberty and brain organization would be correlated, but not because the former is causally active in determining the latter. The Waber findings, in conjunction with those on patients with Turner's syndrome, lend strong support to the view that sex differences in cerebral and psychological structure are conditioned by prenatal factors and, probably, by the quality and amount of fetal sex steroids.

The emphasis given to biological determinants in the generation of sex differences in neuropsychology should not be construed to imply either that all males and females display the modal pattern of their sex; or that sociocultural factors are unimportant. There can be little argument that social institutions and customs serve to reinforce and magnify whatever biologically based differences there may be; that males are punished for manifesting stereotypically feminine interests and females for failing to accept the stereotypical feminine role. Traditionally, men are expected to be competent in mechanical problems, in mathematics, and in finding solutions to technical problems, whereas women have been expected to collapse helplessly and wait for male assistance should their cars break down, their bankbooks become unbalanced, or their hair dryers become inoperative. The societal pressures generate a high motivation in men and women to gain the competencies expected of them and those expectations are strongly sex-typed. Women are expected to smile at the charming helplessness of a man faced with a crying baby in wet diapers and to take charge of the situation; similarly, men are expected to calm their hysterical wives as they apply their plumbing skills to an overflowing toilet. The man who has an interest in and sensitivity to young children and who chooses to be a nursery-school teacher needs to have considerable bravery to follow his leanings, and the woman who chooses a career as a mathematician does so in the face of both practical and psychological barriers.

It should be kept in mind that the within-sex variance in cerebral and cognitive organization is probably much larger than the between-sex variance and that, for this reason, every individual, whether male or female, must be judged for himself or herself alone. The fact that biological factors may underlie modal sex differences to a major extent merely means that an equal sex distribution across all occupations cannot be rationally expected, but it provides no justification for social rewards and punishments to be allocated in accordance with how well people conform to the modal characteristics of their sex. Equality of opportunity and of civil rights does not depend on biological identity, and it is a dangerous proposition to maintain that they do. A recognition that there are biologically based differences in the neuropsychology of males and females should, in a just society, lead both to an appreciation of the special skills brought to the social system by each sex as well as to an acceptance and encouragement of those with sex-atypical abilities and values.

D. Psychopathology and Lateralization

Psychopathology has been traditionally classified as either "organic" or "nonorganic," implying that in the absence of an easily identifiable neurological lesion, psychopathology was to be attributed to a purely mental disorder. The fact that disordered mental function must necessarily result from a disordered brain was either ignored or actively denied by a great proportion of therapists. However, this dualistic view became increasingly difficult to maintain as psychopharmacology and neurochemistry began to untangle complex brain chemistry. The advent of psychotherapeutic drugs and psychotomimetics proved beyond any doubt that behavioral abnormalities were caused by abnormalities of neural function.

Evidence has been accumulating that psychotic symptomatology is directly related to unusual patterns of lateralization. An elegant series of studies by Glick and colleagues (Glick, 1973; Glick, Cox, and Greenstein, 1975; Glick, Crane, Jerussi, Fleisher, and Green, 1975; Glick and Jerussi, 1974; Glick, Jerussi, Waters, and Green, 1974; Jerussi and Glick, 1974, 1975, 1976) in animals suggests a possible neurochemical basis for the deviant laterality patterns in psychosis. That there may be lateralized disturbances associated with psychopathology has been evident since the earliest neuropsychological studies of brain-lesioned patients. The differing symptoms resulting from left and right hemisphere lesions and the similarity between the various syndromes and those diagnostic of various types of psychosis were apparent. However, it was not until 1945 that the first direct evidence of a lateralized dysfunction in schizophrenia was obtained.

In the normal individual, rotational acceleration induces nystagmic movements (by convention, defined as the saccadic fast component) in the direction of rotation, associated with an increase in baseline neural firing from the ampullar nerve ipsilateral to rotational direction and a decrease in baseline firing rate from the opposite ampullar nerve. Caloric stimulation of one labyrinth with water, cooler or warmer than body temperature, by setting up convection currents in the endolymph, also produces nystagmus, warm water inducing ipsilateral nystagmus (presumably increasing firing rate from the nerve of the stimulated vertibular organ) and cool water inducing contralateral nystagmus (presumably decreasing firing rate from the nerve). Vestibular information projects to the ipsilateral cerebellum and predominantly to the contralateral temporal lobe cortex, and activity in these regions facilitates nystagmus in the direction of the more active ampullar nerve. From a number of studies, it seems likely that the cortical command center for contralateral saccades has its origin in the parieto-occipital region which receives facilitation from almost all areas of the ipsilateral cerebral hemisphere and which projects to the contralateral cerebellum for the control of smooth saccades (Aschoff, 1974). Stimulation of one side of the cerebral cortex, of the ipsilateral pontine nuclei which receive a direct projection from Brodman's area 18 (visual association cortex), or of the contralateral vermis of the cerebellum which is a major projection area of the pontine nuclei, elicts saccadic movements in a direction contralateral to cortical or pontine stimulation and ipsilateral to cerebellar stimulation. It is probable, also, that the two sides of the cerebrum and of the cerebellum are reciprocally inhibitory in the control of nystagmus: were this not so, a spasm of fixation would be likely to result.

Given these relationships, it could be expected that a unilateral temporal lobe lesion would inhibit contralateral vestibular nystagmus and facilitate, via disinhibition of the opposite temporal lobe, ipsilateral vestibular nystagmus, while having no effects either on optokinetic nystagmus or on voluntary saccades. Indeed, Fitzgerald and Hallpike (1942) found that patients with unilateral temporal lobe lesions showed a reduction in the duration of calorically induced nystagmic movements contralateral to the lesion and a prolongation of those ipsilateral to the lesion. Lesions of the frontal cortex had no effect on vestibular nystagmus.

The relevance of this finding to the present discussion is that Fitzgerald and Stengel (1945) found a directional preponderance in 18 of 50 schizophrenics to calorically induced nystagmus, 15 patients showing prolongation of nystagmus to the left, 2 showing a prolongation to the right, $\chi^2(1) = 9.94$, $p = .002$, and one showing opposite directional preponderances on two examinations. The data strongly suggest a left temporal lobe dysfunction in schizophrenics, though the authors failed to draw this conclusion.

Kleist (1960) suggested that schizophrenic symptomatology was quite similar in many respects to that found with left hemisphere lesions, but at that time the only direct evidence in support of this view were the data of Fitzgerald and Stengel which had been little noted and rarely cited. A number of studies had found schizophrenic-like symptoms associated with left hemisphere lesions and symptoms of affective psychoses associated with right hemisphere lesions (see Flor-Henry, 1976, for review). The critical question, however, was not whether various psychoses could be induced by brain damage, but whether localized cerebral dysfunctions could be identified in so-called "nonorganic" psychoses.

Following the Fitzgerald and Stengel paper, almost 30 years elapsed before additional evidence bearing on this question was obtained. Luria and Homskaya (1966) had reported that unilateral frontal and–or temporal lobe lesions were associated with an attenuation of ipsilateral skin conductance orienting responses to tones, though patients with lesions confined to the temporal region did respond to tones that had signal value. Gruzelier and Venables (1973, 1974) found that 50% of schizophrenics were bilaterally nonresponsive, indicating massive cortical inhibition of the autonomically controlled electrodermal response. However, of the patients showing a unilateral lack of response, most manifested a left side attenuation to neutral tone stimuli, with restoration of the response to tones of signal value, a pattern clearly indicative of left temporal lobe dysfunction.

Serafetinides (1972, 1973) found that remission of schizophrenic symptomatology was associated with a voltage increase over the left hemisphere. Since high voltage EEGs are associated with a **reduction** in arousal, these results suggest that schizophrenics have overly aroused left hemispheres. Observations of Flor-Henry, Koles, Bo-Lassen, and Yeudall (1975) confirm this interpretation. They found that power in the beta frequency (20–30 Hz and associated with arousal) over the left hemisphere in schizophrenics and over the right hemisphere in manic-depressives was increased as compared to normals. Gur (1977, 1978) found behavioral evidence of left hemisphere overactivation in schizophrenia, as well as indications that the overly aroused hemisphere was defective in processing. As compared to normals, schizophrenics manifested a bias toward conjugate lateral eye movements to the right, indicating asymmetric control of the left hemisphere over voluntary saccades. This observation strongly suggests that the command center for saccadic movements is functionally intact, though overaroused, in the schizophrenic left hemisphere, and that the leftward nystagmic predominance to vestibular stimulation found by Fitzgerald and Stengel (1945) was specifically related to a functional lesion of the cortical projection area for vestibular information in the left temporal lobe.

In further support of the view that the schizophrenic left hemisphere dominates behavioral control, Gur found that on a task involving detection of differences between two similar pictures, schizophrenics applied the same solution strategy as patients with right hemisphere lesions. Control subjects and patients with left hemisphere lesions used a different strategy that indicated reliance on the right hemisphere. Thus, schizophrenics seemed to rely on the left hemisphere in spite of the maladaptivity of the strategies it could apply.

As indications that the overcontrolling left hemisphere was defective even in the processing of information for which it is specialized, Gur found in tachistoscopic laterality tests a left field superiority on both spatial and verbal tasks. Control subjects had a right visual field superiority on the verbal test. Additional evidence that the schizophrenic left hemisphere is defective was Gur's finding of an increase in left-handedness, eyedness, and footedness, all indicative of damage to the left side of the brain. Hillsberg (unpublished manuscript, 1976) found that schizophrenics had longer RTs to stimuli in the right visual field than in the left, while control subjects had no difference between fields on a nonverbal same–different decision task, again indicating left hemisphere dysfunction in the patient group.

To summarize, the evidence shows that the left hemisphere of schizophrenics is disordered, with respect to behavioral dominance and with respect to functional capacity. In the typical neurological patient suffering from unilateral brain damage, the intact hemisphere assumes control of behavior, an adaptive response that can lead to symptomatic recovery by the utilization of alternative pathways. In schizophrenics, however, the damaged left hemisphere, rather than releasing control to the other side of the brain, overwhelmingly dominates control pathways. It would appear that the extreme psychopathology of schizophrenia is a consequence of this maladaptive response to functional disability. Rather than "favoring" the normal half-brain, the schizophrenic seems to force the injured half to carry all the weight of behavior—quite possibly interfering with recovery.

Very recent evidence shows that the autistic child, also, has a unilateral cerebral dysfunction, though of a very different sort from that seen in schizophrenia. The profound language disorder seen in autism, along with normal or superior visuo-spatial function, is highly suggestive of a left hemisphere disability. Indeed, left-handedness and ambilaterality are increased in autism (Colby and Parkison, 1977), the left lateral ventricle is enlarged (Hauser, De Long, and Rosman, 1975), and evoked response patterns indicate abnormality of the left hemisphere (Tanguay, 1975). However, in contrast to schizophrenics, the left hemisphere of autistic children apparently suffers from a pathological incapacity to gain control over behavior. Levy, Meck, and Staikoff (1978) found that autistic children manifest a remarkably strong sensorimotor bias to the left— in natural play, almost all (97%) turns during walking or running were to the left; 95% of turns made at the end of a sliding board were to the left; all turns made on a tricycle were to the left; in one-choice maze turns, 95% were to the left; in drawings, all autistic children displaced their pictures to the left half of the page. In response to tactile, visual, and acoustic stimuli, all children showed a leftward orientation bias. None of these biases was observed in normal children, two retarded children, or in a nonautistic child with defective articulation and abnormal behavior. Blackstock (1977) also found leftward biases in autistic children. In normal children, he found a right ear preference for listening to stories and a left ear preference for listening to music, with stories being preferred to music. In autistic children, a left ear bias was apparent for both music and stories, the left ear bias for musical listening being significantly stronger in autistic than in normal children, and with music being preferred to stories.

Both the Levy et al. and the Blackstock studies show the right hemisphere to be strongly dominant over behavior, and the left hemisphere to be effectively unconscious. The symptoms of autism also indicate that a fully specialized right hemisphere processes all input and controls all output, and that the cognitive–emotional world of autistic children is the world of the right side of the brain. Levy et al. have suggested that the autistic child's left hemisphere, though unable to gain behavioral control, is fully competent to inhibit the development of language and its cognitive correlates in the right side of the brain, resulting in complete right hemisphere specialization, in contrast to the child with left hemispherectomy whose right hemisphere subsumes left hemisphere functions. If, as some suggest, the affective symptoms of autism are a secondary consequence of the cognitive disorder, it is not difficult to imagine how an infant born with only those cognitive programs of the right hemisphere could develop all the various manifestations of autism.

Thus, like schizophrenics, autistic children seem to have a major problem with hemispheric control of behavior, but it is the right hemisphere that overwhelms control pathways. In addition, the fact that dextrality is decreased in autistic populations and that the left lateral ventricle is enlarged (reducing the cortical mass surrounding it), suggests that if the left hemisphere could be activated so that its functional capacity could be determined, defective processing would be seen. The autistic child, then, does rely on his intact hemisphere, but reliance on a specialized right hemisphere, with its restricted cognitive programs, throughout the entire period of maturation must necessarily yield an extremely peculiar model of reality to the child—perhaps a model that is lacking altogether the temporal dimension, the notion of temporal causality, any apprehension of language and its cognitive substrates, understanding of the conscious worlds of other people, or any ability to escape the frightening concatenation of stimuli that cannot be temporally organized into a conceptually meaningful pattern.

From the data currently available, it is not possible to know whether, in either schizophrenics or in autistic children, functional disability of a hemisphere **causes** asymmetric dominance or vice-versa, or whether both dysfunctions derive from a single underlying cause. However, asymmetric dominance has been seen in animals and is correlated with asymmetries in neurochemical systems on the left and right. Glick and colleagues (see Glick, Jerussi, and Zimmerberg, 1977, for review) have found in a variety of species that most animals have an asymmetry in the dopaminergic systems, dopamine levels being higher and receptors more dense on one side than on the other. The asymmetry in the left and right nigrostriatal bundles and in the striatal receptor regions is correlated with motor biases contralateral to the side with the higher levels, and it is tempting to speculate that the unusually strong lateral motoric biases in schizophrenia and autism might reflect unusually strong asymmetries in the left and right dopaminergic systems. Glick et al. (1977) report that d-amphetamine increases motoric biases, presumably by causing a greater release of dopamine from the side with the intrinsically higher concentration (d-amphetamine blocks dopamine reuptake). Interestingly, in normal rats, the accuracy of timing behavior is positively correlated with degree of asymmetry in side preference, but when d-amphetamine is administered and asymmetry is abnormally increased, timing behavior in the majority of rats is disrupted. Also, animals with strong side preferences were less active that those with weak side preferences, they learned passive avoidance responses faster and active avoidance responses more slowly.

In people, since the hemispheres are laterally specialized, abnormal asymmetries in the left and right dopamine levels would be expected to lead to differing behavioral abnormalities, depending on the direction of the asymmetry. In schizophrenics, it would be expected that the dopamine concentration on the left would be elevated and that on the right depressed, with the reverse asymmetry obtaining in autistic children. It is interesting that blockage of dopamine receptors by chlorpromazine and haloperidol has a potent antipsychotic effect (Matthysse, 1973), suggesting in the case of shizophrenics, that antipsychotics may help to restore normal asymmetry relations between the arousal levels of the two hemispheres. The failure of chlorpromazine to ameliorate the symptoms of autism might be due to inactivation of the only functional dopamine system in the brains of autistic children: Dopamine levels in the left hemisphere may be so low that dopamine receptor blockage, though increasing hemispheric symmetry, might depress the right hemisphere to a degree that **neither** side of the brain is competent for behavioral control. Certainly, the motoric biases observed in autistic children are much more obvious and extreme than those observed in schizophrenics. While the foregoing comments are, of course, speculative, it is to be hoped that the relation between abnormalities in behavior, patterns of functional lateralization of the brain, and neurochemical systems will soon be clarified. One is encouraged in this hope by the remarkable progress that has occurred in recent years.

IV. Sociobiology and Cerebral Asymmetry

I have attempted in this chapter to describe the nature of cerebral asymmetry, some of the methods used to assess it, normal and abnormal variations in the patterns of lateralization, and their possible causes and relationships with sex, cognition, and behavior. The evidence discussed suggests that the two sides of the human brain, though similar in many respects in their performance capabilities, have radically different ways of perceiving and dealing with the world, that people vary in the extent and direction of hemispheric differentiation and in the functional organizations of their "verbal" and "nonverbal" hemispheres, that these differences are reflected in cognitive structure and behavior, and that biological factors, in large part genetic, are a major source of the observed variance.

Central questions that remain are **why** the human brain is asymmetric, why there are variations in the patterns of asymmetry, and what the implications of the answers to these questions might be for human society. While there are a variety of structural and/or functional asymmetries in the nervous systems of invertebrates (Chapple, 1977a,b), fish (Stahl, 1977), birds (Nottebohm, 1977), rodents (Glick et al., 1977), rabbits (Nelson, Phillips, and Goldstein, 1977), and cats (Webster, 1977), in the phyletic series closely related to man only the anthropoid apes manifest asymmetries that appear to be homologous with those of our species (LeMay and Geschwind, 1975; Yeni-Komshian and Benson, 1976). Though Dewson (1977) believes that left hemisphere lesions in the superior temporal gyrus of monkeys selectively interfere with auditory short term memory, only 5 monkeys were tested, 3 with left hemisphere lesions and 2 with right hemisphere lesions, and no statistical comparisons between the two groups on pre- versus postoperative performance were presented. Further, Warren (1977) could find no evidence of consistent hand preference of 15 monkeys over tasks, and certainly no indication of right-handedness in the monkeys as a group. Also, Hamilton (1977a,b), in an extensive series of investigations on split-brain monkeys, found no evidence of functional hemispheric asymmetry. In addition, though Yeni-Komshian and Benson (1976) found the left Sylvian fissure to be longer than the right in both human and ape brains, in monkey brains the lengths of the left and right Sylvian fissures were not significantly different. Clearly, if monkeys do have functionally asymmetric brains, the asymmetry is quite minor compared to that in human brains and exceedingly difficult to reveal.

To date, the anatomical asymmetries of the great ape brain have not been correlated with function, but there are no published accounts of any attempts to detect laterally differentiated functions in the hemispheres of chimpanzees, gorillas, or orangutans. Given that the anatomical asymmetries that have been seen closely resembly those in the human brain, it seems likely that at least some functional asymmetry will be observed. In summary, if the modern monkey is representative of the common ancestor of the anthropoids, the development of cerebral asymmetry in the human evolutionary line probably first appeared during the Miocene when the hominoids (apes and man) diverged from the cercopithecoids (Old World monkeys). Should apes be found to have functionally symmetric brains, then cerebral asymmetry in the hominoid line would be of much more recent origin, possibly only appearing during the last 10 million years or so.

In either case, it seems clear that the type of cerebral lateralization seen in the human species coevolved with brain size, intelligence, and with increasingly greater dependence on cognitive power as the basis for adaptation.

A functionally symmetric brain is, by definition, a redundant brain: Both hemispheres are identical in function, process input in an identical manner, store memories in identical codes, and program identical responses to environmental demands. The advantages of having two identical hemispheres instead of one reside in the safety provided by a parallel circuit, from speed advantages that might derive from parallel and increased memory storage, but predominantly from the necessity to perceive and respond to both halves of space without a lateral bias. In animals whose adaptation crucially depends on an accurate perception of ongoing environmental events and rapid and adaptive responses to those events, a single hemisphere, though cognitively almost as competent as two, has access to and can respond to only one-half of space. Loss of one of two symmetric hemispheres would effectively abolish half the animal's world.

Lateral specialization of hemispheric function carries with it some of the same disadvantages as total hemispherectomy. Motoric and perceptual biases can be induced by pure thought. Analytic, propositional thought asymmetrically activates one hemisphere, reducing perceptual awareness of the ipsilateral half of space and biasing motor responses toward the contralateral half of space. Similarly, imagistic thinking and visualization activate the opposite side of the brain, producing opposite sensorimotor biases. Thus, an animal with laterally differentiated functions in the halves of the brain can be randomly biased to the left or right independently of asymmetries in the external environment, a dangerous and maladaptive neural organization for an animal whose life may well depend on the rapid and veridical detection of environmental events and appropriate responses to them. It is not difficult to imagine why the prosimians and subhominoid anthropoids should have basically symmetric brains with respect to cognitive, perceptual, and motoric functions.

On the other hand, functional symmetry is an extremely wasteful cognitive design. Lateralization of function almost doubles the size of the cognitive computer: One half-brain can be fully devoted to one set of functions and the other to another set of functions. The neural organizations within each hemisphere can be optimally designed for either analytical, propositional processing or for the encoding of literal sensory images and the extraction of sensory–spatial invariants. Were a single hemisphere burdened with both sets of operations, neither could be optimally integrated. It could hardly be expected that the hemisphere that conceived of the Mona Lisa could also have developed quantum mechanics. Just as social specialization increases the efficiency and output of a society, so would hemispheric specialization be expected to increase the cognitive power of a brain. The adaptive advantage conferred by such specialization would, however, be proportional to the adaptive dependence of an animal on cognition, and inversely proportional to its adaptive dependence on perceptions of and responses to the immediate stimulus environment.

Human behavior is, for the most part, under control, not of the immediately present reality, but of a model of reality (Jerison, 1973) that subsumes the past and an imagined future, that extends well beyond the here-and-now to distant regions of space and time. The adaptiveness of our behavior depends more on the generality and accuracy of that model than on sensory acuity and rapidity of response. We are defective creatures in these domains compared to dogs and cats, lions, tigers, or any number of other animals. We survive by our wits, and at that point in our evolutionary past when intelligence came to be the most important basis for our survival, any disadvantages of cerebral asymmetry must have been far outweighed by the cognitive power it conferred.

Yet, why are we not all equally differentiated laterally and to the maximum that human genes allow, and why are females less lateralized than males, and why is the direction of lateralization reversed in some fraction of the population? Surely if hemispheric asymmetry confers the advantages claimed, several million years of selection for asymmetry would have been sufficient to make us as invariant in our laterality patterns as we are in our bipedalism.

Although there is no way to establish with certainty the validity of any answers that might be given, the same limitation holds for any inductive conclusions in any area of science. We know that for any genetic trait, genetic variance can be maintained in a population only if the trait is selectively neutral or if special forms of selection operate that prevent allelic fixation. It is extremely unlikely that fundamental variations in brain organization could be selectively neutral in a species whose survival is strongly dependent on its cognitive properties. We are therefore led to the inference that selective factors themselves have maintained genetically based variations in patterns of cerebral lateralization.

There are a variety of mechanisms that are variance-preserving, including heterosis, in which heterozygotes have higher reproductive rates than either dominant or recessive homozygotes, stabilizing selection, in which genotypes manifesting average phenotypes have higher biological fitness than those manifesting extreme phenotypes (an example of which may be height), frequency-dependent selection, in which fitness increases with rarity of genotype and decreases with prevalence of genotype, and a form of selection in which fitness is differentially associated with genotypes in the sexes.

Though any or all of these mechanisms may have operated, a consideration of the social conditions under which our species has evolved and continues to live strongly implicates frequency-dependent selection in the maintenance of cerebral variability, selective pressures deriving from the structure of the social group itself. By definition, a socially organized group is one in which different members play socially specialized roles, each member of the group contributing his special skills and deriving from the group the benefits of the special skills of others. In a cohesive and adaptive group, the frequency of members engaged in particular roles is balanced in such a way that both individual and group needs are optimally met. Though changing external conditions, as well as technological and social evolution, demand a great deal of plasticity in the variety of social roles any given individual can fill, it would nonetheless be adaptively advantageous for some members of the group to be motivated toward and be highly able in certain types of activities asymmetrically associated with left and right hemisphere functions. Bilateralization of verbal functions, though quite likely reducing pure spatial ability since neither hemisphere would be fully organized to serve those functions, might well increase capacity for logical, analytical reasoning, verbal communication and fluency, or other functions associated with the verbal hemisphere. Similarly, bilateralization of spatial function, though reducing some aspects of verbal competency, might result in unusually high capacities for those functions associated with the mute hemisphere. Such superiorities deriving from bilateralization could come about through a variety of mechanisms.

Through parallel processing, more information might be taken in during a fixed unit of time; memory encoding capacities might be increased; activation of the "wrong" hemisphere for the task at hand would not decrease performance adequacy so much as would be the case in a strongly lateralized brain; decrements in performance due to hemispheric fatigue might be overcome by shifting processing to the other side of the brain. Obviously, such cognitively specialized people might be at a disadvantage were they hermits or were all members of the group of which they were a part similarly specialized, but as members of a social group consisting of a majority of cognitive generalists with strongly lateralized brains and a minority of specialists of the same or of the opposite type, any deficiencies they might have would be met by the group and they, in turn, could contribute their valuable and specialized skills. It is easy to imagine the types of social reinforcements and punishments that could serve to select rare cognitive types, thus increasing their number, and that could counterselect overly prevalent types, thus decreasing their number. By such means, a variety of cerebral–cognitive types would be maintained in the population and social cohesion and adaptation would, thereby, be increased. If this interpretation is valid, it implies that there exists no "best" cerebral organization, that the human species has evolved and survived through the differences among its different members, and that the variations that occur are of critical value to the population as a whole. If so, any attempt to abolish individual variation in cognitive propensities and structures, if successful, must necessarily reduce the adaptive strength of the human population.

Until recently, there was no reason to believe that variations in the **direction** of lateralization had any psychological consequences at all. However, as mentioned, Reid (1980) found that the left hemisphere of females and the right hemisphere of males, regardless of their specialized functions, mature earlier, and that cognitive abilities were higher for the earlier-maturing hemisphere. Thus, in girls with language lateralized to the left hemisphere and boys with language lateralized to the right hemisphere, verbal abilities exceeded spatial abilities. In girls with spatial functions localized to the left hemisphere and in boys with spatial functions in the right hemisphere, spatial abilities exceeded verbal abilities. Cognitive capacity for a given set of functions was predictable from an interaction between sex and direction of lateralization. Children with a mirror-reversed laterality pattern were also mirror-reversed with respect to the typical pattern of cognitive sex differences. It may be that people with a sex-atypical cognitive structure were of great value to the social group during times when the two sexes were separated over long periods.

The selective forces operating on males and females have been very different: Males ranged widely over unmapped terrain in search of prey and were compelled to design weapons of defense and offense; to females was left the responsibility of socializing the young, of teaching language, the history of the culture, the means of interacting with other people; they had to devise means for maintaining the stability of the social group during the long absences of males and for recognizing threats to that stability in the actions of other members of the group. To them was left the preservation of the cultural heritage, the maintenance of cultural mores, the continuity of cultural values and morals. The differing brain organizations and abilities and propensities of the two sexes might well reflect the different demands placed on them throughout hominid evolution.

Cultural institutions, no doubt, have developed to magnify and reinforce whatever biological differences may be present, and the differences that are there represent, in any case, only average differences for the sexes. The overlap in cerebral–cognitive organization is great, and it is probable that within-sex variations are significantly greater than those between sexes. Nevertheless, it is extremely improbable, both from the empirical evidence and on theoretical grounds, that all cerebral–cognitive differences in males and females are attributable to training and expectation. As discussed earlier, variations in fetal sex steroids are known to have permanent organizing effects on the brains of animals (see, e.g., Whalen, 1967), on the behavior of people (Money and Ehrhardt, 1972), and even on cerebral lateralization (Netley, 1977).

The differences between the sexes, like those within the sexes, have very probably served the fitness and adaptation of our species, each sex giving to the social group the benefits of their abilities and receiving from the other the benefits of theirs. While purely social reinforcements and sanctions may serve to assure that essential social roles are filled, genetic variations that produce differences in propensities and abilities would serve as a cohesive social force and would tend to optimize the social structure for the fulfillment of human needs.

Clearly, to the extent that cerebral–cognitive variations are genetic, their current distribution reflects the selective demands that acted over millions of years of hominoid evolution and that acted within a human ecology that was very different from that of an advanced technological society. That differences among people are of value seems certain, but the nature and distribution of those differences that would best serve modern society are almost certainly different from those that best served our forebears. We are both the beneficiaries and victims of our evolutionary heritage, and it is of critical importance that we distinguish the two aspects of our inheritance. Even a definitive proof that human adaptation was increased in some neolithic culture when sex roles were highly differentiated does not imply that the same holds true today. The modern child may need the nurturing of fathers as much as the nurturing of mothers, and the modern technology may need the cognitive skills of females as much as that of males. While a rigid social structure may have been required in our distant past, an accommodating structure may best serve current needs. We may need, and be able to tolerate, more cognitive specialists now than then, and rather than being sinister, it may be that, as Hugo's Jean Valjean said in *Les Miserables*, "The left-handed are precious; they take places which are inconvenient for the rest."

I believe that our survival as a species may well depend on our acknowledging both the potentialities and the limitations conferred by our evolution, on encouraging what is best from that heritage, on inhibiting that which no longer serves an adaptive function, and on being able to distinguish the two. To accept the thesis that biology is destiny is to forfeit the gift of evolution that made us human, but to deny biology altogether is to forfeit the wisdom of our entire evolutionary history.

Bibliography

Achenbach, T. M. Cue learning, associative responding, and school performance in children. *Developmental Psychology,* 1969 *1,* 717–725.

Akelaitis, A. J. Psychobiological studies following section of the corpus callosum: A preliminary report. *American Journal of Psychiatry,* 1941 *97,* 1147–1157.(a)

Akelaitis, A. J. Studies on the corpus callosum: II. The higher visual functions in each homonymous field following complete section of the corpus callosum. *Archives of Neurology and Psychiatry,* 1941, *45,* 788–796.(b)

Akelaitis, A. J. Studies on the corpus callosum: VIII. The effects of partial and complete section of the corpus callosum on psychopathic epileptics. *American Journal of Psychiatry,* 1941, *98:* 409–414.(c)

Akelaitis, A. J. Studies on the corpus callosum: V. Homonymous defects for color, object and letter recognition (homonymous hemiamblyopia) before and after section of the corpus callosum. *Archives of Neurology and Psychiatry,* 1942, *48:* 108–118.(a)

Akelaitis, A. J. Studies on the corpus callosum: VI. Orientation (temporal-spatial gnosis) following section of the corpus callosum. *Archives of Neurology and Psychiatry,* 1942, *48:* 914–937. (b)

Akelaitis, A. J. Studies on the corpus callosum: VII. Study of language functions (tactile and visual lexia and graphia) unilaterally following section of the corpus callosum. *Journal of Neuropathology and Experimental Neurology,* 1943, *2,* 226–262.

Akelaitis, A. J. A study of gnosis, praxis and language following section of the corpus callosum and anterior commissure. *Journal of Neurosurgery,* 1944, *1,* 94–102.

Akelaitis, A. J., Risteen, W. A., Herren, R. Y., & Van Wagenen, W. P. Studies on the corpus callosum: III. A contribution to the study of dyspraxia in epileptics following partial and complete section of the corpus callosum. *Archives of Neurology and Psychiatry,* 1942, *47,* 971–1008.

Akelaitis, A. J., Risteen, W. A., & Van Wagenen, W. P. Studies on the corpus callosum: IX. Relationship of the grasp reflex to section of the corpus callosum. *Archives of Neurology and Psychiatry,* 1943, *49:* 820–825.

Alajouanine, T., & Lhermitte, F. Some problems concerning the agnosias, apraxias, and aphasia. In L. Halpern (Ed.), *Problems of dynamic neurology.* Jerusalem: Herbrew University Hadassah Medical School, 1963.

Alexander, D., Ehrhardt, A. A., & Money, J. Defective figure drawing, geometric and human, in Turner's Syndrome. *The Journal of Nervous and Mental Diseases,* 1966, *142.* 161–167.

Amster, H., & Wiegand, V. Developmental study of sex differences in free recall. *Proceedings of the 80th annual meetings of the American Psychological Association,* 1972.

Andrew, D. M., & Paterson, D. G. *Minnesota Clerical Test: Manual.* New York: The Psychological Corporation, 1946.

Annett, M. Handedness in families. *Annals of Human Genetics, London,* 1973, *37,* 93–105.

Aschoff, J. C. Reconsideration of the oculomotor pathway. In F. O. Schmitt, F. G. Worden (Eds.), *The neurosciences (Vol. 3).* Cambridge, Mass.: The MIT Press, 1974.

Backman, M. E. Patterns of mental abilities: ethnic, socioeconomic, and sex differences. *American Educational Research Journal,* 1972, *9,* 1–12.

Bahrick, H. P., Bahrick, P. O., & Wittlinger, R. P. Fifty years of memory for names and faces: A cross-sectional approach. *Journal of Experimental Psychology: General,* 1975, *104,* 54–75.

Bakan, P., Dibb, G., & Reed, P. Handedness and birth stress. *Neuropsychologia,* 1973, *3,* 363–366.

Bakan, P., & Svorad, D. Resting EEG alpha and asymmetry of reflective lateral eye movements. *Nature,* 1969, *223,* 975–976.

Barton, M. I., Goodglass, H., & Shai, A. Differential recognition of tachistoscopically presented English and Hebrew words in right and left visual fields. *Perceptual and Motor Skills,* 1965, *21.* 431–327.

Bennett, G. K., Seashore, H. G., & Wesman, A. G. *Differential aptitude tests,* (3rd Ed.). New York: The Psychological Corporation, 1959.

Berlin, C. I., & Cullen, J. K., Jr. Acoustic problems in dichotic listening tasks. In S. J. Segalowitz, & F. A. Gruber (Eds.), *Language development and neurological theory.* New York: Academic Press, 1977.

Berlucchi, G., Crea, F., DiStefano, M., & Tassinari, G. Influence of spatial stimulus-response compatibility on reaction time of ipsilateral and contralateral hand to lateralized light stimuli. *Journal of Experimental Psychology: Human Perception and Performance,* 1977, *3,* 505–517.

Best, C. T., & Glanville, B. B. Cerebral asymmetries in speech and timbre discrimination by 2-, 3-, and 4-month-old infants. Paper presented at The First International Conference on Infant Studies, Providence, R.I., March, 1978.

Bever, T. G. The nature of cerebral dominance in speech behavior of the child and adult. In R. Huxley and E. Ingram (Eds.) *Language acquisition: Models and methods.* New York: Academic Press, 1971.

Billet, R. Signes moteurs homolatéraux dans quelques cas de méningiomes. *Semaine des Hopitaux de Paris, 83,* 2001–2002, 1961.

Blackstock, E. G. Cerebral asymmetry and the development of infantile autism. Downsview, Ontario, Canada: Report No. 64 from the Department of Psychology, York University, 1977.

Bogen, J. E. The other side of the brain. I: Dysgraphia and dyscopia following cerebral commissurotomy. *Bulletin of the Los Angeles Neurological Society,* 1969, *34,* 73–105. (a)

Bogen, J. E. The other side of the brain. II: An appositional mind. *Bulletin of the Los Angeles Neurological Society,* 1969, *34,* 135–162.(b)

Bogen, J. E., & Gazzaniga, M. S. Cerebral commissurotomy in man: Minor hemisphere dominance for certain visuospatial functions. *Journal of Neurosurgery,* 1965, *23.* 395–399.

Bogen, J. E., & Vogel, P. J. Cerebral commissurotomy in man. Preliminary case report. *Bulletin of the Los Angeles Neurological Society,* 1962, *27:* 169–172.

Bolin, B. J. Left handedness and stuttering as signs diagnostic of epileptics. *Journal of Mental Science,* 1953, *99:* 483–488.

Brimer, M. A. Sex differences in listening comprehension *Journal of Research and Development in Education*, 1969, 3, 72–79.

Broadbent, D. E., & Gregory, M. Donders' B and C reactions and S–R compatibility. *Journal of Experimental Psychology*, 1962, 63, 575–578.

Broca, P. Remarques sur le siege de la faculté du langage articulé suives d'une observation d'aphemie. *Bulletin Societie Anatomique* (Paris), 1861, 6: 330–357.

Brown, J. W., & Hécaen, H. Lateralization and language representation. *Neurology*, 1976, 26: 183–189.

Bryden, M. P. Laterality effects in dichotic listening: Relations with handedness and reacing ability in children. *Neuropsychologia* 1970, 8: 443–450.

Bryden, M. P. Left–right differences in tachistoscopic recognition: directional scanning or cerebral dominance? *Perceptual and Motor Skills*, 1966, 23, 1127–1134.

Buck, R. W., Savin, V. J., Miller, R. E., & Caul, W. F. Communication of affect through facial expression in humans. *Journal of Personality and Social Psychology*, 1972, 23, 362–371.

Callan, J., Klisz, D., & Parson, O. A. Strength of auditory stimulus-response compatibility as a function of task complexity. *Journal of Experimental Psychology*, 1974, 102: 1039–1045.

Carter-Saltzman, L. Patterns of cognitive abilities in relation to handedness and sex. In M. Wittig, & A. Peterson, (Eds.), *Determinants of sex-related differences in cognitive functioning*. New York: Academic Press, 1978.

Chapple, W. D. Central and peripheral organs of asymmetry in the abdominal motor system of the Hermit Crab. In S. Dimond, and D. A. Blizard, (Eds.), *Evolution and lateralization of the brain (Vol. 299), Annals of the New York Academy of Sciences*. New York: New York Academy of Sciences, 1977.(a)

Chapple, W. D. Role of asymmetry in the functioning of invertebrate nervous systems. In S. Harnad, R. W. Doty, L. Goldstein, J. Jaynes, & G. Krauthamer, (Eds.), *Lalization in the nervous system*. New York: Academic Press, 1977.(b)

Churchil, J. A., Igna, E., & Senf, R. The association of position at birth and handedness. *Pediatrics*, 1962, 29: 307–309.

Clarke-Stewart, K. A. Interactions between mothers and their young children: characteristics and consequences. *Monographs of Society for Research in Child Development*, 1973, 38, (No. 153).

Colby, K. M., & Parkison, C. Handedness in autistic children. *Journal of Autism and Childhood Schizophrenia*, 1977, 7, 3–9.

Conel, J. L. *The postnatal development of the human cerebral cortex:* (Vol. 7): *The cortex of the four-year-old child.* Cambridge, Mass.: Harvard University Press, 1963.

Conrad, K. Über aphasische Sprachstörungen bei hirnverletzten Linkshändern. *Nervenarzt*, 1949, 20, 148–154.

Corah, N. L. Differentiation in children and their parents. *Journal of Personality*, 1965, 33, 300–308.

Coren, S., & Kaplan, C. P. Patterns of ocular dominance. *American Journal of Optometry and Archives of the American Academy of Optometry*, 1973, 50, 283–292.

Curtiss, S. *The case of Genie: A modern day wild child.* New York: Academic Press, 1977.

Czochra, M. Homolateral pyramidal syndrome in cases of extracerebral hematoma of the 3rd frontal convolution. *Neurologia, Neurochirurgia i Psychiatria Polska*, 1962, 12, 517–522. (Polish)

Davidoff, L. L. *Introduction to psychology.* New York: McGraw-Hill. 1976.

Davies, A. D. The perceptual maze test in a normal population. *Perceptual and Motor Skills*, 1965, 20, 287–293.

Dennis, M., & Kohn, B. Comprehension of syntax in infantile hemiplegics after cerebral hemidecortication: Left-hemisphere superiority. *Brain and Language*, 1975, 2, 472–482.

Dewson, J. H., III. Preliminary evidence of hemispheric asymmetry of auditory function in monkeys. In S. Harnad, R. W. Doty, L. Goldstein, J. Jaynes, & G. Krauthamer (Eds.), *Lateralization in the nervous system*. New York: Academic Press, 1977.

Donders, F. C. Die Schnelligkeit psychischer Processe. *Archiv für Anatomie und Physiologie*, 1868, 657–681.

Dorman, M. F., & Geffner, D. S. Hemispheric specialization for speech perception in six-year-old black and white children from low and middle socioeconomic classes. *Cortex*, 1974, *10*, 171–176.

Douglas, J. W. B., Ross, J. M., & Simpson, H. R. *All our future*. 1968. (Cited by C. Hutt. *Males and females*. Baltimore: Penguin Books. 1972.)

Droege, R. C. Sex differences in aptitude maturation during high school. *Journal Counciling Psychology*, 1967, *14*, 407–411.

Dykstra, R., & Tinney, R. Sex differences in reading readiness—first grade achievement and second grade achievement. *Reading and Realism*, 1969, *13*, 623–628.

Eccles, J. C. *Facing Reality: Philosophical adventures by a brain scientist*. New York: Springer, 1970.

Eccles, J. C. Brain, speech, and consciousness. *Die Naturwissenschaften*, 1973, *60*, 167–176.

Ectors, L., & Achslogh, J. Le syndrome pyramidal homolatéral précoce et les méningiomes de la III³ frontale. *Neurochirurgie*, 1959, *5*: 388–400.

Eisenberg, L., Berlin, C. I., Dill, A., & Frank, S. Class and race effects on intelligibility of monosyllables. *Child Development*, 1968, *39*: 1077–1089.

Ehrlichman, H. I. Hemisphere functioning and individual differences in cognitive ability. *Dissertation Abstracts*, 1972, *33*, 2319.

Entus, A. K. Hemispheric asymmetry in processing of dichotically presented speech and nonspeech stimuli by infants. In S. J. Segalowitz, & F. A. Gruber, (Eds.), *Language development and neurological theory*. New York: Academic Press, 1977.

Ettlinger, G., Blakemore, C. B., Milner, A. D., & Wilson, J. Agenesis of the corpus callosum: A behavioural investigation. *Brain*, 1972, *95*, 327–346.

Ettlinger, G., Warrington, E., & Zangwill, O. L. A further study of visuo-spatial agnosia. *Brain*, 1957, *80*, 335–361.

Falek, A. Handedness: A family study. *American Journal of Human Genetics*, 1959, *11*, 52–62.

Felzen, E., & Anisfeld, M. Semantic and phonetic relations in the false recognition of words by third- and sixth-grade children. *Developmental Psychology*, 1970, *3*, 163–168.

Ferriss, G. S., & Dorsen, M. M. Agenesis of the corpus callosum: I. Neuropsychological studies. *Cortex*, 1975, *11*, 95–122.

Fiebert, M. Cognitive styles in the deaf. *Perceptual and Motor Skills*, 1967, *24*, 319–329.

Finley, G. E., & Frenkel, O. J. Children's tachistoscopic recognition thresholds for and recall of words which differ in connotative meaning. *Child Development*, 1972, *43*, 1098–1103.

Fitzgerald, G., & Hallpike, C. S. Studies in human vestibular function: I. Observations on the directional preponderance ("Nystagmusbereitschaft") of caloric nystagmus resulting from cerebral lesions. *Brain*, 1942, *65*, 115–137.

Fitzgerald, G., & Stengel, E. Vestibular reactivity to caloric stimulation in schizophrenics. *Journal of Mental Science*, 1945, *91*, 93–100.

Flechsig, P. *Die leitungsbahnen in gehirn and rückenmark des menschen*. Leipzig: W. Engelmann, 1876.

Flor-Henry, P. Lateralized temporal-limbic dysfunction and psychopathology. In S. Harnad, H. Steklis, & J. Lancaster, (Eds.), *Origins and evolution of language and speech, (Vol. 280): Annals of the New York Academy of Sciences*. New York: The New York Academy of Sciences. 1976.

Flor-Henry, P., Koles, Z. J., Bo-Lassen, P., & Yeudall, L. T. Studies of the functional psychoses: Power spectral EEG analysis. *International Research Communications System/Medical Science*, 1975, *3*, 87.

Frances, K. Effects of "White" and "Black" examiner voices on IQ scores of children. *Developmental Psychology*, 1973, *8*, 144.

François, J., Eggermont, E, Evens, L., Logghe, N., & De Bock, F. Agenesis of the corpus callosum, the median facial cleft syndrome and associated ocular malformations. *American Journal of Ophthalmology*, 1973, *76*, 241–245.

Frederiksen, N., & Evans, F. R. Effects of models of creative performance on ability to formulate hypotheses. *Journal of Educational Psychology*, 1974, *66*, 83–89.

Gardiner, M. F., & Walter, D. O. Evidence of hemispheric specialization from EEG. In S. Harnad, R. W. Doty, L. Goldstein, J. Jaynes, & G. Krauthamer, (Eds.), *Lateralization in the nervous system*. New York: Academic Press, 1977.

Gazzaniga, M. S., Bogen, J. E., & Sperry, R. W. Some functional effects of sectioning the cerebral commissures in man. *Proceedings of the National Academy of Sciences*, 1962, *48*, 1765–1769.

Gazzaniga, M. S., Bogen, J. E., & Sperry, R. W. Observations on visual perception after disconnection of the cerebral hemispheres in man. *Brain*, 1965, *88*, 221–236.

Gazzaniga, M. S., & Hillyard, S. A. Language and speech capacity of the right hemisphere. *Neuropsychologia*, 1971, *9*, 273–280.

Gazzaniga, M. S., & Sperry, R. W. Language after section of the cerebral commissures. *Brain*, 1967, *90*, 131–148.

Geffner, D. S., & Dorman, M. F. Hemispheric specialization for speech perception in four-year-old children from low and middle socio-economic classes. *Cortex*, 1976, *12*, 71–73.

Geffner, D. S., Hochberg, I. Ear laterality performance of children from low and middle socioeconomic levels on a verbal dichotic listening task. *Cortex*, 1971, *3*, 193–203.

Geiwitz, J. *Looking at ourselves: An invitation to psychology*. Boston: Little, Brown, & Co., 1976.

Geschwind, N., & Levitsky, W. Human brain: Left-right asymmetries in temporal speech region. *Science*, 1968, *161*, 186–187.

Gesell, A., & Ames, L. B. The development of handedness. *Journal of Genetic Psychology*, 1947, *70*, 155–175.

Glick, S. D. Enhancement of spatial preferences by (+)-amphetamine. *Neuropharmacology*, 1973, *12*, 43–47.

Glick, S. D., Cox, R. S., & Greenstein, S. Relationship of rats' spatial preferences to effects of d-amphetamine on timing and behavior. *European Journal of Pharmacology*, 1975, *33*, 173–182.

Glick, S. D., Crane, A. M., Jerussi, T. P., Fleisher, L. N., & Green, J. P. Functional and neurochemical correlates of potentiation of striatal asymmetry by callosal section. *Nature*, 1975, *254*, 616–617.

Glick, S. D., & Jerussi, T. P. Spatial and paw preferences in rats: their relationship to rate-dependent effects of d-amphetamine. *Journal of Pharmacology and Experimental Therapeutics*, 1974, *188*, 714–715.

Glick, S. D., Jerussi, T. P., Waters, D. H., & Green, J. P. Amphetamine-induced changes in striatal dopamine and acetylcholine levels and relationship to rotation (circling behavior) in rats. *Biochemical Pharmacology*, 1974, *23*, 3223–3225.

Glick, S. D., Jerussi, T. P., & Zimmerberg, B. Behavioral and neuropharmacological correlates of nigrostriatal asymmetry in rats. In S. Harnad, R. W. Doty, L. Goldstein, J. Jaynes, & G. Krauthamer, (Eds.), *Lateralization in the nervous system*. New York: Academic Press, 1977.

Goodglass, H., & Quadfasal, F. A. Language laterality in left-handed aphasics. *Brain*, 1954, *77*, 521–548.

Gruzelier, J. H., & Venables, P. H. Skin conductance responses to tones with and without attentional significance in schizophrenic and nonschizophrenic psychiatric patients. *Neuropsychologia*, 1973, *11*, 221–230.

Gruzelier, J. H., & Venables, P. H. Bimodality and lateral asymmetry of skin conductance orienting activity in schizophrenics: replication and evidence of lateral asymmetry in patients with depression and disorders of personality. *Biological Psychiatry*, 1974, *8*, 55–73.

Gur, R. E. Motoric laterality unbalance in schizophrenia: A possible concomitant of left hemisphere dysfunction. *Archives of General Psychiatry*, 1977, *34*, 33–37.

Gur, R. C., Levy, J., & Van Auken, C. Eyedness, handedness, and perinatal stress. In preparation.

Gur, R. E. Left hemisphere dysfunction and overactivation in schizophrenia. *Journal of Abnormal Psychology*, 1978, *87*, 226–238.

Gur, R. E., & Gur, R. C. The direction and degree of lateral field asymmetries as a function of eye dominance in right handers. In preparation.

Hale, G. A., Miller, L. K., & Stevenson, H. W. Incidental learning of film content: a developmental study. *Child Development*, 1968, *39*, 69–77.

Hamilton, C. R. An assessment of hemispheric specialization in monkeys. In S. J. Dimond, D. A. Blizard, (Eds.), *Evolution and lateralization of the brain (Vol. 299): Annals of the New York Academy of Sciences*. New York: The New York Academy of Sciences, 1977.(a)

Hamilton, C. R. Investigations of perceptual and mnemonic lateralization in monkeys. In S. Harnad, L. Goldstein, J. Jaynes, & G. Krauthamer, (Eds.), *Lateralization in the nervous system*. New York: Academic Press, 1977.(b)

Hauser, S. L., De Long, G. R., & Rosman, N. P. Pneumographic findings in infantile autism syndrome. *Brain*, 1975, *98*, 667–688.

Hayashi, T., & Bryden, M. P. Ocular dominance and perceptual asymmetry. *Perceptual and Motor Skills*, 1967, *25*, 605–612.

Hécaen, H., & Angelergues, R. Agnosia for faces (prosopagnosia). *A.M.A. Archives of Neurology*, 1962, *7*, 92–100.

Hécaen, H., Angelergues, R., & Douzens, L. A. Les agraphies. *Neuropsychologia*, 1963, *1*, 179–208.

Hécaen, H., Penfield, W., Bertrand, C., & Malmo, R. The syndrome of apractognosia due to lesions of the minor cerebral hemisphere. *Archives of Neurology and Psychiatry*, 1956, *75*, 400–434.

Hécaen, H., and Sauguet, J. Cerebral dominance in left-handed subjects. *Cortex*, 1971, *7*, 19–48.

Heilman, K. M., Coyle, J. M., Gonyea, E. F., & Geschwind, N. Apraxia and agraphia in a left-hander. *Brain*, 1973, *96*, 21–28.

Heron, W. Perception as a function of retinal locus and attention. *American Journal of Psychology*, 1957, *70*, 38–48.

Hilgard, E. R. *Introduction to psychology* (3rd ed.). New York: Harcourt, Brace, and World, Inc., 1962.

Hilgard, E. R., Atkinson, R. C., and Atkinson, R. L. *Introduction to psychology* (6th ed.). New York: Harcourt Brace Jovanovich, 1975.

Hillsberg, B. W. Visual field differences in information processing and decision making in schizophrenic and normal subjects. Unpublished, 1976.

Hilton, T. L., & Berglund, G. W. Sex differences in mathematics achievement—a longitudinal study. *Educational testing service research bulletin*, 1971.

Humphrey, M. E., & Zangwill, O. L. Dysphasia in left handed patients with unilateral lesions. *Journal of Neurology, Neurosurgery, and Psychiatry*, 1952, *15*, 184–193.(a)

Humphrey, M. E., & Zangwill, O. L. Effects of a right sided occipito-parietal brain injury in a left handed man. *Brain*, 1952, *75*, 312–324.(b)

Hutt, C. *Males and females.* Baltimore: Penguin, 1972.

Jeeves, M. A. Hemispheric differences in response rates to visual stimuli in children. *Psychonomic Science,* 1972, *27,* 201–203.

Jerison, H. *Evolution of the brain and intelligence.* New York: Academic Press, 1973.

Jerussi, T. P., & Glick, S. D. Amphetamine-induced rotation in rats without lesions. *Neuropharmacology,* 1974, *13,* 283–286.

Jerussi, T. P., & Glick, S. D. Apomorphine-induced rotation in normal rats and interaction with unilateral caudate lesions. *Psychopharmacologia,* 1975, *40,* 329–334.

Jerussi, T. P., & Glick, S. D. Drug-induced rotation in rats without lesions: Behavioral and neurochemical indices of a normal asymmetry in nigro-striatal function. *Psychopharmacology,* 1976, *47,* 249–260.

Johnstone, J., Galin, D., & Herron, J. Choice of handedness measures in studies of hemispheric specialization. Submitted, 1978.

Kagan, J., & Havemann, E. *Psychology: An introduction* (3rd ed.). New York: Harcourt Brace Jovanovich, 1976.

Keogh, B. K., & Ryan, S. R. Use of three measures and field organization with young children. *Perceptual and Motor Skills,* 1971, *33,* 466.

Kerr, F. W. L., & O'Leary, J. L. The thalamic source of cortical recruiting in the rodent. *Electroencephalography and Clinical Neurophysiology,* 1957, *9,* 461–476.

Kimura, D. Cerebral dominance and the perception of verbal stimuli. *Canadian Journal of Psychology,* 1961, *15,* 166–171.

Kimura, D. Dual functional asymmetry of the brain in visual perception. *Neuropsychologia,* 1966, *4,* 275–285.

Kimura, D. Functional asymmetry of the brain in dichotic listening. *Cortex,* 1967, *3,* 163–178.

Kimura, D. Spatial localization in left and right visual fields. *Canadian Journal of Psychology,* 1969, *23,* 445–458.

Kimura, D. The asymmetry of the human brain. *Scientific American,* 1973, *228:* 70–78.

Kleist, K. Schizophrenic symptoms and cerebral pathology. *Journal of Mental Science,* 1960, *106,* 246–255.

Knox, C., & Kimura, D. Cerebral processing of nonverbal sounds in boys and girls. *Neuropsychologia,* 1970, *8,* 227–237.

Kohn, B., & Dennis, M. Selective impairments of visuo-spatial abilities in infantile hemiplegics after right cerebral hemidecortication. *Neuropsychologia,* 1974, *12,* 505–512.

Kuhn, T. S. *The structure of scientific revolutions.* Chicago: University of Chicago Press, 1962.

Lansdell, H. Sex differences in hemispheric asymmetries of the human brain. *Nature,* 1964, *203,* 550.

Lansdell, H., & Davie, J. C. Massa intermedia: Possible relation to intelligence. *Neuropsychologia,* 1972, *10,* 207–210.

Lansdell, H., & Smith, F. J. Asymmetrical cerebral function for two WAIS factors and their recovery after brain injury. *Journal of Consulting and Clinical Psychology,* 1975, *43,* 923.

Lazerson, A. (Ed.). *Psychology today: An introduction* (3rd ed.). New York: Random House, 1975.

Le Doux, J. E., Wilson, D. H., & Gazzaniga, M. S. Manipulo-spatial aspects of cerebral lateralization: clues to the origin of lateralization. *Neuropsychologia,* 1977, *15,* 743–750.

Lehmann, H. J., & Lampe, H. Observations on the interhemispheric transmission of information in 9 patients with corpus callosum defect. *European Neurology,* 1970, *4,* 129–147.

Le May, M., & Culebras, A. Human brain—morphologic differences in the hemispheres demonstrable by carotid arteriography. *New England Journal of Medicine,* 1972, *287,* 168–170.

Le May, M., & Geschwind, N. Hemispheric differences in the brains of great apes. *Brain, Behavior, and Evolution*, 1975, *11*, 48–52.

Lenneberg, E. H. Speech development: Its anatomical and physiological concomitants. In E. C. Carterette, (Ed.), *Brain function (Vol. 3): Speech, language, and communication*. Los Angeles and Berkeley: University of California Press, 1966.

Levy, J. The correlation of the function of the difference score with performance and its relevance to laterality experiments. *Cortex*, 1977, *13*, 458–464.

Levy, J. Psychobiological implications of bilateral asymmetry. In S. J. Dimond, J. G. Beaumont, (Eds.), *Hemisphere function in the human brain*. New York: John Wiley and Sons, 1974.

Levy, J. A review of evidence for a genetic component in the determination of handedness. *Behavior Genetics*, 1976, *6*, 429–453.

Levy, J., Meck, B., & Staikoff, J. Dysfunction of the left cerebral hemisphere in autistic children. Submitted, 1978.

Levy, J., & Reid, M. Variations in writing posture and cerebral organization. *Science*, 1976, *194*, 337–339.

Levy, J., & Reid, M. Variations in cerebral organization as a function of handedness, hand posture in writing, and sex. *Journal of Experimental Psychology: General* 1978, *107*, 119–144.

Levy, J., & Trevarthen, C. Metacontrol of hemispheric function in human split-brain patients. *Journal of Experimental Psychology: Human Perception and Performance*, 1976, 2, 299–312.

Levy, J., & Trevarthen, C. Perceptual, semantic and phonetic aspects of elementary language processes in split brain patients. *Brain*, 1977, *100:* 105–118.

Levy, J., Trevarthen, C., & Sperry, R. W. Perception of bilateral chimeric figures following hemispheric deconnection. *Brain*, 1972, *95*, 61–78.

Levy-Agresti, J., and Sperry, R. W. Differential perceptual capacities in major and minor hemispheres. *Proceedings of the National Academy of Sciences*, 1968, *61*, 1151. (Abstract).

Lewis, M. Infants' responses to facial stimuli during the first year of life. *Developmental Psychology*, 1969, *1*, 75–86.

Lewis, M., & Freedle, R. Mother-infant dyad: the cradle of meaning. *Symposium on language and thought: Communication and affect*. Erindale College, University of Toronto, March, 1972.

Liebert, R. M., & Neale, J. M. *Psychology*. New York: John Wiley and Sons, 1977.

Lindzey, G., Hall, C., & Thompson, R. F. *Psychology*. New York: Worth. 1975.

Luria, A. R. *Traumatic aphasia*. The Hague, Paris: Mouton, 1970.

Luria, A. R., & Homskaya, E. D. Disturbance of action control in frontal lobe lesions. In A. R. Luria, (Ed.), *Human brain and psychological processes*. New York: Harper and Row, 1966.

Maccoby, E. E., & Jacklin, C. N. *The psychology of sex differences*. Stanford, Calif.: Stanford University Press, 1974.

Mastrobuono, M., & Munarini, D. Sindrome piramidale omolaterale nell' ematoma sottodurale cronico. *Rivista Sperimentale di Freniatria e Medicina Legale delle Alienazioni Mentale*, 1963, *87*, 1349–1361.

Matthysse, S. Antipsychotic drug actions: a clue to the neuropathology of schizophrenia? *Federated Proceedings*, 1973, *32*, 200–205.

McFie, J., Piercy, M. F., & Zangwill, O. L. Visual-spatial agnosia associated with lesions of the right cerebral hemisphere. *Brain*, 1950, *73*, 167–190.

McGaugh, J. L., Thompson, R. F., & Nelson, T. O. *Psychology I: An experimental approach*. San Francisco: Albion, 1977.

McGlone, J., & Davidson, W. The relation between cerebral speech laterality and spatial ability with special reference to sex and hand preference. *Neuropsychologia*, 1973, *11*, 105–113.

McGlone, J., & Kertesz, A. Sex differences in cerebral processing of visuo-spatial tasks. *Cortex*, 1973, *9*, 313–320.

Mellone, M. A. A factorial study of picture tests for young children. *British Journal of Psychology*, 1944, *35*, 9–16.

Merrell, D. J. Dominance of hand and eye. *Human Biology*, 1957, *23*, 314–328.

Meyer, V., & Jones, H. G. Patterns of cognitive test performance as functions of the lateral localization of cerebral abnormalities in the temporal lobe. *Journal of Mental Science*, 1957, *103*, 758–772.

Miele, J. A. Sex differences in intelligence: the relationship of sex to intelligence as measured by the Wechsler Adult Intelligence Scale and the Wechsler Intelligence Scale for Children. *Dissertation Abstracts*, 1958, *18*, 2213.

Milburn, T. W., Bell, N., & Koeske, G. F. Effects of censure or praise and evaluative dependence in a free-learning task. *Journal of Personality and Social Psychology*, 1970, *15*, 43–47.

Milner, B. Brain mechanisms suggested by studies of the temporal lobes. In F. L. Darley, (Ed.), *Brain mechanisms underlying speech and language*. New York: Grune and Stratton. 1967.

Milner, B., & Taylor, L. Right-hemisphere superiority in tactile pattern-recognition after cerebral commissurotomy: Evidence for nonverbal memory. *Neuropsychologia*, 1972, *10*, 1–15.

Mishkin, M., & Forgays, D. G. Word recognition as a function of retinal locus. *Journal of Experimental Psychology*, 1952, *43*, 42–48.

Molfese, D. Infant cerebral asymmetry. In S. J. Segalowitz, & F. A. Gruber, (Eds.), *Language development and neurological theory*. New York: Academic Press, 1977.

Money, J., & Ehrhardt, A. A. *Man, woman, boy, and girl*. Baltimore: The Johns Hopkins University Press, 1972.

Moore, T. Language and intelligence: a longitudinal study of the first eight years. Part 1. Patterns of development in boys and girls. *Human Development*, 1967, *10*, 88–106.

Morel, F. La massa intermedia ou commissure grise. *Acta Anatomica*, 1947, *4:* 203–207.

Morgan, A. H., MacDonald, H., & Hilgard, E. R. EEG alpha: Lateral asymmetry related to task and hypnotizability. *Psychophysiology*, 1974, *11*, 275–282.

Morgan, A. H., McDonald, P. J., & MacDonald, H. Differences in bilateral alpha activity as a function of experimental task, with a note on lateral eye movements and hypnotizability. *Neuropsychologia*, 1971, *9:* 459–469.

Morgan, C. T., & King, R. A. *Introduction to Psychology* (5th ed.). New York: McGraw-Hill, 1975.

Morgan, M. Embryology and inheritance of asymmetry. In S. Harnad, R. W. Doty, L. Goldstein, J. Jaynes, & G. Krauthamer, (Eds.), *Lateralization in the nervous system*. New York: Academic Press, 1977.

Morris, C. G. *Psychology: An introduction* (2nd ed.). Englewood Cliffs, N.J.: Prentice-Hall, 1976.

Moscovitch, M., & Smith, L. C. Differences in neural organization between individuals with inverted hand posture during writing. *Science*, 1979, *205*, 710–713.

Meyer, V. & Jones, H. G. Patterns of cognitive test performance as functions of the lateral localization of cerebral abnormalities in the temporal lobe. *Journal of Mental Science*, 1957, *103*, 758–772.

Nathan, P. W., & Smith, M. C. Effects of two unilateral cordotomies on the motility of the lower limbs. *Brain*, 1973, *96*, 471–494.

Nelson, J. M., Phillips, R., & Goldstein, L. Interhemispheric EEG laterality relationships following psychoactive agents and during operant performance in rabbits. In S. Harnad, R. W. Doty, L. Goldstein, J. Jaynes, & G. Krauthamer, (Eds.), *Lateralization in the nervous system*. New York: Academic Press, 1977.

Netley, C. Dichotic listening of callosal agensis and Turner's syndrome patients. In S. J. Segalowitz, & F. A. Gruber, (Eds.), *Language development and neurological theory*. New York: Academic Press, 1977.

Neville, H. Electroencephalographic testing of cerebral specialization in normal and congenitally deaf children: A preliminary report. In S. J. Segalowitz, & F. A. Gruber, (Eds.), *Language development and neurological theory*. New York: Academic Press, 1977.

Nottebohm, F. Asymmetries in neural control of vocalization in the canary. In S. Harnad, R. W. Doty, L. Goldstein, J. Jaynes, & G. Krauthamer, (Eds.), *Lateralization in the nervous system*. New York: Academic Press, 1977.

Nyberg-Hansen, R., & Rinvik, E. Some comments on the pyramidal tract with special reference to its individual variations in man. *Acta Neurologica Scandinavica*, 1963, *39*, 1–30.

Okonji, M. O. The differential effects of rural and urban upbringing on the development of cognitive styles. *International Journal of Psychology*, 1969, *4*, 293–305.

Orbach, J. Retinal locus as a factor in recognition of visually perceived words. *American Journal of Psychology*, 1953, *65*, 555–562.

Paterson, A., & Zangwill, O. L. Disorders of visual space perception associated with lesions of the right cerebral hemisphere. *Brain*, 1944, *67*, 331–358.

Peters, M., & Durding, B. M. Footedness of left- and right-handers. *American Journal of Psychology*, 1979, *92*, 133–142.

Piaget, J. *The construction of reality in the child*. New York: Basic Books, 1954.

Pizzamiglio, L., & Cecchini, M. Development of the hemispheric dominance in children from 5 to 10 years of age and their relations with the development of cognitive processes. *Brain Research*, 1971, *31*, 363–364. (Abstract).

Poffenberger, A. T. Reaction time to retinal stimulation with special reference to the time lost in conduction through nervous centers. *Archives of Psychology*, 1912, *23*, 1–73.

Porteus, S. D. *Porteus Maze Test: Fifty years' application*. Palo Alto, Calif.: Pacific Books, 1965.

Puccetti, R. Brain bisection and personal identity. *British Journal of the Philosophy of Science*, 1973, *24*, 339–355.

Pyle, W. H., & Drouin, A. Left handedness: An experimental and statistical study. *School and Society*, 1932, *36*, 253–256.

Rasmussen, T., & Milner, B. The role of early left-brain injury in determining lateralization of cerebral speech functions. In S. J. Dimond & D. A. Blizard (Ed.), *Evolution and lateralization of the brain*, (Vol. 299) Annals of the New York Academy of Sciences. New York: The New York Academy of Sciences, 1977.

Reid, M. Cerebral lateralization in children: An ontogenetic and organismic analysis (Doctoral dissertation, in preparation, University of Colorado). 1980.

Reitan, R. M., & Tarshes, E. L. Differential effects of lateralised brain lesions on the Trail Making Test. *Journal of Nervous and Mental Diseases*, 1959, *129*, 257–262.

Remington, R., Krashen, S., & Harshman, R. A possible sex difference in degree of lateralization of dichotic stimuli? Paper read at the 86th meeting of the Acoustical Society of America, Los Angeles. November, 1973.

Rife, D. C. Genetic interrelationships of dermatoglyphics and functional handedness. *Genetics*, 1943, *28*, 41–48.

Rife, D. C. Handedness, with special reference to twins. *Genetics,* 1940, *25,* 178–186.

Rosenberg, B. G., & Sutton-Smith, B. The relationship of ordinal position and sibling sex status to cognitive abilities. *Psychonomic Science, 1964, 1,* 81–82.

Rosenberg, B. G., & Sutton-Smith, B. Sibling age spacing effects upon cognition. *Developmental Psychology,* 1969, *1,* 661–668.

Rudel, R., Denckla, M., & Spalten, E. The functional asymmetry of Braille letter learning in normal sighted children. *Neurology,* 1974, *24,* 733–738.

Saarni, C. I. Piagetian operations and field independence as factors in children's problemsolving performance. *Child Development,* 1973, *44,* 338–345.

Sarnat, H. B., & Netsky, M. B. *Evolution of the nervous system.* London and New York: Oxford University Press, 1974.

Satz, P., Achenback, K., Pattishall, E., & Fennell, E. Order of report, ear asymmetry, and handedness in dichotic listening. *Cortex,* 1965, *1,* 377–396.

Saul, R. E., & Gott, P. S. Language and speech lateralization by amytal and dichotic listening tests in agenesis of the corpus callosum. In D. O. Walter, L. Rogers, & J. H. Finzi-Fried, (Eds.), *Conference on human brain function: Brain information service.* Los Angeles: BRI Publications, University of California, 1976.

Saul, R. & Sperry, R. W. Absence of commissurotomy symptoms with agenesis of the corpus callosum. *Neurology,* 1968, *18,* 307.

Schneidler, G. R., & Paterson, D. G. Sex differences in clerical aptitude. *Journal Educational Psychology,* 1942, *33,* 303–309.

Serafetinides, E. A. Voltage laterality in the EEG of psychiatric patients. *Diseases of the Nervous System,* 1972, *33,* 622–623.

Serafetinides, E. A. Voltage laterality in the EEG of psychiatric patients. *Diseases of the Nervous System,* 1973, *34,* 190–191.

Shanon, B. Writing positions in Americans and Israelis. *Neuropsychologia,* in press.

Sherman, J. A. Field articulation, sex, spatial visualization dependency, practice, laterality of the brain and birth order. *Perceptual and Motor Skills,* 1974, *38,* 1223–1235.

Sherrington, C. *The integrative action of the nervous system.* Cambridge: Cambridge University Press, 1947.

Siqueland, E. R. Operant conditioning of head turning in four-month infants. *Psychonomic Science,* 1964, *1,* 223–224.

Siqueland, E. R., & Lipsett, L. P. Conditioned head-turning in human newborns. *Journal of Experimental Child Psychology,* 1966, *4,* 356–377.

Smith, K. U., & Akelaitis, A. J. Studies on the corpus callosum: I. Laterality in behavior and bilateral motor organization in man before and after section of the corpus callosum. *Archives of Neurology and Psychiatry,* 1942, *47,* 519–543.

Smith, L. C., & Moscovitch, M. Writing posture, hemispheric control of movement and cerebral dominance in individuals with inverted and noninverted hand postures during writing. In preparation, 1978.

Soloman, D., & Ali, F. A. Age trends in the perception of verbal reinforcers. *Developmental Psychology,* 1972, *7,* 238–243.

Sperry, R. W. Restoration of vision after crossing of optic nerves and after contralateral transposition of the eye. *Journal of Neurophysiology,* 1945, *8,* 15–28.

Sperry, R. W. Lateral specialization in the surgically separated hemispheres. In F. O. Schmitt, & F. G. Worden, (Eds.), *The neurosciences* (Vol. 3). Cambridge, Mass.: The MIT Press, 1974.

Sperry, R. W., Gazzaniga, M. S., & Bogen, J. E. Interhemispheric relationships: the neocortical commissures; syndromes of hemisphere disconnection. In P. J. Vinken, G. W. Bruyn, (Eds.), *Handbook of clinical neurology* (Vol. 4). Amsterdam: North-Holland, 1969.

Stahl, B. J. Early and recent primitive brain forms. In S. J. Dimond, & D. A. Blizard, (Eds.), *Evolution and lateralization of the brain* (Vol. 299). *Annals of the New York Academy of Sciences.* New York: The New York Academy of Sciences, 1977.

Starck, R., Genesee, F., Lambert, W. E., & Seitz, M. Multiple language experience and the development of cerebral dominance. In S. Harnad, R. W. Doty, L. Goldstein, J. Jaynes, & G. Krauthamer, (Eds.), *Language development and neurological theory.* New York: Academic Press, 1977.

Stevenson, H. W., Hale, G. A., Klein, R. E., & Miller, L. K. Interrelations and correlates in children's learning and problem solving. *Monographs of the Society for Research in Child Development,* 1968, *33.*

Stevenson, H. W., Klein, R. E., Hale, G. A., & Miller, L. K. Solution of anagrams: a developmental study. *Child Development,* 1968, *39,* 905–912.

Svensson, A. *Relative achivement: School performance in relation to intelligence, sex, and home environment.* Stockholm: Almquist and Wiksell, 1971.

Tanguay, P. Clinical and electrophysiological research. In E. Ritvo (Ed.), *Autism, diagnosis, current research and management.* New York: Spectrum Publications, 1975.

Taylor, J. (Ed.). *Selected writings of john hughlings jackson.* New York: Basic Books, 1958.

Teng, E. L., Lee, P. Yang, K., & Chang, P. C. Genetic, cultural, and neuropathologic factors in relation to laterality. In D. O. Walter, L. Rogers, & J. H. Finzi- Fried (Eds.), *Conference on human brain function: Brain information service.* Los Angeles: BRI Publications, University of California, 1976.

Terrace, H. S. The effects of retinal locus and attention on the perception of words. *Journal of Experimental Psychology,* 1959, *58,* 382–385.

Turkewitz, G., Birch, H. G., Moreau, T., Levy, L., & Cornwell, A. C. Effect of intensity of auditory stimulation on directional eye movements in the human neonate. *Animal Behavior,* 1966, *14,* 93–101.

Turkewitz, G., Gordon, E. W., & Birch, H. G. Head turing in the human neonate: Effect of prandial condition and lateral preference. *Journal of Comparative and Physiological Psychology,* 1965, *59,* 189–192.

Van Duyne, J., & D'Alonzo, B. J. Amount of verbal information and ear differences in 5- and 6-year-old boys and girls. *Perceptual and Motor Skills,* 1976, *43,* 31–39.

Van Wagenen, W. P., & Herren, R. Y. Surgical division of commissural pathways in the corpus callosum. Relation to spread of an epileptic attack. *Archives of Neurology and Psychiatry,* 1940, *44,* 740–759.

Varney, N. R., & Benton, A. L. Tactile perception of direction in relation to handedness and familial handedness. *Neuropsychologia,* 1975, *13,* 449–454.

Verhaart, W. J. C. & Kramer, W. The uncrossed pyramidal tract. *Acta Psychiatrica Scandinavica,* 1952, *21,* 181–200.

Very, P. S. Differential factor structures in mathematical abilities. *Genet. Psychol. Monog.,* 1967, *75,* 169–207.

Waber, D. P. Sex differences in cognition: A function of maturation rate? *Science,* 1976, *192,* 572–574.

Wada, J. A., Clarke, R., & Hamm, A. Cerebral hemispheric asymmetry in humans. Cortical speech zones in 100 adult and 100 infant brains. *Archives of Neurology,* 1975, *32,* 239–246.

Warren, J. M. Handedness and cerebral dominance in monkeys. In S. Harnad, R. W. Doty, L. Goldstein, J. Jaynes, & G. Krauthamer, (Eds.). *Lateralization in the nervous system.* New York: Academic Press, 1977.

Webster, W. G. Hemispheric asymmetry in cats. In S. Harnad, R. W. Doty, L. Goldstein, J. Jaynes, & G. Krauthamer, (Eds.). *Lateralization in the nervous system.* New York: Academic Press, 1977.

Weisenberg, T., & McBride, K. E. *Aphasia: A clinical and psychological study.* New York: Commonwealth Fund, 1935.

Werdelin, I. *Geometrical ability and the space factors in boys and girls.* Lund: C.W.K. Gleerup, 1961.

Whalen, R. E. (Ed.). *Hormones and behavior.* New York: Van Nostrand Reinhold Co., 1967.

Wickelgren, L. W. Convergence in the human newborn. *Journal of Experimental Child Psychology,* 1967, *5,* 75–85.

Wigan, A. L. *The duality of the mind.* London: Longman, 1844.

Wilson, R. S. Twins: patterns of cognitive development as measured on the Wechsler Preschool and Primary Scale of Intelligence. *Developmental Psychology,* 1975, *11,* 126–134.

Witelson, S. F. Sex and the single hemisphere: right hemisphere specialization for spatial processing. *Science,* 1976, *193,* 425–427.

Witelson, S. F. Early hemisphere specialization and interhemispheric plasticity: An empirical and theoretical review. In S. J. Segalowitz, & F. A. Gruber, (Eds.), *Language development and neurological theory.* New York: Academic Press, 1977.

Witelson, S. F., & Pallie, W. Left hemisphere specialization for language in the newborn: Neuroanatomical evidence of asymmetry. *Brain,* 1973, *96,* 641–647.

Witkin, H. A., Goodenough, D. R., & Karp, S. A. Stability of cognitive style from childhood to young adulthood. *Journal of Personality and Social Psychology,* 1967, *7,* 291–300.

Yeni-Komshian, G. H. & Benson, D. A. Anatomical study of cerebral asymmetry in temporal lobe of humans, chimpanzees, and rhesus monkeys. *Science,* 1976, 387–389.

Zaidel, E. Auditory vocabulary of the right hemisphere following brain bisection or hemidecortication. *Cortex,* 1976, *12,* 191–211.(a)

Zaidel, E. Language, dichotic listening, and the disconnected hemispheres. In D. O. Walter, L. Rogers, & J. H. Finzi-Fried, (Eds.), *Conference in human brain function: Brain information service.* Los Angeles: BRI Publications, University of California, 1976.(b)

Zaidel, E. Unilateral auditory language comprehension on the Token Test following cerebral commissurotomy and hemispherectomy. *Neuropsychologia,* 1977, *15,* 1–18.

Zenner, P. Ein Fall von Hirngeschwulst in der linken motorischen Sphäre, linkseitiger Lahmung, Abwesenheit der Pyramidenkreuzung. *Neurologisches Zentralblatt,* 1898, *17,* 202–203.

Zurif, E. B., & Bryden, M. P. Familial handedness and left-right difference in auditory and visual perception. *Neuropsychologia,* 1969, *7,* 179–187.

PART III

PSYCHOLOGY AND THE RECENT RESEARCH ON THE BRAIN

The third and final section of this book develops relationships between recent research on the brain and cognitive processes of interest to many psychologists. These relationships between the brain and psychology are developed from three different perspectives: that of a brain researcher, a developmental psychologist, and an educational psychologist. These chapters bring together many of the issues and findings reported in the earlier chapters of this volume and relate them to issues in cognition, development, and learning.

Chapter VII

Cognition and the Brain

MARCEL KINSBOURNE

The purpose of this chapter is to outline some principles of the functional organization of the brain with respect to its control of intelligent behavior. Drawing upon a combination of known facts and controversial but heuristically useful concepts, it attempts to show that the way the human brain is organized determines the manner in which we expand our potential to learn as our brains mature during childhood. If the educator takes note of the principles of acquisition of skill, and of how these are influenced by brain organization, he will be in a better position to use to best advantage his pupil's cognitive potential and understand an unexpected block to learning when it occurs.

I. Point of Departure

Neurologically simple organisms behave in a few stereotyped ways predetermined by species-specific genetically mediated control. The number of perceptual discriminations they can make is small, though sufficient to satisfy adaptive necessity. Their limited response repertoire is geared to the few broad categories of perceptual differentiation that they can make. But even quite early in the further elaboration of the nervous system, organisms achieve an additional capability: to learn.

325

This enables organisms to modify their response patterns in the light of individual experiences they have had, experiences that would not necessarily have happened in the same way to all members of the species. In this way, individual differences in behavior can arise that permit optimal adaptation to diverse environments. Cognition, at its most elaborate in the human species, is a massive development of this ability to modify innately determined perceptual and response priorities in the light of personal experience.

II. From Awareness to Automatization

The ultimate goal of learning is rapid, fluent, adept response to all possible contingencies. If such an ideal state came to pass, there would be no remaining role for conscious processes, as attention (awareness) is only a means to an end and is no longer required when the response has been perfected and automatized. By classifying inputs in terms of previous experience, and forming plans for action, cognitive processes lay the foundations for subsequent automatization of response. The event that we perceive and to which we respond is an episode that is forgotten unless and until a situation very like it occurs again. Close similarities constitute the *retrieval cues* that permit "episodic" remembering to occur (Tulving, 1972). But most episodes do not recur in faithful detail and therefore we do not remember most of the specific events of our lives. This is just as well as otherwise we would spend most of our lives in introspective preoccupation, and be unprepared to deal with unexpected but important events. When a situation on which we have focused attention recurs time and again, we become increasingly adept at detecting its presence even in irrelevant or distracting contexts, and we respond more quickly and accurately in those ways that we have learned are effective and will lead to reward, or at any rate will minimize punishment. Initially, we might have pondered over each of a number of features of the situation one by one and in painstaking sequence tried out a number of possible action patterns to determine which might best enable us to realize our goal. As experience gathers, we become more able to process the relevant features in parallel and to program a response without hesitation; even without attending to it. In essence, we become aware of or consciously experience that with which we have not yet become familiar. What we notice ourselves doing, as opposed to what we do without knowing it, except in broadest outline, is that in which we have not yet become highly skilled. Note that not all learning need be conceived as originating in the conscious awareness of recurrent episodes. Nor need we credit animals (or infant humans) with episodic memory. When an event occurs, one aspect or feature of which is salient, a response to that stimulus can be made and can be perpetuated by reinforcement without at any stage calling for the imaginative recreation of the context of that stimulus. Instead, episodic remembering mediates learning only in those situations in which the feature or relationship that will become relevant at some subsequent time is not immediately clear. When the need arises to recover information embedded in that initial experience, it is necessary to represent mentally the essence of the total experience, so that the to-be-remembered item may then be picked out by inwardly focused selective attention. This ability to use mental representation to mediate learning expands to the extent to which the organism can benefit from complex experiences.

III. Genetically Preprogrammed Behavior

There are perhaps two basic ways in which a neural network could have been engineered to adapt in this manner. One is for it initially to be equally responsive to all discriminable sensory differences and for it to permit with equal probability all conceivable responses. Insofar as such a tabula rasa system might work, it would be most likely to do so in an extremely sheltered altricial species, the young of which could afford to take the time to learn because they are meanwhile effectively protected. We know of no such organism. The human species comes closer to this prototype than most but not close enough to be able to dispense totally with innate behavior patterns. Its nervous system, like that of all animals, is engineered in a different fashion. The human infant comes equipped with the ability to make numerous sensory discriminations but is so programmed that certain modalities and certain states of input within each modality command his attention to the exclusion of others (i.e., are salient—Gibson, 1969). Although the human infant has essentially the locomotor equipment he will have in full maturity, his motor executive system is so programmed that certain response combinations, *synergisms*, are far more probable than others, and only a small set of all the conceivable combinations of movement at the various joints are possible for him. Those perceptual dimensions to which the infant preferentially attends are the ones that are most relevant for purposes of adaptation. Those movement patterns of which the infant is capable are ones that have, or have had, survival value—such as the tonic neck response—the eye, and body turning by means of which the direction of orientation of the receptors can be shifted, the suck and grasp synergism, or the startle response, by which he clutches and clings to the caretaker under the presumably menacing impetus of a powerful stimulus.

IV. From Stimulus-Bound Response to Mental Representation

As perceptual maturation proceeds, the individual, though still most vividly impressed by salient stimuli, becomes able to shift attention away from them with increasing facility and to attend selectively to ever more subtle features of the environment. Similarly, although movement in accordance with a genetically predetermined pattern remains relatively easy, by virtue of motor maturation he becomes able also to move according to patterns that deviate from or even violate the predetermined order. Maturation of the brain generates the potential for this differentiation. Specific experiences that are recurrent or are deliberately rehearsed endow the child with the ability to respond fluently in ways that are adaptive to the particular environment. It is the individuality of this learning process which enables humans to adapt to so many vastly differing ecological niches. Within a particular habitat, it enables different humans to specialize in and become adept at different roles within their community. We will now look more closely at the manner in which these learned adaptations are acquired.

A simple organism can choose between alternative courses of action only on a trial and error basis. Only one kind of action can be entertained at a given time, and if it is not rewarded, another plan may be tried the next time (if the individual survives to have that opportunity). Such straighforward trial and error behavior entails a high risk when the situation is relatively unfamiliar, and a choice has to be made between numerous possible solutions. Animals with complex nervous systems are to some extent able to protect themselves from this risk by postponing an overt decision, while they consider the possibilities. In effect, they imaginatively represent the environmental rearrangements that various action patterns would bring about, matching each against the ideal state, goal, or schema that would seem to meet the adaptive needs of the moment (Shepard, 1978). The chess player, pondering his move, considers action sequences and represents the position of the chess men at the end of each sequence in an attempt to choose the configuration that appears most advantageous. The interior decorator imaginatively represents various arrangements of furniture, wallpaper, and other decorations without needing to construct them physically one after the other. From among the set of mental representations, that one which is considered the most pleasing and convenient is chosen and realized in action. This ability to represent, implicit in which is the ability to execute in the mind actions of which the body gives little evidence, develops gradually during childhood. The infant appears to have no such capability. His behavior is controlled by the here-and-now and the positions of his body not only betray his thoughts but probably are inseparable from them. He cannot as yet hide, dissimilate, or misrepresent his state of mind. To do that one has to be able to dissociate brain state from body state, by erecting inhibitory barriers between mental representations and the output control mechanisms. Selective inhibition becomes increasingly possible as the child grows older and his brain matures. So, covert representation of actions and their economical coding, particularly in terms of the words of the language, becomes increasingly possible as the nervous system matures (Kinsbourne & Swanson, 1979). The particular percepts and action patterns that are represented and the particular language that is used for coding is, of course, a matter of individualized learning. Though there is much that human beings learn in common, there is also much that is individual about each person's experience and therefore in his choice of what to represent and how to represent it at any given time.

V. The Need for Response Inhibition

We must consider the limits of these capabilities. People never become able to detect in parallel all possible arbitrary constellations of features with maximum efficiency. Nor do they become able to execute with fluent automaticity all possible combinations of displacements at the various joints. The limits on these abilities are not merely structural (e.g., the logical impossibility of moving a limb in opposite directions at the same time). Beyond such obvious mechanical limitations, there are limitations of central neuronal programming. Certain forms of differentiation are very hard to achieve (i.e., require immense practice) or perhaps can never be achieved. In a nervous system, which is an undifferentiated nerve net and behavioral tabula rasa, such limitations would not be expected. In the actual nervous system they become understandable when we consider that any deviation from preprogrammed behavior must necessarily involve, in mature as well as immature individuals, the selective and specific inhibition of the favored preprogrammed response. Thus, when we perform a skill we do not merely program the requisite muscular contractions as if they were on a keyboard. Rather, we pick out a relevant synergism (movement pattern), inhibit its irrelevant or potentially counterproductive components, and leave uninhibited only those which are called for by the action plan. It is the difficulty of selectively inhibiting unwanted movements with perfect efficiency that limits highly skilled performance and the ability to do several things efficiently at the same time. Similar limitations invest our mental ability to represent any chosen percept: The difficulty is to switch attention away from other previously experienced configurations that bear close family resemblance to the required pattern. The matter comes to a head during problem solving. Problems are situations in which the obvious course of action turns out not to be the one that is successful. In order to solve problems, people have to be able to reject the most probable (obvious) response in favor of less probable ones. As the person's attention travels down the range of conceivable alternatives, he may come to a point beyond which he can entertain no further possibilities. The problem is too difficult for him to solve. The individual who does solve the problem succeeds by entertaining mentally an even less expected circumstance. In the limit, the brilliant and innovative individual is able mentally to represent contingencies which run counter to overlearned experience, that is, to what passes for knowledge. A striking example is Einstein's ability to entertain the possibility that light might bend. Thus, one source of difficulty in problem solving is to inhibit so-called "popular" responses in favor of ones that do not so readily come to mind. The other challenge in complex problem solving is to hold in mind simultaneously the full set of critical items of information. This makes it possible for them to become imaginatively aligned into the configuration which accurately fits the schema that the individual had set for himself as goal or solution. Again, this process calls for selective inhibition. To hold in mind simultaneously separate thoughts, ideas, and representations, one has to permit each to maintain its integrity and not permit any one or subset of them fully to take over conscious awareness. The persons who can solve the most complex problems that require holding in mind many items of information at the same time are the persons who can restrain their mental representations from merging into one another.

VI. Functional Distance in the Brain

We can now consider on what neuronal arrangements higher mental activity, conceived of in the above terms, might be based. Where unique neural connections are called for, they exist. Where diffuse and mass response is the characteristic behavior, nerve networks are found. In the more complex nervous systems, that basic network pattern is modified by preferential connections varying in degree. But even the most sophisticated central nervous system is highly linked in that no more than five or six synapses are interposed between any neuron and any other. There are therefore theoretically five or six degrees of proximity between the various control centers. The number of nerve fibers connecting any two control centers is also a relevant variable. When two parts of the nervous system are highly connected, it is relatively easy for both of them to adopt the same pattern of activation and engage in cooperative, compatible, or identical, activity. By the same token, it is difficult for them to adopt unrelated patterns of activity, because each pattern would tend to overflow into and contaminate the other. This can to some extent be obviated by an inhibitory barrier; the further apart the centers are, the more readily such insulation by inhibition can be achieved without the inhibition encroaching on the active loci themselves and reducing the efficiency of their programming. This is the *functional cerebral space principle* (Kinsbourne & Hicks, 1978).

VII. Life-Span Changes in Functional Cerebral Space

Given these principles of behavioral maturation, we can now consider what types of changes in the nervous system might underlie them. We begin with the following facts. The number of neurons is fixed and their full complement is present at birth. Throughout the lifespan, and at an accelerating rate and to a variable extent, this neuronal complement is depleted. From these facts we conclude that in the course of early maturation the major change is the establishment of differential synaptic connectivity (made possible by the maturational process and implemented on the basis of experience). During aging and particularly under circumstances where cortical atrophy and thinning of neuronal density are prominent, one would expect the selectivity set up earlier to remain but to become inflexible and refractory to modification by further experience because the depleted neuronal population becomes less and less able to inhibit selectively and to keep different loci of patterned activation from interfering with each other. To use a different terminology, *functional cerebral distance* (a determinant of the probability that two loci of patterned activation could simultaneously maintain their activity) expands in the developing brain because intercalated inhibition more effectively separates active loci from each other: Functional cerebral distance contracts in the aging brain because the depleted neuronal number effectively leaves the remaining neurons more highly linked (Kinsbourne, 1979a).

These life-span developmental changes profoundly affect the individual's ability to hold in mind more than one idea at a time, or to pay attention to, or to perform more than one task at a time. As we have already mentioned, the attention of the immature individual tends to be fully occupied by salient aspects of the here-and-now. He cannot simultaneously hold in mind the experience of a moment earlier, let alone far more distant events in the past. Phenomena such as Piagetian nonconservation are based on this fact. The child bases his perceptual judgment on present appearances and is unable to take into account an immediately preceding event which would logically lead him to modify his judgment. The retarded individual remains in this stimulus-bound state. Behavior is permanently controlled by that which is immediate and salient. Although he can be trained in a variety of responses by massive practice, the retarded one is unable in a given situation to deviate from the tendency to emit that response which either innate mechanisms or training have made most probable. Therefore, such a person is at a loss when faced with a novel challenge or when the previously reinforced response is unaccountably no longer reinforced. The aging demented individual retains the rich repertoire of perceptual selectivities and response priorities acquired before the onset of the dementing process. As long as surroundings are familiar and while demands remain consistent with what has already been learned, he can function adaptively. But should the circumstances and the demands change, the person is not equipped to remodel the response repertoire in response to these changes. This is the biological reason for the fact that the behavior of such people appears to others to be rigid and inflexible (Kinsbourne, 1979a).

As previously mentioned, the endpoint of attentive behavior is preattentive automaticity. This is a response precisely geared to the demands of a familiar situation which has the merit of being expeditious and which at the same time leaves the individual's attention available for other concurrent problems. The more limited the individual's resource of attention (i.e., the shorter the cerebral functional distances that characterize his brain), the more important it is to be automatized, as much as possible, so that the attentional resources will be maximally available for unpredictable happenings.

VIII. Why Function Is Localized in the Brain

We can now understand the need for localization of function in the brain. We will distinguish between vegetative and basic functions, such as the control of respiration, blood pressure, and pulse rate, and those cognitive functions with which we are chiefly concerned. The first type of function is adequately served by a precisely engineered and genetically predetermined neuronal arrangement. The less it is influenced by whatever else is happening in the brain, the better; although as is well known to psychophysiologists, even the simplest such functions are by no means invulnerable to the effects of changing brain states during higher mental functioning, as well as during variation in emotional states. When we consider the much more highly linked organization of the association areas of the cerebral cortex and the much more complex demands on it for variously patterned activation, it becomes clear why it is adaptive for different categories of mental activity to be represented in different parts of the cerebral cortex (and the more different, the further apart). The exact location of the representation of each category is not necessarily material. Indeed, the typical organization of cerebral cortex is grossly infringed in a substantial minority of non-right-handed individuals, apparently without loss of cognitive efficiency (Hardyck, Petrinovich, & Goldman, 1976). The more important principle is that those functions most likely to be subsumed by a common superordinate program should be closely adjacent somewhere in functional cerebral space, whereas those which are guided by different rules should be further apart, wherever they are in absolute cerebral space. Thus, the whole gamut of verbal function is represented in most people within the language area of one hemisphere. This arrangement is consistent with the great ability of humans to entertain complicated verbal propositions that have a unified meaning or that conform to a unitary principle, but the severe difficulty that they experience when they try simultaneously to maintain in mind unconnected verbal propositions. In contrast, people can very readily speak of one thing and at the same time act nonverbally in some unconnected fashion. This is because the loci of activation for those control centers are relatively distant and therefore more easily separated by inhibitory barriers. This, of course, is an adaptive arrangement, as the latter type of behavioral combination is frequently called for, whereas the former kind is imposed on people almost exclusively in the psychological laboratory, a context which was not represented at the time when natural selection guided the way the human brain became organized.

As has already been explained, the extent to which any one process makes demands on attention limits the available attentional resource for any concurrent mental activity. When the brain malfunctions, either because of maldevelopment or because of damage, then particular processes become more difficult and even deautomatized. Not only is a performance then observably impaired, but because the patient's attempt to conduct it requires an undue amount of attention, he is severely handicapped in doing anything else at the same time. In this respect, the patient is like a young child whose operational efficiency with respect to any component of a skilled act is less than that of the adult, and who therefore is unable to conduct at the same time or hold in mind other necessary components. This malfunction imposes a limit on how sophisticated a skill he can learn in his immature state.

IV. Hemisphere Differences

These considerations relate to recent claims made for differing cognitive styles or even different "consciousnesses" for the two cerebral hemispheres (Sperry, 1968). These claims are problematic because crucial logical distinctions are not being made clear. It is undoubted that by virtue of cerebral specialization some cognitive processes are primarily controlled by one and some by the other hemisphere (e.g. Kinsbourne, 1976). This difference in control should not be taken to imply, however, that each hemisphere is incapable of the activities for which the other is specialized. Certainly, when a hemisphere dominant for a particular function is extensively injured, the opposite hemisphere can, to a remarkable extent (particularly in the immature brain), assume that function (Rudel, 1978). Further, one should clearly distinguish between specialization for cognitive processes and the selection of a cognitive style. It has been argued that the functions for which the right-hander's right hemisphere is specifically equipped are for relational and parallel processing (Bogen, 1969). Some have taken more fanciful excursions into half-brained personality and credited the left hemisphere with a cold rationality and the right hemisphere with a creative and intuitive flair (Ornstein, 1972). These value judgments are not based on any systematic evidence. Specifically, there is no evidence that one hemisphere would approach a given task, by preference, in one style and the other hemisphere would approach the same task in another style. The existing evidence instead supports the more humdrum conclusion that the individual as a whole has a personality or cognitive style, which does not change when the balance between the hemispheres, is disturbed by lateralized damage. He merely is less adept than before at those functions which were subserved by the now damaged hemisphere. As a consequence he might well avoid situations which would compel him to deploy those processes (Goldstein, 1942). However, this would be an act of adaptive compensation rather than a personality change. In fact, to ask whether an individual selects left hemispheric analytic or right hemispheric relational processes to solve problems that permit solutions in either mode is to impose too simplistic a dichotomy on an individual's ability to use his brain for purposes of problem solving. The anatomical discontinuity between the two bulky hemispheres, connected as they are by a major commissure, is deceptive. The interconnection of the two hemispheres through the corpus callosum is immensely rich and the two halves of the cerebrum function as a unit. This means that in the intact human being various parts of each side of the cerebrum may be conjointly active. Only the person whose corpus callosum has been surgically disconnected is confronted with the choice of utilizing the right or left hemisphere for a particular attention-demanding task (Kinsbourne, 1974a).

The fact of asymmetrical representation of cerebral function and even the recently much discussed existence of minor physical asymmetries of the cerebrum in its gross morphology has been overused for speculative interpretations. Some simple reasons why disparate functions might be advantageously separated in functional cerebral space have been given. However, there is nothing unique about such dispersion along the lateral plane and no evolutionarily valid reason for supposing that deviation from bisymmetry itself is of substantial adaptive advantage for higher mental function. A conservative supposition would be that as higher mental functions (specifically coding and representation) do not adhere to particular locations in external space, in contrast to for instance, orienting toward or acting on a particular external locus, bisymmetric representation of such functions becomes redundant, and cerebral space becomes available for other purposes (Kinsbourne, 1978).

X. Selector Mechanisms

Given the rich array of various processes available at a cortical level and the individual's ability to deploy them selectively, by what mechanism does he choose the appropriate process to use for the situation (in technical terms, adopt the appropriate mental set)? A selector system would be required that is sufficiently open to input to be informed of the general category of problems to be solved. That selector system, then, selectively activates the appropriate parts of the cerebral cortex, and they process the input in detail.

Although it is sparse, the evidence we have points to the brainstem as the site for the selector systems. One interesting source of evidence comes from recent studies on normal human newborns.

Infants can make rather fine phonological discriminations (Eimas, 1975) and when they do, the left halves of their brains reveal more activity (e.g., in terms of averaged evoked potentials), than the right halves of the brains (Molfese et al., 1975). When exposed to music to which the infant is as incapable of responding adaptively as to speech, it is the right half of the brain that exhibits the greater activation. Knowing, as we do, that those areas will ultimately become responsible for the processing of verbal and musical information, it is remarkable that evidence of differential activation is picked up by electrodes placed over them on the scalp. We may conclude that the selector system is already sufficiently mature soon after birth to activate selectively the proper side of the brain when exposed to categorical stimulation, even before that part of the brain has sufficiently matured to process the information in what later will be the conventional fashion. In other words, we see lateral specialization of the hemispheres as related to and maybe even caused by lateral specialization of the selector systems at brainstem level. When the offspring of non-right-handed parents show deviations in the lateral organization of their major cognitive functions, we would surmise that they are due to a lack of reversal of gradients at the brainstem selector system level (Kinsbourne, 1976b). This inference, however, is speculative at this time.

Selection involves not only the adoption of the appropriate mental set; it also determines the focus of attention in space and time. In space, attention may be focused on a specific location or on a feature that is perceived or searched for, or it may be widely spread across space and may include a generous array of stimuli of different categories (Easterbrook, 1959). In its temporal aspect, attention may be brief, and suspended as soon as the novelty of the situation has worn off slightly or it may be concentrated so that attention is maintained on a given issue until it is explored very thoroughly (Swanson & Kinsbourne, 1979). The focus of attention in space and in time is flexible. This flexibility arises from the way in which the control system is organized centrally. This organization conforms to a principle that prevails at all levels of the vertebrate nervous system: reciprocal inhibition between opponent processors (Kinsbourne, 1974b). A simple instance is the facility that permits us to orient to various points along the horizontal meridian to right or left. This is done by a change in the balance of excitation and inhibition between the right orienting facility (located in the left hemisphere) and the left orienting facility (located in the right hemisphere). The direction of orientation is the result of the opposing tendencies sub-served by these two opponent processors. Opposition between parts of the frontal lobe and parts of the parietal lobe seem to constitute the brain basis of the reciprocal balance between narrow and wide focus of attention. The factors that make for lengthy concentration are not clearly understood but they, too, seem to depend upon the rivalry between an approach system which "jumps to conclusions" and possibly involves the parietal lobe, lateral hypothalamus, and a "stop system" which programs hesitation pending further computation of the costs and benefits of the proposed action (Kinsbourne & Swanson, 1979). This stop system may involve the orbital frontal lobe, septal region, and medial hypothalamus. Another control system serves to select the appropriate level of cerebral activation; expressed behaviorally as degree of readiness for action. At very low activation levels the organism is under-aroused, and if unable to sleep, responds to the environment in a disorganized and unpredictable fashion. The overaroused organism's responses become highly predictable and repetitive. In the limit, they are inflexible and do not respond to the specific needs inherent in the situation. This is the predicament of people whose level of anxiety is very high. There is a homeostatic device which serves to reduce such excessively high levels of activation. The repetitive movements that animals emit when thwarted or frustrated (displacement activity) or that humans emit when very anxious (and perhaps the stereotypic whirling, flapping, and head-banging of autistic children) all appear to serve a dearousing function. As they proceed, activation levels decrease (as measured by the usual psychophysiological criteria) and the individual may even fall asleep (Kinsbourne, in press).

Perhaps the most studied selector system is the one that is responsible for remembering. It selects from a large set of previous experiences the particular one called for by cues inherent in the present situation. It is based in the limbic system and involves at least the medial hippocampus, mammillary bodies, and cingulate gyrus (Victor, 1969). The manner in which this system works is not known in detail. But there are two components to the remembering of specific events (episodic memory) without which it could not occur, and the limbic system is presumably involved in at least one of them. The first is the detaching of attention from those features of the present situation that have nothing in common with the experience to be remembered (i.e., which do not serve as retrieval cues). This includes withdrawing attention from the outside world and terminating existing states of mind. The second component is reconstructing the remaining essentials of the previously experienced event based on the cues that are available. The end product is a partial reexperiencing of an event that has passed, in the sense that it has left the focus of immediate attention; perhaps moments or even years ago.

With respect to their substrate in the brain, these two components of episodic remembering are in sharp contrast. The mechanism which sets the stage for remembering, by minimizing the effect of potential blocking and distracting factors, is well localized in the limbic brain. The patient with an amnesic syndrome lacks the assistance of this mechanism. But the reconstructive aspect of remembering is not made possible by, or localized in, any one area of the brain. It is coextensive with whatever parts of the brain were chiefly active when an event was originally experienced. The reconstruction presumably relies on a general property of neuronal systems to resume a state of specific patterned activity when a sufficient part of the total pattern is recreated. There is no memory store. Varying parts of the brain as a whole are active when we reexperience a previous experience. It follows that we cannot aspire to improve memory by expanding a hypothetical memory store. Instead, we would seek to improve memory by enriching the initial experience and by guiding attention toward the features that most probably will recur to act as cues when the situation calls for information embedded in the experience. For persons whose limbic retrieval system is impaired, assistance would involve explicit instruction to focus a mental set, and to establish an environment relatively free from distracting stimulation.

A clear distinction should be made between this episodic remembering and the fluent exercise of a skill or automatic availability of information. As episodes which have in common a particular invariant ingredient recur in different contexts ("encoding variability"), the organism becomes familiar with the invariant ingredient regardless of the context in which it appears. The outcome of this rehearsal or reexperiencing process is the automatic availability of categorical material by virtue of processes located in the cerebral cortex without much need to detach attention from the experience of the moment.

Whereas access to a recapitulated experience is determined by the limbic mechanism, access to items of knowledge or skill is determined by various areas of the cerebral cortex (Kinsbourne & Wood, 1975). Focal cortical lesions may incapacitate a person selectively in such previously easy endeavors as naming familiar objects or executing highly practiced movement sequences. Unlike the immature or naive individual who feels that the activity in question is unfamiliar or unknown, the patient with focal cortical disease retains a feeling of long-standing familiarity and experiences considerable frustration on account of his newfound inability to perform mechanically easy tasks. Also, in contradistinction to the naive individual who can be trained, the individual with a selective cognitive deficit probably cannot be retrained in the same way. At any rate, reported training successes either can be accounted for by motivational change or are confounded with recovery of the underlying damaged brain substrate of the activity or with compensation by intact brain. The problem with such retraining is not necessarily that the damaged area is the only area in the cortex capable of subserving the activity in question. On the contrary, if the whole of the hemisphere, including but extending far beyond the area of focal damage were also destroyed, the other hemisphere might well be able to program the affected function, if not as well as before, at least with a degree of success. The fact that focal lesions within a hemisphere often generate specific deficits far more profound than these that occur after the loss of the whole hemisphere suggests that the presence of the intact hemisphere in some way obstructs the other side from compensating. One possibility is that as long as the selector mechanism continues to activate the customary area which is now damaged and incapable, compensation cannot occur because potentially compensating parts of the brain are not thrown into readiness at the appropriate times. If the selector mechanism itself is changed or capable of modification, compensation might be much easier.

There have been claims for individual age and sex differences in the rate of recovery from various symptoms of cerebral cortical dysfunction following acute focal damage. Insofar as these differences are valid, they more probably are due to differences in the ability of selector mechanisms to reorganize than to differences in the cerebral substrate of the processes in question or in the manner in which they are lateralized.

XI. Educational Implications

The level of maturation of the brain determines the rate at which an individual is able to learn a given material and whether, at whatever rate, he is capable of learning that material, (a) by the usual methods; and/or (b) by specially designed methods.

For the learning of those skills and concepts which even immature cognitive systems can assimilate (such as discriminating real-life objects that differ from each other in salient and redundant ways) specific instructional methods are not usually needed. The presence of the objects in the environment and an occasional comment from an adult about its name and use, suffice. For reasons which are hotly debated, the same reasoning seems to apply to the learning of a natural language. Exposure to customary discourse and verbal interaction with the child appear to be sufficient for the child to acquire language, albeit over a number of years and not perfectly until the end of the first decade. It appears that his perceptual and executive systems are geared to observe and emit the critical sounds, sound constellations, and word sequences without the imposition of additional structure by the teacher. None of this is necessarily true for the child who is perceptually, motorically, or linguistically handicapped. For him, these experiences are not automatically salient and these acts do not conform to predetermined motor dispositions. For these children, it is necessary for the teacher or therapist to manipulate salience to enable the children to notice critical features and to train specific movement sequences, while teaching the child to inhibit unwanted synergic muscular contractions.

The older the child, the more types of experiences his more sophisticated nervous system can acquire without specific instruction because his ability to attend selectively and to control spontaneously the pattern of his motor activity has increased. It is a more economical use of the child's and the teacher's time to have the instructional process occur relatively late during maturation, though there are of course many social reasons why this might not be advantageous. The converse, the existence of critical periods during which the immature brain is more receptive to certain forms of learning than later, has not been convincingly demonstrated in humans. However, there are certain skills for which specific instruction and practice are necessary at any age. Piano playing is an obvious example, as is any highly sophisticated skill, such as any sport. Reading and writing, for most children, probably belong in this category, though there are examples of children who "just pick it up." This must have to do with the age at which we elect to teach children to read or write (between 5 and 7 years). At that stage in the lifespan the critical distinction made in reading, and the critical motions made in writing are by no means consistent with the child's perceptuomotor predispositions. For that reason the teacher has to provide specific practice to modify both the child's attentional proclivities and the ways that he would normally move the pencil across the paper if he were in an untutored state. As reading and writing instruction becomes more advanced in succeeding grades, the demands on the child's cognitive systems keep outstripping what any other than the most gifted child would acquire naturally. For this reason, the child needs instruction to keep pace with the increasingly demanding curriculum. It would follow that if reading instruction were deferred until near or full maturity, much less formal teaching would have to be done. There has, however, been no systematic test of this proposition. When children have reading disability, the need for externally imposed structure is naturally much greater (Kinsbourne & Caplan, 1979). If taught at the level customary for their age, the structure that is provided by the teacher is insufficient: They cannot understand and remember, because their perceptual, motor, or linguistic levels of maturity are insufficient to permit them to observe, execute, and comprehend in ways that seem natural to their normal peers who need no additional help. In other words, the educational needs of the learning disabled child are like those of a younger, normal child, because the learning disabled child's cognitive system in some crucial respect or respects is immature.

Remedial education at any age should proceed along the lines of removing high probability preconceptions and alerting the student to apparently improbable but actually better fitting alternative solutions to problems. When teaching old or demented people this procedure becomes very difficult as the individual's longstanding habits are deeply ingrained, not so much because of practice but because of limitations in the neuronal mass available to the brain for purposes of selective inhibition and modification of response habits. For this reason, retraining a skill as if it were a totally new skill may be better than an attempt at removing a longstanding but maladaptive habit by modifying it even slightly in such a person. If the skill trained is new, it might be possible to avoid interference. Simplifying the situation sufficiently, and graduating the schedule of training in a painstaking fashion might even permit the senile or demented person to learn.

Negative conclusions also follow. Whereas inadequately stimulating environments leave the individual's performance potential unused or used incompletely, there is no reason to suppose that an additionally enriched environment, as distinct from an appropriately structured one, has any stimulating effect on brain growth or development or that it helps to overcome deficits other than those caused by initial deprivation. Enough is as good as a feast.

Teaching to strength is achieved by finding those cognitive modes available to the child that could be used to attain the same practical objectives as would normally have been obtained by cognitive routes closed to him. Teaching to a weakness has to be done in a very slow, laborious fashion as if with a much younger, normal child. In the severest cases it should be discontinued before too much failure has totally discouraged the child from further effort. Attempts to manipulate brain organization are futile, distracting, and misdirected. Not only are details of localization and lateralization of cerebral function invulnerable to any manipulations presently available, but in any case, these factors are not decisive with respect to learning potential (Kinsbourne & Hiscock, 1978). Even if it were possible to manipulate them there would be no educational point in doing so. Thus, a consideration of the relations between cognition and the brain lead the educator back to fundamental principles of instruction which have to be based on an understanding of the principles of children's mental development.

Bibliography

Bogen, J. The other side of the brain II: An appositional mind. *Bulletin of the Los Angeles Neurological Society,* 1969, *34,* 135–162.

Easterbrook, J. A. The effect of emotion on cue utilization and the organization of behavior. *Psychological Review,* 1959, *66,* 183–201.

Eimas, P. D. Speech perception in early infancy. In L. B. Cohen & P. Salapatek (Eds.), *Infant perception* (Vol. 2). New York: Academic Press, 1975.

Gibson, E. J. *Principles of perceptual learning and perceptual development.* New York: Appleton-Century-Crofts, 1969.

Goldstein K. *After-effects of brain injuries in war; Their evaluation and treatment.* New York: Grune and Stratton, 1942.

Hardyck, C., Petrinovich, L. F., & Goldman, R. D. Left-handedness and cognitive deficit. *Cortex,* 1976, *12,* 266–279.

Kinsbourne, M. Mechanisms of hemispheric interaction in man. In M. Kinsbourne, & W. L. Smith, (Eds.), *Hemispheric disconnection and cerebral function.* Springfield, Ill.: Charles C Thomas, 1974.(a)

Kinsbourne, M. Lateral interactions in the brain. In M. Kinsbourne, & W. L. Smith, (Eds.), *Hemispheric disconnection and cerebral function.* Springfield, Ill.: Charles C. Thomas, 1974.(b)

Kinsbourne, M. The neuropsychological analysis of cognitive deficit. In R. G. Grenell, & S. Gabay (Eds.), *Biological foundations in psychiatry.* New York: Raven Press, 1976.

Kinsbourne, M. The biological determinants of functional bisymmetry and asymmetry. In M. Kinsbourne (Ed.), *The asymmetrical function of the brain.* New York: Cambridge University Press, 1978.

Kinsbourne, M. Attentional dysfunctions and the elderly: Theoretical models and research perspectives. In J. W. Poon, J. L. Fozard, L. S. Cermak, D. Arenberg & L. W. Thompson (Eds.), *New directions in memory and aging: Proceedings of the George Talland Memorial Conference.* Boston: 1979.

Kinsbourne, M. A model for the ontogeny of cerebral organization in non-righthanders: In J. Herron (Ed.), *The neuropsychology of left-handedness,* Academic Press, New York, 1980.

Kinsbourne, M. Do repetitive movement patterns in children and animals serve a dearousing function? Journal of Developmental and Behavioral Pediatrics, in press.

Kinsbourne, M., & Caplan, P. J. *Children's learning and attention problems.* Boston: Little, Brown, 1979.

Kinsbourne, M., & Hicks, R. E. Functional cerebral space: A model for overflow, transfer and interference effects in human performance. In J. Requin, (Ed.), *Attention and performance VII.* Hillsdale, N.J.: Erlbaum 345–362, 1978.

Kinsbourne, M., & Hiscock, M. Cerebral lateralization and cognitive development. In J. S. Chall & A. Merskey, (Eds.), *Education and the brain. Yearbook of the National Society for Study of Education,* 1978, 169–222.

Kinsbourne, M., & Swanson, J. M. Developmental aspects of selective orientation. In G. Hale & M. Lewis (Eds.), *Attention and the development of cognitive skills.* New York: Plenum Press, 1979.

Kinsbourne, M., & Wood, F. Short term memory and pathological forgetting. In J. A. Deutsch, (Ed.), *Short term memory*. New York: Academic Press, 1975.

Molfese, D. K., Freeman, R. B. & Palermo, D. S. The ontogeny of brain lateralization for speech and nonspeech stimuli. *Brain and Language*, 1975, 2, 356–368.

Ornstein, R. E. *The psychology of consciousness*. San Francisco: W. H. Freeman and Co., 1972.

Rudel, R. G. Neuroplasticity: Implications for development and education. In J. S. Chall & A. F. Mersky (Eds.), *Education and the brain*. Chicago: University of Chicago Press, 1978.

Shepard, R. N. The mental image. *American Psychologist*, 1978, *33*, 125–137.

Swanson, J. M., & Kinsbourne, M. The cognitive effects of stimulant drugs on hyperactive (inattentive) children. In G. Hale, & M. Lewis, (Eds.), *Attention and the development of cognitive skills* New York: Plenum Press, 1979.

Sperry, R. W. Mental unity following surgical disconnection of the cerebral hemisphere. *Harvey lectures* (Series 72). New York: Academic Press, 1968.

Tulving, E. Episodic and semantic memory. In E. Tulving, & W. Donaldson (Eds.), *Organization of memory*. New York: Academic Press, 1972.

Victor, M. The amnesic syndrome and its anatomical basis. *Canadian Medical Association Journal*, 1969, *100*, 1115–1125.

Chapter VIII

The Developing Brain and Child Development

W. E. JEFFREY

I. Introduction

This chapter, of necessity, must proceed at a different level of analysis than the previous chapters to avoid redundancy as well as to attempt some integration of concepts. Developmental psychologists are frequently called upon to account for the total developing organism. That they have accepted this challenge too readily accounts for the cycles of contradictory advice given to parents over the years. Too much has been said on the basis of too little factual information. Unfortunately, even if one resists the temptation to provide answers to the broad, and typically unanswerable questions commonly asked by parents, special problems remain for the developmental psychologist.

Although the majority of developmental research has age as a significant variable, few developmental psychologists have been satisfied with describing behavior change only as a function of age. It is not orderliness of development that is of greatest interest, but the individual differences that appear with development, differences in ability to perform, as well as differences in ability to profit from experience. Given this focus, age in itself is an inadequate index of neurological and physical maturation, as both are substantially influenced by the environment in which the child is reared as well as by genetic programs. Moreover, in recent years

345

it has been recognized increasingly that the state of physical and neurological maturation also affects the impact of the environment on the child.

Research designs that typically have been used to relate behavior to age place individual differences in rate of development and in the amount or type of experience in the error term. Such designs obviously are intended to obscure individual differences in the pursuit of more general laws. In the research directed toward differences in rate of development there have been essentially two different approaches: One is to correlate differences in environment with difference in performance at any specific age. The other is to establish correlations among various behavioral indices. The first of these approaches, in attempting to assess the effect of the environment, ignores those individual differences not attributable to specific environments. The second approach is essentially silent on the underlying cause, but interpretations in most instances lean toward biological or genetic rather than environmental causes. Recent advances in the neurosciences, however, have encouraged and nurtured much greater speculation as to basic processes that could account for performance differences that may be correlated with development but actually reflect differences in information processing strategies and other enduring performance attributes (cf. Zelniker & Jeffrey, 1979).

Previous research relating neurophysiological variables to differences in development and performance has typically depended on behavioral or physical stigmata as indices of neurological damage or dysfunction (e.g., cerebral palsy, or Downs syndrome). In the absence of such obvious signs, inferences were frequently made from the behaviors to be explained (e.g., minimal brain damage from hyperactivity). Because there is a thorough history of this research covered by many books and articles, this chapter will tend to ignore that tradition in favor of attractive, and in most instances, more speculative current attempts to consider neurophysiological factors underlying individual differences more closely within normal bounds, or at least identified with normal variation rather than with something as discontinuous as an extra chromosome, or specific neurological damage.

Unfortunately, when it comes to explaining less specific problems of development, we have much greater difficulty assessing either the behavior or its biological basis in any reliable fashion. It is a tribute to evolution that, given anywhere near decent conditions for survival, we all come out as similar as we do. We all walk, talk, reproduce, and cope with a variety of environmental circumstances. The more or less of any of these behaviors appear to be as attributable to environment as to genes.

Because of the apparent capacity of classical and instrumental conditioning models to account for the development of such a broad range of behaviors, many psychologists of the 1930s and 1940s assumed that differences in habit acquisition were the key to differences in individual performance. Even though there has been increasing recognition of the role genes play in behavior, and in spite of a tremendous accretion of information about the human nervous system, the concepts of current learning theory remain the psychologist's most important tool for modifying behavior even in cases where specific neurological dysfunction can be assessed. The fact that the learning or habit acquisition approach tends to be insensitive to the underlying conditions of the individual is to many of us, however, a serious inadequacy. Nevertheless, to say that the learning or behavior theorist is not concerned with more than emitted responses and adequate reinforcers is also increasingly untrue. The whole idea of shaping behavior suggests a search for elements that can be strengthened and combined. Therefore, insofar as knowledge of the brain and its various processes might suggest trainable elements and appropriate reinforcers, information about relevant neurological processes can be important.

II. Past Endeavors to Relate Behavior to the Brain

Those who have addressed themselves specifically to developmental disorders have tended to maintain the search for neurological causes even when the symptoms are diffuse, such as lack of fluency in the language skills of speaking and reading or writing. Because very specific speech dysfunctions (aphasias) result from damge to Broca's and Wernicke's areas of the brain, it has been tempting to look for relatively precise causes for similar but less specific difficulties. If areas of the left hemisphere are so important to speech, is it possible that lack of hemispheric dominance could account for less specific dysfunctions of language such as stuttering and reading disorders? Orton (1937) asserted that to be the case with respect to reading, and the same explanation was used for stuttering by others (Travis, 1931). There are many anecdotal reports as well as some reasonably careful research that indicate poor left–right discrimination among retarded readers. Delacato (1959) drew considerable attention in the early 1960s with a therapeutic program that attempted to establish cerebral dominance in retarded readers by a training regimen that started with "cross-patterned" creeping (i.e., advancing the contralateral arm and leg simultaneously). A survey of recent books on reading and reading disorders suggest that Delacato's program has been discounted if not discredited, for one can hardly find a current reference to it.

Although research has continued to find some correlation between poor reading and poor left-right discrinination (Koos, 1964; Shankweiler, 1963; Zangwill, 1960), others have found no such correlation (Balow, 1963), or have found a correlation that disappears when intergroup differences in intelligence level are taken into account (Coleman & Deutsch, 1964). Furthermore, problems of cerebral dominance in no instance prove to be an infallible sign of dyslexia or less severe reading problems (Benton, 1975).

Treatment of reading disorders or other symptoms assumed to have a neurological basis with training devised to improve cerebral lateralization, or to promote sensory and sensorimotor integration (cf. Ayres, 1975) has generally had limited success. Interpreting success or failure, however, is difficult in that for some instances the training may not be appropriate to the disorder (i.e., it may be applied to to gross a category of symptoms); if the training was more properly focused it might be more effective. Also, it is quite possible that any training regimen that is not noxious may have a positive influence on a child's self-confidence and emotional well-being that could facilitate motivation and performance. Thus, even if a training procedure does precisely what it is supposed to do in developing neural integration, its consequences for reading may be due to motivational effects rather than to enhanced neural integration. This statement is not meant to discourage treatment based on hunches about neurological dysfunctions but to indicate the problems that arise in interpreting results of various treatment procedures.

As is indicated in Chapter 4 by Madden and Nebes and Chapter 6 by Levy, nonclinical investigations into the differential functions of the hemispheres makes it quite clear that there are complicated interrelationships between the hemispheres as well as considerable shared function. Furthermore, we do not know to what extent the lateralization that does exist is influenced by experience. For example, do Witelson's (1976) findings of slower lateralization in girls than boys reflect a sex-linked gene or differential rearing conditions and early experiences for boys and girls?

Although it is well-known that for almost all people the left hemisphere plays the major role in the reception and production of language, that fact tells us nothing about the process of learning to speak or to read. Even in the case of specific lesions to specific areas there may be considerable individual differences in behavioral consequences. Moreover, as the complexity of the behavior increases, the effect of the lesion is typically minimized, indicating rather clearly the multiplicity of events and brain areas involved in most behaviors. Given this fact, it becomes reasonable to ask whether knowledge of the brain can help us in our search for a better understanding of the development of human behavior.

The basis for suggesting that knowledge of the brain may be helpful is as follows. Our approach to control of behavior through the concepts of learning has changed markedly over the last two decades; these changes came not so much from the failure of learning theories per se, but from advances in the available information about the brain and nervous system that made alternative conceptions not only possible but necessary. For example, behaviorism had vigorously rejected the concept of attention because of its mentalistic implications. For the most part, it could be excluded through experimental controls that assured an alert organism and no competing stimuli. To the extent that such control was not possible, the notion of receptor orienting responses was introduced (Wyckoff, 1952). At about the same time research on the brain indicated that the reticular formation played a crucial role in attention (Moruzzi & Magoun, 1949). Chapter 3 by McGuinness and Pribram provides a more current analysis of the reticular activating system and companion systems, but of importance here is the fact that the neuroscience research that followed made it clear that in addition to selection by receptor orientation, there was selection amongst incoming stimuli (Hernandez-Peón, Sherrer, & Jouvet, 1958). The latter fact was elaborated in studies on human behavior by Broadbent (1958) into the concepts of limited channel capacity and selective attention.

Another point at which a neurophysiological concept forced the reevaluation of the behaviorists' conception of behavior development came from Hebb's revolutionary book, *The Organization of Behavior* (1949). Hebb pointed out the inconsistency between the learning theorists' mechanistic notion of the satiated or sleeping organism as a "turned off" organism, and electrophysiological data. Electroencephalograms demonstrated that a considerable amount of neural activity occurred even during sleep. Hebb's own stimulus deprivation studies indicated the organismic need that existed for continuous stimulation. In this context Hunt (1963) proposed that the human organism was naturally information seeking and hence could be expected to attend to stimuli and solve problems without recourse to, or support from, such basic drives as hunger or thirst, or related secondary drives or reinforcers. Hebb also made a distinction between early and later learning that along with the work of ethologists on imprinting provided the foundation for early experience research. Much of the research on early experience has shown that the dramatic changes in behavior that have resulted from some rather limited early experiences can be associated with more or less permanent changes to certain physiological structures (Levine, 1960; Rosenzweig, Bennett, & Diamond, 1972).

Miller, Galanter, and Pribram (1960) combined notions from the neurosciences, information theory, and cybernetics to stress the plans and structures that developed in human problem solving as well as a more organized approach to problem solving that recognized the sentience that behaviorism denied. These general shifts in our conception of the organism also made it possible for the development psychologist to give belated attention to the work of Piaget. His biological viewpoint gave the organism its due respect while also stressing the effects of experience. Indeed, the Piagetian approach, much like that of the neurosciences, has not been so much to show that behavior can be controlled as to observe relationships. Given the inconsistencies that are found even when the task is only to describe the relationships among variables, it is not surprising that the psychologist is not as successful as he would like to be in the considerably more complicated task of trying to alter or promote behaviors such as those involved in learning to read. Although there is probably something from each of the previous chapters that is relevant to that task, none of them tells us precisely how or where the engram for a letter is formed, how the engram for the sound is formed, how either is stored, how they get associated, or how the motor response is produced. Although they can point to motor, speech, and association areas of the brain as being relevant, it is also known that there is very little of the brain not finally involved in the relatively simple act of seeing a letter and pronouncing its label. Therefore, we must recognize that specific instructions for the developmental or educational psychologist will not be found in the neurophysiological literature.

III. Neurological Processes in Perception

A. The Visual System

It is well known that all senses are at least minimally operative at birth, but having said that, we must ask what is involved in perception at that time. With regard to vision, Bronson (1974) proposes that early perception is under control of a phylogenetically older "second visual system." This system is concerned with processing stimuli that fall on the more peripheral areas of the retina. Its main function is presumed to be the transmission of information regarding the loci of salient peripherally located stimuli. The more recently evolved primary system is concerned with the analysis and encoding of complex stimuli. Anatomical evidence of myelinogenesis supports a developmental pattern that would indicate earlier development of the subcortical processes involved in this second system than those involved in the primary system (Conel, 1939–1967). Thus, these data as well as considerable other electrophysiological and behavioral research cited by Bronson, suggest that assertions of infant responses to patterns (e.g., Fantz, 1965) before at least one month are probably incorrect.

Bronson's hypothesis was challenged, however, by Lewis, Maurer, and Kay (1978) who found that neonates would fixate a line that subtended only 8″ of the retina. The measures they took of position of the eye, as well as the excellent sensitivity demonstrated, suggests foveal fixation rather than a response of the secondary system. Whereas a line width of 8″ was adequate to control fixation when a line was presented centrally, a line presented 10° to the left center had to be at least 17″ wide to elicit a head turn. This finding does not support the lack of foveal sensitivity that Bronson's theory suggests. Neither do Lewis et al. necessarily provide definitive support for the opposite view. Anatomical studies indicate that at birth the macula is less mature than the rest of the retina (Mann, 1964). That is, the cones are shorter and less numerous than they will be by 4 months of age. By 4 months, however, many layers of ganglion, amacrine, and bipolar cells will have moved to the periphery and the cones will have become much longer and more densely packed. Thus, even if the primary system is operative, there must be limits on how adequately it operates (i.e., it is reasonable to question its acuity and its ability to process stimuli that impinge on the fovea).

Behavioral assessment of the newborn perceptual capacity has typically proved to be difficult. The capacity of the infant to make an adequate indicator response is extremely limited and is typically confounded with the infant's state of arousal. For these reasons the results of most tests are relatively unsatisfactory. Our more successful attempts occur only after the second month of age when the infant is alert for longer periods of time, and when it is possible to use the habituation and recovery paradigm as a means of assessing perception. Because of the additional mechanisms involved, studies that require habituation will be discussed in the section on attention which follows a description of the early development of the ear.

B. The Auditory System

The mechanical aspects of the human auditory apparatus are reasonably mature at birth. This is particularly true of the ossicular chain and stapedial footplate. The external auditory canal, the tympanic membrane, and the middle ear cavity do not reach adult dimensions until about one year of age, which may impede the transfer efficiency somewhat, but probably results in no more than a 10 db conductive loss in sensitivity (Hecox, 1975).

Information regarding the development of the eighth auditory nerve is relatively meager, but what is available indicates that it is even more mature than the peripheral transducer (Hecox, 1975). In general it can be said that it completes its proliferative activity early and is well myelinated at the time of birth. The evidence for brainstem development is also limited, but indications of incomplete myelination of the inferior colliculus and medial geniculate would result only in slower conduction velocity, hence longer response latencies. As for auditory areas of the cortex, although there is apparently no proliferation of neurons after birth, differentiation and migration of young neurons continues for several years. Myelination of projection fibers is sparse at birth but is essentially complete by four years of age, whereas myelination of intracortical fibers continues into adolescence (Hecox, 1975, p. 169). Only layers 5 and 6 of the auditory cortex appear to have reached the functional stage at birth, and they, too, will undergo considerable histological changes during the early years. These facts would account for the prolonged latency and diminished amplitude of the newborn cortical evoked response.

According to Witelson and Pallie (1973), the planum temporale, the language mediating area of the temporal lobe, is larger in the left hemisphere than in the right for newborns as well as adults. Furthermore, Molfese (1972) has provided evidence for the lateralization of language in the first week of life. The degree to which the auditory system may be specially tuned to detect some of the special features of language as early as the first month is discussed thoroughly in a chapter by Eimas (1975), and will be discussed here also in the section on attention.

IV. Arousal, Attention, and the Developing Brain

Except for the current popularity of research evaluating the asymmetry of the brain, which is reflected in a few chapters in this book as well as by more than a half-dozen books directly concerned with brain asymmetry published in the last four years, probably no other topic has captured the interest of the experimental psychologist as much as that of attention. Because of the discussion of attention in the chapters by Kinsbourne and by McGuinness and Pribram, it is not necessary to comment here on its history, but only on how the concept of attention is used in child development.

The visual fixations of the neonate suggest that given an adequate level of arousal, attention is obligatory. That is, the infant reflexively fixates those edges or contours that impinge upon certain areas of the retina. These fixations are short lived, however, because the infant's state of arousal is cyclical. It must be noted, that arousal is also affected by the impingement of strong stimulation which elicits what James referred to as involuntary or reflex attention. What James called voluntary attention, in the case of the young infant, appears hardly less involuntary, although it might well be distinguished by the fact that attention is captured rather than compelled, and that the arousal system is not driven by the stimulus.

McGuinness and Pribram replace the concepts "involuntary" with "arousal" and "voluntary" with "activation" in order to more readily relate these attentional descriptors to underlying physiological systems. They define the former as "a phasic short-lived and reflex response to input" and the latter as "a tonic long-lasting and involuntary readiness to respond." They add the concept of effort as a third system that coordinates arousal and activation. This way of looking at attention appears to be particularly useful when considering the developing infant and child.

Given our concern with the developing organism it is important to consider the early development of the brain, with particular attention to the cortex, before any additional discussion of the behavioral aspects of attention. In this context it is of interest to note the phylogenic differences in proportion of sensorimotor neocortex, as compared with associational neocortex, from rat to man as shown in Table 8.1. These data clearly suggest that much of man's greater abilities, compared even with the ability of chimpanzees, are attributable to the considerable increment in the proportion of the association areas of the neocortex.

Turner (1948, 1950) has shown that in the human the cortex manifests considerable growth after birth. There are marked changes in both sur-

TABLE 8.1

Percentage of Increase from Rodent to Man in Proportion of Association Neocortex[a]

Mammal	Sensorimotor neocortex	Associational neocortex
Rodent	90	10
Cat	70	30
Monkey	40	60
Man	15	85

[a] From Milner (1967).

face area and fissurization, and they are especially rapid during the first six years. The distribution of that growth and relative growth rates for the various lobes is presented in Table 8.2. Although these morphological changes cannot be related to specific neurological changes or to behavior, they do give a rough index of the postnatal development of the brain that correlates reasonable well with such indices as myelination of nerve fibers, size of nerve cells, and quality and size of nerve processes.

As late as 1963 (Peiper, 1963) it was commonly assumed that the cortex of the newborn was not functional. Cited as evidence for this assertion was the fact that babies without cerebral hemispheres (hydranencephalics and surviving anencephalics) behave in the same way as normal newborns, and that cerebral motor defects such as the spastic cerebral palsies are not apparent in the newborn, presumably because the defects are in structures that are not yet functioning (Robinson, 1969). This view has undergone change for a variety of reasons, but mainly because closer observation has shown a number of subtle differences in sleep cycles, crying, and in the EEG, between normal infants and babies with no hemispheres (Robinson, 1969).

The normal infant EEG suggests a functioning but poorly organized cortex that will become progressively more organized with age (Parmelee, Wenner, Akiyama, Stern, & Flescher, 1967). There is also evidence, from the comparison of premature with normal term infants, that most of the changes in cortical activity are controlled by age rather than by environment (Dreyfus-Brisac, 1964; Parmelee, Schulte, Akiyama, Wenner, Schultz, & Stern, 1968). On the other hand, it appears that after a normal term birth the environment plays an ever-increasing role in developmental change. Schulte (1969) proposes that nerve conduction velocity, as an indicator of myelination, and basic EEG patterns, as an indicator both of dendritic arborization and of the formation of intracortical synaptic connections depend on structural maturation and are therefore suitable for estimating conceptual age. Such complex nervous activity as behavioral state stability and circadian distribution of EEG patterns, as well as the coincidence of these patterns with respiration, heart rate, and muscle activity are assumed to be influenced by both internal and external factors.

Given these indicators of the neurological immaturity of the human brain at birth, particularly those parts of the brain that seem most likely to be involved with behavior development, it is reasonable to question how and when the capacity for attention develops. The potential for arousal, as McGuinness and Pribram define it, is there from birth, but activation (i.e., the capacity to remain alert, to register input, and to

TABLE 8.2
Relative Growth Rates of Neocortical Lobes[a]

Age period	Parietal lobe		Occipital lobe		Temporal lobe		Frontal lobe	
	Surface area	Fissuration	Surface area	Fissuration	Surface area	Fissuration	Surface area	Fissuration
0–2 yr	Most rapid	Rapid	Same as overall pattern (see text)	Same as parietal lobe	Moderate	Rapid in auditory portion	Rapid	Moderate
2–6 yr	Same as overall pattern (see text)	Moderate			Very rapid	Rapid in temporal pole	Moderate, even until near-max.	Rapid
6 and after	Practically none; total at 24.	Moderate to submax. at 10	None		None	None	At 10 (total at 20)	Moderate to submax. at 10

[a]From Milner (1967)

maximize input through control of the somatomotor and sensorimotor systems), develops slowly over the first two months. The capturing of sensory systems by edges and the onset of visual and auditory stimuli may well provide rudimentary tuning of the sensorimotor system of the newborn. The ability to respond to a wider range of stimuli comes, however, with cortical maturation (cf. Bronson, 1974) and the resulting capacity for longer periods of activation.

It has been proposed previously (Jeffrey, 1968, 1969) that perceptual development in infants was the result of the capture of attention by stimuli, and the serial habituation of attention to the invariant characteristics of these stimuli. Subsequently this analysis was refined in a way that appears more consonant with the McGuinness and Pribram view in that two mechanisms were proposed (Jeffrey, 1976). The orienting reflex was presumed to occur only to the onset of stimuli, which corresponds with McGuinness and Pribram's concept of arousal. Subsequent analysis of the stimulus was proposed to be controlled by an information processing system, which corresponds, at least somewhat, with the McGuinness and Pribram notion of activation. It should be noted that, by identifying activation with tonic readiness to respond, and Pavlov's "what's to be done?" response, McGuinness and Pribram place more emphasis on the period immediately following arousal, whereas Jeffrey is concerned with the relatively prolonged scanning of novel stimuli that occurs after the initial capture of an infant's attention by a novel stimulus. If there is a difference in these views, however, it is only in the degree of activation and the potential final response. Whereas in the mature organism, whether dog, cat, monkey or man, attentional responses are typically observed in the context of a required approach or avoidance response, research on infant attention is directed toward investigating perceptual capacity through measures of fixation times, or with autonomic indicators of perceptual responding. This approach is more appropriate to the human infant because most of the infant's attending is not related to alimentary or defensive needs, but to the extraction of information from the environment (Hunt, 1963). Thus, measures of attention are typically our only index of a response. Interestingly enough, of the battery of physiological indices Sokolov (1963) proposes as measures of the orienting reflex (i.e., attention), the only response that can be readily obtained from the human infant is heart rate deceleration. This fact in itself may be a good indication of the immaturity of the infant attentional system. Nevertheless, heart rate deceleration does give us an early index of attention that has proved useful in the study of early perceptual development.

V. Attention and Habituation in Perceptual Development

The major share of research on infant perception has been done on 3- and 4-month-old infants. There are several reasons for waiting until the infant is at least 2 months of age, and even better, 3 or 4 months. The infants are more available (i.e., mothers are willing to take them out of the home, their attention spans are longer, hence one can get a more reliable measure of attention, and what is particularly critical, it is difficult to elicit an orienting, as opposed to a defensive reaction, before 2 months of age (Graham & Clifton, 1966). The shift from a defensive reaction to an orienting reaction to most moderate stimuli (i.e., a shift from heart-rate acceleration to deceleration), occurs more or less concurrently with the disappearance of a number of the more primitive reflexes, which is generally interpreted as evidence for increasing cortical control. That the infant is more attentive may also reflect the increased influence of the primary visual system as Bronson proposes, or it may be only a matter of the increased maturation of a number of systems.

Our current interest in infant perceptual development is due largely to the seminal research of Fantz (1965) which provided an attention paradigm to replace the conditioning paradigm that had been used earlier with negligible success. The fact that the attention of an infant to one stimulus was significantly greater than to another, regardless of changes in position of the stimulus, was taken to indicate ability to discriminate one stimulus from another. However, it was quite possible that two highly discriminable stimuli could be equally attractive and thus produce no differential attending, therefore the habituation–recovery paradigm became popular because it promised more power. If an observing response or heart-rate deceleration has habituated after repeated presentation of a stimulus, any attending response or heart-rate deceleration that occurs to a novel stimulus, or to a stimulus that differs in some way from the one previously presented, provides clear evidence that the difference was discriminated.

Two relatively current studies are presented here as examples of what can be done with the attention paradigm, of how attention may change with age, and of the potential complexity of an infant's perceptual capacity by 5–6 months of age. Since Fantz (1965) first demonstrated an early infant preference for schematic faces, there has been considerable interest in the cues to which the infant might be responding. The study by Caron, Caron, Caldwell and Weiss (1973) appears to be definitive. Four-month-old infants were habituated to one or another distorted schematic face, then response recovery was noted when a normal schematic face was presented. It was assumed that recovery of attention to a normal face would occur only to the extent that the distorted feature in the habituated stimulus was sufficiently salient to have been perceived. All distortions were displacements or inversions of features. There were eye distortions, nose–mouth distortions, head distortions, and head–face distortions, a total of 16 heads in all. The results are not easy to summarize, but in general it was found that distortions of eyes were most salient, along with lack of hair and a scrambled asymmetric face, which included an eye distortion. Nose–mouth distortions were apparently not perceived. To see whether a slightly older group of infants might be more sensitive to the nose and mouth, a 5-month-old group was presented with a smaller set of stimuli which had either no eyes, no mouth, an inverted inner face, or an inverted head. For this group, recovery was just as great to the nose and mouth distortions as to the eye distortions, indicating a marked increase in visual perception over the period of just one month.

Current research on auditory perception may be best exemplified by that of Eimas (1975). Capitalizing on the apparent reinforcing power of the orienting reflex, he made the delivery of synthetic speech sounds contingent upon rate of high amplitude sucking. As interest in the stimulus was shown to decline by a decrease in the rate of sucking, a component of the stimulus was changed. If the change elicited an orienting response the rate increased, otherwise it remained low or continued to decline. Of particular interest is Eimas' demonstration that infants respond categorically to certain ranges of differences among speech stimuli. Specifically, he has found that although voice onset time can take a continuous range of values, infants respond differentially to stimuli only on either side of a rather small range of voice onset times. Similarly astonishing is Moffit's (1971) demonstration with habituation of heart-rate deceleration that infants could discriminate tongue place distinctions associated with the sounds *dah* and *gah*. Sound spectography identifies these differences with second formant transitions that occur in the first 50 msec.

In spite of this evidence of rather sophisticated detection and processing ability for these segmental features of language, according to research by Horowitz (1972), 4-month-old infants habituate only to the first of two tones presented successively for 5 sec each. Recovery of heart-rate deceleration did not occur to changes that were made in the second tone. In a subsequent study, O'Connor (1973) presented a 12-sec train of two tones, each of which was on for 2 sec. After habituation to this stimulus, tones were selectively altered such that the extent of the infant's attention could be evaluated. The results were essentially similar to those obtained by Horowitz in that recovery of heart-rate deceleration did not occur to changes beyond the third tone (i.e., 6 sec).

Thus, in spite of the apparently exquisite sensitivity to certain features of auditory stimulation, the 4-month-old infant is not yet capable of attending broadly, or integrating serially, the sounds that impinge upon him. It can be presumed that later development in the association areas is related to the more complex features of language, which of course include not only response to an auditory stimulus but the association of that stimulus with some visual, tactile, or proprioceptive memories. More will be said about this process later, but it should be noted that neurophysiological information regarding the development of these types of processes is exceedingly sparse.

The evidence cited in this section is only a small part of much more that generally can be interpreted to indicate that the nervous system of the young infant is programmed to respond to certain types of figure–ground relationships (i.e., brightness contours, differential voice onset times, or arrival time asynchrony at the ears—auditory localization). These stimuli elicit appropriate arousal and excitation mechanisms, and at least minimal receptor orientation, but adequate localization and perceptual–motor response depend on subsequent experience. For example, a sound that arrives from off center will cause the infants to turn in the direction of the sound (Bower, 1974), but it is unlikely that the infant can identify the precise origin of the sound. As Bower points out, the change in head size with growth would make it impractical for the latter capability to be programmed in advance, as it is a judgment that has to adjust to changing parameters more or less continuously through childhood.

Even the hand does not have to be taught to reach or grasp, but the preadapted response pattern is clumsy. With feedback the response improves sufficiently that much less attentional capacity is required, which then makes possible higher levels of integration of more complex input with more complex response, and with much less effort (Bruner, 1973).

VI. Affective Development

Although the perceptual and cognitive development of children has been a dominant focus of research over the last decade, the affective side of development has not been overlooked entirely, and recently, interest in affective development has broadened insofar as the development of affective control is now being seen by some as an integral part of cognitive development. For example, the presentation of a stimulus that engages attending (i.e., elicits an orienting response), will in most instances produce quieting if the infant is already in a state of excitement. Thus, affect is modulated by cognitive events as well as by internal variables. Obviously, the exquisite control of arousal and excitation that McGuinness and Pribram attribute to the amygdala and hippocampus is soon integrated with the engrams of many cognitive experiences, and hence can come under individual control. Moreover, lack of control of arousal makes the registration of input impossible, and with this failure, the nervous system is temporarily swamped and reacts only with automatisms. This state is common in the infant, and it continues on occasion into childhood and even adulthood, but certainly with greatly reduced frequency. It seems reasonable to assume that this normal reduction in uncontrolled distress is the result of increased cognitive control.

Probably the most salient of external stimuli in early life is the caretaker. Caretakers present visual features of interesting symmetry, movement that is engaging but typically not too abrupt, and auditory stimulation that is endlessly novel. These stimuli are variously associated with relief from pain and the satisfaction of primary drives. Given this, it is not surprising that the caretaker more than any other stimulus would come to be sought and manipulated for the express purpose of the modulation of affect. This condition is typically referred to as attachment. It also seems reasonable to presume that as cognitive competence develops, the infant would become increasingly able to cope with arousal without the close contact with the caretaker that was previously necessary. That is, in times of threat he need only check visually to see that the caretaker is nearby, or maybe the potential availability of the attachment figure can even be handled symbolically. This is the case, of course, only if transactions with the attachment figure provide adequate support during that critical period in infancy when there is so much coping to do. Although Sroufe and Mitchell (1979) do not place as much emphasis on cognition as on the controlling mechanism, they discuss both attachment and emotional development in similar terms (Sroufe & Waters, 1977). That arousal would be controlled by cognitive mechanisms also fits extremely well with the McGuinness and Pribram description of the subtle balance between the amygdala and hippocampal systems, and the influence of external stimuli on these structures. A strong stimulus produces arousal that can either lead to additional processing and a decision regarding necessary motor activity, or in the absence of an adequate cognitive response, arousal may increase to the point of complete lack of control. The latter condition is either terminated by exhaustion or another strong stimulus that interrupts the aroused state and leads to hippocampal control.

In their discussion of emotional development Sroufe and Mitchell (in press) and Emde, Gaensbauer, and Harmon (1976) are particularly concerned with the development of the fear response, which seems to appear somewhere between 7 and 9 months and is assumed by them to be a maturational event. As has been noted earlier in this chapter there is considerable evidence of rapid maturation of neurological systems over the first year, and the fact that there might be saltatory changes in the expression of distress does not conflict with the notion of the ability to cope cognitively as a controlling factor. Indeed, as research by Schachter and Singer (1962) indicates, even in adulthood the differentiation and identification of emotions is cognitive rather than physiological. What seems of greatest interest and concern, however, is the fact that in their extreme form emotions represent a lack of control, an inability to react intelligently. Thus, it would appear from this analysis that an environment in infancy and early childhood that provided a secure base, but also encouraged the development of skills for coping with the environment, would be instrumental in producing a stable, secure child. Given this state of affairs, the child's interest and effort could be expected to be directed outward toward solving problems, and learning, rather than directed inward toward one's fears and inadequacies.

VII. Cognitive Development

The development of language offers a prototypical example of the importance of the maturation of specific neurological substrates as well as the necessity for appropriate experiences. Because the specific neurological structures are delineated in several other chapters in this book, they need not be repeated here. The importance of experience to the adequate development of the structures basic to language is well exemplified by the case of Genie (Curtiss, 1977). This child, who was deprived of vocal stimulation from around 20 months of age until 13 years of age, was able to become only minimally competent even though beginning at age 13 years 7 months she was provided with extensive training that extended over a period of more than 4 years.

Given minimal experience, and even with severe biological limitations, at least limited language facility is likely to develop (Lenneberg, 1967); and in spite of differences in experience, and the language being learned, the progression of early language development is quite orderly (Brown, 1973). Brown proposes that although the order of acquisition of linguistic knowledge may prove to be approximately invariant across children learning a single language, the rate of progression will vary radically among children (Brown, 1973, p. 408). He then conjectures that this rate of acquisition will prove to be dependent to some extent on general intelligence. Both of these assertions, as he goes on to note, are congruent with the Piagetian approach to intelligence.

At the heart of much of Piaget's conception of cognitive growth is the notion of decentration. With cognitive development, the child becomes able to inhibit attention to the most salient features of a stimulus and to utilize less salient features as a basis of response, or in a problem-solving situation to utilize various features and to weight them differentially in making a decision. Kinsbourne (this volume) makes much of the importance of the ability to inhibit responses that are most obvious in order to solve complex problems, and Piaget's tests of conservation provide excellent examples of the need to decenter, or inhibit responses to the most salient features of the transformed stimuli in order to respond appropriately.

A second aspect of intelligent behavior is the ability to provide mental representation. The utilization of mental representation in problem solving must represent the utmost exercise of our brains in that it involves not only inhibition but the ability to remember, produce images, use subvocal language, look backward and ahead, produce diagrams or maps either covertly or overtly, and at the end of this process to perform a response. It is very likely that little of the brain remains uninvolved when we attempt to solve complicated problems. Moreover, behavior at this level involves thorough integration of all of these various brain functions.

It should be clear after reading this book, if it were not before, that the development of a high level of problem-solving ability must depend on the continuous and inseparable interaction of physiological growth and experience. For example, there is undoubtedly a continuum of abilities to inhibit response. Some develop rather easily in the normal course of development; some take prolonged training and frequently require that we remind ourselves to stop and think. Likewise with memory; whereas some experiences are easily remembered, by middle childhood we learn to varying extents to engage in special activities to remember more complex things. Thus, it is not only necessary to have experiences to keep needed information available for expert problem solving, but also one must make special attempts (i.e., use special strategies), to assure that experiences are encoded adequately and stored effectively. Therefore, it should not be surprising if individuals differed substantially both in their capacity to solve problems and their approach to problem solving.

Neither should these potential differences in the development of the brain be discouraging; rather, they should be taken by the parent or educator as representing a challenge to discover the potential ways for optimizing capacities as they develop.

VIII. Individual Differences in Attention and Perception

Evidence has accumulated over the years that individuals differ in what they attend to in the environment. As a result, they differ in what they perceive, and thus in how they respond. Although there are strong developmental trends in the development of attention and perception, differences among individuals tend to be maintained over changes in age, hence it is likely that at least some of these differences reflect more than developmental lag (cf. Zelniker & Jeffrey, 1979), even though behavioral manifestations of cognitive style frequently appear as only differences in maturity.

There are two cognitive style dimensions that have been the subject of considerable research. One of these is field articulation—field independence–dependence (cf. Witkin, Dyk, Paterson, Goodenough, & Karp, 1974). The primary requirement of tests that are used to assess field articulation is the ability to isolate a stimulus from its surroundings, such as in the embedded figures or rod and frame tests. The other dimension is that of reflection–impulsivity (cf. Messer, 1976) which typically is assessed with the Matching Familiar Figures Test. Low errors and long latencies to respond identify a reflective individual, whereas high errors and short latencies are associated with impulsivity. These two cognitive styles, although not highly correlated with each other, and most particularly not with intelligence, do predict a range of other behaviors associated with problem-solving ability.

Field articulation has roots in developmental theories that used differentiation as a central theoretical construct (Witkin, Goodenough & Oltman, 1977). This construct was used to explain developmentally the increasing functional independence of a person's parts, as well as the person from his environment. Current research on lateralization of the brain, however, has given the concept of differentiation new and different meaning. There are clear individual differences in the degree of differentiation of function of the hemispheres (cf. Levy, this volume) and Zoccolotti and Oltman (1978) have shown that greater lateralization of function in the hemispheres is likely to be associated with greater field independence. This fact does not provide an explanation for all of those behaviors associated with the field-articulation dimension, but the correspondence of measures of field independence such as spatial abilities, degree of impulse control, social independence, and intellectualization, with behaviors that relate to hemisphere lateralization, opens up areas for meaningful investigation that may increase our understanding of field articulation at a physiological level.

For example, given that the human female tends to mature earlier than the male, Waber (1977) proposed that the rate of physical maturation could account for the differences in spatial abilities that are so frequently associated with sex. In a comparison of early and later maturing individuals of both sexes, she found that late maturing individuals did indeed show better spatial abilities than the early maturing. She also found that the difference between the two maturation groups was far greater within sexes than that typically found between sexes. For instance, late maturers of both sexes showed greater lateralization for speech perception on a dichotic listening task than did early maturers. Inasmuch as the differences in spatial and speech perception have been linked closely with differences in degree of hemispheric lateralization, Waber's research is suggestive of a genetic, and probably hormonal influence on the development of lateralization. It is to be noted that both Levy and Kinsbourne point out that lateralization does not develop but is clearly indicated at birth. What has been taken by some to be development in hemispheric lateralization is more likely evidence of development of a particular cognitive function in the appropriate hemisphere. The degree to which the function is lateralized once it is there, however, is probably not the result of training but reflects a condition that is predetermined. Thus, one should consider that rate of maturation is quite likely a product of genetic variables.

In recent years, Witkin has tended to stress the social aspect of field dependence (i.e., field-dependents have better social skills and show more interpersonal competence in contrast with field-independents), who show more autonomy and greater competence in cognitive restructuring. To explain how these differences come about, Witkin (Goodenough & Witkin, 1977) places heavy emphasis on socialization practices. It may be, however, that cerebral lateralization provides a better explanation. As our knowledge of cerebral lateralization has advanced, it has become clearer that it is the degree of hemispheric specialization that is critical rather than the dominance of one hemisphere over the other. Given also our increasing insight into the role of the right hemisphere in the expression of emotion, it seems reasonable that less lateralized individuals might tend to rely more on social and emotional cues, and show less of the autonomy and fewer spatial skills associated with more lateralized individuals (Waber, 1977a); thus it may be that the behaviors Witkin associates with differentiation are primarily a reflection of the degree of hemispheric lateralization. And the bulk of the evidence for the development of lateral specialization weighs heavily on the physiological side (Waber, 1977b).

Lest we forget that experience does play a role in determining ability to perform various functions, it should be noted that Genie, after 13½ years of isolation, was capable of acquiring only that speech typically associated with the right hemisphere. This fact supports Lenneberg's (1967) assertion that there is a critical period for the activation of left hemisphere speech and reinforces the importance of experience in the development of various processes. It does not necessarily imply, however, that Genie would have been less lateralized had she been raised under more normal conditions. We undoubtedly have much to learn about the intricacies of the interaction of the biological substrate, the subsequent effects of experience, and the presence of steroid hormones, which the work of Waber (1977a), among others, clearly implicates, as important factors in mental as well as physical development.

We know much less of the physiological underpinnings of the reflection–impulsivity cognitive style dimension, but Zelniker and Jeffrey (1976) have emphasized the perceptual aspects of the Matching Familiar Figures Test. Impulsive children may be more attentive to global or peripheral aspects of a stimulus, whereas reflective children attend more to detail or internal features. Although these different attention strategies can also be related conceptually to hemisphere specialization, convincing evidence for such a relationship is lacking. It also may be that an even more critical difference between reflective and impulsive children is in the effort they extend. The fast response of the impulsive child may indicate primarily a failure to engage more than superficially in cognitive processing. Although some of the processes involved in the effort dimension of attention are understood (cf. McGuinness & Pribram, this volume) the variables that might account for individual differences are not obvious but may well be the result of differences in the balance of ACTH-related neuropeptides which is known to affect problem-solving performance. Current research on neurochemistry has opened a whole new frontier beyond which there is the promise of considerably greater understanding and potential for control.

In conclusion, one other area of individual difference in information processing has been under investigation recently by Das and his colleagues (Das, Kirby, & Jarman, 1975). It is somewhat surprising that so much interest and effort has been concentrated on the possible different functions of the right and left hemispheres, at least recently, when there are so many other functional differences that could prove equally important to our understanding of behavior development and individual differences. Of particular interest here are the differences in abilities to engage in simultaneous and successive synthesis that Luria (1966) has identified with the occipital and temporal–parietal areas respectively. Das has attempted to show that these differential competencies are meaningfully related to the types of tasks involved in the measurement of intelligence, information processing, and memory, and that differences in these modes of synthesis show up in the mentally retarded (Das, Kirby, & Jarman, 1975), in children with reading disabilities (Cummins & Das, 1977; Kirby & Das, 1977), and with cultural differences (Das, Jachuck, & Panda, 1970).

As we learn more about these various cognitive styles and their underlying mechanisms, we should develop an increasing appreciation for individual diversity and learn to work with strengths rather than with weaknesses. It is important to note that it is not necessarily to society's advantage to have every individual fit the same mold. We recognize readily now that not every child has the potential to become a great violinist. That does not mean we cannot teach him to enjoy music. We probably would not do that, however, by forcing long hours of practice on the violin. It should be obvious by now that there are equal differences in other capacities, and although it is to society's advantage to teach everyone to read, it may well be that the time at which reading is taught, and the method by which it is taught, should be tailored to what we know and expect to learn in the future about individual differences in cognitive styles and capacities. To do this could do much to avoid frustration with schooling on the part of the child as well as those social difficulties and alienation such frustration frequently engenders with teachers, parents, and other children. If we have not realized it before, it is certainly time to recognize that our heads differ as much on the inside as they do on the outside. Therefore we must be as concerned with the fit of our training as we are with the fit of our hats or hairdos.

IX. Conclusion

In spite of the fact that, for the most part, it is only the environment we are able to manipulate as parents or educators, what we expect from a child, and how we manipulate that environment, should be tempered by what we know about how underlying structures develop, what the potentially important mediating structures are, and what differences there may be in these structures from one individual to another. We have a long way to go before we can have as much information as we should have in this regard, but from this book it is obvious we have also come a long way in our discovery of some of the important basic structures, and in comprehending something of their operation. To suggest that we tailor educational programs to individual differences in these structures does not mean that we give in to weakness, but rather that we recognize that there will be differences in how, what, and when children learn.

Bibliography

Ayres, A. J. Sensory foundations of academic ability. In William Cruikshank & D. P. Hallihan (Eds.), *Perceptual and learning disabilities in children* (Vol. 2.). Syracuse: Syracuse University Press, 1975.

Balow, I. H. Lateral dominance characteristics and reading achievement in the first grade. *Journal of Psychology*, 1963, *55*, 323–328.

Benton, A. L. Developmental dyslexia: Neurological aspects. In W. J. Freidlander (Ed.), *Advances in neurology* (Vol. 7.). New York: Raven Press, 1975.

Bower, J.G.R. *Development in infancy*. San Francisco: Freeman, 1974.

Bronson, G. The postnatal growth of visual capacity. *Child Development*, 1974, *45*, 873–890.

Broadbent, D. E. *Perception and communication*. London: Pergamon Press, 1958.

Brown, R. *A first language*. Cambridge, Mass.: Harvard University Press, 1973.

Bruner, J. S. Organization of early skilled action. *Child Development*, 1973, *44*, 1–11.

Caron, A. J., Caron, R. F., Caldwell, R. C., & Weiss, S. J. Infant perception of the structural properties of the face. *Developmental Psychology*, 1973, *9*, 385–399.

Coleman, R. I., & Deutsch, C. P. Lateral dominance and right-left discrimination: A comparison of normal and retarded readers. *Perceptual and Motor Skills*, 1964, *19*, 43–50.

Conel, J. *The postnatal development of the human cortex* (8 Vols.). Cambridge, Mass.: Harvard University Press, 1939–1967.

Cummins, J., & Das, J. P. Cognitive processing and reading difficulties: A framework for research. *The Alberta Journal of Educational Research*, 1977, *XXIII*, 245–256.

Curtiss, S. *Genie: A psycholinguistic study of a modern-day "wild child"*. New York: Academic Press, 1977.

Das, J. P., Jachuck, K., & Panda, T. P. Caste, cultural deprivation and cognitive growth. In H. C. Hagwood (Ed.), *Social-cultural aspects of mental retardation*. New York: Appleton, 1970.

Das, J. P., Kirby, J., & Jarman, R. F. Simultaneous and successive syntheses: An alternate model for cognitive abilities. *Psychological Bulletin*, 1975, *82*, 87–103.

Delacato, C. H. Neurological organization and reading. Springfield, Ill.: Charles C. Thomas, 1966.

Dreyfus-Brisac, C. The encephalogram of the premature infant and full-term newborn. In P. Kellaway & E. Petersen (Eds.), *Neurological and electroencephalographic correlative studies in infancy*. New York: Grune & Stratton, 1964, 186–207.

Eimas, P. Speech perception in early infancy. In L. B. Cohen & P. Salapatek (Eds.), *Infant perception from sensation to cognition* (Vol. 2). New York: Academic Press, 1975.

Emde, R. N., Gaensbauer, T. J., & Harmon, R. J. *Emotional expression in infancy*. New York: International Universities Press, Inc., 1976.

Fantz, R. L. Visual perception from birth as shown by pattern selectivity. *Annals of the New York Academy of Sciences*, 1965, *118*, 793–814.

Goodenough, D. R., & Witkin, H. A. Origins of field-dependent and field-independent cognitive styles. Princeton, N.J.: Educational Testing Service, 1977.

Graham, F. K., & Clifton, R. K. Heart-rate change as a component of the orienting response. *Psychological Bulletin*, 1966, *65*, 305–320.

Hebb, D. O. *The organization of behavior*. New York: Wiley, 1949.

Hecox, K. Electrophysiological correlates of human auditory development. In L. B. Cohen and P. Salapatek (Eds.), *Infant perception from sensation to cognition* (Vol. 2). New York: Academic Press, 1975.

Hernandez-Peón, R., Scherrer, H., & Jouvet, M. Modification of electrical activity in cochlear nuclei during attention in unanesthetized cats. *Science*, 1958, *123*, 331–332.

Hunt, J. McV. Motivation inherent in information processing and action. In O. D. Harvey (Ed.), *Motivation and social interaction*. New York: Ronald Press, 1963.

Horowitz, A. Habituation and memory: Infant cardiac responses to familiar and discrepant auditory stimuli. *Child Development*, 1972, *43*, 43–53.

Jeffrey, W. E. The orienting reflex in cognitive development. *Psychological Review*, 1968, *75*, 323–334.

Jeffrey, W. E. Early stimulation and cognitive development. In J. P. Hill (Ed.), *Minnesota symposium on child psychology* (Vol. 3). Minneapolis: The University of Minnesota Press, 1969.

Jeffrey, W. E. Habituation as a mechanism for perceptual development. In T. J. Tighe & R. N. Leaton (Eds.), *Habituation: Perspectives from child development, animal behavior, and neurophysiology*. Hillsdale, N.J.: Erlbaum, 1976.

Kirby, J. R., & Das, J. P. Reading achievement, I.Q., and simultaneous-successive processing. *Journal of Educational Psychology*, 1977, *69*, 564–570.

Koos, E. M. Manifestations of cerebral dominance and reading retardation in primary-grade children. *Journal of Genetic Psychology*, 1964, *104*, 155–165.

Lenneberg, E. H. *Biological foundations of language*. New York: Wiley, 1967.

Levine, S. Stimulation in infancy. *Scientific American*, May 1960, *202*,(5), 80–101.

Lewis, T. L., Mauer, D., & Kay, D. Newborns' central vision: Whole or hole? *Journal of Experimental Child Psychology*, 1978, *26*, 193–203.

Luria, A. R. *Higher cortical functions in man*. New York: Basic Books, 1966.

Mann, I. *The development of the human eye*. London: British Medical Association, 1964.

Messer, B. Reflection-impulsivity: A review. *Psychological Bulletin*, 1976, *83*, 1026–1052.

Miller, G. A., Galanter, E., & Pribram, K. *Plans and the structure of behavior*. New York: Holt, Rinehart & Winston, 1960.

Milner, E. *Human neural and behavioral development, a relational inquiry*. Springfield, Ill.: Charles C. Thomas, 1967.

Moruzzi, G., & Magoun, H. W. Brainstem reticular formation and activation of the EEG. *Electroencephalography and Clinical Neurophysiology*, 1949, *1*, 455–473.

Moffit, A. R. Consonant cue perception by twenty- to twenty-four-week-old infants. *Child Development*, 1971, *42*, 717–731.

Molfese, D. L. Cerebral asymmetry in infants, children and adults: Auditory evoked responses to speech and noise stimuli. Unpublished doctoral dissertation, The Pennsylvania State University, 1972.

O'Connor, M. Auditory habituation in four-month-old infants. Unpublished manuscript, 1973.

Orton, S. T. *Reading, writing and speech problems in children.* New York: Norton, 1937.

Parmelee, A. H., Schulte, F. J., Akiyama, Y., Wenner, W. H., Schultz, M. A., & Stern, E. Motivation of EEG activity during sleep in premature infants. *Electroencephalography and Clinical Neurophysiology,* 1968, *24,* 319–329.

Parmelee, A. H., Wenner, W. H., Akiyama, Y., Stern, E., & Flescher, J. Electroencephalography and brain maturation. In A. Minkowsky (Ed.), *Regional development of the brain in early life.* Oxford: Bladewell Scientific Publications, 1967.

Peiper, A. *Cerebral function in infancy and childhood.* [A translation by Wartis (Ed.), of *Die eigenart der kindlichen hirntatigkeit* (3rd ed.), Leipsig, Thieme.] New York: Consultants Bureau, 1963.

Robinson, R. J. (Ed.), *Brain and early behavior: Development in the fetus and infant.* New York: Academic Press, 1969.

Rosenzweig, M. R., Bennett, E. L., & Diamond, M. C. Brain changes in responses to experience. *Scientific American* Feb. 1972, *226*(2), 22–29.

Schachter, S., & Singer, J. E. Cognitive and social determinants of emotional state. *Psychological Review,* 1962, *69,* 379–399.

Schulte, F. J. Excitation, inhibition, and impulsive conduction in spinal motoneurones of preterm, term and small-for-dates newborn infants. In R. J. Robinson (Ed.), *Brain and early behavior: Development in the fetus and infant.* New York: Academic Press, 1969. Pp. 87–109.

Shankweiler, D. P. A study of development dyslexia. *Neuropsychologia,* 1963, *1,* 267–286.

Sokolov, E. N. *Perception and the conditioned reflex.* New York: Macmillan, 1963.

Sroufe, L. A., & Mitchell, P. Emotional development in infancy. In J. Osofsky (Ed.), *Handbook of infancy research.* New York: John Wiley, 1979.

Sroufe, L. A., & Waters, E. Attachment as an organizational construct. *Child Development,* 1977, *48,* 1184–1199.

Travis, L. E. *Speech pathology.* New York: Appleton-Century, 1931.

Turner, O. A. Growth and development of cerebral cortical pattern in man. *Archives of Neurology and Psychiatry,* 1948, *59,* 1–12.

Turner, O. A. Postnatal growth changes in the cortical surface area. *Archives of Neurology and Psychiatry,* 1950, *64,* 378–384.

Waber, D. P. Biological substrates of field dependence: Implications of the sex difference. *Psychological Bulletin,* 1977, *84,* 1076–1087. (a)

Waber, D. P. Sex differences in mental abilities, hemispheric lateralization, and rate of physical growth at adolescence. *Developmental Psychology,* 1977, *13,* 29–38. (b)

Witelson, S. F. Sex and the single hemisphere: Right hemisphere specialization for spatial processing. *Science,* 1976, *193,* 425–427.

Witelson, S. F., & Pallie, W. Left hemisphere specialization for language in the newborn: Neuroanatomical evidence of asymmetry. *Brain,* 1973, *96,* 641–647.

Witkin, H. A., Dyk, R. B., Paterson, H. F., Goodenough, D. R., & Karp, S. A. *Psychological differentiation.* Potomac, Md.: Erlbaum, 1974.

Witkin, H. A., Goodenough, D. R., & Oltman, P. K. *Psychological differentiation: Current status.* Princeton, N.J.: Educational Testing Service, 1977.

Wyckoff, L. B. The role of observing responses in discrimination learning. Part I. *Psychological Review,* 1952, *59,* 431–442.

Zangwill, O. L. *Cerebral dominance and its relation to psychological function.* Edinburgh: Oliver and Boyd, 1960.

Zelniker, T., & Jeffrey, W. E. Reflective and impulsive children: Strategies of information processing underlying differences in problem-solving. *Monographs of the Society for Research in Child Development* (Vol. 41), 6, 1976.

Zelniker, T., & Jeffrey, W. E. Attention and cognitive style in children. In C. Hale & M. Lewis (Eds.), *Attention and cognitive development*. New York: Plenum Press, 1979.

Zoccolotti, P., & Oltman, P. K. Field dependence and lateralization of verbal and configurational processing. *Cortex*, 1978, *14*, 155–163.

Chapter IX

Learning and the Brain

M. C. WITTROCK

I. Introduction

In this chapter, I will compare recent findings about the brain with recent findings about the cognitive processes of learning. From a comparison of research findings at these two different levels of study, I will discuss implications of interest to educational psychologists who study learning and individual differences among learners.

The development of relationships between research in neuroscience and research in cognitive psychology is a delicate process because the researchers in these two areas study learning at different levels of abstraction. At the same time, it is precisely because research about the brain and research in the psychology of learning involve different levels of related phenomena that we can deepen our understanding of human learning through a comparison of their findings and through a search for themes that recur in both areas.

II. The Functions of the Brain

In several experiments, my students and I have found that some types of human learning from instruction involve generative cognitive pro-

371

THE BRAIN AND PSYCHOLOGY

cesses, in which learners actively select and transform verbal information as well as receive and record it (Wittrock, 1974; Wittrock & Carter, 1975; Wittrock, Marks, & Doctorow, 1975; Wittrock & Lumsdaine, 1977; Doctorow, Wittrock, & Marks, 1978).

In these studies, the learners often constructed relations between events and memories of experience. The same instructional treatments or environmental events meant different things to different people because of their different previous experiences and the different ways they transformed nominal stimuli into functional stimuli.

From quite different contexts, people who study the brain have developed similar inferences. McGuinness and Pribram in Chapter 3 write, "Rather, behaving organisms are spontaneously active, generating changes in the environment often by way of highly programmed (i.e., serially ordered) responses [p. 101]." From the study of the evolution of the brain, Jerison (1977) maintains that the brain is a model builder. Its central function is to construct a model of reality. An implication from these two lines of research on the brain is that experiences themselves are constructions or representations which reflect the model brought to the episodes, in interaction with the environmental stimuli sensed by the learners.

The theme recurs in a number of studies about the brain. Trevarthen (1974) discusses how eye movements and hand actions contribute to the generation of consciousness in commissurotomy patients. Their experience depends upon the intrinsic functions of the brain, such as attention, perception, and set, and the operations performed upon stimuli. In commissurotomized patients, the organization of the brain processes has been altered, and consequently the consciousness they construct will also be altered. Trevarthen begins with the hierarchical organization of the intrinsic processes of the brain, and tries to understand learning and consciousness as the constructions of these internal processes, almost the reverse of common methods of studying learning used in educational psychology.

Elio Maggio (1971) makes a related point. He writes,

As a matter of fact, it has been proved that input signals can be modified in the brain even before they reach the specific sensory areas of the cortex, and that this alternation of sensory stimuli is due to the prewired organization of the nervous system of each individual but is also significantly influenced by learning experiences. Experience, in other words, molds neurophysiological mechanisms, even those which appear more stable and closely depending upon genetic and biochemical factors. The central nervous system is not only the site where passive interconnecting functions occur, but also, and perhaps primarily, a structure allowing an active function upon varied incoming sensory stimuli [p. 81].[1]

A good example of Maggio's point is the well-known finding reported by Hernandez-Peón, Scherrer, and Jouvet (1956). An audible "click" regularly produced a distinctive brainwave response in the cochlear nucleus of a cat, until mice, fish odor, or shock was presented simultaneously with the click. When any of these stimuli appeared, the brainwave response to the click was greatly reduced. The cat selectively attended to the distracting visual, olfactory, or nociceptive stimulus, though it is possible that orienting movements to attend to the acoustic stimuli may have contributed to the observed changes in brainwaves.

Although learners live in a structured reality, the constructive processes of their brains contribute to the meanings they acquire from instruction. The clear implication is that to understand how people learn from instruction, we should identify the ways that individual learners use their brains to transform information and to relate it to their memories of experience.

The dismal record of attempts to correlate the acts of teachers directly with the learning of students may be due to the simplistic paradigms used in these studies, rather than to their methodological problems or to their selection of behaviors for study. Meaningful relations between teaching and learning are more likely to be found when the cognitive processes and transformations of the learner are included in the research paradigm. Recent research on the brain and its information processing strategies, to which we now turn, offers new ideas about the nature and variety of some of the cognitive transformations used by learners.

III. The Functional Organization of the Brain

In the first chapter of this book, Thompson, Berger, and Berry described the basic anatomy, physiology, and chemistry of the brain. Their chapter provides a basis for the following discussion of the functional organization of the brain and for the subsequent discussion of the cognitive processes of learning.

Luria (1973) presents an informative but controversial model of brain function. The tentative nature of the model should be kept in mind while reading about it. He distinguishes three principal functional units

---

[1]From *Psychophysiology of Learning and Memory* by Elio Maggio (1971). Courtesy of Charles C Thomas, Publisher, Springfield, Illinois.

of the brain: (*a*) the unit for regulating tone, waking, and mental states; (*b*) the unit for receiving, analyzing, and storing information; and (*c*) the unit for programming, regulating, and verifying activity.

The first unit, which maintains arousal, lies in the subcortex and brainstem. The unit consists largely of the ascending reticular activating system, identified by Moruzzi and Magoun (1949), and the descending reticular activating system. Both systems connect the neocortex and the brain stem, with projections through intermediate structures such as the thalamus. Each of the systems of fibers of the reticular activating system exerts either a facilitative or inhibitory influence upon activation and arousal. Stimulation of the reticular activating system can originate in the metabolic processes of the organism or in the external environment and can lead to an orienting reflex. Stimulation can also arise in the cortex and can lead to so-called conceptually driven behavior.

For the study of learning, these findings imply that metabolic processes or external events, such as directions from an instructor, can stimulate or inhibit activation and arousal. The cortex, including the frontal lobes with plans and intentions mediated through them, also can stimulate or inhibit the arousal and activation systems of the brain. All of these sources of stimulation should be taken in account to determine the reactions of the learner to instructional treatments.

Luria's second of three principal functional units of the brain, called the unit for receiving, analyzing, and storing information, occupies the posterior, convex surface of the cortical hemispheres, which includes the occipital, temporal, and parietal lobes. The cells of this second functional unit of the brain are hierarchically organized into three areas called the primary, secondary, and tertiary levels. The primary level contains modally specific regions, whose components often separately process visual, auditory, vestibular, gustatory, and olfactory stimuli.

The secondary level of the hierarchically arrayed unit for receiving, analyzing, and storing information is modally less specific than the primary level. This second level organizes and codes sensory information primarily from one mode, such as visual information from different parts of the retina, into functional units.

The tertiary level of Luria's second functional unit of the brain is a distinctly human structure. It organizes or codes symbolic information coming from sensory analyzers in different sensory modes in the two lower levels of the hierarchy. Cells in the tertiary level respond to general features of multimodal information, such as their spatial characteristics. These cells also convert successively or linearly organized stimuli into simultaneously organized stimuli. Another characteristic of the secondary and tertiary levels of the unit for receiving, storing, and analyzing information is its lateralization of function, which we will discuss later in this chapter.

The third principal functional part of the brain, called the unit for programming, regulating, and verifying activity, organizes consciousness. The third unit occupies the anterior regions of the brain, the area in front of the precentral gyrus. Its motor outlet is the motor cortex, roughly the area immediately anterior to the precentral gyrus. Luria (1973) summarizes the functions of the third principle unit of the brain as follows:

> "Man not only reacts passively to incoming information, but creates *intentions*, forms *plans* and *programs* of his actions, inspects their performance, and regulates his behavior so that it conforms to these plans and programs; finally he *verifies* his conscious activity, comparing the effects of his actions with the original intentions and correcting any mistakes he has made [pp. 79–80]."[2]

The frontal lobes connect extensively with nearly all other parts of the brain, including subcortical regions, which implies that plans and intentions can stimulate or inhibit information processing, arousal, and activation. Removal of the frontal lobes of monkeys has led to an inability to ignore distracting stimuli, to inhibit responses to irrelevant stimuli, to continue to anticipate reinforcement across a delay interval, and to maintain a plan of action directed toward the future, rather than to behave reflexively in response to environmental stimuli.

In a chapter entitled "The frontal lobes and the regulation of behavior" (Pribram & Luria, 1973), Luria discusses in greater detail the functions of these lobes, including their roles in activation, in verbally controlled behavior, and in problem solving. He writes that although logical reasoning may remain intact with lesions of the frontal lobes, the ability to analyze problems, to select programs of action, and to execute them is seriously impaired or destroyed by the lesions. Behavior becomes stereotyped, evidencing a lack of ability to make goal-directed choices among alternatives.

When one reads about the processes and functions of the brain, it is important to remember that each process or function involves several areas of the brain working in harmony. Several studies show the pattern of involvement of many parts of the brain in learning tasks common in schools, such as arithmetic and reading. Livanov, Gavrilova, and Aslanov (1964, 1973) graphically demonstrated an increasing synchrony of

---

[2]From *The Working Brain: An Introduction to Neuropsychology* by Alexander Romanovich Luria, translated by Basil Haigh, Copyright © by Penguin Books Ltd., 1973, translation Copyright © by Penguin Books Ltd., 1973, Basic Books, Inc., Publishers, New York.

activities in the cortex during problem solving and mental arithmetic. Lassen and Ingvar (1972), Ingvar (1973), and Ingvar and Schwartz (1974) recorded changes in blood flow, as a qualitative measure of patterns among localized cortical functions. In one study (Lassen, Ingvar & Skinhøj, 1978), the images were produced in color by computers from data that traced the flow of a radioactive gas, [133] Xenon, through the brain when sensory stimuli were presented and when motor tasks were performed by the subjects. At rest, the flow of blood was highest in the front part of the human cortex. Sensory stimuli or motor responses increased blood flow to primary sensory or motor cortex, respectively, and to its adjacent association areas. During speech, blood flow increased to Broca's area, and to a lesser extent and in a different pattern, to the area in the right hemisphere that corresponds in location to Broca's area. In the left hemisphere, blood flow during silent reading increased in Broca's area, the primary and associational visual areas, the supplementary motor area, and the frontal eye field area. In the right hemisphere, the pattern was much the same. The images of blood flow clearly indicated the patterned involvement of multiple regions of the brain in psychological activities such as reading. It seems that learning involves many areas of the brain working in different patterns; the patterns depending upon the problem and its content.

IV. Biological Processes in Learning and Memory

Cell division in the brain, the formation of new cells, slows at birth and ceases before 2 years of age, probably at about age 12 to 15 months (Winick & Rosso, 1975, p. 41). However, brain weight increases about 35% after the cessation of brain cell division, probably because of cellular growth, such as the growth and branching of the dendrites and the increasing complexity of networks of connections among the neurons. Winick and Rosso (1975) classify brain growth into three periods. In the earliest period, hyperplasia, the number of brain cells increases while their size remains constant. In the second period, hyperplasia with hypertrophy, the rate of cell division slows while the size of the cells increases. In the third period, hypertrophy, cell division stops, while cell size and weight increase.

The point is that experience, learning, and nutrition influence the neural growth of the brain differently in each of these three stages of early brain development. Monckeberg (1975) treated 14 infants who had suffered severe marasma, a type of early malnutrition that occurs usually during the first five months of life. After extensive treatment for malnutrition, each child was returned home and was given 20 liters of milk per month thereafter. At ages 4–7 years, all 14 treated children were clinically normal, with normal indexes of nutrition. But their average Binet IQ was 62. The highest IQ score of any child was 76. The implication of these data was that the effects of malnutrition on IQ during hyperplasia were irreversible because the number of brain cells could not be increased later through proper nutrition. The problem with this implication is that malnutrition is correlated with a number of variables, such as socioeconomic level and heredity, which could have contributed to the finding that the average IQ was below normal with or without malnutrition. Further, a treatment that does not remove a deficiency may indicate only that one needs a more effective treatment. Nonetheless, the data suggest that severe and early malnutrition, whether reversible or not, lowers IQ scores.

Monckeberg (1975) also studied subalimentation, or undernutrition, and its influence upon mental ability. He studied 500 preschool children from Santiago, Chile. One of his three groups of children was from a low socioeconomic level and had suffered severe malnutrition. About 40% of these children had IQs below 80. Only 3% of the two groups not suffering from undernutrition, one group from a middle socioeconomic level and the other from a low socioeconomic level, had IQs below 80. The latter of these two groups had, for 10 years, received a program of nutrition and medical care. The results imply that nutrition may influence IQ, and, depending upon the age of onset of undernutrition, its effects upon IQ can sometimes be remedied by a lengthy program of nutrition.

In a chapter on the influence of early protein–calorie malnutrition on intellectual development, von Muralt (1975) discusses kwashiorkor, a malnutritional disease of an older infant that occurs after a new baby is born. Kwashiorkor, which comes from the Ga-tribe in Ghana and means "first–second," involves a lack of protein–nitrogen in the diet, often during the first 18 months of life. von Muralt (1975) summarizes the findings about kwashiorkor as follows: "Malnutrition during fetal and the first 18 months of a child's life seems to be a noxious insult, which affects the normal development of the brain and is in most cases incurable by a later improvement of the child's nutrition [p. 313]." In sum, these data indicate the importance of proper nutrition, especially during the first two years of life, to the growth of the brain, IQ, and learning.

A. Experience and Neural Growth

With increasing age, from 3 to 24 months at least, there is a definite thickening of human cortical dendrites and an increase in their branching (Pribram, 1971, p. 27). Evidence from animal studies indicates that experience influences dendritic growth. Globus and Scheibel (1967) showed that a restriction of rabbits' vision deformed apical dendritic spines. By stimulating newborn rats with 20–30 min of handling, shaking, noise making, and light-flashing for each of eight consecutive days Schapiro and Vukovich (1970) increased the number of cortical dendritic spines and the number of cortical neurons. Hubel and Wiesel (1970) found that visual deprivation induced by closing a kitten's eye, especially between the fourth and eighth weeks of life, sharply reduced the number of neurons in the visual cortex that reacted later in life to stimulation of the formerly closed eye.

Rosenzweig (1970), Rosenzweig, Bennett, and Diamond (1972), Rosenzweig and Bennett (1976), and Bennett, Diamond, Krech, and Rosenzweig (1964) compared (a) rats raised in groups of threes for 25–105 days in a standard laboratory cage; with (b) rats raised in isolation in a so-called impoverished environment, a plain wire cage; with (c) rats raised in groups of 12 in a complex, so-called enriched environment, a wire cage with a variety of apparatus which was changed daily. The rats raised in the enriched environment had larger brains with thicker cortices, greater concentration of acetylcholine, and more glial cells than did the rats raised in the impoverished environment. Rosenzweig (1970) also reports comparable increases in these measures of brain growth among adult rats placed in enriched environments for 105–185 days. See Rosenzweig and Bennett (1976), especially Chapters 16 (by W. Greenough) and 17 (by E. Bennett), for further discussion of the effects of training on the brain.

These data indicate that brain growth occurs partially as a result of experience, implying that enriched experience for rats might enhance learning and memory, as they are correlated with neural growth. A bolder implication worth testing is that experience can contribute through neural growth to an increased ability to learn and to remember. The increase in brain size and weight, the increased density of aborization of dendritic spines, the profusion of intercellular connections, and changes in neurotransmitters might indicate a greater store of information in the brain, an increased ability to learn, or an increase in the neural substrates of the ability to learn and to remember.

How might increases in neural growth due to enriched experience or improved nutrition influence psychological function? No doubt the influences depend upon the types of neural growth and their relevance to the psychological functions. Speed of reaction, organization of information, and perception of spatial relations involve different combinations of activities and various brain structures that are differentially susceptible to the experience-induced increases in neural growth.

In animals at least, well-timed enriched experiences increase neural growth, which in turn increases the possibilities of improved learning and improved ability to learn. The implication for educational psychologists is that we should explore in humans the possibility that well-timed, stimulating instruction influences brain growth, and with it psychological functions that transcend the behaviors measured on commonly used tests of learning.

B. Neural Transmission and Learning

What happens in brain cells when learning occurs? How are memories stored in the brain? How can one influence the biological changes that occur in learning and in memory storage? Thompson, Berger, and Berry (this volume) and McGuinness and Pribram (this volume) discuss these issues, including the search for the elusive engram, the hypothetical neural memory trace or representation of learning in memory.

The structural mechanisms of the brain involved in learning and memory include the growth of dendritic spines, increases in the complexity of the networks of synaptic connections among neurons, and the division of neuroglial cells. In addition to structural growth, chemical changes also occur in cells, such as the synthesis of protein molecules to code and store information, and changes at the synapses in the concentrations of neurotransmitters and their modulators. A third mechanism involves changes in the patterns of coherent electrical activity, or modes of oscillation, of voltages across neurons. The electrical mechanism implies that the resultant statistical configuration of waveforms across cells represents different memories at different times (John, 1971).

All of the above mechanisms might be involved in a variety of ways in different neurons and in different types of learning and memory. Pribram (1971, pp. 441–447) presented an induction model of memory in which RNA induces chemical changes in the membranes between neurons and glia. The chemical changes influence the action of the neurotransmitters which excite glial cell division. The cone of a neuron then grows between the daughter glial cells to form new connections with other neurons. The result is a change in the structure of neurons that involves many of the brain mechanisms previously described.

We have already discussed some of the effects of neural growth upon learning. We will now discuss chemical influences upon learning, especially as they involve synapses and neurotransmitters. As Thompson et al. (this volume), Eccles (1977), and Pribram (1971) indicate, even when a nerve cell is not firing, it is rhythmically and continuously influenced by the voltage changes of the neurons surrounding it, which result in a waxing and waning of graded-decision processes. When these graded changes increase sufficiently, they depolarize the cell membrane and produce firing of a neuron, an action potential. The firing of a neuron in the human brain involves a fascinating sequence of chemical changes that occur rapidly, within 1–2 msec. The chemicals active at the synapse during the sequence of changes include the neurotransmitters, which facilitate or inhibit the firing of a neuron, their modulators, their precursors—from which the neurotransmitters are synthesized—and the degradative enzymes, which inactivate the neurotransmitters.

Acetylcholine is a neurotransmitter that facilitates muscular action and perhaps brain activity. Choline is one of its precursors. Other neurotransmitters thought to be active in the brain include the catecholamines, epinephrine, norepinephrine, and dopamine, and perhaps the indolamine, serotonin. The amino acids glycine and gamma aminobutyric acid (GABA) are putative inhibitory neurotransmitters in the central nervous system (Eccles, 1977, p. 84).

Do the neurotransmitters and their precursors, for example acetylcholine and choline, influence learning? In two experiments, Sitaram, Weingartner, and Gillin (1978) gave 10 gm of choline, or 4 gm of arecholine, a cholinergic agonist, or a placebo to subjects 10 min before they serially learned a list of 10 words. Scopolamine, a cholinergic antagonist was given to some of the learners before they were given arecholine or the placebo. Compared with the placebo, arecholine or choline enhanced learning, and scopolamine impaired learning. Arecholine also inactivated the scopolamine produced impairment of serial learning. The effects of all these chemicals interacted with student learning ability. The poorer learners showed greater improvement with choline and arecholine, and greater impairment with scopolamine than did the better learners.

Acetylcholinesterase (AChE) is an enzyme that decomposes acetylcholine into acetic acid and choline. Physostigmine is an AChE inhibitor. Davis, Mohs, Tinklenberg, Pfefferbaum, Hollister, and Kopell (1978) gave normal human male subjects either physostigmine or a placebo before and during testing of their short-term memory with digit span or Sternberg-type tasks. The effects of physostigmine on long-term memory was tested with a list of 15 concrete nouns, learned 30 min before the intravenous placebo or physostigmine injections began, and recalled twice: 18 min, and again 80 min after the injections began. Physostigmine increased long-term memory storage on both recall trials, but did not influence short-term memory scores on either test. A second task introduced 30 min after the injections began indicated that physostigmine enhanced memory storage, but retrieval, attention, and motivation could not be eliminated as possible contributing variables.

These two studies by Sitaram et al. (1978) and Davis et al. (1978) indicate that at least some types of learning and memory can be facilitated in some learners by increasing the level of facilitory neurotransmitters, such as acetylcholine. One implication of these findings is that a change in synaptic transmission is one of the mechanisms involved in at least some types of learning and memory.

The synthesis of RNA and of protein is a second type of chemical change involved in learning or in memory (Brazier, 1964; Hyden & Egyházi, 1962). It is difficult to establish protein synthesis as a mechanism of learning. A given protein molecule lives about one month, which means that its replacement must encode the same memories as its predecessor. Some studies indicate, however, that RNA, which synthesizes proteins, directs the formation of memories.

These complex issues can be studied in several ways. One way is to determine the variables effecting the synthesis of RNA or protein that occurs during learning, as Hyden and Egyházi (1962) did with RNA and Shashoua (1976) demonstrated with protein. For example, in a training condition, Shashoua attached a small float to the ventral midline of goldfish, causing them to swim upside down until they learned to swim right side up. To index the amount of protein synthesis occurring during learning, he injected the fish with an amino acid, valine, which is used to construct protein molecules. About 5 hours after training, the time when the concentration of RNA molecules that increase with learning should be at its maximum, he found that the trained fish incorporated more valine into the construction of protein molecules than did the untrained fish or goldfish trained in control procedures. A control condition suggested that stress was not a factor determining the difference between the trained and untrained groups. The results indicated that the increase in protein synthesis was due to the learning of the new behavior. See Hyden (1976) for a description of protein synthesis and differentiation occurring during learning.

A second way to study protein synthesis in learning and memory is to give learners drugs or chemicals before or after training. Flexner, Flexner, and Roberts (1967) found that puromycin disrupted intermediate and long-term memory through the inhibition of protein synthesis caused by a loss of messenger RNA, which was hypothesized to sustain the synthesis of protein molecules. In other studies, tricyanoaminopropene increased the rate of consolidation in long-term memory, probably by increasing RNA synthesis; and nitrous oxide facilitated retention in human subjects.

Other drugs influence some types of learning and memory, although the mechanisms of influence are not known. Caffeine, strychnine, and picrotoxin, all of which may block inhibitory synaptic mechanisms, can influence learning. Both strychnine and amphetamine produce dose-specific interfering or facilitating effects upon learning. Potassium ions, and to a lesser extent, calcium ions, improve learning under some conditions. Depressant drugs, such as sodium pentobarbital, facilitate or disrupt short-term memory, depending on the timing and the amount of the dose; and nitrous oxide sometimes enhances long-term memory (Quarton, 1967).

Dimond (1976) gave Piracetam (2-pyrrolidone acetamide) to 16 college students. Piracetam seems to facilitate transfer of information from one cortical hemisphere to another in animals. In a serial learning task, the drug facilitated learning 14 days after the doses began, but not seven days after the doses began. Pursuit rotor task performance was not influenced by the drug. (The results were equivocal regarding the interhemispheric hypothesis.) Harshman, Crawford, and Hecht (1976) found that marijuana, which seriously debilitates behavior, reduced verbal and analytic abilities but increased visual and spatial functions, perhaps by increasing interhemispheric transfer of information. Smith (1970) found that ethosuximide increased verbal IQ scores in learning disabled children from 8 to 14 years old with abnormal EEG readings who had poor school performance in English, arithmetic, reading, and spelling.

Stimulant drugs such as methylphenidate hydrochloride (Ritalin), Benzedrine, dextroamphetamine sulphate (Dexedrine), and Pemoline produce a variety of effects which interact with the type of task and specific behaviors. They often facilitate selective attention by inhibiting the effects of distracting task relevant information and perhaps by increasing the level of arousal. We will discuss stimulant drugs further in the following section on attention.

The studies summarized in this section imply that all of the structural, chemical, and electrical mechanisms mentioned earlier are involved in different kinds of learning and in memory. These processes sometimes can be facilitated with proper nutrition, well-timed experience, training, and drugs. However, the precise neurological mechanisms involved in different types of learning are not known.

V. Fundamental Processes of Learning

The following discussion will involve two of the learning processes that have been studied in neuroscience and in cognitive psychology and that have relevance for educational psychology: attention and encoding.

A. Attention

Zeaman and House (1963) showed that the learning curves of retarted children, when plotted backward from the point of learning, indicated the importance of attention in the learning process. Instead of the relatively gradual increments typical of learning curves plotted by trials for the average performance of groups of learners, they found sudden, large gains in learning. Compared with normal learners, the mentally retarded children showed similar sudden large increments in learning, but the gains occurred after a larger number of trials. Zeaman and House inferred that the poorer discrimination learning of the retarded children was due to their inability to attend selectively to the relevant cues, not to an inability to learn. Other psychologists (Dykman, Ackerman, Clements, & Peters, 1971) also have found that attention is a fundamental cause of some learning disabilities.

In addition to psychologists who study learning in children, neuroscientists study attention as a variable in information processing. In many neuropsychological studies, attention is measured by recording brainwave patterns (EEG). The following types of brainwaves have been identified:

1. Delta waves, .5–4 Hz, occur during sleep.

2. Theta waves, 5–7 Hz, indicate stress or affectivity. They increase when alpha waves decrease, but they are negatively correlated with attention to external stimuli. Delta and theta waves are common among children with behavioral or neurological disorders.

3. Alpha waves, 8–12 Hz, indicate an awake but inactive person not attending to external stimuli.

4. Kappa waves, also 8–12 Hz, may index only eye movements; they are not well understood. They increase during arithmetic, reading, and related intellectual work.

5. Beta waves, 18–30 Hz, and gamma waves, 30–50 Hz, have not been frequently studied, but probably index attention to external stimuli.

In addition to the frequency of a brainwave, its shape and its amplitude in millivolts (mV) or microvolts (μV) can be used as an index of attention. The evoked potential (EP) technique consists of the presentation of an external stimulus and the recording of the amplitude, shape, and latency of the brain's responses. The exogenous components of the wave, which usually have short latencies (time measured from stimulus onset), measure the attentional responses of the brain to the external stimulus. The endogenous components of the brainwave, which usually have long latencies, measure internal processes not controlled by the external stimulus. For example, a brainwave component with a latency of 100 msec may be an index of selective attention to the external stimulus. At a latency of 200 msec, a spike often occurs when unexpected events are presented, including the nonappearance of an expected event. The spike may reflect involvement of stored information and expectancies. A brainwave component at 250 msec latency can represent storage of information in short-term memory. At 300 msec latency, the component may relate to a variety of endogenous information processing factors and response sets (Näätänen, 1975; John & Schwartz, 1978).

Changes in waveforms **preceding** an event also can measure endogenous components. The contingent negative variation (CNV) or expectancy wave, is a waveform slowly increasing in negativity that occurs after a warning stimulus but before the stimulus that elicits a response. In the following paragraphs we will examine some of the results of studies that used these techniques and measures. See John et al. (1977) for a description of a diagnostic technique called "neurometrics" that provides electrophysiological measures of brain functions.

John, Bartlett, Shimokochi, and Kleinman (1973) trained cats to press a lever or to jump a hurdle, depending upon the type of warning signal, to escape shock. The shape of the late components of the waveforms indicated the response the cat would make, but did not indicate the type of warning signal the cat saw. Pribram (1969) taught monkeys to press the right half of a panel when a circle, or the left half when stripes appeared on a screen. The early components of the waveforms indicated whether the circle or stripes were seen. The later occurring response or "intention" waveforms showed a sharp peak when the monkeys were about to press the right half of the panel, and a flatter waveform when they prepared to press the left half. The "intention" waveform, which indicated the half of the panel the monkey was about to press, was not under the control of the external stimulus. The processing of information included more than automatic responses to external stimuli.

Barry and Thompson (1978) found that spontaneous EEG data, recorded from the dorsal hippocampus of rabbits prior to classical conditioning, reliably predicted the subsequent rate of learning, implicating nonspecific factors such as arousal or attention.

With humans, Teyler, Megela, and Hesse (1977) measured evoked responses associated with the acquisition of meaning for visual stimuli. The physically different visual stimuli could have the same meaning, and the physically similar stimuli could have different meanings. Regardless of their appearance, the sematic similarity of the stimuli determined the amplitude of the learners' brainwave response. That is, a concept was indexed by the brainwave.

Hillyard, Hink, Schwent, and Picton (1973) gave tone signals to each ear of each subject. An early negative component of the waveform indicated the matching of the signal to a model, while a later component at 300 milliseconds indicated the learner's overt response to the signal. That is, it was possible to measure components of the cognitive processing of the signal and from them to predict the overt response that would be made.

A number of studies report related findings. Brown, Marsh, and Smith (1973) found that words with ambiguous meanings evoked different waveforms depending upon the contexts of the words. Begleiter, Porjesz, Yerre, and Kissin (1973) showed that the evoked potential indexed the expected bright or dim light flash, but not the actual medium intensity light stimulus. Expected events which did not actually occur have influenced the evoked potentials of human subjects in studies by Klinke, Fruhstorfer, and Finkenzeller (1968); and Weinberg, Walter, and Crow (1970). John et al. (1973) concluded that the consistency and reliability of these phenomena, called neural readout from memory, "reflect the activation of particular memories related to cognitive decisions about the meaning of the aberrant input [p. 922]." In these studies, it is not the environmental stimulus but the meaning attached to it by the subject which evokes the brain response.

The EP technique has also been used to study attention in children with learning disabilities. Third and fourth grade children with reading disabilities showed correlations of −.6 between the amplitude of the left parietal lobe component at the 200 msec latency and reading achievement (Conners, 1970). Preston, Guthrie, and Childs (1974) presented words and flashes of light to 9-year-old children. With light flashes only, the poor readers showed a lower brainwave response amplitude at 180 msec latency than did the normal readers, indicating a deficit in attention, not in ability to read words. Shields (1973) compared learning disabled children from 10 to 13 years old with normal children. All children in the study had IQs of 90 or better. The evoked responses indicated that all latencies were longer and amplitudes of the two positive waveforms were greater for the learning disabled group than for the normal group. The author concluded that, compared with the normal learners, the learning disabled children take longer to respond and differ in their attentional responses.

Hyperarousal and hypoarousal are abnormalities of attention that offer new explanations for some behavioral problems, such as hyperkinetic activity, usually considered to be a learning disorder. Hyperactivity often is reduced by stimulant drugs, such as Benzedrine, Dexedrine, Pemoline, and Ritalin. Although they produce a variety of effects, depending upon the individuals, dosages, and tasks, these drugs influence selective attention by inhibiting distracting stimuli and impulsive actions and by increasing arousal. The drugs facilitate cortical inhibitory mechanisms; they do not seem to influence learning, memory, nor cognitive style directly (Conners, 1976). Haward (1970) found that among air-traffic controllers, Pemoline increased concentration and reduced errors caused by fatigue. van Duyne (1976) found that the effect of Ritalin interacted with the task and with the specific behavior of the hyperactive child, but not with the child's cognitive style. Conners (1972) also found several specific but no global effects of drugs upon different learners and different learning disabilities.

The specific nature of drug effects is clearly indicated in a study by Sprague and Sleator (1977). They found a peak enhancement of learning in 8-year-old children given a dose of .3 mg of Ritalin per kilogram of body weight. Social behavior among the children increased most with a higher dose (1.0 mg) of the drug per kilogram of body weight, indicating the specific effects of the drug upon different behaviors and cognitive processes.

Conners (1976) recorded auditory and visual evoked potentials under stimulant drug or placebo conditions. The drug had the greatest effect on selective attention; less on arousal. Conners states that although hyperkinetic children are less aroused than normal children, their primary deficit is a lack of ability to inhibit impulsive responses to the effects of distracting contextual information. That is, attention involves several processes, such as arousal and activation, as McGuinness and Pribram (this volume) state.

In the related literature on learning disabled children, which includes studies of educationally handicapped, mentally retarded, or brain damaged children, some of the findings support the attentional hypothesis just discussed. In sustained attention tasks (vigilance), Krupski (1979) reports that children who are mentally retarded, hyperactive, educationally handicapped, brain damaged, or highly active low achievers make more errors of omissions and show greater decrement of performance than do normal children. She also states that hyperactive children perform less well on sustained, voluntary attention tasks. But compared with normal children, the hyperactive children perform equally well on involuntary attention tasks.

Krupski's (1975) reaction time studies also support a sustained attention model of some learning disabilities. In reaction time studies, where the time between the warning signal and the reaction signal is constant, heart rate deceleration often occurs: (a) immediately after a warning signal, which is interpreted to index involuntary attention; and (b) with the onset of the signal to react, which is interpreted to measure voluntary attention. Mentally retarded children often show a normal heart rate deceleration to the warning signal, but often show a less than normal heart rate deceleration to the signal to react, indicating a deficit of voluntary attention.

Similar results are sometimes obtained with skin conductance measures indicating that learning disabled children sometimes show deficits in active responses but not in passive tasks. The implication of the results summarized here is that deficits involving voluntary attention may be the causes of some learning problems.

An attentional hypothesis also helps to explain how motivational instructions, cognitive rehearsal strategies, and stimulant drugs can often improve behavior among some types of learning disabled children. However, this tempting hypothesis must be qualified by consideration of the tasks and the learners studied in the research. In the literature on learning disorders, again we find that the responses to the stimulant drugs interact with the learners and the tasks. Porges, Walter, Korb, and Sprague (1975) found that the best dosage of drug for improving reaction time of slow responders did not improve their classroom social behavior, but did improve the classroom social behavior of fast responders.

Whalen and Henker (1976) developed a cognitive interpretation of the effects of stimulant drugs, hypothesizing that the drugs influence the attributions of hyperactive children. By attributing success in school to the drug, which is an external factor, they hypothesized that achievement should decline when drug treatment ended. The reason for the decline is that success in school is not perceived by the children as the result of internal factors, such as effort. Instead, success becomes something dependent upon the drug, an external factor not influenced by ability or effort.

At the same time, they state that an attribution to external sources of the cause of the learning problem is helpful. Their interesting hypothesis is that one should teach the children external causal attributions for the origin of failures in school, but internal causal attributions for the origin of the remedies of the problems.

In addition to further study of the attribution processes of hyperkinetic children, we also need to learn about their cognitive styles. In one study (Zahn, Abate, Little, & Wender, 1975), hyperkinetic children tended to be more field dependent and more impulsive than normal children. That finding is compatible with an arousal and attention explanation of hyperkinesis, as discussed previously, in which there is poor ability to control voluntarily the processing of incoming stimuli, especially by the inhibition of distracting, task-relevant stimuli, which appear within the stimulus array. Rosenthal and Allen (1978) discuss this hypothesis, which summarizes an important part of the current state of knowledge about attention in hyperactivity. As they state the relationship (pp. 703, 711), the low scores found on some measures of arousal indicate a relatively flat gradient of attention across the task-relevant, contextual stimuli (i.e., all of the dimensions of the stimulus array). Hyperkinetic children, like normal children, are not often distracted by task-irrelevant stimuli that occur outside the stimulus array. An increase in the steepness of the gradient of attention, produced by instructions, drugs, or other techniques, would increase performance on voluntary attention tasks, such as discrimination learning.

An attentional hypothesis explains many of the findings about hyperactivity. However, in the literature discussed, attention and arousal are still elusive concepts indexed by a broad variety of measures and apparatus. To organize the field more tightly, models of attention, such as the one by McGuinness and Pribram in Chapter 3, are needed. They can explicate relationships among multiple brain structures and psychological functions.

McGuinness and Pribram provide a comprehensive model of attention. They analyze attention into three components: arousal, activation, and effort.

1. Arousal, a phasic, 1–3 sec, short-term component of attention, responds to changes in the external environment. A reduction in heart rate and an increase in skin conductance are measures of arousal. As does the orienting response, arousal habituates upon repetition of an external event, and recurs when the stimulus changes.

2. Activation, a tonic component of attention, represents a readiness to respond by the individual. A decrease in heart rate and CNV each index activation.

3. Effort, the third component of the model, represents the voluntary coordination of arousal and activation. The attempts to coordinate arousal and activation require voluntary control, which we experience as effort.

The model also indicates useful new measures of learning and reasoning. Categorization decreases heart rate, perhaps through facilitation of selective attention and consequent reduction of information to be processed. Reasoning and problem solving involve effort in the making of trial responses and increase heart rate.

Especially significant for educational psychology are their findings that attention involves voluntary, internally controlled processes. These findings were summarized in a quote from the authors in the introduction of this chapter. For example, McGuinness and Pribram's model implies that generative processes of the brain influence arousal and its habituation. The phasic component of attention occurs in response to external stimuli and habituates to their repetition, implying that a model of the stimulus has been constructed and used to determine when to cease attending to it. The orienting response recurs with changes in one or more dimensions of the stimulus. That is, in their model a stimulus is actually a recognized change in stimulation which indicates that the model of the stimulus needs modification. We attend to the change in the stimulus to refine the model of it. The point is that to detect a change in a stimulus one needs a model of the stimulation. The implication for educational psychology is that attention involves the active construction of models of reality. Outcome-generated inputs contribute to the construction of neural models more complex than those produced by repetitions of stimuli.

B. Implications for Learning

Selective attention influences learning in a variety of ways. Shallice and Warrington (1977) studied selective attention in literal dyslexia, the ability to read words or their isolated letters, without the ability to read the individual letters of the intact words. They suggested that the passage from a perceptual, spatially parallel system of recognizing words to a semantic, serial system of information processing involves hierarchical control and selective attention to the perceptual information available in different channels or routes. Krupski's (1975) research described earlier also shows clearly that rehearsal strategies and instructions can enhance attention and improve learning in schools.

Kinsbourne (1973) presented a model of attention and information processing in the cortical hemispheres that relates attention to learning. Each cortical hemisphere of the brain voluntarily activates its attentional mechanism to attend selectively to expected stimulation from the contralateral side. With increasing age and development, different people learn different strategies for the shifting of attention to receive types of anticipated information. Sets to learn, verbal instructions, tasks, and objectives differentially induce different allocations of information to right and left hemispheric information processing strategies. When verbal instructions stimulate the cortical hemisphere appropriate for the nature of the task and for the type of information processing, the result is a facilitation in information processing.

In addition to these implications about attentional processes in learning disabilities and in hemispheric encoding strategies, the models of attention and the research reviewed here suggest some of the mechanisms by which questions, objectives, and instructions influence learning. One hypothesis is that they influence learners' voluntary control over attention. By focusing the learners' plans and intentions upon the objectives to be mastered, by inducing a problem to be solved in the reading of a text, or by inducing an information processing strategy, attention is directed and voluntary control over the direction is enhanced. For example, when students read questions inserted into a text, either before (a prequestion) or after (a postquestion) the paragraphs containing the information relevant to the answer to the question, their learning reflects the effects of selective attention. The prequestion often directs attention to the specific information in the question, while the postquestion often directs attention in the subsequent paragraphs to the type of information cued in the question. Instructions and objectives given to learners also seem to direct attention, and sometimes increase arousal. These ideas are described further in an article by Wittrock (1978).

With the neuroscientists' and cognitive psychologists' constantly developing models and measures of attention and arousal, we should be able in the future to determine more precisely educationally useful ways to influence attention among different students, subject matters, and learning tasks. These data and models indicate the constructive nature of attentional processes. The CNV, expectancy brainwave component, and late, endogenous components indicate that attention involves generative processes of the brain. Voluntary attention, which relates to success in school learning tasks, also involves generative information processing by the brain. The data from neuroscience and cognitive psychology on attention and arousal often complement each other and provide a new understanding of some of the cognitive mechanisms involved in some learning tasks of interest to educational psychologists.

C. Encoding

People use their brains to generate models of reality. People use information processing systems, such as encoding, to construct and to store abstract and concrete representations and interpretations of the events they experience. The following studies indicate some of the ways people use their brains to generate meaning from experience, and to organize, code, and store it in long-term memory.

Mischel and Baker (1975) asked hungry 3- and 4-year-old nursery school children to delay as long as possible the eating of the marshmallows or pretzels placed in front of them. The children, who were instructed to imagine that the pretzels were logs or that the marshmallows were white clouds, delayed their eating for about 14 min. A control group of nursery school children who were not given these instructions averaged a delay of 6 min. By the generation of images of inedible objects, the children were able to respond differently to the food placed before them.

Instructions can also be used to influence the verbal processes used to construct models of reality or meaning from experience. Kaufman, Baron, and Kopp (1966) instructed learners in an operant task that they would be reinforced on fixed-interval or variable-ratio schedules, when instead the reinforcement was actually provided on a variable-interval schedule. The authors found that the instructions they gave the learners "far outweighed the influences of the reinforcing contingencies actually present in the operant training condition [p. 243]."

Bower and Clark (1969) increased retention of words from about 20% to over 90% simply by asking college students to put the words into sentences, maintaining the serial order of the words in the sentences that was present in the original list.

In a number of studies, my students and I have studied the effects of the generation of imagery and verbal elaborations upon learning in school. Bull and Wittrock (1973) found that when elementary school children drew simple pictures of the definitions of vocabulary words they remembered more of the meaning of the words than when they wrote and studied the definitions.

In another study (Wittrock et al., 1975), a familiar story facilitated the generation of meaning for new and undefined vocabulary words. Doctorow et al. (1978) found that instructions given to junior high school students to generate a summary sentence after each paragraph of a story sizeably increased their retention and comprehension of the stories.

In a recently completed study (Wittrock & Lutz, in preparation), college students reading a chapter from Rachel Carson's book, *The Sea Around Us,* increased their memory of the information in the chapter by constructing a verbal analogy for the main idea of each paragraph or by constructing a summary sentence after reading each paragraph. In these studies, self-generated verbal or imaginal representations of the information to be learned facilitated learning.

Allan Paivio (1971) presented a dual process model of encoding in memory. The two processes are imagery and verbal factors. He also reported (1971) a wealth of studies supporting predictions of the model. His research deals with the effects of verbal semantic processes and imagery upon memory, as does much of the contemporary research in cognitive psychology on encoding.

Other psychologists (Das, Kirby, & Jarman, 1975) hypothesize that information is processed successively or simultaneously, but not by its verbal or imagery mode, which they feel tells us little about encoding in memory. The choice between modes of information and strategies of information processing is a fundamental and complex one that has its counterpart in the recent research on the brain. The issue is further complicated because imagery and verbal modes of information might each be coded with either images or verbal processes.

One of the most interesting discoveries reported in the recent research on the brain is that people organize, encode, and store information, employing at least two different modes or strategies, such as imagery and verbal modes, propositional and appositional strategies (Bogen, 1977), simultaneous and successive strategies (Luria, 1973), automatic and episodic strategies (Pribram, 1978), and analytic and holistic strategies. The early research on the hemispheric processes of the brain led to the hypothesis that the two cortical hemispheres specialized somewhat in the type of information they processed. In nearly all right-handers and in about 70% of left-handers, the left hemisphere was better than the right hemisphere at many verbal tasks, especially speech, but worse than the right hemisphere at many visual–spatial tasks.

LeDoux, Wilson, and Gazzaniga (1977) report findings from one patient in which the superiority of the right hemisphere for spatial or perceptual processes appears to be a superiority of manipulospatial activities. (See Gazzaniga & LeDoux, 1978, for further discussion.) The implication of their data, from only one subject, is that the hemispheres are lateralized for language, on the left, and manipulospatial activities on the right.

However, Geffen, Bradshaw, and Nettleton (1972) found that verbal strategies (matching stimuli by name) produced faster responses from the left hemisphere, while visual strategies (visually matching physically identical stimuli) produced faster responses from the right hemisphere. The results implied that the hemispheres may specialize in the strategy of coding they use rather than in the type of information they code.

Bogen (1977) also questioned the verbal–spatial models of hemispheric processes of the brain. Each hemisphere has some language ability and some spatial ability. The right hemisphere reads some words and understands some spoken sentences. The left hemisphere analyzes some complex spatial diagrams. Perhaps the hemispheres differ from each other primarily in the type of information processing strategy they employ, with the left hemisphere employing an analytic, sequential process appropriate for verbal information, and the right hemisphere employing a holistic, synthetic gestalt process, appropriate for spatial information.

In addition to Bogen, other brain researchers find that the cortex specializes somewhat according to strategies of information processing. Luria (1973) described volitional and involuntary hemispheric systems and two information processing mechanisms, called simultaneous and successive strategies, each occurring in each hemisphere. Luria and Simenitskaya (1977) write that psychological functions, such as perception, language, and memory, involve both hemispheres of the brain. Each hemisphere has a variety of hierarchically organized information processing system. The major hemisphere's systems involve conscious, logical processes, including language, that govern volitional behavior. The functions of the minor hemisphere involve subconscious, automatic processes not under voluntary control. Simultaneous synthesis, which occurs in the occipitoparietal area, involves parallel processing of information. Successive synthesis, which occurs in the frontotemporal area, involves sequential analysis of information.

Pribram (1978) states that the anterior lobes of the cortex employ an episodic or situational information processing system and a successive strategy of organization of information. The posterior lobes of the cortex employ an automatic information processing system and a simultaneous strategy of organization of information. However, Madden and Nebes (this volume) emphasize that while dichotomies, such as "in series" or "in parallel," may be relevant to understanding cortical function, these information processing strategies can only be interpreted within the context of the particular task that a subject is attempting to perform.

Attempts to construct models of cortical information processing systems or models of encoding show impressive generative abilities applied to the complex problems of relating psychological function to neurological structure. It seems clear that the sophistication and variety of cortical brain function cannot be reduced to any single dichotomy. The cortex of the brain performs a myriad of different functions within and across its hemispheres. From the images of blood flow in the brain, which we discussed in the introduction, it can be assumed that each of the models of cortical encoding systems is useful, in some contexts, with many problems, and with many learners. Many of the models of brain function are complementary, not mutually exclusive; some of them differ more in the location of than in the nature of the systems they describe.

For educational psychology, the location of the encoding systems in the brain is not as important as is their nature, type, number, and function. If instructional stimuli are processed by at least two different strategies and are learned in two different organizational systems, instruction should be designed accordingly to facilitate these systems. We should use information about individual differences in each system to design instruction. If information is processed in one or another mode, instruction should be designed to facilitate the mode more appropriate for the task and for the ability of the individual learner, and to reduce the sources of interference between alternative modes of organization.

In either case we have interesting, useful models of information processing strategies and of relationships among individual difference variables. Much of the utility of the models derives from the information they provide about the processes used by learners, as different from the abilities of the learners. Some of the models of intellectual ability offer little understanding of the ways information is organized, coded, transformed, and stored. Process-oriented models, such as those of cortical information processing systems, provide more useful information for the design of instruction appropriate for the cognitive strategies and styles of the learners.

One important implication of these studies of encoding is that we should attend to the learners' information processing systems and to the process-oriented individual differences among learners at least as much as we attend to the characteristics of the external stimuli presented to the learners during instruction. The reason is that instructional treatments mean different things to different people, depending upon the information processing strategies they use to construct meaning from the stimuli. For example, visual stimuli, holistically organized and simultaneously presented, can be analyzed linguistically, analytically, and sequentially.

Several more specific implications about types of learning and some learning disabilities also follow from the recent research on the cortical processes of the brain. Glass, Gazzaniga, and Premack (1973) studied global-aphasic adults who had massive damage to their left hemispheres that resulted in severe deficits to their syntactical and grammatical abilities. With iconic symbols of words, much like the symbols Premack used to teach language to chimpanzees, the aphasic patients learned to understand and to construct sentences, each with a subject, verb, and object. The implication is that with appropriate instruction an intact imagery or perceptual coding system in the right hemisphere can be used to understand and generate abstract relationships usually processed by verbal systems in the left hemisphere. With normal people, Raugh and Atkinson (1975) used an imagery mnemonic to teach vocabulary in a second language, sometimes producing a threefold gain in retention.

Research on the cortical information processing systems of the brain suggests possible causes of some reading problems. Marcel, Katz, and Smith (1974) found that 7- and 8-year-old proficient readers showed

greater right over left visual field superiority for word recognition, indicating greater lateralization of function among good readers. In a later
study, Marcel and Rajan (1975) found that the extent of development of
the left, but not the right, hemisphere correlated with reading proficiency among 7–9-year-old children. In dichotic listening tasks, 9–
12-year-old dyslexic children showed less right ear superiority for words
and digits than did a control group of children (Thomson, 1976). Witelson (1977) found 6–14-year-old dyslexic boys to have spatial processes
represented in both hemispheres to a greater degree than normal boys,
which suggests that some dyslexics may read with a spatial–holistic
cognitive strategy instead of with a phonetic–sequential cognitive
strategy. Boder (1971) presented a model of dyslexia in which dysphone-
tic dyslexics use a global rather than an analytic strategy, and spell by
spatial but not the phonetic configuration of words. Dyseidetic dyslexics
read analytically and spell phonetically but have difficulty with the
visual recognition of letters and with the shapes of words. These studies
provide examples of new perspectives from neuroscience and cognitive
psychology that are relevant to some problems of learning common in
schools.

D. Individual Differences

Especially in the areas of cognitive styles, sex, and handedness, the
recent research on the human brain and cognitive psychology reports
findings about individual differences in encoding and memory of interest to educational psychology. We will begin with the unlikely area of
eyelid conditioning, where for about 30 years it has been known that
two groups of subjects, called C-form responders and V-form responders, show different cognitive styles and different conditioning performances. The V-form blink is more rapid, more complete, of earlier onset
and of longer duration, more frequent, and more influenced by the
semantic attributes of stimuli than is the C-form blink. Hellige (1975)
found that the Cs and Vs differ qualitatively in the modes of processing
they typically employ, which might be related to hemispheric brain processes. With verbal stimuli conditioning performance was mediated
normally more by the left hemisphere for Vs than for Cs. One implication of these findings is that, in some situations, even eyeblinks are
conditioned in different ways, which should be considered in the design
of experiments and in the interpretation of their results.

Research in cognitive style and research in the cognitive processes of
the brain show other close relationships. For example, Witkin and co-
workers differentiate between a field-independent or differentiated cog-

nitive style and a field-dependent or global cognitive style. Cohen, Berent, and Silverman (1973) found that electroconvulsive shock, which temporarily incapacitated the right hemispheres of 12 epileptic patients, in each case decreased field dependence, while shock to the left hemispheres of 12 other epileptics in each case increased field dependence. Kagan et al. (1963) identified analytic and nonanalytic conceptual styles. Analytic children tend to be reflective, and nonanalytic children tend to be impulsive. Zelnicker and Jeffrey (1976) found that reflective children tend to use a left hemispheric analytic strategy and impulsive children tend to use a right hemispheric, global cognitive style.

The data reviewed here do not indicate that cognitive styles, such as Cs and Vs, field-independent and field-dependent, and reflective and impulsive, can or should be reduced to cortical processing strategies. The cognitive styles, which are psychological and behavioral functions, involve a variety of neural information processing systems located in many parts of the brain.

The point is that research at different levels of related phenomena indicates the importance of studying stable, process-oriented individual differences in information processing. Learners respond differently to the same stimuli, and the differences in response relate to their cognitive styles. Teaching can be differentiated and learning sometimes improved by matching cognitive styles to organizations of instruction (Pask & Scott, 1972) and to the type of mental elaboration that the learner employs (Krevoy, 1978).

Individual differences in cognitive organization according to handedness and sex have been carefully reviewed by Jerre Levy (this volume). She finds that right-handers and left-handers without a family history of left-handedness are most highly lateralized, with verbal processes primarily in the left hemisphere and visuospatial processes primarily in the right hemisphere. The least lateralized individuals are left-handers with a family history of left-handedness, who have bilateral representation of verbal and spatial processes. Between these two groups are right-handers with a family history of left-handedness, who show greater lateralization than do left-handers. Hardyck and Petrinovich (1977) also review the research on left-handedness and reach the same position.

Levy finds that as a group, females surpass males in the rapid memorization and retention of unstructured, that is, not logically or conceptually organized verbal and spatial information, such as one finds in fluent verbal communication or in facial expressions. As a group, males surpass females in the abstraction and memorization of logically organized verbal and spatial relationships, concepts, and principles embedded in a context. Mathematics is a good example of these relationships. Levy also finds that the male cortex tends to be more lateralized or asymmetric than the female cortex.

She discusses some of the possible educational implications of these differences in cognitive organizations, which need not be repeated here. Although as groups, men, women, left-handers, and right-handers sometimes differ in cognitive proficiency and in the ways they process information, the groups also overlap substantially in cognitive proficiency and methods of processing information. One educational implication of these findings is that although some individuals will be more proficient than others at academic learning, students should not for reasons of sex or handedness be discouraged from the pursuit of any academic subject matter taught in schools.

VI. Summary

The juxtaposition of recent research on the brain with recent research in cognition led to the hypotheses and implications about learning that have been discussed throughout this chapter. Instead of reiterating these hypotheses and implications, it seems more important to discuss the fundamental import for educational psychology of the studies we reviewed.

Although the brain often responds reflexively to incoming stimulation, it is much more than a tabula rasa that passively learns and records incoming information. Instead, the brain has attentional and arousal systems that respond to the plans and intentions of the frontal lobes as well as to environmental and metabolic stimuli. The brain often selects the information to which it will attend, and constructs models of reality from the incoming stimulation.

The encoding of information in memory is also an active, constructive process that involves cortical information processing strategies and stored memories in interaction with the sensory information received from the environment. The construction of meaning for stimuli and events involves expectations, intentions, voluntary attention, previous learning, and strategies for processing information.

This theme about the generative function of the brain has fundamental significance for educational psychologists who study learning and individual differences among learners. It suggests that they try to discover and to understand the information processing systems of learners, as well as their individual differences. Instead of trying to correlate environmental events, including the acts of teachers, directly with student learning, the research described in this chapter implies that it will be more productive to study how learners transform the environmental events of teaching and instruction into functional information. Instruction means different things to different learners depending upon their information processing strategies and their experiences. The research on the brain and its cognitive processes emphasizes the generative nature of learning and the reciprocal interplay between environmental events and the learners' generative cognitive processes.

A most important implication of the research discussed in this chapter is that the people who study learning in educational psychology have some new colleagues in neuroscience and in cognitive science. The growing unity of interests and of findings across these different levels and fields of study promises to benefit all of them and to improve the quality and the productivity of research in educational psychology on human learning and individual differences in learning from instruction.

Bibliography

Begleiter, H., Porjesz, B., Yerre, C., & Kissin, B. Evoked potential correlates of expected stimulus intensity. *Science*, 1973, *179*, 814–816.

Bennett, E. L., Diamond, M. C., Krech, D., & Rosenzweig, M. R. Chemical and anatomical plasticity of the brain. *Science*, 1964, *146*, 610–619.

Berry, S. D., & Thompson, R. F. Prediction of learning rate from the hippocampal electroencephalogram. *Science*, 1978, *200*, 1298–1300.

Boder, E. Developmental dyslexia: Prevailing concepts and a new diagnostic approach. In H. R. Myklebust (Ed.), *Progress in learning disabilities* (Vol. 2). New York: Grune & Stratton, 1971.

Bogen, J. E. Some educational aspects of hemispheric specialization. In M. C. Wittrock, et al., *The human brain*. Englewood Cliffs, N.J.: Prentice-Hall, 1977.

Bower, G. H., & Clark, M. C. Narrative stories as mediators for serial learning. *Psychonomic Science*, 1969, 14, 181–182.

Brazier, M.A.B. *Brain function. II: RNA and brain function; memory and learning.* Berkeley and Los Angeles: University of California Press, 1964.

Brown, W. S., Marsh, J. T., & Smith, J. C. Contextual meaning effects on speech-evoked potentials. *Behavioral Biology*, 1973, *9*, 755–761.

Bull, B. L., & Wittrock, M. C. Imagery in the learning of verbal definitions. *British Journal of Education Psychology*, 1973, *43*, 289–293.

Cohen, B. D., Berent, S., & Silverman, A. J. Field-dependence and lateralization of function in the human brain. *Archives of General Psychiatry*, 1973, *28*, 165–167.

Conners, C. K. Learning disabilities and stimulant drugs in children: Theoretical implications. In R. M. Knights & D. J. Bakker (Eds.), *The neuropsychology of learning disorders*. Baltimore: University Park Press, 1976.

Conners, C. K. Cortical visual evoked response in children with learning disorders. *Psychophysiology*, 1970, *7*, 418–428.

Conners, C. K. Stimulant drugs and cortical evoked responses in learning and behavior disorders in children. In W. L. Smith (Ed.), *Drugs, development, and cerebral function*. Springfield, Ill.: Charles C. Thomas, 1972.

Das, J. P., Kirby, J., & Jarman, R. F. Simultaneous and successive synthesis: An alternative model for cognitive abilities. *Psychological Bulletin, 1975, 82,* 87–103.

Davis, K. L., Mohs, R. C., Tinklenberg, J. R., Pfefferbaum, A., Hollister, L. E., & Kopell, B. S. Physostigmine: Improvement of long-term memory processes in normal humans. *Science, 1978, 201,* 272–274.

Dimond, S. J. Drugs to improve learning in man: Implications and neuropsychological analysis. In R. M. Knights & D. J. Bakker (Eds.), *The neuropsychology of learning disorders.* Baltimore: University Park Press, 1976.

Doctorow, M. J., Wittrock, M. C., & Marks, C. B. Generative process in reading comprehension. *Journal of Education Psychology, 1978, 70,* 109–118.

Dykman, R. A., Ackerman, P. T., Clements, S. D., & Peters, J. E. Specific learning disabilities: An attentional deficit syndrome. In H. R. Myklebust (Ed.), *Progress in learning disabilities* (Vol. 2). New York: Grune & Stratton, 1971.

Dykman, R. A., Walls, R. C., Suzuki, T., Ackerman, P. T., & Peters, J. E. Children with learning disabilities: Conditioning, differentiation, and the effects of distraction. *American Journal of Orthopsychiatry, 1970, 40,* 766–782.

Eccles, J. C. *The understanding of the brain* (2nd ed.). New York: McGraw-Hill, 1977.

Epstein, H. T. Growth spurts during brain development: Implications for educational policy and practice. In J. S. Chall & A. F. Mirsky (Eds.), *Education and the brain,* 77th yearbook, Part II, of the National Society for the Study of Education. Chicago: University of Chicago Press, 1978.

Flexner, L. B., Flexner, J. B., & Roberts, R. B. Memory in mice analyzed with antibiotics. *Science, 1967, 155,* 1377–1381.

Gazzaniga, M. S., & Le Doux, J. E. *The integrated mind.* New York: Plenum Press, 1978.

Geffen, G., Bradshaw, J. L., & Nettleton, N. C. Hemispheric asymmetry: Verbal and spatial encoding of visual stimuli. *Journal of Experimental Psychology, 1972, 95,* 25–31.

Glass, A. V., Gazzaniga, M. S., & Premack, D. Artificial language training in global aphasics. *Neuropsychologia, 1973, 11,* 95–103.

Globus, A., & Scheibel, A. B. The effect of visual deprivation on cortical neurons: A Golgi study. *Experimental Neurology, 1967, 19,* 331–345.

Hardyck, C., & Petrinovich, L. F. Left-handedness. *Psychological Bulletin, 1977, 84,* 385–404.

Harshman, R. A., Crawford, H. J., & Hecht, E. Marihuana, cognitive style, and lateralized hemispheric functions. In S. Cohen & R. C. Stillman (Eds.), *The therapeutic potential of marihuana.* New York: Plenum Press, 1976.

Haward, L.R.C. Effects of sodium diphenylhydantoinate and pemoline upon concentration: A comparative study. In W. L. Smith (Ed.), *Drugs and cerebral function.* Springfield, Ill.: Charles C. Thomas, 1970.

Hellige, J. B. Hemispheric processing differences revealed by differential conditioning and reaction time performance. *Journal of Experimental Psychology: General, 1975, 104,* 309–326.

Hernandez-Peón, R., Scherrer, H., & Jouvet, M. Modification of electrical activity in cochlear nucleus during "attention" in unanesthetized cats. *Science, 1956, 123,* 331–332.

Hillyard, S. A., Hink, R. F., Schwent, V. L., & Picton, T. W. Electrical signs of selective attention in the human brain. *Science, 1973, 182,* 177–180.

Hubel, D. H., & Wiesel, T. N. The period of susceptibility of the physiological effects of unilateral eye closure in kittens. *Journal of Physiology, 1970, 206,* 419–436.

Hyden, H. Plastic changes in neurons during acquisition of new behavior as a problem of protein differentiation. In M. A. Corner & D. F. Swaab (Eds.), *Perspectives in brain research.* (Vol. 45 of *Progress in brain research*). Amsterdam: Elsevier Scientific Publishing Company, 1976.

Hyden, H., & Egyhazi, E. Nuclear RNA changes in nerve cells during a learning experiment in rats. *Proceedings of the National Academy of Sciences*, 1962, *48*, 1366-1373.

Ingvar, D. H. Localisation of cortical functions by multiregional measurements of the cerebral blood flow. In M.A.B. Brazier & H. Petsche (Eds.), *Architectonics of the cerebral cortex*. New York: Raven Press, 1978.

Ingvar, D. H., & Schwartz, M. S. Blood flow patterns induced in the dominant hemisphere in speech and reading. *Brain*, 1974, *97*, 273-288.

Jerison, H. Evolution of the brain. In M. C. Wittrock, et al., *The human brain*. Englewood Cliffs, N.J.: Prentice-Hall, 1977.

John, E. R. Brain mechanisms of memory. In J. L. McGaugh (Ed.), *Psychobiology: Behavior from a biological perspective*. New York: Academic Press, 1971.

John, E. R., et al. Neurometrics. *Science*, 1977, *196*, 1393-1410.

John, E. R., Bartlett, F., Schimokochi, M., & Kleinman, D. Neural readout from memory. *Journal of Neurophysiology*, 1973, *36*, 893-924.

John, E. R., & Schwartz, E. L. The neurophysiology of information processing and cognition. In M. R. Rosenzweig & L. W. Porter (Eds.), *Annual review of psychology*. Palo Alto, Calif.: Annual Reviews, 1978.

Kagan, J., Moss, H. A., & Sigel, I. E. Psychological significance of style of conceptualization. In J. C. Wright & J. Kagan (Eds.), Basic cognitive processes in children. *Monographs of the Society for Research in Child Development*. 1963, *28*, 73-112.

Kaufman, A., Baron, A., & Kopp, R. Some effects of instructions on human operant behavior. *Psychonomic Monograph Supplements*, 1966, *1*, 243-250.

Kinsbourne, M. The control of attention by interaction between the cerebral hemispheres. In S. Kornblum (Ed.), *Attention and performance IV*. New York: Academic Press, 1973.

Klinke, R., Fruhstorfer, H., & Finkenzeller, P. Evoked responses as a function of external and stored information. *Electroencephalography and Clinical Neurophysiology*, 1968, *26*, 216-219.

Krevoy, S. B. Analytic vs. holistic encoding strategies in relation to vocabulary learning and recall. (Doctoral dissertation, University of California, Los Angeles, 1978.)

Krupski, A. Heart rate changes during a fixed reaction time task in normal and retarded adult males. *Psychophysiology*, 1975, *12*, 262-267.

Krupski, A. Sustained attention: Research, theory and implications for special education. In B. K. Keogh (Ed.), *Advances in special education* (Vol. 1). Greenwich, Conn.: JAI Press, in press.

Lassen, N. A., & Ingvar, D. H. Radio-isotopic assessment of regional cerebral blood flow. In E. J. Potchen & V. R. McCready (Eds.), *Progress in nuclear medicine* (Vol. 1). Baltimore: University Park Press, 1972.

Lassen, N. A., Ingvar, D. H., & Skinhøj, E. Brain function and blood flow. *Scientific American*, 1978, *239*, 62-71.

Le Doux, J. E., Wilson, D. H., & Gazzaniga, M. S. Manipulo-spatial aspects of cerebral lateralization. *Neuropsychologia*, 1977, *15*, 743-750.

Livanov, M. N., Gavrilova, N. A., & Aslanov, A. S. Correlation of biopotentials in the frontal parts of the human brain. In K. H. Pribram & A. R. Luria (Eds.), *Psychophysiology of the frontal lobes*. New York: Academic Press, 1973.

Livanov, M. N., Gavrilova, N. A., & Aslanov, A. S. Intercorrelations between different cortical regions of human brain during mental activity. *Neuropsychologia*, 1964, *2*, 281-289.

Luria, A. R. *The working brain: An introduction to neuropsychology* (B. Haigh, trans.). New York: Basic Books, Inc., 1973.

Luria, A. R., & Simernitskaya, E. G. Interhemispheric relations and the functions of the minor hemisphere. *Neuropsychologia*, 1977, *15*, 175–178.

Maggio, E. *Psychophysiology of learning and memory*. Springfield, Ill.: Charles C. Thomas, 1971.

Marcel, T., Katz, L., & Smith, M. Laterality and reading proficiency. *Neuropsychologia*, 1974, *12*, 131–139.

Marcel, T., & Rajan, P. Lateral specialization for recognition of words and faces in good and poor readers. *Neuropsychologia*, 1975, *13*, 489–497.

Mischel, W., & Baker, N. Cognitive appraisals and transformations in delay behavior. *Journal of Personality and Social Psychology*, 1975, *31*, 254–261.

Monckeberg, F. The effect of malnutrition on physical growth and brain development. In J. W. Prescott, M. S. Read, & D. B. Coursin, *Brain function and malnutrition*. New York: Wiley, 1975.

Moruzzi, G., & Magoun, H. W. Brain stem reticular formation and activation of the EEG. *Electroencephalography and Clinical Neurophysiology*, 1949, *1*, 455–473.

Näätänen, R. Selective attention and evoked potentials in humans—A critical review. *Biological Psychology*, 1975, *2*, 237–307.

Paivio, A. *Imagery and verbal processes*. New York: Holt, Rinehart, & Winston, 1971.

Pask, G., & Scott, B.C.E. Learning strategies and individual competence. *International Journal of Man-Machine Studies*, 1972, *4*, 217–253.

Porges, S. W., Walter, G. F., Korb, R. J., & Sprague, R. L. The influences of methylphenidate on heart rate and behavioral measures of attention in hyperactive children. *Child Development*, 1975, *46*, 727–733.

Preston, M. S., Guthrie, J. T., & Childs, B. Visual evoked responses in normal and disabled readers. *Psychophysiology*, 1974, *11*, 452–457.

Pribram, K. H. The neurophysiology of remembering. *Scientific American*, January 1969, 73–86.

Pribram, K. H. *Languages of the brain*. Englewood Cliffs, N.J.: Pentrice-Hall, 1971.

Pribram, K. H. Modes of central processing in human learning and remembering. In T. Teyler (Ed.), *Brain and learning*. Stamford, Conn.: Greylock Publishers, 1978.

Pribram, K. H., & Luria, A. R. *Psychophysiology of the frontal lobes*. New York: Academic Press, 1973.

Quarton, G. C. The enhancement of learning by drugs and the transfer of learning by macromolecules. In G. C. Quarton, T. Melnechuk, & F. O. Schmitt (Eds.), *The neurosciences: A study program*. New York: The Rockefeller University Press, 1967.

Raugh, M. R., & Atkinson, R. C. A mnemonic method for learning a second-language vocabulary. *Journal of Educational Psychology*, 1975, *67*, 1–16.

Rosenthal, R. H., & Allen, T. W. An examination of attention, arousal, and learning dysfunctions of hyperkinetic children. *Psychological Bulletin*, 1978, *85*, 689–715.

Rosenzweig, M. R. Evidence for anatomical and chemical changes in the brain during primary learning. In K. H. Pribram & D. E. Broadbent (Eds.), *Biology of memory*. New York: Academic Press, 1970.

Rosenzweig, M. R., & Bennett, E. L. (Eds.). *Neural mechanisms of learning and memory*. Cambridge, Mass.: MIT Press, 1976.

Rosenzweig, M. R., Bennett, E. L., & Diamond, M. C. Brain changes in response to experience. *Scientific. American*, 1972, *226*(2), 22–29.

Schapiro, S., & Vukovich, K. R. Early experience effects upon cortical dendrites: A proposal model for development. *Science*, 1970, *167*, 292–294.

Shallice, T., & Warrington, E. K. The possible role of selective attention in acquired dyslexia. *Neuropsychologia*, 1977, *15*, 31–41.

Shashoua, V. E. Identification of specific changes in the pattern of brain protein synthesis after training. *Science*, 1976, *193*, 1264–1266.

Shields, D. T. Brain responses to stimuli in disorders of information processing. *Journal of Learning Disabilities*, 1973, *6*, 501–505.

Sitaram, N., Weingartner, H., & Gillin, J. C. Human serial learning: Enhancement with arecholine and choline and impairment with scopolamine. *Science*, 1978, *201*, 274–276.

Smith, W. L. Facilitating verbal–symbolic functions in children with learning problems and 14–6 positive spike EEG patterns with ethosuximide (zarontin). In W. L. Smith Ed.), *Drugs and cerebral function*. Springfield, Ill.: Charles C. Thomas, 1970.

Sprague, R. L., & Sleator, E. K. Methylphenidate in hyperkinetic children: Differences in dose effects on learning and social behavior. *Science*, 1977, *198*, 1274–1276.

Teyler, T. J., Megela, A., & Hesse, G. Habituation and generalization of the ERP to linguistic and non-linguistic stimuli. In D. Otto (Ed.), *Perspectives in event-related brain potential research*. Washington, D.C.: U.S. Government Printing Office, 1977.

Thompson, R. F. *Introduction of physiological psychology*. New York: Harper & Row, 1975.

Thomson, M. E. A comparison of laterality effects in dyslexics and controls using verbal dichotic listening tasks. *Neuropsychologia*, 1976, *14*, 243–246.

Travarthen, C. Analysis of cerebral activities that generate and regulate consciousness in commissurotomy patients. In S. J. Dimond & J. G. Beaumont (Eds.), *Hemisphere function in the human brain*. New York: Halsted Press, 1974.

van Duyne, H. J. Effects of stimulant drug therapy on learning behaviors in hyperactive/MBD children. In R. M. Knights & D. J. Bakker (Eds.), *The neuropsychology of learning disorders*. Baltimore: University Park Press, 1976.

von Muralt, A. Influence of early protein-calorie malnutrition on the intellectual development: The point of view of a physiologist. In M.A.B. Brazier (Ed.), *Growth and development of the brain*. New York: Raven Press, 1975.

Weinberg, H., Walter, W. G., Crow, H. H. Intracerebral events in humans related to real and imaginary stimuli. *Electroencephalography and Clinical Neurophysiology*, 1970, *29*, 1–9.

Whalen, C. K., & Henker, B. Psychostimulants and children: A review and analysis. *Psychological Bulletin*, 1976, *83*, 1113–1130.

Winick, M., & Rosso, P. Malnutrition and central nervous system development. In J. W. Prescott, M. S. Read, & D. B. Coursin, *Brain function and malnutrition*. New York: Wiley, 1975, pp. 41–51.

Witelson, S. F. Developmental dyslexia: Two right hemispheres and none left. *Science*, 1977, *195*, 309–311.

Wittrock, M. C. Learning as a generative process. *Educational Psychologist*, 1974, *11*, 87–95.

Wittrock, M. C. The cognitive movement in instruction. *Educational Psychologist*, 1978, *13*, 15–29.

Wittrock, M. C., & Carter, J. Generative processing of hierarchically organized words. *American Journal of Psychology*, 1975, *88*, 489–501.

Wittrock, M. C., et al. *The human brain*. Englewood Cliffs, N.J.: Prentice-Hall, 1977.

Wittrock, M. C., & Lumsdaine, A. A. Instructional psychology. In M. R. Rosenzweig & L. W. Porter (Eds.), *Annual review of psychology* (Vol. 28). Palo Alto, Calif.: Annual Reviews, Inc., 1977.

Wittrock, M. C., & Lutz, K. Reading comprehension and the generation of verbal analogies and summaries, in preparation.

Wittrock, M. C., Marks, C. B., & Doctorow, M. J. Reading as a generative process. *Journal of Educational Psychology*, 1975, *67*, 484–489.

Zahn, T. P., Abate, F., Little, B. C., & Wender, P. H. Minimal brain dysfunction, stimulant drugs, and autonomic nervous system activity. *Archives of General Psychiatry*, 1975, *32*, 381–387.

Zeaman, D., & House, B. The role of attention in discrimination learning. In N. Ellis (Ed.), *Handbook of mental deficiency*. New York: McGraw-Hill, 1963.

Zelniker, T., & Jeffrey, W. E. Reflective and impulsive children: Strategies of information processing underlying differences in problem solving. *Monographs of the Society for Research in Child Development*, 1976, *41*(5), Serial Number 168.

Subject Index

EDUCATIONAL PSYCHOLOGY

continued from page ii

Kay Pomerance Torshen. The Mastery Approach to Competency-Based Education

Harvey Lesser. Television and the Preschool Child: A Psychological Theory of Instruction and Curriculum Development

Donald J. Treffinger, J. Kent Davis, and Richard E. Ripple (eds.). Handbook on Teaching Educational Psychology

Harry L. Hom, Jr. and Paul A. Robinson (eds.). Psychological Processes in Early Education

J. Nina Lieberman. Playfulness: Its Relationship to Imagination and Creativity

Samuel Ball (ed.). Motivation in Education

Erness Bright Brody and Nathan Brody. Intelligence: Nature, Determinants, and Consequences

António Simões (ed.). The Bilingual Child: Research and Analysis of Existing Educational Themes

Gilbert R. Austin. Early Childhood Education: An International Perspective

Vernon L. Allen (ed.). Children as Teachers: Theory and Research on Tutoring

Joel R. Levin and Vernon L. Allen (eds.). Cognitive Learning in Children: Theories and Strategies

Donald E. P. Smith and others. A Technology of Reading and Writing (in four volumes).

> Vol. 1. *Learning to Read and Write: A Task Analysis (by Donald E. P. Smith)*
> Vol. 2. *Criterion-Referenced Tests for Reading and Writing (by Judith M. Smith, Donald E. P. Smith, and James R. Brink)*
> Vol. 3. *The Adaptive Classroom (by Donald E. P. Smith)*
> Vol. 4. *Designing Instructional Tasks (by Judith M. Smith)*

Phillip S. Strain, Thomas P. Cooke, and Tony Apolloni. Teaching Exceptional Children: Assessing and Modifying Social Behavior